ENGLISH GRAMMAR

WORD
by
WORD

D1245950

Sylvia Chalker

Nelson

Thomas Nelson and Sons Ltd
Nelson House   Mayfield Road
Walton-on-Thames   Surrey
KT12 5PL   UK

51 York Place
Edinburgh
EH13JD   UK

Thomas Nelson (Hong Kong) Ltd
Toppan Building 10/F
22A Westlands Road
Quarry Bay   Hong Kong

First published by Thomas Nelson and Sons Ltd 1990

ISBN 0–17–555705–5

NPN 9 8 7 6 5 4 3 2

Printed in Hong Kong

Contents

Introduction

This book approaches grammar through vocabulary. It is not a grammar book arranged alphabetically. It is more like a dictionary of some of the commonest words in English – words that are known to cause trouble – but with much fuller treatment of each word's grammar than is possible in a conventional dictionary.

In everyday conversation and writing about 1000 English words make up over 70% of the language used. The grammar of some of these common words is straightforward. For example, most count nouns in English add -s or -es to make their plurals (*mothers*, *fathers*, *churches*); and these plurals can be used with plural words such as *many* and *several*, and take plural verbs. That is the good news.

The 'bad news' is that many of the most frequently used words – words needed by elementary learners – often have a lot of grammar. They may belong to more than one part of speech and have several meanings (*mind*, *like*) or their meaning and usage may be complicated (modal verbs all have their individual differences). So it is not enough to know the meaning(s) of a word; or even to know in general what, say, verb tenses mean; you still need to know how each particular word is used in practice.

But even this 'bad news' has its good side. By concentrating on the grammar of a few hundred individual words you learn the essentials of English grammar.

Word frequencies

Research into word frequencies (how often different words are used) has been transformed in recent years by computers, which have enabled large quantities of real English (both written and spoken) to be accurately analysed. Nevertheless, research findings depend on the 'texts' fed into the computers in the first place, and the resulting frequency counts have to be interpreted in the light of learners' experiences and needs.

In **English Grammar Word by Word** I have omitted some high frequency words that have simple grammar (*door*, *father*, *house*, *local*, *mother*, *party*, *water* . . .) But I have included a number of words with rather lower frequencies. I have done this either because these words belong to the 'core' grammar of English (*anyhow*, *barely*, *dare*, *first*, *hence*, *oneself*, *seldom*, *theirs*, *yourselves*) or because – despite the statistics – learners do encounter them, and their usage is not straightforward (*asleep*, *awake*, *belong* . . .). I have also restricted most entries to meanings and usages that a not-too-advanced learner might be expected to need.

Grammar tables

A feature of this book which I hope will appeal to users – both learners and teachers – are the tables showing verb patterns, the usage of determiners and pronouns and the ways in which various other words (e.g., *certain*) are used. Comparison of some of these tables will give an overall picture of some areas of grammar, but always firmly based on actual individual words.

Thanks

My grateful thanks to David Newby, for making valuable comments on the manuscript – and to Professor Sidney Greenbaum for allowing me to quote from the spoken and written texts that form the Survey of English Usage at University College London.

Sylvia Chalker.
London 1990

Key to symbols

/	or	→	*person/people* = person or people
*	not standard English	→	**I have gone yesterday.*
?	some people consider this is not standard	→	*? I didn't come due to the weather.*
( )	optional	→	*He said (that) he liked it.*
C	count noun		
U	uncountable noun		
adj	adjective		
adv	adverb		
ıo	indirect object		
o	direct object		
pl	plural		
sing	singular		

For Crispin

a/an: indefinite articles ▶ Compare **the**

1 a/an: pronunciation

a The use of *a* or *an* depends on the pronunciation of the following word, not on the spelling.
a is used before all consonant sounds, and *an* before all vowel sounds:
> *a European   a union*

But:
> *an Eskimo   an uncle*

With abbreviations, the same rule is true: it is the sound that matters:
> *a learner   a member of parliament*

But:
> *an L-plate* (on a learner-driver's car)   *an MP*

b *a* is pronounced /ə/ and *an* is pronounced /ən/ unless we want to stress the word, when we say /eɪ/ or /æn/:
> *I didn't say the Queen, I said a /eɪ/ queen.*

Three nouns beginning with *h* are pronounced without an *h*-sound and use *an*:
> *an heir   an hour   an honour* (also related words, e.g. *an hourly train service.*)

If the *h* is pronounced, we usually use *a* /ə/:
> *a hat   a house*

But a few *h*-words with an unstressed first syllable sometimes take *an*:
> *a/an hotel   a/an historical novel*

2 a/an: usage

a/an are mainly used with singular count nouns:
> *She gave him a pen for Christmas.*
> *If you have an idea, let me know.*

With plural nouns or uncountable nouns we show indefinite meaning by zero article:
> *In that school, they always give **pens** for prizes.*
> *He shows a lack of **intelligence**.*

a Some nouns that are usually uncountable can be used as count nouns if we are thinking of separate units:
> *a tea . . . two teas* (= a cup . . . two cups of tea)

or of different types or classes of something:
> *That's a very sweet wine.*
> *Stilton is a blue cheese.*

b *a/an* are also used with some uncountable nouns when we limit the meaning, e.g. by referring to one case or example:
> *a knowledge of computers   a love of money*

c *a/an* are used with some nouns formed from verbs to mean one example of the action:
> *have a go   have a wash   take a look*

d *a/an* can be omitted before a count noun when it is the second word in a pair; otherwise count nouns must have an article (*a/an* or *the*):
    a bat and ball . . . a spoon and fork

e *a/an* can be used with proper names when we use them as ordinary count nouns:
    There's a Mrs Young to see you. (= a person called Mrs Young)

3 **a/an**: meaning

a/an have two meanings.

a If we say *A train has just arrived at Platform 5*, we mean an actual train. We don't say *the train* because we don't expect our listeners to know which train we are talking about. So it is an actual, specific, but indefinite train.
This meaning, when we are talking about an actual person or thing, becomes definite the next time we mention it, and we then use *the*:
    The train is probably ours. (= the one mentioned before)

b On the other hand, if we say *A train runs on rails* we are not thinking of an actual train, but of a train compared with a bus or a plane. We are saying the thing belongs to a certain class or type. This is indefinite classifying meaning. It is this classifying meaning that is used in sentences like:
    I am a student.   My sister is an engineer.   She is a nice person. (That's the kind of people we are.)

With this meaning, even when we use the word again, we are still talking indefinitely, so we continue to use *a/an*:
    I am a student.   I've been a student for two years now.
                                                  ▶   See **any**

4 **a/an** or **one**?

a We normally use *a/an* (NOT **one*) when talking about singular things or people:
    Have you got a sister?
    I'd like an apple.
    I'll write to you in a day or two.

b If we wish to emphasise number, i.e. to contrast with two, three, etc., then we must use *one*:
    I've only got one cousin – not six, like you.
    I simply ate one snail, and immediately felt sick.
    We shall only stay one or two days.

c *a/an* and *one* are sometimes interchangeable, with *one* being slightly more emphatic:
    He wrote this amazing book in a week/one week.
    It's a/one hundred miles from here.
    I don't believe him for a/one moment.

d Some number expressions normally take *a* in the singular – *a dozen* (12), *a hundred*, *a thousand* etc., but can take *one* if we wish to contrast *one dozen*, say, with *two dozen*:
    I'll take a dozen eggs.
    I only want a/one dozen.

There is no possibility of living to be two hundred years old, so we only use *a* (not *one*) in:
> *I don't think I'll live to be a hundred.*

e *a/an* are used in expressions like the following:
> *We go to the cinema **twice a month**.*
> *This oil costs **80p a litre**.*
> *Unskilled workers earn **£3 an hour**.*

▶ See **quite**; **rather**; **such**

---

ability: noun (C, U) ▶ Compare able

- the right skill or power necessary to do something.
  We often use *ability* + *to*-INFINITIVE:
  > *She has an amazing **ability** to get on with all sorts of people.*
  > *The child showed mathematical **ability** from an early age.*

---

able

1 be able to: verb ▶ Compare **can**; **could**

a *be able to* is used like a one-word verb, and expresses an ability to do something through having the physical power or knowledge or opportunity, rather like *can/could*:
> *An elephant **is able to/can** pick up food with its trunk.*
> *She **was able to/could** play the piano when she was only four.*

b In the past tense, *was able to*, unlike *could*, not only expresses a general ability to do something, but has the extra meaning of actually achieving something on a particular occasion:
> *The burglar **was able to** get in because we had left the window open.*
> (NOT *. . . could get in . . .*)

c *be able to* is also used for something that is not possible now but will be in the future:
> *We'll **be able to** drive from London to Paris when the tunnel's built.*
> (NOT *We can drive . . .*)

d As *be able to* is based on *be*, it has a full range of verb forms, including participles, and combines with *have* and modal verbs. This means it can be used to express ideas where *can* and *could* cannot be used:
> *It's nice **being able to** work when you feel like it.*
> *She's **been able to** sit in the garden during this recent good weather.*
> *We might **be able to** change the date if you can't manage the fifth.*

2 able: adjective

- capable, good at something, clever
  > *She is an extremely **able** doctor.*
  > *Don't worry about Gordon. He's very **able** – he'll soon sort it out.*

about

1 about: preposition

a • concerning; on the subject of
  *I heard **about** you.*
  *Nobody can do anything **about** it.* (= change the situation)
  *The great thing **about** youth hostels is that they're all reasonably clean.* (=The
  advantage that they have . . .)

b • here and there in ▶ Compare **around**
  *Will you stop sitting **about** the house feeling sorry for yourself and do
  something useful!*

c • approximately; roughly
  *Marie and I went and stayed there last summer for **about** a fortnight.*
  *We walked **about** ten miles a day.*
  *Come **about** 6 o'clock.*
  Around is also possible here, but is more formal.

d How about/What about . . . ?
  How about/What about . . . ? can be used to make suggestions:
  ***How about/What about** (having) a nice cup of tea?*

  What about . . . ? is also used for more genuine questions:
  ***What about** the cat while you're on holiday?* (= What is going to happen to
  the cat? What have you arranged?)
  *'We've all got a right to eat meat if we want to.' '**What about** the rights of
  animals?'* (= consider an alternative point of view.)

e about or **on**?
  Books, articles and discussions can be *about* or *on* something. But *on* suggests
  more serious study of the topic. Novels and stories are usually *about*
  something, even if the subject is serious:
  *He's been writing a novel **about** conditions in the slums.*

2 about: adverb ▶ Compare **around; round**

  • here and there; in no special direction; in no special place
  *There are people who go **about** interviewing people in the streets.*
  *He was quite happy to sit **about** doing nothing in particular.*
  *He hasn't been out and **about** much lately.*

  around or *round* are alternatives in the first example and *around* in the second.
  Around is common in American English.

3 just about

  • nearly; almost
  *This will **just about** finish me off.*
  *That will **just about** pay for their advertisement in the paper.*
  *I've had (**just**) **about** enough of your rudeness.* (= I will not tolerate it any
  more.)

4 be about to

To *be about to do* something is to be on the point of doing something:
*We **were about to** go and play tennis, when it started to rain.*
*If you'd only listen, **I'm about to** tell you something interesting.*

---

above ► Compare **over**

1 above: preposition

above is the opposite of *below*. The general meaning is 'higher than' or 'in a higher place'.

a Place
As a preposition of place, *above* often means 'on a higher level than':
*The remains of this 13th century castle stand on the hill **above** the town.*
*Seals will lie just **above** the highwater mark.*
*Make a cut half an inch **above** the bud and with the thumb of the right hand press on the stem below the bud.*

When the meaning is 'vertically higher', both *above* and *over* may be possible:
*The helicopter was **above/over** our heads.*
*There was a picture of Charles 1 **above/over** the fireplace.*
*They live in a flat **above/over** the shop.*

b Measurements
With measurement on a scale we use *above*:
*The town lies in a high valley 700 feet **above** sea level.*
*Temperatures hardly rose **above** freezing for three months.*
*It was **above** average in quality.*
Note: *over* is not possible in these examples, but when the meaning could be either 'higher than' (*above*) or 'more than' (*over*) both are possible:
*The price of tickets has been well **above/over** £10 for several months now.*
*People **above/over** a certain level of income are expected to pay more.*

c Rank
If you are *above* somebody, you have a higher rank or a higher position in society:
*A major is **above** a captain.* (= It's a higher rank in the army.)
*A lot of students find they only know people in their own year and know nobody **above** them and nobody **below** them.* (= nobody in a higher or lower class)
Contrast *over* and *under*, which show a relationship between individual people rather than ranks or titles:
*The Director of Studies is **over** Bob and me. In fact, she's got twelve teachers **under** her.*

2 above: adverb

● in/to a higher place
The meanings are similar to those of the preposition.

---

a **Place**
*The people in the flat **above** are very noisy.*
*See **above** (page 161).* (= higher on the same page *or* earlier in the book.)

b **Measurements**
*With temperatures of 120°F and **above**, New Delhi can be rather uncomfortable in the summer.*

c **Rank**
*I don't know anyone in the class **above**.*

3 **above**: adjective

above is rare as an adjective, except to refer to something mentioned earlier:
*Perhaps you could ring my secretary on the **above** number.* (= the telephone number at the top of the letter.)

4 **above all**

- more important; more seriously than anything else
*A person today needs different qualifications; **above all**, he must understand the world in which he works.*
*He couldn't read and he couldn't eat. **Above all**, he could not sleep.*

absence: noun (C, U)

a - an occasion or period of being away
*It was good to see everybody after such a long **absence** abroad.*
*He had to shut the shop because there was nobody to look after it during his **absence**.*

b - a lack of something
*In the **absence** of any proof of guilt . . .*

absent: adjective

absent is the opposite of *present*. The meaning is 'not at a place':
*There were a lot of people **absent** from school today because of 'flu.*

accept: verb   ▶ Compare **agree**

> accept + OBJECT
> *that*-CLAUSE

a - agree to take or use something.
We can accept advice, an invitation, an offer, a suggestion, or actual things offered.

The usual pattern is *accept* + OBJECT (NOT **accept* + *to*-INFINITIVE):
*She would not **accept** a reward.*

b We also *accept* some unpleasant fact or situation if we realise that we cannot change it:

*I just cannot **accept** (the fact) that I'll never see him again.*
*He knew his father didn't like him, but somehow he couldn't **accept** it.*

▶ See **except**

accident

1 accident: noun

- an unexpected event that causes damage
  *There's been another terrible **accident** on the motorway – six people have been killed.*
  *I'm afraid I've had a bit of an **accident** and spilled coffee on your book.*

2 by accident

- by chance (good or bad)
  *I met Susan this morning quite **by accident** in the supermarket – I thought she was away.*

according to: preposition

a We use *according to* when we quote what some other person has said or written:

Your overdraft (= the money you owe the bank), ***according to** the bank's books, is £3122.*
***According to** the exams department, she hasn't even entered.*
***According to** the timetable, there was only one bus a day.*
***According to** her, her pain is very bad.*

But:

We say *In my/our opinion*, *In my/our view* (NOT **According to me/us*).
*According to me, he's a disappointed man.

b *According to* can also mean 'in a way that agrees with', 'depending on':

*If you use the product **according to** the instructions, I can guarantee it's safe.*
*Everything went **according to** plan.*
*The rents are somewhere between £60 and £70 a week **according to** the kind of house.*
*He taught various subjects, **according to** the interests and standards of his students.*

account

1 account: noun

a - money deposited in a bank
  *How much money have I got in my **account**, please?*

b • a report of an event
*Just give us an **account** of what happened in your owns words.*

c on account of
• because of
*They wanted to live near the sea **on account of** the boy's health.*

d not on any account/on no account
These phrases are used to emphasise an imperative:
***Don't on any account** eat those beans uncooked.*
***On no account** should you eat those beans uncooked.* (Note the word order.)

2 account for: verb

a • explain
*How do you **account for** the fact that there is £500 missing?*
*There's no **accounting for** taste.* (= no way of explaining)
*I've got £300 I can't **account for**.*
*He must **account for** the money he spends.* (= keep a record of)

b • be the cause or origin of
*Cotton **accounts for** fifty-seven percent of their gross national product.*

ache

1 ache: noun (C, U)

a *Headaches* and the general word *ache* are count nouns:
*I'm full of **aches** and pains – I think I've got 'flu.*
*Sarah's got a **headache** – she gets lots of **headaches**.*

b Other kinds of *ache* are usually uncountable in British English:
*I've got **backache/toothache/earache**.*

but countable in American English:
*Dwight's got a **stomach ache**.*

Note: Only *back*, *ear*, *head*, *stomach* and *tooth* can form nouns with *ache* in this way.

2 ache: verb
*My legs **ache** after all that climbing.*

across ▶ Compare **over; through**

1 across: preposition

a • from one side of to the other
*There's a fence right **across** the airport runway.*
*He had a large nose with a red mark **across** it.*
*I'll take you **across** the Channel to Europe.*
*I have to drive **across** the States from Los Angeles and spend a couple of days in New York.*

b • on the other side of
*It should be just **across** the street.*
*The army was just **across** the frontier.*

c **across** or **over**?
Both *across* and *over* can mean 'from one side to the other' or 'on the other side from here'. *Across* suggests a fairly flat surface; *over* emphasises that one passes on top of something. So, in some cases we can use either. We can *walk across* or *over a road, a bridge, a frontier*. But we *walk across a room* (NOT **over*) because we are inside it, while we *climb over a wall* (NOT **across*) because it is high rather than wide.

d **across** or **through**?
Both *across* and *through* mean 'from one side to another'. *Through* suggests being surrounded by other things. So we *walk through a forest* or *a crowd of people*.

2 **across**: adverb

*She looked **across** at me and smiled.*
*I'm just going **across** to the baker's. (**over** is also possible)*

---

act ▶ Compare **action; activity**

1 **act**: verb

*Sometimes she **acts** in a very peculiar way. (= behaves)*
*This medicine **acts** quickly. (= takes effect/has an effect)*
*The police **acted** on information: they went to the house and arrested three people. (= took action)*
*I **acted** in a lot of plays at school. (= performed in)*

2 **act**: noun

• something that somebody does when we see it as single and complete

*an **act** of bravery/kindness/terrorism (NOT *action here)*
*an **Act** of Parliament (= a law)*
*a play in three **acts** (= major division of a play)*

---

action: noun (C, U)

As a count noun, *action* is sometimes almost the same as *act* (*a brave act* or *action*). But *action* stresses a process, something that is/was happening, often for a purpose:
*We need **action**, not words.*
*The film is full of **action**.*
*The committee made lots of decisions, but they did not take any **action**.*
*Her **actions** showed she was sincere.*

1 **activity**: noun (C, U) ▶ Compare **act; action**

activity suggests busy and continuous actions and movements, or things done
for pleasure:
*It was a sort of holiday camp with plenty of organised **activities** – you know,
swimming, dances, games, and so on.*
*The **activities** of this political group were criminal really.*
*There seemed to be plenty of **activity**, but no real action.* (= People were
busy, but perhaps without any results.)

2 **active**: adjective

● usually doing things; energetic
*She's eighty now, but still very **active**, and takes an **active** interest in
everything that goes on around her.*
*He's an **active** member of the committee.*

actual: adjective ▶ Compare **real**

● exactly the same (one/ones), real
*Tom said something very rude, though I don't remember the **actual** words.*
Even a cheap little bottle of wine costs about £2, but most of that is tax. The
***actual** cost of the wine is a few pence.*

actual does not mean 'current', 'happening now'.

actually ▶ Compare **really; in fact**

1 **actually**: adverb

● really; in fact
*I didn't **actually** hear the speech – I read it in the papers next day.*
*The wine itself **actually** only costs a few pence. The rest is tax.*

actually does not mean 'currently', 'now', 'at present'.

2 **actually**: sentence adverb

actually often introduces information that we think will be surprising, because
it contrasts with what has been said. So it is sometimes a polite way of
correcting someone or disagreeing:
*'Your daughter's a nurse, I think you said.' 'Well, she's a doctor, **actually**.'*
*'I expect you're looking forward to your holiday.' '**Actually**, I don't really
want to go.'*

add: verb

a • join something to something else, to increase the number or size or to complete in some way:
If you add 5½ to 4½ the answer is 10.
Taste this to see if you want to add salt.
No Added Sugar (label on some tins of food)

b • say or write something more
'It's expensive. And anyway, I don't need it,' she added.

addition

1 **addition**: noun
• an extra person or thing
She's a useful addition to our staff.

2 **in addition (to)**
• as well (as); also
In addition to the normal programme, there were special games for the children.

admission: noun (C, U)

a • (price for) allowing someone into a building such as a museum
Admission £2 – children half price.
No Admission except on Business. (or *No Admittance . . .*, which is more formal.)

b • agreeing that something is true
his frank admission of his guilt
an admission of failure

admit: verb

```
          OBJECT
admit + -ing
          that-CLAUSE
```

a • allow into a place
This ticket admits two people.
She was admitted to hospital with a broken leg.

b • agree that something bad is true
He now admits his mistake. He admits it.
He admits telling lies.
He admits (that) he stole the car.

advice: noun (U)

> *If you listened to **advice**, you might not make so many mistakes.*
> *Let me give you a piece of **advice**.*
> *All she needed was some **advice** and a cup of tea.*

advise: verb

```
              OBJECT
              -ing
advise + o + to-INFINITIVE
         (o) + that-CLAUSE
         (o) + wh-CLAUSE
```

advise is sometimes used without an object, but usually it needs an OBJECT, or *-ing*, or a personal object plus a *to*-INFINITIVE, a *that*-CLAUSE or a *wh*-CLAUSE:

> *I did as/what you **advised**.*
> *I would **advise** against admitting anything.*
> *The doctor **advised** plenty of rest.*
> *I don't **advise** going by bus – it's so slow.*
> *He **advised** me not to take the job.*
> *They **advised** (me) that I shouldn't sign it.*
> *They'll **advise** you where to go.*

affect: verb ▶ Compare **effect**

- influence; cause a change to
  > *The way you talk **affects** the way people treat you.*
  > *The climate badly **affected** her health.*
  > *She **was badly affected** by the death of her only son.*
  > *A prison sentence **would affect** the rest of your life.*

afford: verb

```
can
could   afford +  OBJECT
                  to-INFINITIVE
```

a ● have enough money or time for something

The usual pattern when using *afford* is *can/be able to afford* + (*to*-INFINITIVE) + OBJECT. It is most often used in questions and negatives, but rarely in the passive:

> *I can actually afford a holiday now.*

*I don't know how they can **afford** (to have) two cars.*
*I can't **afford** (to buy) a new coat this year – I'll have to wear my old one.*
*I couldn't **afford** to spend so much time watching TV.*

b When we say we *cannot afford* to do something we can also mean that it would be dangerous or inconvenient:
*You **can't afford** to miss that lecture.* (= You mustn't . . .)
*I can't **afford** to wait any longer for you, I'm late already.*

---

afraid: predicative adjective ▶ Compare **fear**

```
            of + OBJECT
            of + -ing
afraid + to-INFINITIVE
            that-CLAUSE
            so/not
```

a If you are *afraid of* something, you are frightened of something unpleasant, perhaps something which often causes fear:
*Why are you **afraid**? What are you **afraid** of?*
*Tom is **afraid** of spiders.*

If you are *afraid of doing* something, you do not want to do this thing; if you are *afraid of something* happening, you do not want it to happen:
*I'm **afraid** of flying.*
*He's really **afraid** of making a mistake.*

b If you are *afraid to do* something, you may be too frightened to do it. You may decide not to do it:
*She was **afraid** to go out alone.*
*He is **afraid** to tell his wife what he's done.*

c If you are *afraid that* something will happen, you are frightened or worried about a possible future event; you expect something unpleasant:
*We're **afraid** (that) many more people will die of this disease.*
*I'm **afraid** I might make a mistake.*

d *afraid* is also used politely, to mean, roughly, 'sorry', when telling people bad news or when apologising:
*I'm (very much) **afraid** that this is going to be a great shock to you.*
*I'm **afraid** I've lost your book.*
*'Is it too late for lunch?' 'Yes, I'm **afraid** so. We're closed.'*
*'Can we have lunch here?' 'I'm **afraid** not. We're closed.'*

---

after

1 **after**: preposition

• later than, following
after is the opposite of *before*.
*What are we going to do **after** breakfast?*

---

*Q comes **after** P in the alphabet.*
***After** doing her homework she watched TV.*

In American English *after* is used in time expressions to express minutes past the hour:
*It's twenty **after** seven.* (= 7.20) (British English = twenty past seven)

2   after: conjunction

after is the opposite of *before*.

***After** he left school, he got a job in a bank.*
***After** we've had breakfast, I want to go out for a walk.*
*I'll ring you **after** I get back.*

3   after: adverb ▶ See **afterwards**

after is sometimes used as an adverb of time, but the usual adverb is *afterwards*:
*They lived happily ever **after**.*

4   after all

after all is used in two ways.
a ● surprisingly; despite what happened earlier
With this meaning, *after all* usually comes at the end of its clause:
*About your visit, sorry it's not this week **after all**.*
*I think perhaps we might invite him **after all**.*

b ● but it must be remembered that
With this meaning, *after all* usually comes at the beginning of its clause or in mid-position:
*Perhaps we should change and go on the plane. **After all**, I'm not sure that I can face the journey.*
*You have, **after all**, lived with my family for nearly twenty years.*

After all does not mean 'in the end', 'finally', 'at last'.

afternoon: noun (C, U) ▶ See **morning**

afterwards: adverb

● later
afterwards is usually used either before the subject or at the end of the clause:
*The injection relieved his pain, but **afterwards** his leg felt stiff.*
*I was rather unkind to them, and **afterwards** I felt sorry.*
*The pen wasn't working properly, but it did work **afterwards**.*

again: adverb

a • another time; a second time; once more
In simple sentences, *again* usually comes at the end:
> *Lovely to see you **again**.*
> *For goodness sake, don't play that record **again**.*

In more complicated sentences, if we want *again* at the beginning, we often use *once again*; otherwise people may think we are using sense **b**:
> *I walked down, and **once again**, just like the first time, there was nobody in the street.*
> *(**Once**) **again**, we're talking about blame. But we're missing the point.*

When we add *again* at the end of a question we are asking a person to repeat information:
> *What's his phone number **again**?*

b *again* at the beginning of a sentence often means 'additionally' or 'and here is another fact':
> *Scientists are worried that all the goodness will be taken out of the soil when the trees come down . . . **Again**, industrial developments could have a bad effect on the rivers.*

c *Then again* and *there again* introduce additional information, and often additional arguments or reasons:
> *I mean you could make fifty pounds a week easily having two tenants and, **then again**, you've got to have the money to furnish the place.*
> *The children shouldn't play in the street, but **there again** they haven't got anywhere else to go.*

against: preposition

a • next to and touching
> *Rain rattled **against** the windscreen.*
> *She stood leaning **against** the churchyard wall.*

b • opposed to; not for
> *Hughes was carried off with an injured ankle at Liverpool's match **against** Spurs last night.*
> *I have nothing **against** you – it's just that I'm afraid we're incompatible.*
> *I've got deep prejudices **against** it.*

age: noun (C, U)   ▶ Compare **old**

a *He would never tell anyone his **age** – he was 39 for years.*
*I never spoke to my parents like that when I was your **age**.*
*Old **age** is not much fun – what is there to look forward to?*
*She learnt to read at the **age** of four.*

Note:
If you want to know someone's age, say *How old are you?/How old is your son?*
It is possible to say *He's twelve years of age*, but it is much more usual to say *He's twelve (years old)*.

b ages/age
  • a long time
    *I haven't seen Audrey for **ages** – I hope she's all right.*
    *Let's have a game of tennis. It's an **age** since I've had any exercise.*

---

ago: adverb   ► Compare **since**

  • back in time from now
a *ago* follows a time expression and usually needs a past tense (not present perfect):
    *They came to London eight years **ago**.*
    *How long **ago** did it happen?*
    *Oh, many years **ago**/two weeks **ago**/not very long **ago**.*

  A modal perfect is possible:
    *I must **have met** them twenty years **ago**.*

b *ago* relates to *now* and does not mean 'back from then' or 'back from some past time'. If we are referring to a point of time before a time in the past we use *before* or *earlier*:
    *I stayed in that hotel three years **ago**.*
  But:
    *When I went to New York I stayed in the same hotel where I had stayed five years **before/earlier**.*

---

agree: verb   ► Compare **accept**

>   –
>   *with*
> **agree** + *about/to*
>   (*on*) + OBJECT
>   *to*-INFINITIVE
>   *that*-CLAUSE

agree is used in various patterns with slightly different meanings. It is not usually used in the progressive:
    *'I think we should give her a month's trial.' 'Yes, I **agree**.'*
    *I **agree** with the government's policy.* (= view it favourably)
    *I **agree** with you on/about most things but not on/about this.* (= share your views)
    *In the end he **agreed** to their plan.* (= accepted)
    *Can we **agree** on a date for the next committee meeting?* (= decide on)

*I thought you **agreed** to take the job?*
*It was **agreed** that no action would be taken.*

In British English (but not American English) *on* is sometimes omitted:
*Last week MPs on the committee refused to **agree** a timetable.*

ahead

1 ahead: adverb

ahead is usually used in end position.

a ● in front
*Keep straight **ahead**, up the road to the pass.*

b ● in the future; in advance; in front of us (in time)
*This is the task which now lies **ahead** for our generation.*
*I can't arrange as far **ahead** as 30th November.*
*There is no easy road **ahead**.*
*You should look **ahead** instead of living from day to day.* (= plan for the future)

▶ See **look forward to**

c go/get ahead
to *go ahead* is to begin doing something, or to go in front.
to *get ahead* is to make progress or succeed:
*They said 'OK, **go ahead**, do what you want. But don't blame us if it all goes wrong.*
*In the twenty-eighth minute Leeds **went ahead** and scored a goal.*
*I wanted to **get ahead**, because I was very ambitious.*

2 ahead of: preposition

● in front of (in space or time)
*Gerald saw a tall dark girl walking **ahead of** them towards Knightsbridge.*
*London is five hours **ahead of** New York.*

aim

1 aim: noun (C)

a ● purpose; something a person hopes to achieve
*The **aim** of the scheme is to help the young unemployed to find jobs.*
*He seems to have no **aims** in life.*

b ● the act of pointing a weapon
*Take careful **aim**, then squeeze the trigger.* (= point at a target)

2 aim: verb

```
            OBJECT
aim + at
            to-INFINITIVE
```

*The man picked up his gun and **aimed** (it) at the animal.*
*They **aim** to help the unemployed.*

ain't

In non-standard Modern English, *ain't* is a short form of *am not, are not, is not* or *have not*. It is sometimes used jokingly by standard speakers
*It **ain't** going to be the Liberal party, says he, laughing.*
*You **ain't** seen nothing yet.*

air

1   air: noun (usually U)

a   *Open the windows – we need some fresh **air**.*
*I don't like **air** travel, but going by **air** is so much quicker.*

b   the air
  • the space above and around the earth
  *We were 20,000 feet up in **the air** and had a marvellous view of the mountains down below.*
  ***The air** is full of radio waves.*

2   air: verb

a   • expose or be exposed to the air to freshen or to dry
  *Do you mind if I open the window and **air** the room? It's full of smoke.*
  *It's a tiny flat and there's nowhere to **air** the clothes when you've washed them.*

b   • speak about one's opinions or complaints
  *The monthly meeting is the place to discuss progress and **air** grievances.*

alike

1   alike: adjective   ► Compare **like**

  • like each other
  alike is predicative only:
  *His letters were beautifully formed, but they were all **alike**, so it was impossible to read his handwriting.*
  *Mary and her sister sound exactly **alike** on the phone.*

2   alike: adverb

  • in the same way

  *You really ought to treat them all **alike**.*

---

alive and **live** /laɪv/: adjectives　　▶ Compare **live** /lɪv/: verb

Both *alive* and *live* mean 'having life', but *alive* is predicative only:
　*Both my grandmothers **are** still **alive**.*

whereas *live* is used attributively:
　*Is it right to keep **live** animals in cages?*
　*'He shouldn't have said it. He knew it was a **live** broadcast.'* (= a radio or TV
　programme not recorded in advance)
　*Never touch a **live** wire.* (= carrying electricity)

---

all

1 **all**: determiner and pronoun　　　　▶ Compare **both**

a **all** *(+ of)* + NOUN/PRONOUN

A all		oranges (pl) food (U)
B	the these/those my/your/his/her/our/their	oranges (pl)
all (of)	the this/that my/your, etc.	food (U) orange (sing)
	this/these, etc. mine/yours, etc.	
C **all of**	it/them you/us	

A **all** + NOUN
　All can come immediately before a plural noun or an uncountable noun,
　and then means 'every one of' a group, or 'the whole amount of'
　something:
　　***All** children love ice-cream.*
　　***All** ice-cream is fattening.*

　We cannot use *all* + SINGULAR NOUN (NOT **all orange*). But notice *all day*, *all*
　night used like adverbs:
　　*I want to dance **all night**.*

B **all (of)** + *the/this/my*, etc. + NOUN and *all (of)* + *this/mine*, etc.
All or *all of* can come before *the*, *this*, *my*, etc. plus a noun. With a singular
noun (*all the orange*) the meaning is 'the whole thing'. *All* (*of*) can also come
before pronouns *this/that/these/those* and possessive pronouns (*mine*, etc.):
  *I've spent **all** (**of**) my money.*
  *I've read **all** (**of**) the book.*

C **all of** + *it/them/you/us*
We have to say *all of it, all of us*, etc. (NOT **all it, *all us*):
  *Be quiet, **all of** you!*

Note: we can also use *all of which/whom/whose*:
  *There were lots of traffic signs, **all of which** he ignored.*
  *She had dozens of friends, **all of whom** sent cards.*

b NOUN/PRONOUN + **all**

A The children (pl) They		**all**	enjoyed the party. have oranges.
The food (U) It		**all**	looked delicious.
B The children (pl) They	are	**all**	ready. enjoying the meal.
	have		finished now.
The food (U) It	is	**all**	delicious
	has		been eaten.
	should		look attractive.

A A noun or pronoun is often followed by *all*, particularly when it is the subject.
All comes immediately after the noun or pronoun when a one-word verb
follows, unless that verb is *be*.
B *all* follows *be* or an auxiliary or modal verb. (Compare mid-position adverbs.)
Note: In short answers the position of *all* depends on whether the answer is
positive or negative:
  *How many of the children are still in the classroom? They **all** are.*
  *Are all the men out on strike? No, they aren't **all**. A few are still working.*

c Sentence functions of *all*-phrases

SUBJECT	All (**of**) the children **All of** us The children **all** We **all**	enjoyed the party.	
DIRECT OBJECT	He ate	**all** (**of**) the oranges/the food. **all of** them/it. them **all**/it **all**.	
INDIRECT OBJECT	We gave	**all** (**of**) the children **all of** them them **all**	oranges.
	We gave	oranges to	**all** (**of**) the children. **all of** them. them **all**.
SUBJECT COMPLEMENT	Is that the lot? Yes, that's	**all** (**of**) the oranges/the food. **all of** them/it.	

all (of) + NOUN/PRONOUN (as in **a** above) is used in different positions in a sentence.

But NOUN + *all* (**b**) is mainly used only as a subject. (NOT **He ate the oranges all.* **We gave oranges to the children all.*)

  PRONOUN + *all* (also **b**) – e.g. *they all, them all* – can be subject and object, but not usually subject complement at the end of a sentence (NOT **That's them all/ us all.*). But the following are possible:
   *It's **you all** (that) I want to see.*
   *That's **us all** in Athens last summer.* (describing a photograph)

d all + PHRASE or RELATIVE CLAUSE
  all is not often used in modern English as a pronoun on its own. We prefer *everything* or *everybody*:
   *Have you got **everything**?* (NOT **Have you got all?*)
   *Do you know **everybody** here?* (NOT **Do you know all here?*)

  But we can say *all about*, meaning 'everything about':
   *I'll tell you **all about** my holiday some time.*

  We can also use *all* + RELATIVE CLAUSE:
   *I'll tell you **all I know**.* (= everything I know)
   ***All you ever do** is complain.* (= The only thing you do . . .)

  It is possible to say *all those* when referring to people:
   ***All those** who failed to get tickets will get their money back.*

e   all and every

all and *every*, when used to talk about people and things as a group, are similar in meaning. But *every* is only used with a singular noun (and a singular verb form if necessary) while *all* is followed by a plural noun with a plural verb form:

All (the) seats have been taken.

or by an uncountable noun with a singular verb:

All the standing-room is occupied too.

f   not all

It can be confusing to begin a negative sentence with *all* (*All young people are not alike.*). Instead we prefer:

Not all young people are alike. (= but some are alike)
Young people are not all alike.

g   at all

at all, meaning 'of any kind', 'in any way' is mainly non-assertive:
Is there a cinema or a disco here at all?
There's nothing at all to do.
Stop if you should feel at all tired.

▶ See   *not at all* at **not**

h   for all

For all someone knows/cares, has the meaning 'as far as one knows/cares, but one does not really know/care . . .':
I could be dead for all you care.
For all I know, they may already be in London.

Do not confuse this with *for all* + NOUN, which means 'in spite of':
For all my hard work, I still failed the exam.

▶ See   **above all; after all**

2   all: adverb

As an adverb, *all* means 'completely, utterly'. *All* is used to emphasise an adjective, another adverb or a preposition that follows it:

I feel all excited.
Our holiday was over all too soon.
There was mud all over the floor.
I'm all for it. (= very much in favour of . . .)

▶ See   *all along* at **along**
            all but at **but**
            all right at **right**

---

allow: verb   ▶ Compare **let**

allow +	OBJECT *-ing* O + *to*-INFINITIVE IO + OBJECT

a • permit
  *They don't **allow** dogs in the swimming pool.*
  *We don't **allow** eating in class.*
  *We aren't **allowed** to eat in the classrooms.*
  *You cannot **allow** children to do exactly what they want all the time.*
  *Remember to **allow** them time to clear up.*

b • pay regularly
  *My father **allows** me £60 a week.*

Note: We do not use *allow* plus an infinitive when there is no object: **He does not **allow** to eat* in class.

allowance: noun

a • an amount of money given regularly or for a particular purpose
  *I get an **allowance** of £60 a week.*
  *Do the students get a book **allowance**?*
  allowance does not mean 'permission'.

b **make allowances for**
  *You should **make allowances for** her – she's very young.* (= consider this fact when judging her)

almost: adverb ▶ Compare **nearly**

 • nearly, but not quite
a *almost* often has a similar meaning to *nearly*, and both words could be used in the examples here. With verbs, *almost* usually comes in mid-position:
  *He's **almost** as tall as you.*
  *I **almost** phoned them up and said, 'Come a bit later'.*
  *Max's life was so dull that it is **almost** impossible to make a story of it.*
  *There were **almost** fifty people at the party.*
  *I **almost** didn't go.*
  *I shall eventually get **almost** all the money from Jim.*
  *I go **almost** every weekend.*
  ***Almost** everybody is forced to be more generous.*
  *I **almost** always do go in the end.*
  *I'm **almost** ready.* (. . . and will be soon)

b *almost* is used when we talk about an end, a finishing point, a result which could never be reached. *Nearly* cannot be used in these examples:
  *My dog can **almost** talk.* (but it never will)
  *This was **almost** news to me.* (but it wasn't quite)
  *I **almost** wish I hadn't told you.* (but I have told you)
  *They brought the bill **almost** before we'd finished eating.* (but we had finished)

c *almost* (NOT *nearly) is used before *any* and before negative words like *no, none, never, nobody, nothing*:
  *Our defences are weaker than at **almost** any time in our history.*
  *He knows what has been written about **almost** anything.*

*The heavy blade made **almost** no impression.*
*I need some more pins – I've **almost** none.*
*I **almost** never go.*
*He saw **almost** nobody and did **almost** nothing.*

---

alone ▶ Compare **lone**; **lonely**

alone: adjective and adverb

a • without other people
*Peter took out the boat **alone** and nearly drowned himself.*
*I want to be **alone**.*
*He and I had dinner **alone**. (= just the two of us)*
*'You didn't go on holiday **alone**?' 'Yes I did – I rather enjoyed it.'*

b When *alone* belongs to the noun it follows, it means 'only' or 'by itself':
***Heaven alone** knows what will happen!*
***Money alone** will not solve the problem.*
***The fares alone** cost £500, and then there's hotels and everything on top.*

c *leave/let something alone* means 'not to touch it', 'not to interfere with it':
***Leave** those spots **alone**. You'll make them worse if you touch them.*
▶ See **let alone**

d Like most words with *a* as a prefix, *alone* is never an attributive adjective (NOT **She's an alone person*).

---

along

1 along: preposition ▶ Compare **through**

• in the same direction as the side or length of
*The rat began to run **along** the bottom of the ditch.*
*They walked two or three times **along** disused footpaths.*
*I was walking **along** a long corridor.*

2 along: adverb

As an adverb, *along* occurs with verbs of movement:
*We **hurried along** down the platform looking for seats on the train.*
*The young people were **walking along** chatting and singing.*
***Come along**, please. Hurry up.*

3 all along

• all that time; throughout that long period
*He seems **all along** to have been aware of its real purpose.*

---

alongside: preposition and adverb

• along the side (of); together with
*The two hundred kilometres **alongside** each new road have been made into state property.*

*This job could be held **alongside** a teaching job.*
*Bring your boat up **alongside**.*

---

already: adverb ► Compare **still**; **yet**

- even now/even then; earlier than the time expected; surprisingly soon
already usually comes in mid-position or end-position:

a *I'm afraid we've **already** had dinner.*
*Surely Tom hasn't **already** left – he said he'd wait for us.*
*He was probably **already** suspicious.*
*I knew the story **already**.*
*We can't get tickets – the play is completely booked up **already**.*
***Already** I long to get back to civilisation.*

b In British English, action verbs with *already* prefer perfect, not past, tenses:
*I have **already** decided what to do.*
*Surely Tom hasn't **already** left.*

But in American English we can say:
*I **already decided**.*
*Tom **already left**.*

c Do not confuse with *all ready*, as in:
*We are **all ready** to go.* (= All of us are ready *or* We are completely ready.)

---

alright ► See **right**

---

also ► Compare **as well**; **too**

1 also: adverb
a *also* usually comes in mid-position and refers to the verb and what follows. Both the sentences here mean that the person did/has done these things in addition to some other activity.
*He was responsible for financial planning and was **also** actively involved in other departments of the company.*
*He has **also** developed the remarkable practice of swimming backwards at enormous speeds.*

In American English, *also* is used in end-position:
*I need some apples, and some oranges **also**.*
But British English prefers *as well* or *too* for end-position.

b *also* is normally used to add an affirmative statement to another affirmative statement:
*She's hungry, and she's **also** thirsty and tired.*

Also is not usually used like this with two negatives sentences, when we prefer *not . . . either* or *neither/nor*:
*I'm not hungry. And I'm not thirsty or tired **either/Nor** am I thirsty or tired.*

2 also: connector

- in addition; what is more; moreover
  *I am permanently hungry, and too lazy to cook. **Also**, I am spending too much money.*

although: conjunction ▶ Compare **though**; **despite**

- I admit . . . but . . .; despite the fact that
  *I don't feel like writing letters, **although** I must thank you for your card and letter.*
  ***Although** his manner is quiet, this teacher has no discipline problems.*
  *The children never go to see my mother, **although** they're only on the other side of Birmingham.*
  *The weather, **although** sunny, was rather cold.*

altogether

1 altogether: adverb

a - completely; entirely
  *The situation is **altogether** different.*
  *His public appearances became less frequent, and after a time stopped **altogether**.*

b - in total
  altogether is used for the total when adding up numbers:
  *I spent £2.80, £5.20 and £3.50. That's £11.50 **altogether**.*

2 altogether: connector

- on the whole; to sum up
  altogether usually comes in front position:
  *The hotel was terrible, it rained every day, and I broke my arm. **Altogether** the holiday was·a disaster.*

3 altogether or **all together**?

Do not confuse *altogether* with *all together* (i.e., everybody/everything together). Compare:
  *There are seven of us **altogether** – my parents, my four brothers and me.*
  *It's not often that we are **all together** these days.* (= that all of us are together in the same place.)

always: adverb

- every time; all the time
  always usually comes in mid-position.
a *Always* is usually used with simple present or past tenses to talk about habits or permanent states or situations:
  *I **always** have tea in town on Mondays.*
  *He **always** used to make the most horrible noises.*

I've always been afraid of the dark.
Their protests must always be taken cautiously.
He is always terribly busy.

b With ordinary imperative sentences, *always* usually comes before the main verb:
Always remember to check in your mirror before overtaking.
Don't always rely on me to help you out when you're in trouble.

c Used with progressive tenses, *always* means 'continually', 'again and again'.
Always + PROGRESSIVE may suggest 'too frequently', but this is not necessarily part of the meaning:
This is a battle that I'm always fighting.
Proust is always referring back to things and remembering things in the past.
I am always sending you messages but you never send any messages back.
You're always criticising me. It's terribly unfair.

---

am ▶ See **be**

1st person singular present tense of *be*.
The only possible negative for *am* in statements is *I am not* or *I'm not*. (NOT *I amn't* or *I aren't*)
The usual negative question form is *aren't I?* in British English. It is avoided in American English:
Oh dear, I am silly, aren't I?
Aren't I silly!

The form *am I not* is possible but rare.
Positive questions are *am I?*:
Am I right?

---

among and amongst: prepositions ▶ Compare **between**

- in the middle of; one of; existing in; affecting
among and *amongst* are normally followed by plural nouns, referring to three or more people or things. *Amongst* is more formal and less common:
I could just make out a small cabin cruiser among the sailing boats.
The cold water pipes are among the most frequent causes of trouble in a house.
We have, amongst other things, checked with the Midland Bank that she has an account there.
Long hair is now found among all social classes.
The mood among the islanders is one of determination.

---

amount

1 amount: noun (C, U) ▶ Compare number

- a quantity
amount is mainly used with uncountable nouns:
Some people seem to buy large amounts of food that they don't really need.

---

*I've got an enormous **amount** of work to do by the end of the month.*
*There was any **amount** of rubbish lying about in the streets (= large **amounts** of)*

2 **amount to**: verb
- add up to; equal; be worth

amount to is not usually used in the progressive:
*His debts **amounted to** six thousand pounds*
*He was always making wild promises but they didn't **amount to** very much.*

---

an ▶ See **a**

---

and: conjunction ▶ Compare **but; or**

a *and* can join words of the same class (e.g., two nouns, three adjectives):
*bread **and** cheese . . . you **and** me . . . cold, wet **and** miserable . . .*

b Where two clauses are joined by *and*, various meanings may be understood:
*I drove home **and** Paul caught the train back to London. (= both actions at the same time)*
*I drove home **and** went to bed. (= first one action and then the other)*
*I was tired **and** fell asleep immediately. (= the result . . .)*
*Do as you're told **and** you won't get hurt (= If you do . . . you won't . . .)*
*Write him a mad letter, **and** he'll write a mad letter back. (= If you . . . he will . . .)*
*I like cars **and** Paul likes trains. (contrast)*

c If more than two words or clauses are joined, *and* is normally only used between the last two:
*I need a pen, some paper **and** stamps.*
*I drove home, put the car away **and** went straight to bed.*

d VERB + **and** + VERB

Sometimes *and* is used between two verbs where we might expect *to*:
*Try **and** make less noise, please. (But NOT *He tries/tried/is trying **and** . . .)*
*I try **and** telephone my mother every week.*
*Why don't you wait **and** see what happens? (But NOT* He waited/is waiting **and** . . .)*
*Go **and** tell them lunch is ready.*
*He went **and** told them.*

---

another

1 **another**: determiner

a *another* is always written as one word. But it means *an+other*, so it is normally used with singular count nouns only. Compare:
*There isn't **another** bus. (sing)*

There aren't any more/any other buses (pl)
There isn't any more transport. (U)

b *another* has two meanings:
- (1) an additional one of the same kind
  *I've been having **another** busy day.*
  *We could have **another** holiday.*

- (2) different
  With this meaning *another* may be stressed in spoken English:
  *Sometimes I wish I could just go away and start again in **another** town.*
  *The dog ran off in **another** direction.*
  *No, this is **another** guy.* (guy = man)

c **another** + NUMBER or **another** + *few* can be followed by a plural count noun:
  *The book'll probably take about **another** four years to write.*
  *Can I keep this **another** few days?* (= *a few days more*)

2 **another**: pronoun

a *They are rather good chocolates. Have **another**.*
  *She has one boyfriend after **another**.*

b **one another**   ▶ Compare   **each other**
- *each other* referring to people
  *We should be able to accept and respect **one another's** point of view.*

---

answer   ▶ Compare **reply**

1 **answer**: noun (C)
- solution to a problem; reply
  *It was an exercise book with **answers** at the back.*
  *There is no easy **answer** to this problem.*
  *I've written twice, but I haven't had an **answer**.*

2 **answer**: verb

```
                 –
   answer + OBJECT
           that-CLAUSE
```

answer is used with and without an object and with *that*-CLAUSES:
  *I rang the doorbell, but nobody **answered**.*
  ***Answer** me, please.*
  *Have you **answered** his letter?*
  *Why doesn't somebody **answer** the telephone?*
  *Most of the questions were too difficult to **answer**.*
  *I had to **answer** that I didn't know.*

anxious and anxiety

1 anxious: adjective
- worried
  *I was very **anxious** for/about my brother's safety when we heard about the plane crash.*
  *I was **anxious** to know if he was all right.*
  *They were **anxious** for everybody to know the facts.*

2 anxiety: noun
  *There is public **anxiety** about river pollution.*

any ▶ Compare **some**

In general, *any* and words beginning with *any* (e.g. *anywhere*) – contrast with words beginning with *some*.

Any- words are mainly non-assertive. We use them in negative statements, questions, and after *if*. They contrast with the *some* series, which assert statements positively.

Any and *some* words have an indefinite meaning. So they both contrast with *every-* and *no-* words, which have a definite all-or-nothing meaning.

1 any: determiner and pronoun

any some	apples (PLURAL) bread (UNCOUNTABLE)
any some *of*	the/these/his apples the/this/his food it/them/you/us mine/yours . . .

a indefinite quantity
  any can refer to things and people. *Any* is used with uncountable nouns and plural nouns, to mean 'a certain amount of' or 'a number of'. In these non-assertive contexts, *any* can be unstressed:
  *Is there **any** bread?*
  *I don't think there's **any** (bread).*
  *There isn't **any** (bread).*
  *Are there **any** apples?*
  *There seem to be hardly **any**.*
  *I don't suppose there are **any**.*

b it doesn't matter which
  A second meaning of *any* is 'one/some of a kind, but it does not matter which'. With this meaning, *any* can be used in affirmative statements, as well as negatives and questions, and with singular count nouns, as well as plurals and uncountable nouns.

This *any* is usually stressed, and we can often add *just* or *absolutely* in front. Notice that sentences with *any* in this meaning often contain a modal verb:

> Absolutely **any** food would be better than nothing.
> 'Which of these can I have?' '**Any**.'
> **Any** of us would have helped, if you had asked.
> **Any** student could tell you that.
> **Any** book you have on this subject would be useful.

▶ See also *any minute now* at **now**

c   *any of* . . . can be followed by *the/this/these/my* . . . + NOUN and by PRONOUNS:

> I haven't read **any** of his books. (not even one of them)
> I haven't read **any** of that new novel yet. (not even a few pages)
> 'Why didn't you eat **any** of the food in the fridge?' 'I didn't like **any** of it.'
> There were a lot of people there, **any** of whom could have taken the money.

d   **any more/any** + NUMBERS . . .

any can be followed by *more* plus an uncountable noun or a plural noun:

> Is there **any** more (food)?
> We're not expecting **any** more (visitors).

any can also be followed by a number:

> You may borrow **any** two (books) you like.

e   **any** and **either**

any must refer to at least three people or things. So it sometimes contrasts with *either*, which is limited to two:

> I can wear this ring on **any** of my fingers, but I can't get it on to **either** of my thumbs.

f   **any, some** and ZERO   ▶ Compare **a/an**

any and *some* are roughly the plural of *a/an* in its 'specific' sense – that is when we are referring to actual things or people, but we do not definitely say which particular ones:

> 'Have you got a sunhat I could borrow?' 'Well, I have got some old hats somewhere, but I haven't **any** sunhats.'

This contrasts with the classifying use of *a/an*, where *any/some* are not used in the plural:

> I love hats, but my sisters never wear hats. (NOT *****any** hats)
> I need a hat, not sunglasses. (NOT *****some** sunglasses)

2   **any**: adverb   ▶ Compare **no**

a   *any* is used as an adverb in non-assertive sentences, meaning 'to any extent' 'at all'. It is used mainly with comparative adjectives and adverbs, and also with *different*:

> Can't you speak **any** louder?
> This doesn't look **any** different to me.
> We're none of us getting **any** younger.
> It's not cheap **any** more. (It used to be cheap)

b   *any* is also used before *good* and *use*:

> This line isn't **any** good. I can't hear you at all. (= telephone line)
> I don't think it's **any** use asking him – he always says no.

▶ Compare *It's no different/no good/no use* at **no**

---

anybody, anyone: pronouns ▶ Compare **everybody**; **nobody**; **somebody**

- any (indefinite) person

a *anybody/anyone* contrasts with *somebody/someone*, and is used non-assertively:

> *Is anybody/anyone there?*
> *Don't tell anybody/anyone.*
> *Hardly anybody knows this yet.*
> *Wasn't there anyone to ask?*
> *Did you see anyone famous?*
> *Was there anybody of importance there?*

Note that we do not use *anybody/anyone* as the subject of a negative sentence. (NOT **Not anybody knows . . . *Anybody doesn't know . . .* ▶ See **nobody**.)

b *anybody/anyone* can mean 'any person – it doesn't matter who', and with this meaning is used in affirmative statements:

> *Anybody/anyone that thinks that is a fool.*
> *What the world will be like in a hundred year's time is anybody's guess.*

c *anybody/anyone* is also used non-assertively with the meaning of 'an important person':

> *I don't think I shall ever be anybody.*

d Adjectives, relative clauses, *else* and other phrases always follow *anybody/anyone*:

> *anybody nice . . . anyone famous . . . anybody that thinks that . . .*
> *anybody to ask . . . anybody of importance . . . anyone else*

e **anybody/anyone** . . . **they**
anybody/anyone is singular and takes a singular verb, but is often followed by *they* (+ plural verb), *them*, *their*:

> *Has anyone got an umbrella they don't need?* (Note – plural *don't*)
> *Anybody can make mistakes, can't they?*
> *How can anybody forget their own name?*

f **anyone** and **any one**
Do not confuse *anyone* with *any one*, which can refer to things as well as people and means 'whichever one':

> *Isn't there any one person that you really love?*
> *Any one of us would have helped you if you had asked.*
> *'Which is my drink?' 'Oh, take any one you like.'*

---

anyhow, anyway

1 anyhow, anyway: connector ▶ Compare **somehow**

- in any case; in spite of that

> *I don't want to go skiing. Anyhow/Anyway, I can't afford to/I can't afford to, anyway.*
> *I know this meeting isn't very important, but I shall go anyhow/anyway.*

---

2 anyhow (NOT **anyway**): adverb

- it doesn't matter how
  She's not interested in clothes and just dresses (all) ***anyhow****.*

3 anyway and **any way**

Do not confuse *anyway* with *any way* (= *any* method, *any* means). Compare:
I shall go ***any way*** *I can – I'll walk if I have to.*
I shall go ***anyway****.* (= whatever happens).

In American English *anyways* is an informal alternative to *anyway*.

---

anything: pronoun   ▶ Compare **everything; nothing; something**

1

a *anything* is used in non-assertive contexts in contrast to *something*, which is used affirmatively. We do not use *anything* as a subject in a negative sentence (**Not* ***anything*** *happens . . . *****Anything*** *does not happen.* ▶ See **nothing**):
  Is ***anything*** *the matter?*
  If you need ***anything****, tell me.*
  I wonder if he has ***anything*** *of value.*
  There isn't ***anything*** *wrong, is there?*
  I've got a lump on my arm, but the doctor says it isn't ***anything****.* (= it is not important)

b • it doesn't matter what

  anything is also used with a meaning of 'it doesn't matter what', and, in this second sense, it is used in affirmative statements. It often has *just* or *absolutely* in front of it, and sometimes it almost means 'everything':
  Anything *you can do, I can do better.*
  Absolutely ***anything*** *would be better than waiting for news like this.*
  Tell me absolutely ***anything*** *you know about her.*

c Adjectives, relative clauses, *else* and other phrases always follow *anything*:
  anything *wrong . . .* ***anything*** *of value . . .* ***anything*** *you can do . . .* ***anything*** *else . . .*

2 or anything

- or anything like that
  You're not worried ***or anything****, are you?*

3 anything but

- quite the opposite of
  'Why is he lazy?' 'Oh, he's ***anything but*** *lazy. He works tremendously hard.'*

anywhere: adverb ▶ Compare **somewhere**

1

a • any (indefinite) place – in non-assertive contexts
*I can't find my umbrella **anywhere**.*
*Is there **anywhere** we can get a meal after midnight?*
*He'll be at the airport, if **anywhere**.*

b • no matter which place

With this meaning, *anywhere* can be used in affirmative statements:
***Anywhere** would be better than this boring place.*
*We'll go **anywhere** you like.*

2 anywhere like, anywhere near

These two phrases are used in non-assertive contexts and mean 'nearly':
*I'm not **anywhere** like/**anywhere** near ready.*

▶ Compare *nowhere near* at **nowhere** and *not anything/nothing like* at **like**

apart

1 apart: adverb

• separated; some distance away
*Countries as far **apart** as China and Wales will use the dragon to suggest basically the same idea.*
*Plant the young plants not more than a foot **apart**.*

2 apart from: preposition

a • separated from; away from
*He's a married man, living **apart from** his wife.*

b • except for
*I'll be away until about the 20th September. **Apart from** that, I'll be at home.*

c • in addition to
*They had many other policies, **apart from** these.*
***Apart from** the need to remove injustices, there is a need to simplify the law.*

apparent: adjective

a • obvious; clear
With this meaning, *apparent* is used predicatively:
*It is quite **apparent** that the job is too difficult for him.*

b When *apparent* means 'looking real, but perhaps not so', it is used attributively:
*The **apparent** improvement in his health did not last, and three months later he was dead.*

apparently

1 **apparently**: adverb

- seemingly
  When I visited him in hospital he was **apparently** much better.

2 **apparently**: sentence adverb

apparently can introduce some information that we think is true, but we are not sure. The meaning is *It appears that . . .*:
Apparently, they didn't get married after all.
'Did Tom pass his exam?' 'Apparently not./Apparently. (NOT **Apparently so.*)'

appear ▶ Compare **seem**

	—
appear +	*(to be)* + ADJECTIVE *to be* + NOUN *to*-INFINITIVE *as if/as though*
It appears +	*that*-CLAUSE *so/not*

1 • come into view; arrive
As an intransitive verb *appear* is the opposite of *disappear*:
A cow suddenly appeared from nowhere in front of the car.
The new fashions will be appearing in the shops soon.

2 ▶ Compare **seem**
a • judging by what I see or hear; judging from appearances
With this meaning *appear* is not usually used in the progressive. *Appear* can be followed by *(to be +)* ADJECTIVE, *to be* + NOUN and by *to*-INFINITIVE:
You appear (to be) worried. What's the matter?
It now appears certain that the job has gone to someone else.
I asked a girl in a blue dress, who appeared to be a shop assistant.
He appeared to believe that he would get the job.
Everybody appears to have believed that he would.

b With impersonal *It* as subject we can have *It appears* + *as if/as though*; *that*-CLAUSES and *so/not*:
It appears as if/as though Tom has missed the train.
It appears (that) he expected to get the job.
'Did he get the job?' 'It appears so/not.'

c When *appears* + *to*-INFINITIVE is used with a negative idea, we often make *appear*, not the second verb, negative:

> He **doesn't appear** to know what he wants.
> He **appears** not to know . . . (formal)

---

are ► See **be**

---

arise, **arose**, **arisen**: verb Compare **rise**

arise is a rather formal word meaning *happen* and is usually used with abstract nouns such as *difficulties*, *needs*, *opportunities*, *situations*:

> A problem has **arisen** about my university place – I may have to go somewhere else.

---

around ► Compare **about**; **round**

1 around: preposition

a • all round; from one part to another in
round is possible with this meaning (but not *about*):

> Bombs were falling **around us**.
> I love old cities that have walls **around** them.
> She is only just able to walk **around** the house.

b • approximately; roughly
about is possible with this meaning (but not *round*):

> The church was built **around 1500**.
> It's hard to say just how many you'll have in the audience, but I would guess **around** thirty.

2 around: adverb

a • from one place to another; moving in a circle; in the opposite direction
round is possible with this meaning but American English prefers *around*:

> Caroline came **around** yesterday. (= to my home)
> They went **around** to the pub.
> The waiters brought **around** food and drink.
> The cyclist turned right. I could not stop and I hit him. He should have looked **around** to see if anything was coming.
> You've got it the wrong way **around**. August is named after the Emperor Augustus, not the Emperor after the month.

b • somewhere near;   in various places
about is possible with this meaning:

> I sat **around** all day feeling miserable.
> Back to college, but there were not many people **around**.
> He's coming back in January, and I'd like to be **around**.
> I had a copy lying **around** on my desk.
> We followed our guide **around**.
> They seem to know their way **around**.

arrange: verb

```
                 OBJECT
arrange + about/for . . .
         (for . . .) to-INFINITIVE
```

arrange can be followed by an OBJECT, by *about/for*, and by (*for* . . .) *to*-INFINITIVE:

a • put in position
   *I don't like the way I've **arranged** the furniture. The room doesn't look right.*

b • organise
   *Can you **arrange** (about/for) theatre tickets?*
   *Let's **arrange** to meet again soon.*
   *I've **arranged** for a taxi to collect you at 2 p.m.*

arrangement: noun

a • plan; preparations (usually plural)
   *Have you made any **arrangements** for the next committee meeting?*
   *I always leave the travel **arrangements** to someone else.*

b • something agreed; an agreement (C, U)
   *Sharing the costs sounds a good **arrangement**.*
   *The library will be open tomorrow by special **arrangement**.*

arrival: noun (U, C)

a *arrival* is the opposite of *departure* (U)
   *We were late leaving because of the late **arrival** of the plane from Cairo.*

b • person who arrives (C)
   *There were several late **arrivals** at the party.*

arrive: verb

arrive is the opposite of *leave*
   *Some guests always **arrive** late.*
   *We **arrived** in Athens in the middle of the night.*
   *They **arrived** at the airport far too early.*

as

1 **as**: conjunction

a **Time**   ▶ Compare when; while
   • at the same moment that; during the time that; when
   *Roger was leaving the house just **as** I arrived.*

As she grew older, she became rather deaf.
As a child I lived in the country. (= When I was a child)

b Reason ▶ Compare **because; since**
• seeing that; since
as-clauses of reason must have a finite verb (NOT **As clever, you . . .* or **As being clever, you . . .*):

As it's so expensive, I don't think we shall buy it.
As you're so clever, you should know all the answers.

c Manner
• in the way that
Please do as I ask.
Tom was very rude, as he can be sometimes.
We left him alone, as he wished.
You're late as usual. (= *as you usually are*)
As always, you have an excuse, I suppose. (= *as you always have*)

d Concession ▶ Compare **though**
This usage of *as* is rather formal. The meaning is roughly *though*. Notice the unusual word order at the beginning of the sentence:

Much as I would like to, I cannot help you.
Try as they would, we couldn't make them change their minds.
Unlikely as it may seem, we honestly did try.
Exhausted as I was, I kept on running.

e There is an odd usage of *as* where it is rather like a relative pronoun:

He was very rude, as was his wife. (**which** his wife was too)
Suddenly the train stopped and the lights went out, as happens sometimes. (**which** happens . . .)
My background is as follows. (**what** follows.)

Notice that *happens* and *follows* here have no other subjects.
Do not say **as it happens sometimes . . . *as it follows . . .*

2 as . . . as . . .: comparison ▶ Compare **than**

A			
	Roger works	*as*	*hard as I do.*
	His job isn't	*as* / *so*	*interesting as his last job was.*
	Things never seem	*as* / *so*	*good as they were.*
B	*Susan works just*	*as hard.* / *as hard as me.*	
	Her job isn't	*as* / *so*	*tiring (as her last one.)*

as + ADVERB/ADJECTIVE + *as* + *someone/something* (+VERB) is a way of comparing two different people/things.

a   If the second *as* is followed by a pronoun + a verb the pronoun must be a *subject* pronoun:
    Roger works as hard as I do.
    Things never seem as good as they were.

b   When there is no following verb, an object pronoun is normal in modern English, even when it refers to the doer of the verb:
    Susan works as hard as me.

c   After a negative we can use *so* instead of the first *as*. But if there is no negative, we use *as . . . as . . .*
    (For the grammatically minded, the first *as* in *He works as hard as I do* is an adverb, and the second *as* is a conjunction. But the second *as* in *as hard as me* is a preposition.)
    There are sometimes two possible meanings when the noun or object pronoun after *as* could refer to the subject or the object:
    Do you like this place as much as your aunt?
    probably means *Do you like the place as much as your aunt likes it?* but could mean *Do you like the place as much as you like your aunt?*
                        ▶   See *as long as* at **long** and *as soon as* at **soon**.

3   **as if, as though**: conjunctions

    as if and *as though* are also used to make comparisons.
a   If we are talking about a situation that is likely or possible, we use the tenses we would normally use:
    It looks as if I'm going to be busy. (= I'm probably going to be busy.)
    It doesn't sound as if you got much fun out of it.
    Do I look as though I've got a cold?

b   If we are talking about an unlikely situation or one that we know is not true, past tenses may be used with a present meaning:
    They look rather puzzled, as if they didn't/don't know.
    You look as though you had/have seen a ghost.
    Why does he stay in bed all day? It's not as if he were/is ill.
    We felt as though we had been/were stuck to our chairs.

c   *as if/as though* can be followed by non-finite verbs and by phrases:
    Dinah took a breath as if to speak.
    She screamed as though in pain.

4   **as**: preposition   ▶   Compare **like**

    The preposition *as* is used to talk about people and things considered in a particular way – their role or function at a particular time:
a   *I'm interested in people as people, not as numbers.*
    Roger is highly praised as a teacher.
    As a teacher, Roger is outstanding, but as a colleague he is sometimes difficult.
    Would you like to work as a waiter?

Speaking as your brother, I'm really worried about you.
The news of their marriage came as a complete surprise to him. (= it was a surprise)
He soon became known as an outstanding actor.
Eileen took them to the theatre as a birthday treat.

b   Sometimes there is a strong sense of comparison:
We are all as one over this. (= we agree, as if we were only one person.)
Please don't use the floor as an ashtray.
Why is that man dressed as/like a woman?

c   **as** or **like**?
Both *as* and *like* are used to make comparisons. But usage and meaning are not the same. *Like* means 'similar to' or 'in the same way as', but it does not mean 'exactly the same as'. Compare:
As your brother, I am worried about you. (Because I am your brother . . .)
Like your brother, I am worried. (Your brother is worried, and I am too.)

d   Several verbs expressing opinions can take OBJECT + *as*-PHRASES. The *as* can be followed by a noun phrase, a non-finite verb or an adjective:
We regarded the whole thing as a joke.
I never think of myself as (being) clever.
The shop described the books to me as badly damaged.
Also:
look on/recognise/see/view + OBJECT + *as* . . .

With some verbs *as* is optional:
He considers football (as) the best game in the world.

and with others *as* is never used:
You will find this an easy journey.

5   as to, as for

a   Both *as to* and *as for* are used at the beginning of a sentence to introduce a new topic, though one that is still connected with what has just been said. The meaning is roughly 'with reference to' or 'regarding':

As to other personal qualities, he is extremely conscientious and hard-working.
As to being happy, thank you, yes, we are very happy.
As for me, you can tell I'm still alive because you can hear my voice.
As for your other question, I really cannot guess what the future course of Britain's trade with the EEC will be like.

As to is more frequent and is the safer choice, because *as for* sometimes sounds a bit rude, suggesting that the words that follow are not very important. Perhaps for this reason we modestly say *As for me* (NOT **As to me*).

b   *as to* (not *as for*) can also be used later in a sentence to say what we are talking about or on. In all these examples we could use *about* in place of *as to*:
The problem arose (as to) how to clothe him.
I've sounded people out as to what they thought. (sounded out = asked)
She had no doubt as to the issue.
There's still some doubt (as to) whether we should go.

6   as well (as)

a   as well: sentence adverb ▶ Compare **also; too**
  • also; too; in addition
  as well is usually used in end position:
    *I do look forward to seeing you again, and seeing your photographs **as well**.*

b   (just) as well
  If something is *(just) as well*, we mean it is probably a good thing:
    *It's just **as well** to know the truth – however unpleasant.*
    *When racing, it's **as well** to make sure what the rules are.*
    *It was **just as well** we didn't go, because the meeting was cancelled.*

c   may/might as well + BARE INFINITIVE
  If we *may* or *might as well* do something, it means that it is worth doing but not
  very important to us:
    *I **may as well** get my money's worth.*
    *You **might as well** know – we're divorced.*

d   as well as: preposition
  • in addition to
    *Tim was upset **as well as** Roger.*
    *Tim, **as well as** Roger, was upset.* (Notice *was*, not *were*.)
    ***As well as** being upset, he was very angry.*

▶ See also   *as such* and *such as* at **such**

---

ashamed and shameful

People are *ashamed*; things or actions are *shameful*:
  *You should be **ashamed** of yourself – hitting a small child.*
  *I was **ashamed** that I had shouted at her.*
  *I'm **ashamed** to say (that) I just forgot.*

shameful describes behaviour that people ought to be *ashamed of*:
  *The behaviour of the football fans was absolutely **shameful**.*
  *What **shameful** behaviour!*

---

ask: verb ▶ Compare say; tell

```
                 —
              OBJECT
              about/for
ask (+IO) +   if/whether
              wh-CLAUSE
              to-INFINITIVE
```

1   ask + OBJECTS

a   *ask* can take two objects (like *tell*) but an indirect object is not essential:
    *She **asked** (me) a funny question/my name/my opinion/the time/the way to
    the station.*

---

b We can also *ask* (questions) *about* something/somebody, and we can make requests by *asking for* something to be given to us or for something to be done:
> *He **asked** (me) about my holidays/my mother.*
> *I never **ask** (anybody) for money/for help.*
> *I **asked** for the work to be finished by Friday.*
> *He **asked** me for a cigarette.* (NOT *He **asked** me a cigarette.)

c *ask* can also mean 'invite':
> *We've **asked** thirty people to the party.*

d *ask* can be used without any objects, with the general meaning of *asking* (questions) or *asking for* something:
> *I wanted a drink, but I didn't like to **ask**.* (for one)
> *If you lose your way, you must **ask**.* (someone the way)

2 Direct and reported speech

a *ask* is the commonest verb when introducing questions in direct and reported speech:
> *'Are you ready? What are we waiting for?' he **asked** (me).*
> *He **asked** (me) if/whether I was ready, and what we were waiting for.*

b *ask* (+ OBJECT) + *wh*-CLAUSE can also refer to indirect questions of various kinds:
> *You'll have to **ask** (your teacher) what to do.*

c *ask* (+ OBJECT) + *to*-INFINITIVE is used to report requests:
> *He **asked** us to help him.* (He said 'Please help me.')
> *We **asked** to see the room.* (We said 'Can we see the room, please?')
> *(or – We **asked** if we could see the room.)*
> *I didn't **ask** to be born!*

▶ Compare **tell** for commands.

3 Passives

Passives are possible, but not usually with impersonal *it* (NOT *It was **asked** if/whether . . .)
> *I **was asked** some funny questions/about my past/for money/what I knew about Harry.*
> *We've **been asked** (= invited) for the weekend.*
> *Questions **have been asked** about this in Parliament.*

---

asleep and **sleep**　　　　　　　▶ Compare **awake**

1 *asleep* is an adjective and predicative only (so NOT *an **asleep** child). We emphasise *asleep* with *fast* or *sound* (NOT *very **asleep**):
> *I was fast/sound **asleep** when the telephone woke me.*
> *He often falls **asleep** in front of the fire.*

2 *sleep* is a verb (*sleep, slept, slept*) and a noun:
> *Be quiet and go to **sleep**.*

---

*I drank too much coffee and couldn't **sleep**/couldn't get to **sleep** last night.*
*She only **sleeps** four or five hours a night – she doesn't need much **sleep**.* (U)
*Churchill used to like a short **sleep** in the afternoon.*

3 *sleeping* can be used as an attributive adjective and as a 'verbal noun':
*Isn't there a story called the **Sleeping** Princess?*
*I can't go camping – I haven't got a **sleeping** bag.*

---

at: preposition ▶ Compare **in**; **on**

---

at is a preposition of place and time. People/things can be *at* points of place and time. In both meanings *at* contrasts with *on* (surfaces, lines, and fairly short periods of time) and *in* (3-dimensional spaces and longer periods of time).

1 Place

at is used when we are thinking of places as points in space and we are not thinking of their size (for example, exact positions on a map):

*We landed **at** Heathrow.*
*I waited **at** the bus stop.*
*Sherlock Holmes and Dr Watson lived **at** 212b Baker Street.*
*Pauline is **at** home/**at** school/**at** work/**at** Roger's (home).*
*What's on **at** the cinema?*
*There are fairies **at** the bottom of the garden.*
*Put your address **at** the top, and sign your name **at** the bottom/**at** the end.*
*Does anybody actually live **at** the South Pole?*
*Would you like to live **at** the seaside?*
*Celia met Henry **at** a dance when they were both **at** university.*

2 Time

at is used for exact points of time:
***at** 10 o'clock, **at** 3.30 p.m., **at** midnight*

or when we are thinking of longer periods as points in the day or the calendar:
*You should lock all your doors **at** night.* (But – *in the morning/afternoon/evening*)
*We usually go away **at** Christmas/**at** Easter.*
***at** dawn, **at** sunset, **at** the weekend* (American English = *on the weekend*)
*I'm busy **at** the moment/**at** present.*
*Is it better to shop **at** the beginning of the week, or **at** the end?*
*Lots of children leave school **at** (the age of) 16.*
*Stop that **at** once* (= immediately).

▶ See also *at first* at **first**

3 Various other uses

*Look **at** me! Look **at** this.* (NEVER **Look me.* *Look her)
*We were all amused/appalled/astonished/delighted/disappointed/surprised
. . . **at** the news/what has happened . . .*
*He's bad/clever/good **at** . . . games/maths.*
*We were flying **at** a height of 20,000 feet and travelling **at** 500 mph.*
*I saw this last week on sale **at** £9.95.*

---

*one **at** a time . . .*
__at__ regular intervals . . .
*This is **at** your request/__at__ your expense.*
*children **at** risk . . . nations **at** war . . .*

▶ See also *at all* at **all**

4 **at** or **in** or **on**?

a Place

See separate entries at *in* and *on* for the main differences. Sometimes we have a choice depending on what exactly we mean:

*My sister lives **in** Newcastle.* (= the city as a large area)
*The train stops **at** Newcastle on the way to Edinburgh.* (= the city as a point on a map)
*Is it always hot **at**/**on** the Equator?* (seen as a point or a line)
*My mother was sitting **in** the corner of her room.*
*There's a postbox **at**/**on** the corner of our road.*

People live **at** *the seaside*, but **at**/**on** *the coast*. You can swim **in** *a river*, but you live **on** one. (= next to one).

With buildings we use *in* if we are thinking of being inside them, but *at* if we are thinking of their position:

*We're staying **at**/**in** the Sheraton Hotel. We don't usually eat **in** the hotel restaurant, though. Last night we had dinner **at**/**in** a vegetarian restaurant down the road.*
*Guess who we saw **at**/**in** the cinema last night!*

Note:

In addresses we use *at* when we give both the number and the street name:
*Sherlock Holmes lived **at** 212b Baker Street.*

but *in* when we give only the street name (in British English):
*Sherlock Holmes lived **in** Baker Street.*
*Liberty's is **in** Regent Street.*

American English uses *on* for streets and roads:
*Saks is **on** Fifth Avenue.*

b Time

We do not usually use *at*, *in* or *on* before *any*, *each*, *every*, *one*, *this*, *that*, *next*, *last* + time expressions, nor before *tomorrow* or *yesterday*. Compare:
*It's best to telephone her **in** the evening.*
and:
Please telephone him one evening this week.

*We're meeting her **on** Saturday.*
and:
I'm meeting them this Saturday.

*It was very cold here **at** Christmas.*
and:
It was cold here last Christmas.

*She never goes out **at** night.*
and:
She's going out tomorrow night.

5 at or **to?**   ▶ Compare **to**

a In general *at* shows position, and contrasts with *to*, which shows direction or movement:
> *I'll meet you **at** the bus-stop. Can you walk **to** the bus-stop?*

b Sometimes both *at* and *to* are possible with the same verb, but usually the meanings are different. To throw something *at* somebody, to talk *at* them, may be rather unfriendly actions. (Compare *laugh/scream/shout/stare at* people.) But if you throw something *to* someone, you want them to catch it. (Compare *give to/talk to.*):
> *Can you throw my scarf **to** me, please?*
> *Don't throw stones **at** the cat.*
> *I love talking **to** you.*
> *Stop talking **at** me like that. I'm not a fool.*

---

attempt   Compare **try**

1 attempt: verb

> *attempt* roughly means 'try', but is less common. The most usual pattern is *attempt* + *to*-INFINITIVE:
> *They were the first people to **attempt** to climb Everest from the north.*
> *It was brave to **attempt** that in such bad weather.*

2 attempt: noun
> *Crispin passed his driving test at his first **attempt**.*
> *They're making a real **attempt** to clean the place up.*

---

attend: verb

a • be present at
> *attend* is usually followed by an object:
> *They **attended** a meeting/a wedding/a funeral/a play/ a football match . . .*

b attend to

> • look after; pay attention to
> *I've got a lot of work to **attend to** .*

---

attention: noun (usually U)

> *Please **pay attention** in future **to** what the teacher says.*
> *He was driving 'without due care and **attention**'. (= dangerously)*

available: adjective

If something is *available* we either have it or can get it:
*Tickets for the match will be **available** next week.*
*Every **available** seat was taken, and there was standing room only.*
*We cannot achieve much in the short time **available**.* (Note the word order.)

avoid: verb

$$avoid + \begin{matrix} \text{OBJECT} \\ \textit{-ing} \end{matrix}$$

avoid can be followed by objects and by *-ing* forms:
*Let's go later and **avoid** the rush-hour crowds.*
*Why is Henry **avoiding** me – what have I done?*
*You can't **avoid** paying taxes – or if you can, you shouldn't.*

awake and wake and (a)waken

1 *awake* is a predicative adjective (and the opposite of *asleep*). We emphasise *awake* with *wide* not *very* (opposite of *fast asleep*):
*I lay **awake** listening to the rain on the windows.*
*He was so tired he couldn't keep **awake**.*
*One of the children was wide **awake**, but the rest were fast asleep.*

2 *(a)wake* and *(a)waken* are verbs, with various irregular and regular past tenses and past participles:
(a)wake, (a)woke or *(a)waked, (a)woken*;
(a)waken is regular.
All four verbs can be used with and without objects. The most usual verb is *wake, woke, woken(up)*. *Awake* and *(a)waken* are not followed by *up:*
*My neighbour often **wakes(up)** at 4 o'clock and reads in bed.*
Wake up! (NOT **Wake!*) *It's late.*
*The storm **awoke** me/**woke** me(**up**)/**awakened** me.*
*Please don't **wake** the children(**up**).*

aware: predicative adjective

aware is the opposite of *unaware*
• have knowledge of; know that
*She was well **aware** that her parents disliked him.*
*I am **aware** of the problem.*

away

The general meaning is 'from here (or there) to another place', 'not at home'.

1 away: adverb

a *They were worried that I might drive **away** and leave them for ever.*
*He will be **away** in France between the 11th and 17th of January.*
*It wasn't very far **away**.*
*Put **away** your clothes.* (in a cupboard or drawer)

b There is often a meaning of separation or disappearance in *away*:
*The sound died/faded **away**.* (until we no longer heard it)
*The water boiled **away**.* (until there was none left)
*Most people have too many things and should give some of them **away**.*

c Sometimes *away* strengthens the meaning of a verb. It roughly means 'very hard' or 'continuously':
*She is talking **away** to somebody at the moment.*
*I've been working **away** like mad.*

d We use *away* with periods of time to mean in the future:
*My birthday is only ten days **away**.*
*The end of the school term was only a week **away**.*

2 away from: preposition
*He is unfortunately **away from** the office ill.*

3 right away, straight away

- immediately
*It was extremely important, so we went **right away/straight away**.* (sometimes *straightaway*)

---

back

1 back: adverb

a • towards home or to some other starting point or state
*I am rather tired 'cause we did not get **back** till after midnight and my usual bedtime is about 9.00.*
*Can I ring **back** in a few minutes?* (= telephone you – from here to where you are)
*It would be a stupid mistake to think that membership only means paying out a lot of money and getting nothing **back** for it.* (nothing in return)
*I'm on holiday till Monday, and then it's **back** to work.*
*Having run out of tablets, she noticed the pain coming **back**.*
Also *give* **back**; *take* **back**

b • behind; to the rear (in place or time); in a reverse direction
back is the opposite of *forward/forwards*:
*She moved her chair **back** against the wall.*
*Put your head **back** and swallow.*
*Even applications dating **back** at least two years are still awaiting attention.*

Also – we *put the clocks **back*** at the end of the summer (i.e., from 2 a.m. to 1 a.m.). In the spring we *put them **forward/on*** an hour.

2 back: noun

a • part of the body at the rear
*He hurt his **back** by carrying a heavy suitcase.*
*If someone is choking, you have to bang their **back**.*

b • the rear
back is the opposite of *front*:
*There is also an exit at the **back** (of the house) from the kitchen.*
*They are cysts – you know, those huge lumps at the **back** of people's heads.*
*It's a nice car, but there isn't much room in the **back**.*
*His new furniture fell off the **back** of a lorry.* (i.e., it was stolen)

3 back: adjective

a • rear
back is the opposite of *front*:
*a **back** door . . .*
*There were parcels all over the **back** seat (of the car).*
*The dog had hurt one of its **back** legs and was limping.*

b • belonging to an earlier time
***back** pay* (pay owing from an earlier period)
***back** numbers* (earlier issues of a magazine or newspaper)

4 back: verb

a • reverse; move backwards
*I unfortunately **backed** the car into a wall.*

b • support
*I **backed** all the wrong horses and didn't win a thing.* (= bet, put one's money on)
*Of course we'll **back** you up.* (= take your side, support you).

backward: adjective

• slow in developing
*He seemed **backward** as a baby, but now he's a very bright teenager.*

backwards: adverb

Also *backward* in American English
• towards the back/the beginning
backwards is the opposite of *forward(s)*:
*He has also taught himself to swim **backwards** at enormous speeds.*
*I know the poem **backwards**.* (= so well that I could probably say it from the end to the beginning!)
*They bent over **backwards** to do everything possible.* (*bend/lean over **backwards*** = make a very big effort)
*They threw the ball **backwards** and forwards.* (continually in one direction and then another)

bad: adjective ▶ Compare **good**

The comparative and superlative are *worse* and *worst*. *Bad* is the opposite of *good*.

a ● morally wrong; of poor quality; harmful; unpleasant
*The **bad** behaviour of the football fans was a disgrace.*
*I feel **bad** about letting you down.* (= unhappy, ashamed)
*This meat smells awful – it's gone **bad**.*
*Be quiet, you're a very **bad** listener.*
*Sugar is **bad** for your teeth.*
*I'm **bad** at games/maths.*
Also: *a **bad** cold . . . **bad** habits . . . **bad** grammar . . . **bad** news*

b not bad
Informally, *not bad* often means 'quite good':
*That's **not** a **bad** idea at all.*
*'How are you?' '**Not bad** thanks.'*

badly: adverb

a ● in a bad manner
badly is the opposite of *well*:
*You've done this homework very **badly** – you'll have to do it again.*
*Tom's son is a **badly** behaved child; he's often very rude to people.*

b ● very much
*I **badly** want to see you.*
*How **badly** do you need the money?* (= desperately)
*But were they **badly** hurt?*

barely: adverb ▶ Compare **hardly**; **scarcely**

● hardly; scarcely; only just
barely is usually used in mid-position with verbs:
*I **barely** remember the place – we left when I was three.*
*I do need a bigger room – there's **barely** enough space to stand up in.*
*We've **barely** got time, have we?*

base

1 base: verb

a ● have a base in (often passive)
*The company is **based** in Switzerland, but has branches throughout Europe.*

b ● use as a basis
*The novels are **based** on the author's own wartime experiences.*
*He **based** his whole speech on very peculiar arguments.*

c *based on* is sometimes used with the meaning 'as a result of', but this is considered ungrammatical by some people

Based on *your experience at university, what changes do you think need making?*

2 base: noun (plural **bases** /beɪsɪz/) ▶ Compare **basis**

a ● a central position from which one can conduct activities
*military **bases** in Europe . . . the company's **base** in Switzerland . . .*
*We shall use London as a **base** for our holiday in Britain.*

b ● the lowest or bottom part of something
*at the **base** of a cliff/a mountain/a statue . . .*
*Plates often have the maker's name stamped on the **base**.*

---

basic: adjective

● as a starting point; simple; lowest
*Our **basic** position must be to treat people equally.*
*There are still many children in the world who do not get even a **basic** education.*
*The **basic** pay is low, but you can earn more if you work overtime.*

---

basis: noun (plural **bases** /beɪsiːz/) ▶ Compare **base**

a ● reasons, starting-point for something
*These arguments have no scientific **basis**.*
*I shall decide for myself on the **basis** of the information I receive.*

b ● method; system:
*Celia works on a part-time **basis**.*

---

bath: noun and verb /bɑːθ, bæθ/ ▶ Compare **bathe**

*I didn't answer the telephone because I was in the **bath**.*
*I like having a **bath** (British English)/taking a **bath** (American English) in the morning.*
*She **bathed**/was **bathing** (bɑːθɪŋ bæθɪŋ) the baby.*

---

bathe: noun and verb /beɪð/

a ● swim (*swim* is more usual than *bathe* in this sense both as a noun and as a verb)
*We went for a **bathe** but the sea was terribly cold.*
*Some people will only **bathe** in a heated pool.*
*We went **bathing** /beɪðɪŋ/ before breakfast.*

b • was something because it hurts
My eyes were hurting, so I bathed /beɪðd/ *them.*

---

be: verb

1 Forms

a Present and past
The verb *be* is the only English verb with eight different forms.

PRESENT		PAST
I	**am**	**was**
He/She/It	**is**	
We/You/They	**are**	**were**

INFINITIVE & IMPERATIVE	**be**
PRESENT PARTICIPLE	**being**
PAST PARTICIPLE	**been**

b Short forms
The present tense has short forms, which can be added to pronouns and nouns.

I'm	happy
He's/She's/It's/Tom's	a problem
We're/You're/They're	coming

These short forms are only used when followed by another word. They cannot be used alone:
    'Are you happy?' 'Yes, I am.' (NOT **Yes, I'm.*)

Short forms cannot be used if *be* is used as an auxiliary and part of the main verb is omitted:
    'Is Crispin coming tonight?' 'No, but I think he is tomorrow.' (NOT **but I think he's tomorrow.*) But see negatives at **c**.
's is also used after *There* and *Here*:
    There's some cheese in the fridge.
    Here's the book you were asking for.

c Negatives
Negatives of present and past tenses are formed by adding *not* to the verb –
often shortened to *n't* (except after *am*; NEVER **amn't*).

	PRESENT	PAST
I	**am not** **'m not**	**was not**
He/She/It/Crispin That girl/My book	**is not** **isn't** **'s not**	**wasn't**
We/You/They The children/books	**are not** **aren't** **'re not**	**were not** **weren't**

We **were not/weren't** *at all happy about it.*
'Are they coming?' 'No, they **are not/aren't.'**

With the present tense we can also add *not* to the short affirmative forms (see
b), and these negatives can be used alone:
It is **not/isn't/It's not** *the first time that this has happened.*
'Is it raining' 'No, it **isn't/It's not.'**

d Questions and negative questions

Am I/Aren't I	
Are(n't) we/you/they/the children	ready?
Is(n't) he/she/it/that child	coming?
Were(n't) we/you/they	there?
Was(n't) he/she/it/Rachel	

Questions are formed by inversion – putting *be* first and then the subject.
Is Rachel ready?
Were you there?

Negative questions usually take the form *be* + *n't* + subject.
Notice *Aren't I*?:
Aren't I silly?
Isn't he your friend?
Wasn't your sister there yesterday?

In formal use or to give extra emphasis we use unshortened forms and put *not*
after the subject:
Is he, or is he **not,** *your friend?*
Is it **not** *a fact that the world's population is increasing at an alarming rate?*
(meaning 'It is a fact that . . .)

2 be: main verb

a *be* as a main verb has a variety of uses and meanings:
be can show the quality or state or value or age, etc., of the subject, or indicate possession:
> *He is tired, but he'll **be** all right.*
> ***Wasn't** it quiet there!*
> *She **is** English and twenty-five years old.*
> *These oranges **are** 20p each.*
> ***Are** these books yours?*

be can explain the nature of the (grammatical) subject:
> *My sister **is** an engineer. She's a good swimmer.*
> *What are you going **to be** (= become) when you grow up?*
> *The problem **was** to decide what to do next.*

be can show the place or time of someone or something:
> *My parents **are** away, but my sister **is** at home.*
> *'The dance **is** tomorrow evening.' 'I'll **be** there.'*
> *'Where **are** you from?' 'We're from Canada.'*

b When we talk about something existing we often use *There is* or *There are*
> ▶ See **there**

c Tenses
As a main verb *be* has a complete set of tenses, including perfect tenses:
> *It **has been** a long hot summer.*
> *We **hadn't been** to Los Angeles before, so we were very excited.*

We do not usually use progressive tenses of *be* to describe people's feelings or states of mind or their appearance:
> *She **is** happy/excited/beautiful . . .*
> (NOT **She **is being** happy* etc.)

But we can use progressive tenses to describe the way someone is behaving at a particular time:
> *You **are being** very brave.* (= You are behaving bravely.)
> *He **isn't being** at all sensible about this.*

d *be* has an imperative:
> ***Be** quiet!*

The negative uses *don't*:
> ***Don't be** so rude!*

and the positive can use *do* for emphasis:
> ***Do be** quiet! You're giving me a headache.*

The only other use of *do* with the verb *be* is in the phrase *Why don't you be*, which makes a suggestion:
> *Why don't you **be** an airline pilot when you grow up?*
> *Why don't you **be** more careful, you might hurt yourself?*

e Infinitives and participles are used in the same way as infinitives and participles of other verbs:
> *Nobody wants **to be** ill.*
> *How miserable for her **to have been** ill so long.*
> ***Being** ill isn't my idea of fun. It's so boring **being** in bed.*
> *She admitted **to being** afraid.*

Being ill, she missed the party.
Never ***having been*** in hospital before, she slept badly.

f Subjunctive
There are few distinct subjunctive tenses in English. But the subjunctive of *be* is noticeable because it is *be* (instead of *am/is/are*) for talking about events that might happen in the future; and the same tense (instead of *was* or *were*) can be used when talking about the past. We can use this subjunctive after various words of advising, ordering and suggesting, although *should* + VERB, or sometimes an indicative tense are possible alternatives:
> *The committee decided that the man **be** asked to resign.* (or ***should be asked*** . . .)
> *There was a suggestion that the press **not be** told.* (Notice the position of *not*. Or *that the press **was** not told* . . . or . . . *should **not be** told*.)

We can also – very formally – use *be* in sentences of present condition:
> *Whether this **be** the case or not, I shall refuse to lend her any money.* (=*whether this is* . . .)

▶ See also **were**
For *been* or *gone* ▶ *See* **go**

3 **be**: auxiliary verb in progressive tenses

			BE	-ING
PRESENT PROGRESSIVE	I		**am**	waiting
	he/she/it		**is**	
	we/you/they		**are**	
PAST PROGRESSIVE	I/he/she/it		**was**	doing
	we/you/they		**were**	
PRESENT PERFECT PROGRESSIVE	I/you/we/they	**have**	**been**	learning
	He/she/it	**has**		
PAST PERFECT PROGRESSIVE	I etc	**had**		being

a The verb *be* (followed by the *-ing* form of another verb) is used to make the progressive tenses of that verb. The present tense of *be* + *-ing* makes the present progressive:
> *We **are waiting** to see what happens.*

The past tense of *be* + *-ing* makes the past progressive:
> *Tom **was driving** much too fast.*

have + been + -ing makes the present and past perfect progressive tenses:
He has been learning English for three years.
They had not been expecting to win, so they were absolutely delighted.

b   *be* is also used to form the progressive infinitive of other verbs:
It must be awful always to be wondering where your next meal is coming from.
We hope to be seeing more of Pamela now she's come to live in Wimbledon.

c   **Meaning of progressive tenses**
Progressive tenses contrast with simple tenses. They are used to talk about actions in progress at a particular time, and the emphasis is on the activity – in contrast to simple tenses which often refer to habits and repeated actions over a longer period of time.
The activity may be happening at the moment of speaking:
The kettle's boiling. (Contrast: *Water boils at 100 C*, which is true at any time.)

but it may be happening 'during the present period':
My brother's working hard for his exam. (Contrast – *My sister works hard* – i.e., always).

Or you can point to an empty seat and say:
Somebody's sitting there. (i.e., somebody is coming back in a moment.)

Because progressive tenses emphasise activity in progress, the activity may remain unfinished. This again contrasts with simple tenses, which often refer to complete events:
I was writing a novel that year. (We do not know whether the speaker finished writing the book. Contrast: *I wrote a novel that year*, which means that I completed it.)

He was watching 'Neighbours' when they arrived. (We do not know whether he continued watching to the end of the TV programme.)

The present progressive is frequently used to talk about a future activity that is already arranged now:
We are leaving for Rome tomorrow.
I'm having lunch with Anne on Saturday.

Will be doing can be used to predict an activity likely to be in progress at some future time:
Don't ring tomorrow evening. I'll probably be washing my hair.

The past progressive can be used for a future-in-the-past:
We were leaving for Rome next day, so I was busy packing.

By contrast, the present simple is not often used for future arrangements, though it can be used particularly for travel arrangements seen as single events:
We leave for Rome tomorrow.

(But **I have lunch with Anne on Saturday* or **Don't ring tomorrow – I wash my hair* would be very odd.)
Progressive tenses, with their emphasis on activity, are not used when describing states, so 'stative' verbs such as *believe, belong, doubt, know, mean, own* are mainly used in simple tenses only.

4 be: auxiliary verb in passive tenses

		BE	PAST PARTICIPLE
PRESENT SIMPLE PAST		**am/is/are** **was/were**	talked about
PRESENT PERFECT SIMPLE PAST PERFECT	**has/have** **had**	**been**	
PRESENT PROGRESSIVE PAST	**am/is/are** **was/were**	**being**	learnt
PRESENT PERFECT PROGRESSIVE PAST PERFECT	**has/have** **had**	**been being**	

a The verb *be* followed by the past participle of another verb forms the passive tenses of that verb.

The present or past of *be* + PAST PARTICIPLE makes the simple present and the simple past passive tenses:

*These cars **are made** in Britain.*
*'Where **were** you **born**?' 'I **was born** in India, actually.'*

The present or past of *have* + *been* + PAST PARTICIPLE makes the simple perfect passive tenses:

*Two cars **have been stolen** from the car park.*
*Perhaps they **had been left** unlocked.*

The present or past of *be* + *being* + PAST PARTICIPLE gives the progressive passive tenses:

*People **are being questioned**.*
*A man **was being taken** to the police station.*

The present or past of *have* + *been being* + PAST PARTICIPLE gives the perfect progressive tenses, but these are very rare, as many people think *been being* is rather awkward:

*(?) This road has **been being repaired** for the past eighteen months, and it's still not finished.*

b Passive *be* is also used to form passive infinitives and participles of other verbs:

*The lock appears **to have been broken** with a hammer.*
*Criminals must expect **to be sent** to prison.*
*On **being questioned**, he suddenly told the truth.*
*It's not a nice experience **being questioned** by the police.*
***Having been questioned**, the man was allowed to go home.*

c Meaning of the passive
There are various reasons for using a passive rather than an active verb.
Sometimes we are not interested in the doer, or we cannot name one:

*Where **were** you **born**? (We are interested in you, not your mother!)*
*I wonder when this house **was built**.*

*Thousands of people **were killed** in the disaster.*
*You **are not supposed** to ask questions like that.*

But if we do mention the doer, we choose active or passive, depending on what is the more important part of what we are saying. We usually start a sentence with something already known, or with a topic (what the sentence is about), and then we give the important new information at the end.

Active and passive sentences with a 'doer'

TOPIC	NEW INFORMATION
Passive	
This church	*was built by Sir Christopher Wren.*
Active	
Sir Christopher Wren	*also built many other London churches.*

In the first (passive) sentence, we are probably looking at the church, and the new information is the name of the 'doer'. In the second sentence, we have already been talking about Wren, and the new information is another fact about him.

5   be + to—INFINITIVE

a   The *to*-infinitive (*to do* something) usually refers to the future. *Be + to do* often refers to definite plans or arrangements now (for the future) or to past plans (for the future-in-the-past or for the present):
*The Euro-elections **are to take place** on June 14th.*
*'Has it arrived?', she asked. 'It **was to be** my little surprise for you on your birthday.'*

b   Sometimes the meaning is not human plans but fate, or what actually happened later:
*The discovery of oil **was to bring** enormous wealth to the country and rapid change.* (i.e. it did bring . . .)
*But all their plans **were to end** in failure.* (i.e. They ended in failure.)
*Claudia **was to be found** sitting in the garden.* (She was found there.)

c   Sometimes the meaning is duty or *'must'*:
*You **are not to tell** anyone – nobody must know.*
*I **am to emphasise** that the Bank's present attitude is very generous.*
***NOT to be removed** from Euston Station* (Notice on station trolleys at Euston Station, London.)

be able to   ▶ See **able**

bear, bore/borne, born: verb

1

a • support; carry
*The walls had to be strengthened to **bear** the weight of the new roof.*
*These old trees **bore** a lot of apples this year.*

b • endure; put up with
In positive sentences this is rather formal:
Brown. *On 20th January, Mark, aged 87, after a long illness **borne** with great courage.*
*The expense doesn't **bear** thinking about.* (= It is too awful to think about.)

2 can/could bear　　　　　　　　　　　　▶ Compare **stand**

can could	**bear** +	OBJECT *-ing* *you/your-ing* (o) + *to*-INFINITIVE

can/could bear is mainly non-assertive. If you *cannot bear* something you dislike it very much:
*How **can** you **bear** that man? He's so rude.*
*I **can't bear** people who complain all the time.*

can/could bear is also followed by (OBJECT+)-*ing* and by OBJECT + *to* INFINITIVE. Notice that we can say (*can*) *bear you/him*, etc. or *your/his* etc., *doing something*:
*I **can't bear** not knowing.*
*He **couldn't bear** her being so worried.*
***Could** you really **bear** to work in a factory?*
*I **couldn't bear** them to find out.* (. . . *it if they found out.*)

3 (be) born

Grammatically this is a special past participle, used in the passive only, of the verb *bear*:
*Where were you **born**?*
*Napoleon was **born** in Corsica in 1769.*

Active sentences, with this meaning, are possible, but rare.
*Sir Charles Tennant (1823–1906) had two wives, who **bore** him sixteen children.*
We usually use 'have a baby' (*She **had** her first baby when she was only 17*).

because

	CONJUNCTION	CLAUSE
They only turned the water on for two hours a day	**because** **'cause** **cos**	they were short of water.
	PREPOSITION	NOUN PHRASE
	because of	the water shortage. their having so little water.

1 **because** (sometimes informally **'cause** or **cos**): conjunction

a We use *because* before a clause giving a reason, explaining why:
*It's very easy to find the house **because** it's close to the station.*
*I am now rather tired **'cause** we did not get back till after midnight and my usual bedtime is about 9.00.*
*They only turned the water on for two hours a day **cos** they were short of water.*

b *because* clauses usually come after their main clause, but sometimes come at the beginning of a sentence:
But suppose an employer says that nobody older than 28 can apply for a job. ***Because** so many women in their twenties are at home bringing up children, the employer is in fact making it harder for a woman to get the job.*

c Sometimes the *because* clause does not explain the facts of the main clause (as in **a** and **b**) but gives the reason for making a statement or asking a question:
*Is she short-sighted, **because** I have seen her a couple of times and not been seen?* (= That is why I am asking.)

d With *not . . . because* the meaning depends very much on the context:
*I didn't need to tell her I loved her, **because** she knew I loved her.* (This was the reason why I did *not* need to tell her.)
*We did not refuse **because** he was white,* (= we did refuse, but not for this reason), *but **because** he jumped a long queue of coloured men who were in line for the job.* (= This second reason is why we did refuse)

In spoken English, the first *because* clause here (***because** she knew I loved her*) would probably be spoken on a falling tone, indicating completion. But in the second example ***because** he was white* would be on some kind of rising tone, perhaps a fall-rise, to indicate that some other reason is going to follow.

2 because of: preposition

We use *because of* before a noun, pronoun or *-ing* clause to give a reason for something:

***Because of** your great age and my respect for you I have seen you very much as a symbol of hope.*
*The confusion has probably arisen **because of** her complete lack of English.*
*He had to resign **because of** family difficulties.*
*They only turned the water on for two hours a day **because of** the water shortage.*

become, became, become: verb

a *become* can be followed by a complement (noun or adjective):
*She **became** Queen in 1952.*
*My son's **become** a farmer.*
*It's **becoming** increasingly difficult.*

b It is often used with comparative adjectives:
*It's **become** warmer/colder/easier/ more expensive.*

bed: noun (C, U)

*a single **bed** . . . twin **beds** . . . make the **beds***

Notice the uncountable usage (with general meaning) in:
*go to **bed** . . . get out of **bed** . . . be in **bed** . . . read in **bed** . . .*

been   ► See **be**

before

1 before: preposition

a • earlier than
before is the opposite of *after*:
*I'll be there **before** ten.*
*I won't to be able to take any time off **before** the end of term.*
*I'll wait for the order to arrive **before** sending any payment.*

b • in front of
*These are issues that western leaders should be putting **before** President Bush this week.*

The more usual preposition of place in modern English is *in front of*, and *before* is rather formal. (*His statue stands **in front of** the Town Hall.*) Notice, however, expressions like:
*It happened **before my very eyes**. (= I actually saw it happen.)*
*You've got all your life **before you**. (= in front of you, ahead)*

There is also an old (and not completely accurate) spelling rule:
i before e except after c. (so that we correctly spell words like *chief*, *piece*, *field* and *receive*)

2 **before**: adverb

* at some earlier time; in the past
before is the opposite of *afterwards*:
> *I began to see a world I knew nothing of before.*
> *Why didn't you tell me this before?*
> *I recognised her at once as we had been introduced only the week before.*

3 **before**: conjunction

a * at an earlier time than 'when'
> *He lived in Edinburgh before he moved to London in the '70s.*
> *Before it rains I must go out to the postbox.*

b Sometimes the action/event of the *before* clause did not, or may not, happen:
> *He disappeared before I had a chance to thank him.*
> *You really should think again, before you throw away your money like that.*

---

beforehand: adverb

beforehand does not just mean 'before' or 'earlier'. It means 'in advance', perhaps with some plan that would affect a later action:
> *When somebody tells you afterwards, for example, that you have eaten snake, you don't mind – but when they tell you beforehand that you're going to eat it, that's awful.*
> *I don't mind you taking a day off work, so long as you let me know beforehand.*

---

begin, began, begun: verb　　　　▶ Compare **start**

```
              –
          OBJECT
begin  +  -ing
          to-INFINITIVE
```

1 *begin* is the opposite of *end*:
> *The War began in 1939.*
> *Charles began as a reporter on a local paper.*
> *If they don't come soon, we'd better begin (dinner) without them.*
> *It's beginning to snow.*
> *Suddenly she began screaming.*

2 *to begin with* is similar to *to start with*. The meaning is roughly *at first*. . . *but*. It mentions what happened at the beginning that changed later, or it introduces the first of several reasons for something:

*I liked him **to begin with**, but then I realised he wasn't very nice.*
*'Why aren't you having a holiday this year?' 'Well, **to begin with**, I'm too busy. And anyway I can't really afford one. And then . . .'*

beginner: noun

A *beginner* is often somebody just beginning to learn something and therefore not very good at it:

*I've joined a class for **beginners**.*
*I'm just a **beginner** at cricket, I don't play very well.*

beginning: noun (C, U)

- the start; the first part
  *I only met Roger at the **beginning** of term.*
  *The **beginning** of the film was very violent.*
  *The party was a disaster from **beginning** to end.*

behave: verb

a • act in a particular (social) way
  *Tom **behaves** very strangely sometimes – I think he's a bit mad.*
  *She apologised for **behaving** so badly.*

b By itself or as a reflexive verb *behave* means 'behave well':
  *For goodness sake, children, **behave** yourselves!*

behaviour: noun (U)

- way of behaving
  *bad/good/strange **behaviour***

behind

1 behind: preposition

a • at the back of; to the rear of
  *We heard these footsteps **behind** us.*
  *There's a large garden **behind** the house.*

b • later than; making less progress than
  *New York is five hours **behind** London.*
  *We're years **behind** the Americans in space research.*

c • supporting; backing
*It is still possible to question the reasons **behind** much of the organised opposition to government policy.*
*I'm right **behind** you – you can rely on me.*

2 behind: adverb

a • in a place someone is leaving or has left
*In our haste, we left a suitcase **behind**.*
*Let's leave him **behind**.*

b • at the back
*They have a beautiful house with a big garden **behind**.*

c • slow
*Drink up, Jane, you're falling **behind**. (= you're being slower than the others)*
*I was **behind** with my work, and I'd said to them one o'clock, so I almost phoned them up to say 'come a bit later'.*

---

belief: noun (C, U)

• feeling that something is true; what you belief
*It's my **belief** that a lot of the unemployed actually have jobs.*
*Most religions share some sort of **belief** in God.*
*Some people are ready to die for their **beliefs**.*

---

believe: verb

```
                OBJECT
believe +       OBJECT + to be/to have
                that-CLAUSE
                so/not
```

believe is not usually used in the progressive.

a *believe* can be followed by OBJECTS, by *that*-CLAUSES, and by *so/not*. It can mean 'consider something is true', or 'consider somebody to be telling the truth', or 'think/suppose':
*You shouldn't **believe** everything you read in the papers.*
*He's told me so many lies, I can't **believe** him any more.*
*It's hard to **believe** (that) we've been in this house thirty years.*
*'Are the Smiths selling their house?' 'I **believe** so/not.'*

b When we *believe* that something did not or will not happen, we often make *believe* (not the other part of the sentence) negative:
*I don't **believe** he'll resign unless they make him.*
*No, I don't **believe** so, either.*

▶ Compare **expect, imagine; suppose; think**

---

c *believe* can be followed by an OBJECT + *to be/to have*, and this pattern is often
   used in the passive:
   *Most people **believe** her to be right.*
   *They are **believed** to have secret bank accounts.*
   *The criminals are **believed** to be (living) abroad.*
   *They are **believed** to have got away immediately.*
   ▶ Compare **consider**; **think**

d Passives are also possible with an impersonal subject:
   *It was **believed** that they had guns.*

e **believe in**
   • think that something/someone exists; think that something is useful
     *Do you **believe in** life after death?*
     *They don't **believe in** working if they can get money doing nothing.*

---

belong: verb

---

belong is not often used in the progressive.
a • have a usual place
     *Perhaps I'm a foreigner here and should go home where I **belong**.*
     *'Where shall I put your typewriter?' 'Oh it **belongs** on my desk.'*

b **belong to**
   belong to is needed before an object. It means 'be the property of or be a
   member of':
   *Who does this bag **belong** to? Does it **belong** to you?*
   *They **belong** to their local Conservative party.*
   *You can't own property there – everything **belongs** to the State.*

---

belongings: noun (plural)

   • possessions
     *Don't leave valuable **belongings** in your car.*

---

below ▶ Compare **under**; **underneath**

---

below is the opposite of *above*. The general meaning is 'lower than' or in a
lower place.

1 below: preposition

a **Place**
   • in/to a lower place than
     *The little town lies in the valley **below** the castle.*
     *There's a basement which they call a garden flat down **below** us.*
   (Notice *down below*. Contrast *up above*.)

b Measurements

With some measurements, the meaning is also 'lower than':

Parts of the Netherlands are below sea level.
Temperatures in winter were below freezing/below zero for weeks on end.
I'm afraid your work is below average.

Note: *under* is not possible in these examples, but when the meaning could be either 'lower than' (*below*) or 'less than' (*under*), both are possible:

The rate of exchange has been well below/(under) the two dollar level.
There is a new pension scheme that will enable everybody below/(under) a certain level of income to provide for their old age.

c Rank

- junior to in rank or position
A captain is below a major.
Lots of students know nobody in the class below them.

Contrast *under*, which shows a relationship between individual people:
The Director of Studies has got twelve teachers under her. (= she is the boss)

2 below: adverb

- in/to a lower place; lower down
The meanings are similar to those of the preposition.

a Place

The people in the flat below are very noisy.
The Browns live three floors below.
He won't stay below (= under the surface of the sea) *as long as that. In shallow water he usually goes for a series of short dives.*
See below (= lower on the same page, or on a later page).

b Measurements

temperatures of zero and below

c Rank

- in a junior position
The students in the class below are still on Book 1.

beneath

1 beneath: preposition

a • under, underneath
. . . the curve of her hips beneath her tight black skirt.
The leaves beneath our feet made a noise that I loved.

b • not up to one's standard of behaviour
That sort of behaviour is beneath contempt. (= It is disgraceful.)
It's beneath you – we expect you to behave better than that.

2 beneath: adverb

As an adverb *beneath* is both formal and rare. The usual adverb is *underneath*:
the sky above and the earth beneath

beside: preposition

- next to, at the side of
  *Isabel drove, with George **beside** her, and Henry in the back seat.*
  *Come and sit **beside** me.*

besides

1 besides: preposition

- as well as; in addition to
  ***Besides** being involved in teaching, I am preparing a number of articles for publication.*
  *In this fish, **besides** the usual pair of eyes, there is also the so-called third eye.*

2 besides: sentence adverb

- as well; in addition
  *It's best to train properly. **Besides**, training will be interesting.*
  *There are, **besides**, practical difficulties in the way the law works.*

better, best

1 better, best: adjectives　　　　　　　　　▶ See **good**

a *better* and *best* are the comparative and superlative of *good:*
  *They are much **better** cherries than the last ones I bought.*
  *Mr Nolan was so much the **better** teacher of the two.*
  *The **best** thing to do would be to admit her to hospital.*
  ***Best** wishes – to my **best** friend!*
  *He's the **best** dancer in the world – the **best** I've ever seen anyway.*

b *better off (than)* often means 'with more money (than) . . .' but can also mean generally 'in a better state':
  *The tax changes will not make me any **better off**.*
  *The plants ought to be in the garden. They're **better off** outside.*

2 better (NOT **best**): adjective

better when referring to health has two meanings.
a ● not completely recovered and well, but in some way less ill than before
  *She is/feels a bit/a lot/much **better**.*
  *She is **better** than she was when we began her treatment.*

b ● quite/completely/fully recovered and well
  *You give the drug and the patient gets **better**.*

3 better, best: adverbs　　　　　　　　　▶ See **well**

better and *best* are the comparative and superlative of *well:*
  *He feels he could have done the job **better**.*
  *They're **better** paid than they used to be.*

*That's the one I like **best** (of all).*
*This is **best** explained by a little story.*
*The keepers round here are trying to protect the birds as **best** they can.* (NOT
as **best as they can.* It would be more usual to say *as well as they can*.)

4 had better/'d better (not) + INFINITIVE

a *had better (not)* is used with the bare infinitive to give advice, or say that some
action would be sensible. We can also use *had best (not)*, although this is rare:
*I **had better** keep him under observation.*
*I thought **I'd better not** do it over the phone.*
*You**'d better** hurry or the shops will be shut.*

b *had better* is not quite the same as *ought to* or *should*. *Ought to* and *should* can
be used to make general comments; *had better* gives advice or a warning about
future action. It also has a strong suggestion that the action will be done.
Compare:
*People always **ought to/should** think before they speak.* (NOT **People **had**
better always think . . .*)
*You **ought to/should** apologise for being so rude.* (This could be followed by
I'm sure you will or *But I don't suppose you will*.)
*You **had better** apologise, or else!* (= I think you may.) (NOT **You **had better**
apologise, but I know you won't*.)

5 better, best: nouns

*Husband and wife take one another for **better**, for worse.* (a reference to the
church marriage service, where the husband and wife promise to stay
together whatever happens)
*We found him to be a sincere, likeable man, at his **best** when dealing with
people.* (= his most successful)
*I hope you will accept an informal reference, which is the **best** that I can do.*
*I try to do my **best** – but it's not always good enough for them.*

between

1 between: preposition ▶ Compare **among/amongst**

often used in *between . . . and . . .*
a • somewhere in the middle of a space or a period of time
*I sat **between** different people at every meal.*
*It's halfway **between** Marseilles and Narbonne.*
*The time to see it is some time **between** August 15th and September 15th.*
*Many thanks for your help in issuing prescriptions **between** her hospital
visits.*
*. . . an increase of **between** fifty and a hundred thousand.*

b • showing connection or sharing
*Professor Langford and Miss Stuart have run the course **between** them.*
*They broke up into groups to talk over **between** themselves the points I had
raised.*
*I haven't told her so far. This is just **between** you and me.* (= it is our secret)

In the end we decided *between us that it would be best for him and us if he moved into a hotel.*
. . . *the feelings **between** mother and child* . . .
. . . *daily flights **between** London and New York*

c • showing division and difference
*It is important to be aware of cultural differences, religious differences, legal differences that do exist **between** different countries.*
. . . *the tension **between** order and change* . . .

2 between: adverb (usually in between)
It's a deserted spot. There's a lighthouse and one house, and nothing in between. (= in the middle)

3 between or among?

a When we talk of only two people or things, we use *between*:
*a secret **between** you and me* . . . *daily flights **between** Britain and Australia* . . . *the difference **between** friendship and love* . . . *the period **between** 1948 and 1955*

b With more than two people/things
(1) *between* is used when we see them as separate people or things:
*I sat **between** two different people at every meal* . . . ***between** her hospital visits (i.e., **between** the first and the second, **between** the second and the third etc.)* . . . *flights **between** New York, Washington and Los Angeles* . . .

(2) *among* is used when the people/things are seen as one single group, or the meaning is 'included in':
. . . *the mood **among** the islanders* . . . ***among** the most frequent causes of trouble* . . .

c Sometimes either *among* or *between* is possible with the same meaning:
*She divided her jewellery **among/between** her three granddaughters.*
*We hope to develop close relationships **between/among** the 26 authorities concerned.*
*They talked it over **between/among** themselves.*

But sometimes there is a definite difference in meaning:
*They've built a house **between** the trees. (in a space – perhaps with trees on both sides)*
. . . *a house **among** the trees* . . . *(surrounded by trees)*

---

beyond

1 beyond: preposition

a • on/to the far side of
*The bus stop is just **beyond** the traffic lights.*

b • later than; after (usually non-assertive)
*The sale must not be delayed **beyond** the end of November.*

---

c • out of reach of; too far from; too difficult for
*Anything in the nature of a full-time job is **beyond** her.*
*It's silly to blame ourselves for something that's quite **beyond** our control.*
*It's **beyond** me.* (= I don't understand it.)

d • except for; apart from (usually non-assertive)
*There is nothing very much here **beyond** a minor stomach infection.*
(Doctor's report)

2 beyond: adverb

a • far away; in the distance
*They both stared out at the gathering (growing) darkness **beyond**.*

b • later; afterwards
*What can be done to prepare for the changes of the 1990s and **beyond**?*

---

big, bigger, biggest: adjective   ▶ Compare **large**; **great**

big is the opposite of *little*:
a • large in size
Both *big* and *large* are often possible, with *big* being the more informal word:
*a **big** (or **large**) box/family/house/town*

b • important; noticeable
Here *large* is not possible, but *great* is an alternative:
*a **big** advantage/difference/improvement*

c • older
big can mean 'older' when talking about children:
*You mustn't cry – you're a **big** boy now.*

d *big* is usually used with count nouns (*a **big** box*, ***big** improvements*), but there are a few expressions where *big* is used with uncountable nouns:
*Tourism is now **big** business, and there's **big** money to be made in it.*

---

bit

1	a . . . **bit** . . . **bits**	of	the cake paper shopping
2a	a **bit**	of	a nuisance
2b	a **bit**		ashamed (ADJECTIVE) hurriedly (ADVERB) *like* . . . (PREPOSITION)

1 bit: count noun

- part; piece (usually small)

This is an ordinary noun, and we can use many different determiners or adjectives:

That cake looks good – can I have just a small bit?

I'll write all that down on this one bit of paper.

She cut out little bits of my letter and posted them back to me, saying 'How could you say this?'

It's time I was doing my bits of shopping and work.

Going to do a bit of ironing now.

He could save us quite a bit of money. (= quite a lot)

2 a (little) bit: adverb

- rather; to some degree

a *a (little) bit of* is used in this way before a singular count noun:

It's a little bit of a problem.

Mice are a bit of a problem there.

b *a (little) bit* – without *of* – is used as an adverb with verbs; it can also be followed by adjectives and adverbs (including comparative adjectives and adverbs) and by some prepositions – e.g. *like*:

We waited a bit to see if she'd come.

'It doesn't matter, does it?' 'Not a bit, no!' (= It does not matter at all.)

Are you cold in here? You're shivering a bit.

He was looking a bit ashamed of himself.

We'll be a bit late, I'm afraid.

It's a bit warmer today.

'They left a bit hurriedly, I thought.' 'A bit too hurriedly, if you ask me.'

He looks a bit like a bird, really.

3 bit by bit

- gradually

His memory came back to him bit by bit.

4 every bit as

- just as; equally

I'm every bit as careful as you.

board

1 board: noun (C, U)

a The primary meaning is a long flat piece of wood as in floorboards. But many other words come from this:

. . . a breadboard . . . a noticeboard . . . a blackboard/chalkboard/whiteboard

b A second meaning is 'table', now only used in a few phrases such as *bed and board* and *board and lodging*, meaning meals and accommodation. *The board of directors* of a company are the directors as a group. When they have a *board meeting*, they meet round a table.

2 on board

- on a ship
  *We went **on board** in the evening and sailed next morning.*

3 board: verb

The verb has several meanings:
*The shop is all **boarded** up* (= the windows are covered with wood)
*I'm **boarding** with some other students.* (= sharing accommodation with)
*We **boarded** the plane/ship in New York.* (= went on board)

body: noun

a *He's got terrible burns all over his **body**.*
*The (dead) **bodies** were later discovered in a wood only a few miles from where the couple disappeared.*

b • a group of people
*... the governing **body** of this university*

c • the main part of, or a big quantity of
*The factory makes car **bodies**.*
*... a **body** of data/information ...*

book

1 book: noun
*Have you read any good **books** lately?*

2 book: verb

- reserve
We can book seats/tickets for a concert/theatre/football match; seats on a plane or train; a table at a restaurant ...
We can also book in at a hotel – unless we are unlucky and the theatre/hotel etc. is fully booked or booked up.

bored, boring ▶ See **interested**

born ▶ See **bear**

borrow: verb ▶ Compare **lend**

borrow is the opposite of *lend*
If you have something you can *lend* it *to* someone. If you don't have something you can *borrow* it *from* someone:
> *Can I **borrow** your pen/your car/an umbrella?*
> *I've **borrowed** this from the library, but I might buy a copy to keep.*
> *He **borrowed** money from his father and then didn't pay it back.*

both

1 both: determiner and pronoun ▶ Compare **all; half; neither**

a both + NOUN/PRONOUN (Table 1)

A **both**	oranges men	
B **both (of)**	the these/those my/her etc.	oranges brothers
	these/those mine/hers etc.°	
C **both of**	you/us/them	

both (determiner and pronoun) refers to two things or people together. It uses roughly the same grammatical patterns as *all*. We can use:

A **both** + PLURAL NOUN
   *She is complaining of aching pains in **both** knees and **both** lower legs.* (NOT **both of knees . . .*)

B **both (of)** + *the/these/my* etc. + PLURAL NOUN
   ***Both (of)** these young men will make their mark.* (= succeed in life)
   ***Both (of)** my grandfathers wear hats.*
   and
   both of (or **both** which is rare) + *these/mine* etc. (PRONOUNS):
   *Can I have **both (of)** these? **Both** mine have broken.*

C **both of** + PRONOUNS as shown (NOT **both* + PRONOUNS):
   ***Both of** us were depressed last night.*
   ***Both of** them were strong-willed persons.*
   *Come back, **both of** you!*

D *both* by itself can mean two things or people already mentioned:
   *These two young men will make their mark. **Both** are civilised.*

E   Notice that any of these *both* phrases can be used as subject or object:
     ***Both** men/**Both** of the men/**Both** enjoyed the party.*
     *I've eaten **both** my oranges/**both** of them/**both**.*

b   NOUN/PRONOUN + **both** (Table 2)

A			
The girls		**both**	*enjoyed* the party. *have* new dresses.
They	*are*	**both**	ready. *enjoying* the party.
	have	**both**	*finished* now.
B Mrs Smith	has invited is asking for	them/you/us	**both.**
C She	has sent	them you **both** us	invitations.

both can also be used after nouns and pronouns in the following ways.
When *both* is part of the subject (*A*), it comes before the main verb (including
have as a main verb):
     *We **both** agree.*
     *The girls **both** have new dresses.*

but *both* comes after *be* and after auxiliary verbs:
     *His parents were **both** killed.*
     *They have **both** refused.*
     *We are **both** extremely surprised.*

Compare mid-position adverbs.

PERSONAL PRONOUNS + *both* can be used as objects (*B*) or indirect objects (*C*):
     *One slip would send us **both** to our deaths.*
     *It's a difficult situation for them **both**.*
     *She has sent you **both** invitations.*

c   Notice (Tables 1 and 2) that there are often several ways of more or less saying
     the same thing:
     ***Both** these young men/**Both** of these young men/**Both** of them/**Both** will . . .*
     *or They will **both** . . .*
     *It's a difficult situation for them **both**/**both** of them.*

2   **both . . . and . . .:** conjunctions

       ● not only . . . but
     The two words *both . . . and* can join single words or phrases:
     ***Both** he **and** the chief officer made a broadcast.*
     ***Both** he **and** I forgot about that.*

*The play is **both** enjoyable **and** tiring.*
*I have completed **both** part A **and** part B.*
*There is considerable disagreement **both** on economic **and** on social affairs.*
*I am hoping **both** to hear from you **and** see you in the near future.*

Notice that in all these examples the words after *both* and *and* match each other grammatically (two nouns, two verbs etc.). This does not always happen, but it is recommended.

---

bound (to): adjective + *to*-INFINITIVE

a • certain/likely/sure (to)
*Someone is **bound to** find out sooner or later.*

b *I am bound to say* is a way of introducing a comment or criticism, and means *I must say*:
*I am **bound to** say I think you have behaved very foolishly.*

---

break, broke, broken: verb

a *break* can be used with and without an object. If we *break* something, or something *breaks*, it divides into two or more pieces, sometimes as a result of an accident:
*He **broke** the bar of chocolate in half and gave me a piece.*
*My aunt fell and **broke** her leg.*
*Be careful with that plate or it'll **break**.*

b • fail to obey; fail to keep
*If you **break** the law/the rules/the speed limit you'll be in trouble.*
*People don't like someone who **breaks** a promise.*

c *breaking a record* means doing some sporting activity faster or better than anybody else:
*He **broke** the world 1000 metres record by, I think, two seconds.*

d *broken* is a participle and an adjective. Things that are *broken* do not work any more: they need mending. People who are *broken* are destroyed in some way:
*My radio is/has **broken**. I need a new one.*
*There was **broken** glass all over the floor.*
*Nixon seemed a **broken** man – but he returned to public life.*

---

breath: noun /breθ/ (C, U)

a *She took a deep **breath** and jumped into the lake.*
*If you went out for a **breath** of (fresh) air you'd feel better.*

b *You have to hold your **breath** when swimming under water.*
*She ran so quickly she was out of **breath** when she arrived.*

---

breathe: verb /briːð/

> *I can hardly **breathe** – I've got a terrible cold.*
> ***Breathe** through your nose, not your mouth.*

bring, brought, brought: verb ▶ Compare **take**

```
bring (+IO) + OBJECT
```

a   *bring* usually means moving something/someone towards the speaker (or writer):
   > *Waiter! Please **bring** (me) the menu.*
   > *Do **bring** your friends to see us.*
   > *Could you remember to **bring** back my umbrella next time you come?*

   But sometimes the speaker is thinking about the place where the listener is (and the speaker could be):
   > *Can I **bring** my friend to your house to meet you?*
   > *Is there anything you'd like us to **bring** you back from abroad?*

   or where the listener and speaker will both be:
   > *If you'll **bring** the picnic food, we'll **bring** the drink.*

b   Like *give*, *bring* can have one or two objects, but a direct object is essential:
   > ***Bring** (me) the menu.*
   > *Charles! the waiter's already **brought** it (to us).*
   > *They didn't bring me a present, but they **brought** one to/for children.*
   > *We were **brought** breakfast in bed.*

build, built, built: verb

> *People **build** houses/offices/factories/bridges/roads/ships . . .*
> *Birds **build** nests . . .*
> *The British and French are **building** a Channel tunnel . . .*
> *Henry Ford started from nothing and **built up** a large business.*
> *Peter's having a house **built**.*
> *Rome was not **built** in a day.* (= important things take a long time.)

building: noun (C, U)

> *A lot of these modern **buildings** are ugly.*
> *The **building** industry is only interested in new towns, new shops.*

business: noun (C, U)

a   ● company; firm (C)
   > *Martin and his brother run a very successful **business**.*
   > *Both these companies started as small family **businesses**.*

b • activities of a company (U)
I was there on business – not on holiday.
He's a good person to do business with.
They do a lot of business with Japan.
Business is good this year – we have lots of orders.

c • *It's none of their business who I invite here.* (= not their concern)
Please mind your own business. (= do not interfere.)

d • matter; affair (usually count, singular only)
That was a terrible business – all those people getting killed.

but

1 but: conjunction ▶ Compare **and; or**

but introduces a contrast.

a *but* can introduce single words, phrases and clauses:
That's rather clever, but unwise.
I imagine you are painters but not carpenters.
The instruments on the right will be heard mainly with your right ear, but also with your left.
I used to love the cinema, but I'd quite stopped going.
It's horrible, but is it art?

Informally, *but* can express surprise:
'I've just won £10,000.' 'But that's marvellous.'

b not . . . but . . . or **not only . . . but (also) . . .**
When *but* follows a phrase or clause containing *not*, the *but* normally still introduces a contrast – to some negative idea:
They are not carpenters, but painters.
We must not ignore history, but use it more effectively.

This is quite different from *not only . . . but (also) . . .*, where *but* helps to emphasise a surprising addition, not a simple contrast:
They are not only painters, but (also) carpenters. (= they are both).

c but that
This is a rare and formal phrase meaning 'except that', 'only':
I would visit them more often but that it's such a difficult journey.

2 but: preposition ▶ Compare **except**

a • except
Especially after *any*, *every*, *no* and their compounds. Also after *what*, *who*, *where*:
The conclusion surprised everyone but the author.
Why has 'natural selection' not got rid of all but the most efficient of these blood types?
Who but a fool would have trusted them?
She is anything but stupid. (= she is certainly not stupid)
He does nothing but watch TV all day. (Notice *but* + BARE INFINITIVE)

b *the first/last/next but one*

but one, meaning 'except for one' is used after *the first/last/next*. Here is a girl explaining how she went to the theatre the night before the final night of a play:

> *It was the last but one night of 'You Never Can Tell' at the Haymarket Theatre.*

also:

> *The Smiths live next door but one to us.* (= not the next door house, but the one beyond that)

c *but for* introduces a sort of negative condition:

> *We would have missed the train but for you.* (= if you had not helped us)

3 **but**: adverb

- only

This is a formal use.

> *We could but try.* (= It is/was the only thing we could do)
> *There was plenty of new territory for them to take. The army had but to advance.* (= It was all they needed to do.)

4 **all but**

- nearly

> *They all but succeeded.* (= They nearly succeeded, but didn't.)

buy, bought, bought: verb

```
        —
buy + (IO+) OBJECT
```

a *buy* usually needs an object, unless the word is used in a very general sense:

> *I bought this bag in the market.*
> *Buying and selling are very different!*

b *buy* can take two objects, or we can *buy* something *for* somebody:

> *He always buys them flowers.*
> *Please don't buy anything for me.*

by

1 **by**: preposition

a Place

- near; beside

> *He came over and sat by me/by my side.*
> *I'm all by myself.* (= all alone)
> *It's nice living by the sea.*
> *We walked by the lake.*

b **by** + agent   ▶ Compare **with**

We use *by* to introduce the 'doer' or cause of an action (the agent), particularly with passive verbs:

*Everyone was shocked **by** the week's events.*

*Huge losses **by** the bus company have forced the cuts in the bus services.* (= losses that were made by the bus company . . .)

*Is this new poem really **by** Shakespeare?*

*This week's statement **by** the minister is bad news.*

*She was killed **by** a falling chimney.*

c **by** + means/method   ▶ Compare **with**

*The roof was reached **by** a steel ladder.*

*He escaped from prison **by** sawing through the bars.*

*I did this all **by** myself.* (= without help)

*The letter was delivered **by** hand.* (It did not come **by** post.)

*We came **by** air/**by** sea/**by** train/**by** car . . .*

*Things happen **by** chance/**by** accident/**by** mistake . . .*

*I only know them **by** sight.* (= recognise them when I see them, but not really know them)

*You can learn something **by** heart.* (= in your memory)

d ● no later than; when (this time) is/was reached:

By 3 o'clock in the afternoon there was nothing left for him to do.

By 1960 scientists were pursuing all the problems produced by the new theory.

*I've got to give in my homework **by** Friday at the latest.*

*Your father thinks you'll be back **by** Christmas.*

e **Time**

● during

used mostly in the phrases *by day* and *by night*:

*Even **by** day, the aeroplane noise was a nuisance.*

*Those forests were lovely **by** day, but they were even more beautiful **by** night.*

f **Measurements, amounts**

*The room was only twelve foot **by** nine (foot).*

*Dr Jenkin increased the offer **by** £500 million.*

*If you're paid **by** the hour you don't get any sick pay.*

g **Various other uses**

*It's OK **by** me.*

*He's a doctor **by** profession.*

*You can't always judge **by** appearances.*

2 **by**: adverb

● near; past

*Someone has to be **by** to give you the help you need.*

*Stand **by** for an announcement.* (= wait for . . .)

*She sits in the window watching all the people go **by**.*

▶ See *by far* at **far**.

call

1 call: verb

```
        —
call + OBJECT
       O + COMPLEMENT
```

a   When the meaning is 'name', *call* can be followed by an object and a complement:
   ***Call** me Dave.*
   *His name is really David, but he likes to be **called** Dave.*
   *She **called** me a liar! (= She said I told lies.)*
   *What do you **call** that kind of table? Is there a special word for it?*

b   ● telephone
   ***Call** a doctor/the fire brigade/the police.*
   *'Can I speak to Francis, please?' 'Who's **calling**?'*
   *'I'm sorry, he's not in his office. Can I get him to **call** you back?'*

c   ● make a short visit
   *Let's go and **call** on Bob and Sheila.*
   *We'll **call** for you in the car at 9.*
   *The train at Platform 3 is the 9.57 for Edinburgh, **calling** at Peterborough, York and Newcastle.*

d   ● speak loudly, perhaps from one place to another
   *We thought we heard someone **calling** for help.*
   *The nurse will **call** (**out**) your name when it's your turn* (to see the doctor.)

e   **Various other meanings**
   If you ask someone to *call* you in the morning, you want them to wake you up.
   If someone *calls* a meeting, they ask people to come to it.

2 call: noun

a   ● a telephone call
   *I'm expecting a **call** from my mother.*
   *I must make a phone **call**.*
   *Give me a **call** (or a ring) when you get home.*
   *The fire brigade gets hundreds of **calls** a year.*
   *I'm speaking from a **call box**. (= a telephone box)*

b   ● visit
   *We paid a **call** on my grandmother.* (more formal than *called on*)

can: modal verb   ▶ Compare **could**

can is a modal verb referring to the present or the future.
The negative of *can* is *cannot* but in speech we normally use *can't*. *Can't* is pronounced /kɑːnt/ in British English and /kænt/ in American English.
Can is concerned with possibility and freedom in both practical and

theoretical ways. If people *can* do something, they are free to do it because they have permission or ability (1–4). If you ask if something *can* be true, you are talking about whether it is theoretically possible (5–6).

Within these broad meanings, *can* functions to make offers, orders, requests, suggestions . . .

1 Permission (now for the present or future)   ▶   Compare **may**

We use *can* to talk about permission that already exists and to ask for, and give (or refuse), permission now for the future:

'Can I borrow this book?' 'No, I'm afraid you **can't** take reference books out of the library. But you **can** read it in here.'
*You **can't** bring a dog in here – it says so.*
***Can** I speak to Maria, please?* (a request)
***Can** we let you know later?*
***Can** I give you a lift to the station?* (an offer)
***Can** we talk about this later?* (perhaps a suggestion)
*You **can** jolly well wait!* (an order)
*You **can** do exercise 20 for homework, everybody.* (an order)

2 General ability and possibility (now)

can also refers to an ability that exists now, or a possibility that exists for the future:

*'Can you swim?' 'Of course I **can**.' 'No I **can't** actually.'*
*'Their youngest child is only ten months, but she **can** already walk.'*
*'I **can't** believe it.'*
***Can** you pass the salt please?* (a request)
***Can't** you remember anything I tell you?* (a complaint)
***Can** you explain all this to your father?* (a suggestion)
***Can** you please make less noise?* (an order)
***Can't** you keep quiet for a moment.* (an order)
*We **can** give you a lift to the station, if that's any use.*
*The temperature **can** get up to 45°C in the summer.* (and it sometimes does.)
*We **can** all make mistakes.* (and we sometimes do.)

   ▶   See   can't bear at **bear**; can't help at **help**; can't stand at **stand**

3   With verbs of the senses (*see, hear* . . .) *can* is often used to describe ability at the moment of speaking, instead of the verb on its own:

*I **can** see my brother waving to us – but I **can't** hear what he's saying.*

(This is more usual than: *I see him waving* . . . and we cannot say **I'm seeing him* . . .)

Can is also used with some verbs of 'knowing' (also *remember, see*), where it also does not change the meaning very much:

*I **(can)** well understand how you feel.*

4 Future opportunity   ▶   Compare **able**

can is not used for a future ability which does not exist now:
NOT **The baby **can** talk soon.*
NOT **We **can/can't** get there much more quickly when the tunnel is built.*

But *can* is used to make suggestions about future actions where there is nothing in the present that stops them:

*We **can** go to the theatre next week, if you are free.*
*That would be super, but I **can't** go on Wednesday.*
*The food **can** be prepared the day before.*
*We **can** decide about that later.* (perhaps a suggestion).
*Can you **come** to dinner on Saturday?* (invitation)
*I **can** come back tomorrow, if you like.* (suggestion).
*Anything **can** happen!*

5 Theoretical possibility

a Present possibility

When we are guessing about something that may possibly be true now but we do not know, *can* is mainly non-assertive, so we use it in questions and with negatives:

***Can** he really be as old as your grandfather?* (= Is it possible that . . .)
*He **can't** be seventy surely – he only looks about 50.* (= It is impossible that . . .)
*She **can't** like him or she wouldn't be so rude to him.*
*Whoever **can** be telephoning at this hour of the night?*
*Paul **can't** possibly be in Hong Kong yet.*

But we do not use *can* in affirmative statements:

NOT **He **can** be seventy.*
NOT **Paul **can** be in Hong Kong by now.* (▶ See **may could.**)

b Future possibility

can/can't are not usually used to discuss purely theoretical future possibilities
  NOT **He **can** miss the train this evening.* (Say *He **may/might/could** . . .*)
  NOT **It **can** rain tomorrow.* (Say *It **may/might/could** . . .*)
  NOT **Can they forget to come this evening?* (Say *Could they . . .?*)

Note: *?They **can't** forget to come.* (Say *They **won't/couldn't** . . .*)
    *?It **can't** rain tomorrow.* (Say *It **won't/couldn't** . . .*)

We can however say:

*They **can't** be coming tomorrow.* (Notice the present progressive tense.)

Notice that in this purely theoretical sense, *can't* is the opposite of *must*. (Careful thought proves that they are not coming.)

6 **can have** + PAST PARTICIPLE

can have + PAST PARTICIPLE is used to discuss theories now about events in the past. This is mainly non-assertive; it is used with questions and negative sentences:

*Where is Paul? What **can** have happened to him?*
*He **can't** have forgotten.*
*I don't think he **can** have forgotten.*

But not usually:

He **can have forgotten.* (Say *He **could** have . . .* or *He **may** have . . .*)
He **can have had an accident.*

car: noun (C, U)

a   *We've bought a new **car** . . .*
        *I left my book in the **car** . . . get in/out of a **car***

b Notice the uncountable usage:
        *travel by **car** . . . a two-**car** family . . .*

care

1   care: verb

```
            about
            wh-CLAUSE
care +
            for
            to-INFINITIVE
```

a   ● think something is important or interesting
        *She really **cares** about her job – and works hard at it.*
        *All she **cares** about is clothes.*
        *I don't **care** what you say – I'm going to marry him.*
        *He doesn't **care** where he lives.*

b   ● like (mainly non-assertive)
        *Would you **care** to join us?* (a polite invitation)
        *I wouldn't **care** to be in his situation.*
        *I don't **care** for pop music, I'm afraid.*

c   *care for* can also mean 'look after'. This use is rather formal:
        *She gave up her job to **care for** her mother.*

2   care: noun (mainly U)

a   ● process of looking after; responsibility
        *She should take more **care** of herself – then she wouldn't get all these colds.*
        *Who'll take **care** of the children while she's in hospital?*
        *health **care** . . . **care** of the old and sick . . .*

b   ● carefulness
        *Handle with **care**!* (label on a parcel)
        *He was driving 'without due **care** and attention', the police said.*

careful: adjective

        careful is the opposite of *careless*:
        *Do be **careful** – that was my foot you trod on.*
        *Most women are **careful** drivers.*

carry: verb

a With its usual meaning of 'hold or contain something and take it somewhere else', *carry* needs an object:
We all carried our own luggage.
He was carrying the child on his back.
The railway carries thousands of people to work every day.
Do your police carry guns?

b *carry on*, meaning 'continue', can be followed by an *-ing* form:
It was impossible to carry on a conversation with all the noise.
I thought I'd carry on with the course for another term.
We carried on walking, despite the rain.

case

1 case: noun

a • a piece of luggage
a suitcase

b • a quarrel in law:
He brought a case against his employers for sacking him.

c • a situation, an instance or an example of something happening:
It's a case of typhoid . . .
It's sad when you get cases of children running away from home.

2 in case: adverb and conjunction

a We use *in case* to talk about things we do in order to be prepared and ready because something may/might possibly happen:
I imagine your father does not want American stamps, but I will keep some for him in case. (he might want them)
It's perfectly obvious that she doesn't believe in Father Christmas but she's not going to say it, just in case. (= Father Christmas might exist, and he won't give her presents if she says he does not exist.)
In case there is any misunderstanding, I do want to explain. (= there may be some misunderstanding)

b In British English *in case* does not mean 'if':
I'm going to lend you some money now, in case (NOT *if) *you need a taxi tomorrow.* (Then, if you need a taxi, you'll have enough money for one.)

In American English however, *in case* can mean 'if':
In case you need a taxi, you'll have enough money.

3 in case of: preposition

in case of has both the above meanings, even in British English:
Dozens of soldiers took up positions on the surrounding hills in case of attack. (= they were ready for any enemy attack)
In Case of Fire raise the alarm. (a notice in public buildings, meaning 'if there is a fire . . .')

4 in any case

- anyhow; whatever happens
  There's nothing interesting on TV tonight. **In any case,** *I'm too busy to watch.*
  I think there's a late train. But **in any case** *you could always get a taxi.*

5 in this/that case; if this/that is the case

- if this/that happens; if this/that is so
  'The TV set is broken.' 'Well, **in that case** *we can't watch.'*

---

cause   ▶ Compare **make**

1 cause: verb

> **cause** (+ IO) + OBJECT
>   + O + *to*-INFINITIVE

cause can be used in several ways, and can have two objects:
  The storm **caused** *tremendous damage.*
  His behaviour is **causing** *us a lot of problems.*
  Something **caused** *me to lose my balance and I fell over.*

2 cause: noun

a • reason; explanation
  What can be the **cause** *of his odd behaviour?*
  There is no **cause** *for alarm.* (alarm = worry)
  They thought it was murder at first, but then they said his death was due to natural **causes.**

b • important issue; organisation collecting money for others.
  There are so many good **causes** *these days asking for money – like Save the Children Fund and the World Wide Fund for Nature and . . .*
  You are not helping the **cause** *of racial equality.*

---

central: adjective

a • describing something in the middle
  Central *London . . .* **Central** *America* (= the part between North and South America)
  The college is very **central.** (= near the centre of the town, and therefore easy to reach)

b • main; most important; having power throughout a place
  Central *government* (the government of the whole country) *has to work with local government.*
  The **central** *character in the book is an old schoolteacher.*
  67% of homes now have **central** *heating.* (= a system that heats the whole building)

centre: noun

a   the *centre* of something is the middle of it:
> *You stand in the **centre** of the circle and everyone dances round you.*
> *There was a table in the **centre** of the room, and a lot of chairs against the walls.*
> *The **centre** of the earth is unbelievably hot, isn't it?*
> *We live a short busride from the town **centre**.*

b   As a count noun *centre* can mean a building for a special purpose, or a place where a special activity happens:
> *a community **centre** . . . a health **centre** . . . shopping **centres** . . . sports **centres***

century: noun

•   a period of a hundred years, usually measured backwards (BC – Before Christ) or forwards (AD) from the traditional year of Christ's birth. Some people think that the twenty-first *century* begins on 1st January in the year 2000, but other people argue that since we count from one to ten, it actually does not begin until 1st January in 2001!:
> *Our earliest ancestors lived here **centuries** ago.*
> *The middle of the nineteenth **century** too was a time of revolution.*

certain, uncertain

1 certain: determiner

certain can be used with count nouns to mean 'some', but exactly which or how much is not mentioned:
> *A **certain** amount of useful progress has been made.*
> *Exceptions should be made in **certain** cases.*
> *I knew to a **certain** extent that my future depended on them.*
> *There is a new pension scheme . . . that will enable everybody below a **certain** income to provide for their old age.*
> *A **certain** person has been complaining.* (but I'm not saying who.)

2 certain: pronoun   ▶ Compare **several**

This is a rare usage, in the pattern *certain of* + PLURAL NOUN meaning 'some of':
> *They had to leave **certain of** the cooking pots out.*

3 certain; uncertain: mainly predicative adjectives ▶ Compare **likely; sure**

- sure; confident; having no doubts
certain is the opposite of uncertain:

A				
	is feels	**certain** **sure**	(that)	he locked the door.
He	is	**uncertain**	whether if	he will pass the exam.

B				
He	is feels seems	**(un)certain** **(un)sure**	of about	his facts.

C				
He	is seems appears	**certain** **sure**	to	pass the exam.

D				
	is seems	**certain**	(that)	he will pass the exam.
It	looks appears	**uncertain**	whether if	

The exact meaning of the adjective *certain* depends on the pattern it is used in.

A *be + certain + CLAUSE*
In this pattern, *certain* means 'sure' or 'confident', which are also possible:
*I am pretty **certain** I wouldn't like to live like Robin does.*
*Helen said she could not be **certain** I had told her everything.*
*He feels **certain** that he's going to pass the exam.*

If we are *uncertain*, then we have a strong doubt or question in our minds, so we say *uncertain + whether/if*, or + some other question word:
*He was **uncertain** whether he had locked the door.*
*Celia is still **uncertain** how exactly it happened.*
*I'm not **certain** which plane they're coming on.*

B We can also *be* (or *feel* – or *seem* to other people) (*un*)*certain of* or (*un*)*certain about* something. The meaning is still 'sure' or 'confident':
*He seemed so **certain** of his facts that I believed him.*
*You have to get there very early to be **certain** of getting a seat.*
*Are you quite **certain** about the date?*
*No, I feel a bit **uncertain**, actually.*

C If somebody is *certain* (or *sure*) *to do* something, or if something is *certain* (or *sure*) *to happen*, this means the speaker is *certain*, not the person being talked about. ▶ Compare **bound** and **likely**:
*They told me I was **certain** to fail.* (= *They were **certain** that I would fail.*)

*You're almost **certain** to hear from them sooner or later.* (= *We are **certain** that you will hear . . .*)
*She seems **certain** to pass.* (= *I am **certain** that she will pass.*)
*If we have a picnic, it's **certain** to rain.*
*There are **certain** to be complaints.*

D With sentences with an impersonal introductory *it* (*It is **certain** that* + CLAUSE), *sure* is not an alternative. ▶ Compare **likely**
*It seems **certain** that she will pass the exam.*
Also:
*One thing is **certain** – he won't get that job.*

Again (as in A), *uncertain* is followed by question-word clauses (*if* or a *wh*-word):
*She looked **uncertain** whether to go or stay.*
*Tom seemed so **uncertain** what he should do.*

certain can also mean 'definitely known':
*Nothing is **certain** yet – even the date of the exam is still **uncertain**.*

4 for certain, for sure

- without any doubt
*I think so, but I don't know **for certain**/for sure.*
*It is not known **for certain** how the picture came to be in the garden.*

5 make certain, make sure

- check
*Please **make certain** that you have closed all the windows and turned off the lights before you leave the room.*

---

certainly: adverb ▶ Compare **surely**

- of course
a The meaning is 'of course' or 'definitely', but often the speaker qualifies this by adding 'but':
*He'll **certainly** fail his exam if he doesn't work harder.*
*The weather is **certainly** warmer, but it's still rather wet.*

b *certainly* and *certainly not* can be used as replies:
*'May I just try and deal with your questions first?' '**Certainly**.'*
*'Did you open my handbag?' '**Certainly not**.'*
▶ Compare *of course* at **course**

---

change

1 change: noun (C, U)

a - alteration; action etc. that makes things different (C, U)
*There have been so many **changes** here, you wouldn't know the place any more.*

---

*The hospital say there's no **change** in his condition.* (= He is neither better nor worse.)
*This is a time of great **change** in Europe.*

b • something different (C)
*I didn't have a **change** of clothes, so I had to sit in my wet things.*
*There's been a **change** of plan, and they're not coming now.*

c **It is/makes a change; for a change**
These phrases often mean that the difference is good in some way:
*It's a **change** for me not to work at the weekend.*
*Why don't you help **for a change**?*

d • money (U)
*You'll need **change** for the ticket machine.* (= small coins)
*I'm still waiting for my **change** please.* (= money due because I paid with a note or coin of a bigger amount than the price)

2 change: verb

a • become different; make something different
*The weather has **changed**.*
*The village has **changed** so much – you won't recognise it.*
*Wait until the lights **change**.* (= until the traffic lights turn green for 'Go')
*Water **changes** into steam when it boils.*

b • replace something by something else
*If this jumper doesn't fit you, the shop will **change** it.*
*Henry's **changed** his job again.* (= moved to another job)
*Perhaps you need to **change** the batteries.* (= put new batteries in your torch)
*Can you **change** this £50 note, please?* (= give me smaller notes or coins)
*Do you **change** money?* (e.g., pounds into dollars)
*Can we **change** the subject, please?* (= talk about something else)
*We had to **change** (trains) at Crewe.* (= get off one train and on to another)
*All **change**!* (= Everyone on this bus/train must get out here, because it is not going any further.)
*I didn't have time to **change** – I just went as I was.* (= I didn't have time to put on other clothes.)

charge

1 charge: verb ▶ Compare **cost**

```
        –
charge (+IO) + OBJECT
```

a • ask an amount of money for something
*How much do you **charge** to dryclean a coat/for drycleaning?*
*They **charged** (us) £20 each for bed and breakfast.*
*All the banks **charge** you interest if you want to borrow money.*

b • officially accuse
*A man has been **charged** with murder.*

c • rush towards (and attack)
*The lions suddenly **charged** at the car and we only just got away in time.*

2 charge: noun ▶ Compare **cost; price**

a • the amount of money asked – often for doing something
*There's no **charge** for admission but the exhibition catalogue is £3.*
*Postal **charges** have gone up again – so even sending postcards is expensive.*

b • a legal statement, accusing someone of a crime
*He's been arrested on a **charge** of murder.*

c • an attack
*The animals made a sudden **charge** at us.*

d • responsibility
*Who's in **charge** of this shop? Where's the manager?*

---

child (plural **children**): noun

As well as meaning a young person, who is not an adult, a *child* can refer to a son or daughter of any age:
*Our **children** are all married now, with **children** of their own.*

Notice where the possessive apostrophe comes:
*Do you sell **children's** books, please?*

---

choice: noun (C, U) ▶ See **choose**

*There's so much **choice** in the shops – I don't know what to choose.*
*There's a **choice** of fish or beef or chicken.*
*He didn't have any **choice** – he had to agree.*
*Your pudding looks good – you made the right **choice**.*
*A purple bathroom would not be my **choice**, but if you like it . . .*

---

choose, **chose**, **chosen**: verb

> **choose** + (IO) + OBJECT
> *to*-INFINITIVE

*Can I **choose** the television programme this evening? Can I **choose** what we watch?*
*It wasn't easy to **choose** between the applicants for the job.*
*I've **chosen** John a tie/a tie for John.*
*He **chose** to ignore my advice.* (= He decided not to do what I advised.)

circumstance

1 circumstance: noun (usually plural)

- facts and events surrounding some other event
  The **circumstances** *of his life have been rather unusual.*
  I don't know exactly what happened – but she was found dead in rather
  peculiar **circumstances**.

2 in/under the circumstances

- considering all the details of a situation
  The shop said they would give me my money back **in/under the circum-**
  stances, *but only this once.*

class: noun

a *class* is usually an ordinary count noun when it means a lesson and also when it
means a particular social level in society:
  The advanced **class** *is in Room 5.*
  My sister is going to evening **classes**.
  The teacher doesn't mind if we talk in **class**. (uncountable)
  The working **class** *is getting smaller because more and more people consider*
  themselves middle **class**. (*middle class* here is used as an adjective).

b *class* with both these meanings can be a collective noun (using a singular or
plural verb) if the meaning is the people in the group:
  The **class** *like/likes grammar games.*
  The upper **class** *has/have survived for a long while.*

c *class* is uncountable when it refers to one of several levels, of different
qualities:
  If you fly business **class** *there's more room for your legs.*
  Tourist **class** *is rather crowded.*
  *We sat in a first-***class** *compartment by mistake.* (on a train)

clear, clearer, clearest: adjective

a - free from anything that would be in the way, or that would be a nuisance:
  Personally I wouldn't have **clear** *glass in the bathroom window.* (= glass that
  is easy to see through)
  I've got to work, so I need a **clear** *head.* (= free from alcohol)
  I've no **clear** *idea of what they want.*
  The road ahead looked **clear***, which was why he was driving so fast.* (= free
  from cars)
  I've kept next week **clear** *– so come any time that suits you.*
  Stand **clear** *of the doors!* (= Stand well away from the train doors.)
  a **clear** *sky* (= without clouds) . . . *a* **clear** *skin* (= without spots) . . . *a* **clear**
  view (= with nothing in the way)

b ● obvious; easy to understand
It is clearer than ever that the government will have to go.
The instructions on this form are not clear – can I type my answers, or do I have to write by hand?

c ● certain
Are you clear about what you have to do?
I'm not clear whether we are supposed to write or telephone?

clearly

1 clearly: adverb

● in a clear way
Please speak clearly and please speak now. (= recorded message on a telephone answering machine)

2 clearly: sentence adverb
● obviously
That is clearly a big worry for the government.

close, closer, closest /kləʊs kləʊsə(r) kləʊsɪst/

1 close: adverb ▶ Compare **near**
Some animals seem to take no notice of visitors and you can get quite close.
We're too far away – we'll try and get a bit closer.
I don't think you're going to be able to read this – the lines are too close together. (*near* is NOT likely here)

2 close: adjective
If my own sister died I would be terribly upset, although we're not particularly close. (i.e. emotionally close. *near* is NOT possible)
Let's have a closer look.
a close friend

3 close to: preposition

close to is like a preposition, meaning 'near (to)':
It's very easy to find my house. It's close to the station.
My daughter is closer to my wife than she is to me.
Its climate is remarkably close to that of this country.

4 *close on* is used informally like an adverb meaning 'nearly':
She is close on eighty-three years old.

5 close or **near**?

a As adverbs, *close* (1 above) and *near* often mean the same (opposite of *far away*). But when they are used as prepositions (3 above), we must say *close to* (not *close*). With *near* the *to* is optional:
I don't like sitting too close to/too near (to) the television.

91

We're still so **close to**/so **near (to)** the 1970s, it's difficult to think about the period objectively.

b As adjectives (2 above), *close* and *near* are sometimes interchangeable:
a **close/near** *relation* (e.g. a cousin) . . .
a **close/near** *thing* (= a bad thing that nearly happened)

But *close* also has many uses where *near* is not possible:
*They are **close** friends.*
*He has a **close** relationship with his son.*
*There's a **close** connection between eating too much and being fat.*
*We're keeping a **close** (= careful) watch on the situation.*
*On **closer** inspection the picture proved to be a fake.*

6 close /kləʊz/: verb   ▶ Compare **shut**

close is the opposite of *open*
The meaning is the same as *shut* in many cases. We can *close* or *shut* cupboards, doors, gates, windows, our eyes, a book, a shop:
*She **closes**/**shuts** the shop at 6 p.m.*
*The supermarket **closes**/**shuts** at 7.*

But a road is *closed* (NOT *shut*) for repair, and we *close* (or *end*) a letter by writing Yours sincerely, etc. We can also *close* (NOT *shut* or *end*) a bank account.

---

closely: adverb /kləʊslɪ/   ▶ Compare **nearly**

- in a close way; carefully
*Listen **closely**.*
*A **closely** guarded secret . . .*

---

cloth and **clothes**

1 cloth /klɒθ/: noun

a *cloth* is uncountable when it means 'material':
*a piece of **cloth** . . . woollen **cloth** . . .*

Cloth is not a very usual word – *material* is more usual. (*It's made of some sort of nylon **material**.*)

b a *cloth* (countable) is a piece of *cloth* made for some purpose:
*. . . a dish**cloth** . . . a face **cloth** . . . a floor**cloth** . . .*
*Give me a **cloth** – I've spilled my coffee.*

2 clothes /kləʊðz/: noun (plural only and not countable)

clothes – things you wear – is a plural word:
*I've got to buy some new winter **clothes**.*
*She hasn't got many **clothes**.*

Note – we can talk about quantities of *clothes* but we cannot count them. So we can say:

some/not many/lots of/a lot of/plenty of/these/those . . . clothes

But NOT **many/a number of/several/four . . . five . . . clothes*

---

cold

1 cold: noun (C, U)

a • illness often caused by cold weather (usually C)
I've got a terrible cold – I need some paper handkerchiefs.
We've all got colds. You'll catch (a) cold if you go out without a coat.

b Usually *the cold*.
• a place that is cold; cold weather
Why are you standing there in the cold. Come in.
I don't like the cold.

2 cold, colder, coldest: adjective

cold is the opposite of *hot*:
I'm cold. I'm feeling cold. Let's put the heater on.
The weather's turned cold.
This is always a cold house.
There's some cold meat in the fridge. (= cooked and ready to be eaten *cold*)
Last winter was the coldest for twenty years.

---

come, came, come: verb ▶ Compare go

```
        —
come + –ing
    COMPLEMENT
```

a *come* often means movement towards the speaker or writer:
Come here!
Come and see us when you're next in London.
Has the post come yet?

But sometimes the speaker is thinking about the place where the listener is:
We hope to come and visit you at Christmas.

or where one of them will be:
Why don't you and Charles come to Canada with us next summer?

b *come* can be followed by an *-ing* form, with some activity verbs, though this is not very common:
Come swimming with us tomorrow!

---

c come + ADJECTIVE

- become

Will my dreams come true?
Oh, I'm sure everything will come right in the end.

d Various other meanings

The time has come to decide what we're going to do. (The time has arrived.)
He comes from Austria – I thought he was German.
Eventually he came to realise that he had been wrong. (After a time he realised.)
How did you come to find that out? (happen to . . .)
How come he got the job, and not you? (informal: How did it happen?)
Dinner for two came to £30. (cost)
Why don't prices ever come down? (Contrast **go up**)
A button's come off my shirt, and the colour came out in the wash.
Come off it! (= Don't pretend you mean that.)

committee: noun

committee is a collective noun used with singular or plural verb, according to the meaning:
The committee consists of parents and teachers.
The committee has/have decided to build a school swimming-pool.
The committee have all gone home now.

common

1 common: adjective

- familiar; usual; often happening; ordinary

Comparatives and superlatives can be formed by adding -er and -est, or by using *more* and *most*:
At one time wolves were common in Britain.
Jones is probably the commonest Welsh surname.
This problem is commoner/more common than you might think.

b - ordinary in a rather bad way; lacking in taste; uneducated
They're so common – always screaming at each other.
Their manners, their clothes, their house – everything about them is common.

c usually attributive only
- shared in some way by two or more people
The affair was common knowledge for weeks before it got into the newspapers.
Their only common language is English. (= the only language they both speak)
common property . . . a common purpose.

Also *common* sense (= coming from experience) . . . *the common* cold (= the kind of cold that many people get).

2 common: noun

- an open area of grassy ground, where anyone is allowed to go
  *She takes the dogs for a run on the **common** every day.*

3 in common (with)

- shared; like
  *You and I have so much **in common**.* (= we are alike)
  *In **common** with other teenagers, he's mad on rock music.* (= like other teenagers . . .)

company: noun

a
- a business (collective noun with singular or plural verb)
  *John Smith and **Co/Company***
  *The **company** makes/make furniture.*

b
- other people being present (uncountable)
  *'Can I come with you?' 'Oh, do. I'd be glad of your **company**.'*
  *'Shall I keep you **company**, or do you want to go alone?'* (= be with you)

compare: verb

a compare + OBJECT + (*with*)
- decide in what ways two or more things are similar
  *I'm going to **compare** the prices before I decide which bicycle to buy.*
  *I don't see how you can **compare** a bicycle with a motorbike.*

b compare with
When the verb has no object, only *compare with* (NOT **to*) is possible:
  *How do the beaches there **compare** with Spanish ones?*
  *A bicycle cannot **compare** with a motorcycle.* (= a motorcycle is much better.)

c compare . . . to
- say something or someone is like something else
  *She **compared** the human body to a machine.*

d compared with, compared to
Some people prefer *compared with*, and dislike *compared to* in such sentences as the following, but *compared to* is common, especially in American English:
  *Most people work far fewer hours **compared** with years ago.*
  *£10 is cheap **compared** with/to the £35 I had to pay.*

comparison

1 comparison: noun
  *It's difficult to make a **comparison** when you haven't got all the facts.*
  *There's no **comparison** between nylon and real silk.* (= Real silk is better.)

2 by/in comparison with

These two phrases mean the same, but notice always *with* (NOT **to*):
> *The house may seem small to you, but by/in comparison with the flat we had it is really quite large.*

---

complete

1 complete: adjective   ▶ Compare **total; whole**

a • whole; with all the parts that are needed
> *We haven't got a complete list of names – we're still waiting for some.*
> *The complete course takes three years.*
> *The lamp comes complete with plug and spare bulbs.*

b • total
> *I felt a complete fool.*
> *It was a complete success/surprise.*

2 complete: verb   ▶ Compare **end; finish**

  • make something complete; finish
> *I completed my studies in 1984.*
> *The house was never completed because they ran out of money.*
> *I only need his last novel to complete my set.*

---

concern

1 concern: verb (not usually in progressive)

  • to be important or interesting to
> *This information only concerns car owners.*

2 concerned: adjective

a • worried
> *We are all very concerned about/for his health.*
> *Concerned parents have been writing to the minister.*

b • involved
> *I would like to thank all the people concerned in the excellent arrangements.* (= all the people who were responsible for the arrangements. Notice the word order.)

3 as far as somebody/something + be + concerned

This expression points at what the speaker is specially talking about:
> *As far as I am concerned, you may borrow the car – but you'd better ask your mother first if she needs it.* (= I am happy for you to borrow it, but your mother may feel differently.)
> *There's no problem as far as numbers are concerned – we can easily take 200 people.* (= Numbers are not a problem, but there may be other problems.)

---

condition: noun

a • state (usually U and never plural)
*The house was in (a) terrible **condition** when we bought it.*
*She's in no **condition** to travel – she's far too ill.*

b • rule(s) about things that must happen (C, U)
*It's a nice flat but there are all sorts of **conditions** attached – no pets, no radios after 11 p.m. . . . .*
*I'll come on one **condition** – that you let me pay.*
*I'll come on **condition** that you let me pay. (= I'll come only if . . .)*

c **conditions** (plural)

  • the general circumstances surrounding something
*The workers want better pay and working **conditions**.*
*Despite the terrible weather **conditions**, some people were driving much too fast.*
*What are the living **conditions** like in the refugee camps?*

consider: verb ▶ Compare **believe; think**

consider +	OBJECT
	-ing
	wh-CLAUSE
	that CLAUSE
	o + (*to be*) +COMPLEMENT
	o + *to be/to have* . . .

a When *consider* means 'think about seriously' it can be followed by an OBJECT, by *-ing* and by *wh*-CLAUSES:
*We will **consider** your request.*
*Have you **considered** the effect of your behaviour on your mother?*
*Have you ever **considered** working abroad?*
*We are **considering** what to do/whether to go/how we should do it.*

b When *consider* means 'realise' or 'believe', progressive tenses are not usual. We can use a *that*-CLAUSE, an OBJECT (+ *to be*) + a COMPLEMENT, or an OBJECT + *to be* or *to have* . . . .
*When you **consider** (that) this used to be green fields, the change is amazing.*
*We **consider** that she is suitable.*
*We **consider** her (to be) the best tennis player in the world.*
*She is **considered** to have great talent.*

considerable: adjective

- a large amount of; great
  *I have given **considerable** thought to your request.*
  *The storm damage was **considerable**.*

considering

considering introduces a rather surprising fact

1 **considering**: conjunction and preposition
  *It's still very cold, **considering** that it's the middle of the summer.*
  *She's amazingly active, **considering** her age.*

2 **considering**: adverb
  *You did very well in the exam, **considering**. (= considering the difficulties)*

contain: verb

contain is not usually used in the progressive.
- have something inside
  *This book **contains** a lot of useful information.*
  *I must have eaten something **containing** alcohol.*

continue: verb

continue +	— OBJECT *-ing* *to*-INFINITIVE

a - not stop; go on
  *If this rain **continues**, the roads will be flooded.*
  *Celia **continued** with her job after she got married.*
  *I don't want to **continue** paying rent all my life – I'm going to buy a flat.*
  *My mother will **continue** to live in her own home as long as she can.*

b - go on speaking
  *'And what's more,' he **continued**, 'I have found the flat I want.'*

cost

1 cost: noun ▶ Compare **charge; price**

a ● the total amount of money needed for doing something:
*the **cost** of living . . . the **cost** of taking a car to Europe . . .*
*I'm trying to work out the **cost** of a month's holiday.*
*The **cost** of running a car goes up every year.*
*The **cost** of repairing all the storm damage will be millions of pounds.*
*Will £500 cover your **costs**?*

b cost or **charge** or **price**?
The *cost* of something is the money needed in general for something – what it *costs* you; the *charge* is what someone charges you – often for a service; the *price* is what you have to pay for a particular thing: Compare
*The **cost**(s) of running a hotel must be very high.*
*Is £20 a reasonable **price** to pay for bed and breakfast?*
*There is no extra **charge** for parking the car.*

2 cost, cost, cost: verb ▶ Compare **charge**

```
cost (+IO) + OBJECT
```

a *cost* can have two objects:
*My weekly train ticket **costs** (me) £10.*
*It **costs** (me) £10 a week to get to work.*

b cost or **charge**?
*It **costs** (you) £20 a night to stay there.*
*The hotel **charges** (you) £20 a night.*

could: modal verb ▶ Compare **can**

could refers to the past, present and future. The negative of *could* is *could not/ couldn't*.
Like *can*, *could* is concerned with what is possible and what one is free to do, either in practice or in theory. Sometimes the two meanings are combined. Functions include asking and giving permission, requests, orders, suggestions, invitations. If you say something *could* be done, you are saying that it is theoretically possible.
could is sometimes used as an alternative to *can*, when talking about the present or the future, but it suggests that we are less certain about what we are saying. *could* has limited usage as a past tense.

1 Ability and permission (present and future)

could is often less certain than *can*, so it is a politer way of asking for permission, giving orders and so on. But in giving permission it is usually better to use *can*. ('*Yes of course you **can**' sounds direct. '*Yes you **could***' suggests that the speaker does not want to say 'yes'):
*'**Could** I borrow this book?' 'Yes of course you **can**.'*

'Could I speak to Maria, please?' 'Well you could, but I'd have to wake her.'
Could we let you know later?
Could I give you a lift to the station?
Could we talk about this later?
You could do exercise 20 for homework. (an order or suggestion)
You could explain all this to your father. (a suggestion)
Could you come to dinner on Saturday? (an invitation)
I could lend you the money. (offer)
Perhaps Paul could tell us – let's telephone him and ask.

2 Theoretical possibility (present and future)

a *could* is used in affirmative sentences (contrast *can*) as well as questions and
negative sentences to talk about theoretical possibility. The meaning is 'It is
possible, though not very likely that . . .':
I suppose Bob could know. (but I doubt it)
I could murder you! (I am so angry with you.)
He could be 70 by now – he seemed old even when I was a child.
Paul could be in Hong Kong by now.
He could be telephoning from Hong Kong soon.
It could rain this evening. Take an umbrella.
I think something very odd could happen soon.
Could he really be as old as your grandfather? (or *Can he . . . ?*)

b *could not/couldn't* means 'It is impossible that . . .':
He couldn't only be 50. His son's 39. (Or: *He can't . . .*)

This use of *could not* contrasts with *must*.

c **condition**
Because *could* is concerned with theoretical possibilities, it is often used in the
main clause of 'unreal' conditional sentences, referring to the present or
future:
If I were a fish, I could live at the bottom of the sea.
*If you had saved more money, you could be sitting back now and enjoying
life.*
You could learn to use a computer if you took a course. (You would be able
to . . .)
You could borrow my guitar, if you asked me nicely. (I would give you my
permission . . .)

3 Past ability, past permission

a As the past tense of *can*, *could* usually means a general ability to do
something:
My grandfather could speak six languages.
Hilary could walk when she was ten months old.

or a mixture of ability and permission:
In those days you could get an ice cream for only a penny.
Until Sophie was five, I could take her free on the buses and trains.

b *could* is not normally used to talk about ability or permission on a single
occasion:
NOT **Could you take the dog to the hotel last summer?' *'Yes, we could.'*

But
> *'Were you able to . . ./Did they let you . . . ?'*
> *'Yes, we were able to/they let us/they allowed us to . . .'*

NOT **We **could** drive there in three hours yesterday.*
But
> *We were able to drive there/We managed to drive there/We got there . . .*

However, negative *could not/couldn't*, and verbs used with 'near negatives', like *hardly, just, only*, can refer to a single occasion:
> *'Did you take the dog?' 'No we **couldn't**.'*
> *I felt terrible. I **could** only apologise and hope that they would understand.*

Could is also used for ability on a single past occasion with verbs of the senses (*see, hear* . . .):
> *I **could** see my brother waving to us, but I **couldn't** hear what he was saying.*

c *could* is used as the past of *can* in reported speech and after expressions of thinking:
> *They said he **could** speak six languages.*
> *We were very pleased we **could** take the dog.*

4 could have + PAST PARTICIPLE

could have + PAST PARTICIPLE has two rather different meanings

a the possibility/the ability/the opportunity for something to happen existed in the past, but we know now that it did not (or does not or will not) happen:
> *You were a fool to drive so fast – you **could have** been killed.*
> *You **could have** telephoned. Did you forget?* (You did not telephone.)
> *You **could have** come with us next week, if you had bought a ticket yesterday. It's too late to get one now.* (So you can't come).

Notice:
> *You **could have** telephoned if you had wanted to.* (= You did not want to, so you didn't. But it was possible for you to telephone.)
> *You **couldn't have** telephoned, even if you had wanted to.* (You did not want to and you didn't. But it was impossible anyway – the phone wasn't working.)

b It is (theoretically) possible now that something happened/has happened. We do not know whether it has or not. We are guessing:
> *Whatever **could have** happened? They **could have** got lost, they **could have** had an accident.* (Perhaps they have, perhaps they haven't.)

The meaning can even be 'It is theoretically possible that something will have happened by some future date':
> *By this time next week you **could have** forgotten all about this.*
> *By the time they arrive everyone else **could have** left.*

country: noun

a • a nation; the land occupied by a nation (C)
> *. . . the **countries** of Europe . . . Third World **countries** . . .*
> *an industrialised **country** . . . love of one's own **country** . . .*
> *the south-east of the **country***

b **(the) country** (U)

- land that is not the city
  a weekend in the **country** . . . *life in the* **country** . . . **country** *bus services* . . .
  country *towns* . . .
  City life is OK but I'd rather live in the **country**.

c ● land of a special type **(U)**
  . . . *wheat-growing* **country** . . . *hilly* **country** . . .
  Parts of Scotland are quite wild **country**.

---

countryside: noun (U)

This word (usually with *the*) is much less used than *country*. It means country contrasted with towns and cities (as in **b** and **c** above) but particularly the appearance of it:
  All these new roads are ruining the **countryside**.
  He will be taken to Chequers, the British Prime Minister's country house, deep in the Buckinghamshire **countryside**.

---

couple: noun   ► Compare **pair**

a ● two people usually living together (often husband and wife)
  an elderly **couple** . . . *young married* **couples** . . . *the* **couple** *who live next door.*

b ● two similar things/people
  It will only take a **couple** *of days.*
  There are a **couple** *of chops in the fridge.*

---

course

1 **course**: noun

a ● a series of something
  an English **course** . . . *a* **course** *of lectures* . . . *a* **course** *of injections* . . . *a three-* **course** *dinner.*

b ● the way something develops; the path or direction something follows
  in the **course** *of time* . . . *in the normal* **course** *of events* . . . *in the* **course** *of the discussion* . . . *the* **course** *of a river* . . . *a race* **course**
  Your best **course** *is to try for some completely different job.*

2 **of course**: sentence adverb

a ● obviously; the fact is . . . ; naturally
  Most people, **of course**, *wish they had more money, but I wouldn't say there were any really poor people in this country.*
  She always looks lovely, but **of course** *she spends hours at the hairdresser's.*
  I forgot to set my alarm and **of course** *I missed the train.*

---

b *of course* and *of course not* can be used as replies:
> '*Is it OK if I turn the television down? It is rather loud.*' '*Yes, **of course.**'*
> '*You don't mind if I help myself to some more?*' '***Of course not,** go ahead.*'

c **of course not** and **certainly not**
of course not is just an emphatic way of saying something is not so – the facts are different:
> '*You're not cross with me, are you?*' '***Of course not.***'
> '*Do you think it's going to snow?*' '***Of course not.** It's a lovely day.*'

certainly not can sound rather annoyed:
> '*Did you break my torch?*' '***Certainly not,** I never touched it.*'

---

cut, cut, cut: verb

cut usually needs an object
a • use a knife, scissors etc. to remove part of something
> *At least you don't have to **cut** the grass in the winter.*
> *Get your hair **cut** – it's far too long.*
> *I cut the **picture** out of the paper, and now I can't find it.*
> *She can **cut** out a dress or a jacket without a pattern.* (= *cut* the cloth before making the clothes)

b *cut* can be followed by an indirect object and then an object, in the sense of 'cut a piece of food for' someone, but this usage is limited:
> *Could you **cut** me another piece of cake/meat?*

c • reduce; make smaller
> *If your article is too long the editor will **cut** it.*
> *How can we **cut** costs?* (= do something more cheaply)
> *The Channel Tunnel will **cut** the journey time between London and Paris.*
> *You should **cut** down on your smoking – 50 a day is too many.*

d • damage, injure with a knife or something sharp
> *I **cut** myself on a nail.*

e *cut off* means 'disconnect, separate', and is the usual verb when this happens during a telephone conversation:
> '*Hello! Are you there? We were **cut off.**'*

'd

1 '**d** is the short form of **had**:
> *Charlotte's father would have been a hundred if he'**d** been alive today.*
> *They'**d** no choice at all.*

2 '**d** is the short form of **would**:
> *I thought I'**d** telephone you with the news straightaway.*
> *That'**d** be lovely.*
> *I'**d** much rather it was your choice.*

d'

d' is the short form of *do*:
*What **d'**you mean?*
*How **d'**you do?*

damage: noun (U) and verb

*The storms caused/did terrible **damage**.*
*Many houses and cars were badly **damaged**.*
*You'll **damage** the wall if you bang nails in like that.*

Note: Things are *damaged*; people/animals are *hurt* or *injured*.

dare: modal and ordinary verb

dare is both a modal and an ordinary verb, but it is mainly used in the negative and other non-assertive contexts.

NEGATIVE	MODAL VERB	ORDINARY VERB – with or without *to*		
PRESENT	He/I etc. **dare** not **daren't** do . . .	He/she/it	does not doesn't	**dare** (to) do . . .
		I/we/you/they	do not don't	
PAST	He/I etc. **dared** not **daredn't** do . . . (?**daren't**)	He/I etc.	did not didn't	**dare** (to) do . . .

1 In theory *dare*, meaning be brave/bold/rude enough to do something, is both
a) a complete modal verb – followed by an infinitive without *to*; making questions and negatives with *do*; having 3rd person singular present without *-s* (*he/she dare*)
and b) an ordinary verb – followed by a *to*-INFINITIVE; using *do* for questions and negatives; having 3rd person singular *s* (*He/she dares*), combining with true modals (*She would dare*).
But in practice some of these possibilities are not often used.

2
a Notice that as *daren't* (present) and *daredn't* (past) are both pronounced the same /deənt/, some people use the spelling *daren't* for both:
*My new car is meant to go at 120 miles an hour, but I **daren't** try it at that speed.*
*We were very frightened. We **daredn't** speak about her threat. (or **daren't**)*

b In other negative contexts, where *not/n't* does not follow the verb, *dare* is used with and without *to*:
> *I don't think I'd **dare** jump.* (or ***dare** to jump*)
> *Everyone was silent. No one **dared** breathe.* (or ***dared** to breathe*).
> *We can only hope that these cowards would not **dare** to spread their message of hate.* (or ***dare** spread*)
> *'What would you do if a bus ran over the Prime Minister?' 'It wouldn't **dare**!'*

3 Affirmative *dare* is used in the expression *I daresay* (only with the pronoun *I*, and always written as one word). It means 'I expect', 'It is quite likely':
> *'Has he got wind of* (found out) *what you are going to suggest?' '**I daresay**.'*

4 Questions and imperatives are not very common:

a *Who would **dare** (to) do a thing like that?*
> *It was – **dare** I say it? – a failure.* (= I don't think you will like my saying this.)

b *How dare you . . . You dare . . .* and *Don't you dare . . .* are used to show the speaker's anger:
> *How **dare** you speak to me in that rude way.*
> *You **dare**/Don't you **dare** speak to me like that again.* (If you do, I'll be even more angry.)

5 dare + OBJECT + **to**-INFINITIVE

This is an ordinary verb meaning to challenge someone to do something:
> *It is very silly when children **dare** each other to do dangerous things, like running across railway lines.*

---

day: noun (C, U) ▶ Compare **night**; **today**

a The meaning is sometimes a 24-hour period, and sometimes the opposite of *night*:
> *There are 366 **days** in a leap year.*
> *Let's spend a/the **day** fishing.*
> *Have a nice **day**!*
> *I'm not paying £30 a **day** to hire a car.*
> *It's a casual job and you're paid by the **day**.*
> *Is there anyone at home during the **day**?* (or *in the **day**time?*)

b No article is used in the following expressions:
> *They slept by **day** and travelled by night.*
> *I've been working all· **day**.*
> *I seem to do nothing but work **day** after **day**.*

c Time prepositions are frequently not used:
> *I've been working **all day**.*
> *I saw her **the day before yesterday**, and we're meeting again the **day** after tomorrow.*
> ***One day** he just left everything and went off to Australia.*
> *Perhaps **one day**/**some day** my luck will change.*
> *Young people do what they like **these days**!*
> *Guess who I saw **the other day**.* (= *a few **days** ago*)

dead: adjective and **die**, **died**, **died**: verb

1 dead: adjective

- not alive
  *All my grandparents are now **dead**.*
  *That tree is **dead** – it must be cut down.*
  ***dead** flowers . . . a **dead** language* (e.g. Latin)

2 dead: adjective and adverb

- complete(ly); absolute(ly)
  ***dead** silence . . .*
  *You're **dead** right . . . He was **dead** certain . . . I am **dead** tired . . .*
  *We're **dead** on time – it is exactly 12 o'clock.*

3 die (dying), died, died: verb
  *Both my grandfathers **died** in 1981.*
  *And now one of my grandmothers has **died**.*
  *The forests are **dying**.*

deal

1 deal, dealt, dealt: verb

often *deal with*, meaning 'attend to', 'manage':
  *Let me **deal** with this problem.*
  *Shouting at children is not the best way to **deal** with them.*

2 a great/good deal (of): noun and adverb ▶ Compare **a lot**
  *There's **a great deal** of work to be done.*
  *'How's your father?' 'Oh, **a good deal** better than he was, thank you.'*

death: noun (C, U) ▶ Compare **dead**; **die**

a In a general sense, *death* is uncountable:
  *Is there life after **death**?*
  *Keep **Death** Off the Roads!* (= by driving carefully)
  *The police are waiting for a report on the time of **death**.* (= the time that some person died)
  *After the **death** of his wife and children, he couldn't bear to live in the house.*

b *death* can be a count noun when we are more concerned with the numbers of people that died:
  *Both these **deaths** could have been avoided.*
  *The earthquake caused an enormous number of **deaths** in the region.*

decide: verb

```
          to-INFINITIVE
decide +  that-CLAUSE
          wh-CLAUSE
          on/about
```

- choose something or to do something after thinking about it

a We can *decide to do* something; *decide that* . . . or *decide* + *wh*-CLAUSES or *decide* + *wh*-WORD + *to*-INFINITIVE:
  *He's **decided** (not) to go to college after all.*
  *He's **decided** that he ought to do something useful.*
  *But he can't **decide** what he should do next or where to go.*

b We can also *decide on* or *about* something:
  *He's **decided** on (= chosen) a university course.*
  *Have you **decided** about (= made a decision about) your holidays yet?*

decision: noun

- act of choosing or choice made between alternatives

You can *come to/make/reach a **decision**. The *decision* can be a *decision to do* . . ./a *decision that* . . ./or a *decision about*:
  *Please let us know as soon as you reach a **decision**.*
  *The **decision** to build the Channel Tunnel/The **decision** that the tunnel should carry trains/The **decision** about the tunnel . . . pleased some people and upset others.*

deep, deeper, deepest: adjective and adverb ► See **depth**

- going down (a long way) from the top or surface

***deep** water . . . a **deep** hole . . . **deep** snow . . . a **deep** (=low) voice . . . **deep** blue . . . **deep** feelings*
*Dig a hole three feet wide and two feet **deep**.*
*Our feet sank **deeper** and **deeper** into the mud.*

deeply: adverb ► Compare **highly**

deeply is used with words of emotion to mean 'greatly' 'very much':
  ***deeply** grateful . . . **deeply** hurt . . . **deeply** shocked . . .*

depend (on): verb

1 • be affected by
   With this meaning *depend (on)* is not used in the progressive:
   *'Are you going to take the job?' 'Well, it all **depends**.'*
   *It **depends (on)** how much money they offer.*

2 • trust; rely on
   *We can **depend on** Bernard – if he say's he'll do something, he'll do it.*
   *We are **depending on** you to help.*
   *You can't **depend** on the weather here – it could do anything.*

depth: noun ▶ See **deep**

depth corresponds to the adjective *deep*.
• distance down from the surface
   *What is the **depth** of these underground caves?*
   *Don't swim out of your **depth**.* (= in water you cannot stand up in)

despite and in spite of: prepositions
▶ Compare **although**

despite is a rather informal alternative to *in spite of*.

PREPOSITION + NOUN (or *-ing*) PHRASE
Despite **In spite of**	this lovely sunshine, her assuring me . . . the fact (that) . . .

1 The meaning of *despite* and *in spite of* is similar to *although*. But *despite* and *in spite* of are prepositions and must be followed by a noun or an *-ing* phrase:
   *It is still quite cold, **despite** this lovely sunshine.*
   I doubt whether she is taking a full dose (i.e. of her medicine), ***despite** her assuring me that she is.*
   *The Research Unit, **despite** all its money, has produced very little research.*

2 If there is no possible noun, then we can add, *'the fact that'* after *despite*:
   ***Despite the fact that** you consider yourself of no importance, you have been of great importance to my brother.*

3 Compare *although* (conjunction) which is followed by a clause. The usual pattern is *although* + SUBJECT + VERB, etc:
   *It is still quite cold, **although** the sun is shining.*
   ***Although** she assures me/she has assured me . . .*
   *The Research Unit, **although** it receives a lot of money . . .*
   ***Although** you consider yourself of no importance . . .*

---

die ► See **dead**

---

different: adjective and **difference**: noun

► Compare **same**

1 different: adjective

a • unlike; not the same

different behaves like a comparative adjective in some ways and can take *no* and *any* in front of it:

*'Is her hair any **different**? She was thinking of dying it red.' 'It doesn't look any **different** to me. I'd say it was no **different**.'*

b Prepositions used after *different* are *from*, *to* and *than*. *From* is generally considered the best, and many people think that *to* is non-standard, but it is very common:

*Your life is very **different** from/to mine.*
*That's a **different** explanation from the one you gave me last week.*

different than is common in American English. Some British speakers dislike it, but it is more acceptable when introducing a clause:

*You can wear very **different** sorts of clothes on holiday **than** you can for your job.*
*(With from we would have to say . . . **different** from the clothes/the ones you can wear for your job.)*

2 difference: noun

*What's the **difference** between a black bird and a blackbird?*
*I'll come whatever time suits you. It doesn't make any **difference** to me. (= It doesn't matter.)*

---

differently: adverb

*You shouldn't treat boys **differently** from girls.*
*The past is a foreign country. They do things **differently** there.*

---

difficult: adjective ► Compare **easy**; **hard**

• not easy to do, understand or solve

difficult can be used before nouns (a ***difficult** exam*) and predicatively (*the exam was **difficult***). Both patterns can be followed by a *to*-INFINITIVE:

*That was a **difficult** decision to make.*
*I found it a **difficult** question to answer.*
*His accent was rather **difficult** to understand.*

---

difficulty: noun (C, U)

*We had **difficulty** in understanding his accent.*
*He has **difficulty** with some English sounds.*
*We managed to start the car again with **difficulty**.*
*If you swim in that sort of rough sea, you'll get into **difficulties**.*

direct

1 direct: verb

- control; guide
  *Can you **direct** me to Victoria Station, please?* (= tell me the way)
  *There were policemen standing in sort of boxes in the middle of the road **directing** the traffic.*
  *My uncle actually **directs** the whole business from home.*

2 direct: adjective and adverb

- in a straight line; without anything in between
  *Which is the most **direct** way to Edinburgh?*
  *There aren't any trains **direct** to Stamford – you have to change at Peterborough.*
  *Does this plane fly **direct** to Hong Kong, or do we touch down in Kuwait or somewhere?*
  *They've now got a **direct** line* (telephone line) *with the police station.*

directly

1 directly: adverb

*My house is **directly** opposite the station.*
*I'll telephone **directly** after dinner.* (= immediately)

2 directly: conjunction
- as soon as; immediately:
  *I realised **directly** I'd done it that I had made a mistake.*

discuss: verb

- talk about seriously

> **discuss** + OBJECT
> *wh*-CLAUSE

discuss takes a DIRECT OBJECT (NOT **discuss about*), and *wh*-CLAUSES AND *wh*-words + *to*-INFINITIVE (NOT * *that* or *if* clauses):

> *We discussed his job/the state of the country.*
> *We discussed what he ought to do next/what to do/whether* (NOT *if) *he should tell his boss/why he shouldn't tell his wife . . .*

discussion: noun

discussion is usually followed by *about*:

> *We had a long discussion about his job/about what he ought to do next . . .*

dislike ▶ Compare like

1 dislike: verb (not usually in progressive)

> dislike + OBJECT
> -ing

● consider something is unpleasant

dislike is only the opposite of *like* in the sense of 'enjoy'. It does not mean 'choose not to' or 'prefer not to', so it is not followed by a *to*-INFINITIVE:

> *I dislike snakes.*
> *I dislike people who keep you waiting.*
> *I dislike being kept waiting.* (NOT *I dislike to be . . .*)
> *I dislike it if/when people keep you waiting.*

2 dislike: noun (often C)

> *I took an instant dislike to the place. I just knew I couldn't live there.*

distance: noun

a ● the measurement between places

> *What's the distance between Edinburgh and London/the distance from Edinburgh to London?*
> *I can't see what it is from this distance.* (= from this far away.)
> *a great distance . . . a distance of 400 miles . . . within walking distance . . . a good distance away . . . a long-distance runner . . .*

b (U) the distance

● somewhere far away that you can see:

> *We could see smoke in the distance and realised something was on fire.*

distant: adjective

1 • far away
*a **distant** view* . . .

We can also use *distant* to refer to time:
*the dim and **distant** past . . . the not too **distant** future* . . .

2 • not closely related
***distant** relatives . . . a **distant** cousin* . . .

do: verb

1 Forms

	PRESENT	PAST
I/You/We/They	**do**	**did**
He/She/It	**does**	
INFINITIVE and IMPERATIVE: **do** PRESENT PARTICIPLE (main verb only): **doing** PAST PARTICIPLE (main verb only): **done**		

The verb *do* has five different forms as shown. Like *be* and *have* it is used as an auxiliary as well as a main verb.

2 do: auxiliary verb

a As an auxiliary verb, *do* forms negatives by adding *not* or *n't*

	PRESENT	PAST	
I/You/We/They	**do not** **don't**	**did not** **didn't**	go.
He/She/It	**does not** **doesn't**		

b *do* is used as an auxiliary to form questions and negatives for simple present and past tenses of other verbs – except the verb *be*, modals and sometimes *have*. (See **have**):
*(I like it.) **Do** you like it? I **don't** like it. **Don't** you like it?*
*(He likes it.) **Does** he like it? He **doesn't** like it. **Doesn't** he like it?*
(NOT ****Do** you can come tonight?*)

do is not used in questions when *Who*, *What* or *Which* is the subject:
Who told you that? What happened next? Which train gets there first?
(NOT **Who **did** tell you that? *What **did** happen next? *Which train **does** get there first?*)

Contrast these words as objects:
*Who **did** you tell? What **does** he want? Which train **do** you usually catch?*

c *do* is also used to form negative imperatives:
***Don't** talk like that.*

and for emphasis in affirmative sentences:
***Do** listen. I **do** want to help you. **Do** have some.*
*'So, you **didn't** enjoy the party?' 'I **did** enjoy it.'*

d *Do you* in spoken questions is sometimes shortened to *D'you . . .?* /djuː/ (but is not very often written like this).

3 **do**: main verb

a As a main verb, *do* can be used in any tense, including passive and progressive tenses. It uses the auxiliary verb *do* in questions and negatives of simple past and present tenses:
*What on earth have you been **doing**?*
***Don't do** that. **Do** as you're told.*
*Nothing has been **done** about that broken fence, has it?*
*David's **doing** well at school, isn't he?*
***Does** he **do** his homework regularly?*
*Usually, but he **didn't do** any yesterday.*
*If you've nothing else **to do**, you could **do** the shopping for me.*

b The general meaning is connected with activity: ▶ Compare **make**
*What **do** you **do**? (= What is your job?)*
*I get bored if I have nothing **to do**.*
*Go and see what the children are **doing**.*
*I'm just **doing** my teeth (= cleaning them), and then I'll **do** the dishes (= wash them).*
*This car can **do** 120 miles an hour.*

People can **do** their best (= try very hard), **do** their duty; **do** business with someone; **do** (somebody) a favour/a kindness/a service/a good turn; **do** the cooking/the shopping; **do** (their) homework/housework; **do** damage/good/harm; **do** a job/work.

c *How **do** you **do**?* is a formal greeting and the reply is *How **do** you **do**?*

4 *do* is also used in question tags, short answers and other places where we want to avoid repeating another verb (plus the words that follow it):
*'You **didn't** enjoy the party, **did** you?' 'Of course I **did**.' (= I enjoyed the party)*
*I never expect them to bring me a present, but they usually **do**. (. . . bring me a present)*
*Claudia likes seaside holidays much more than Henry **does**. (. . . likes seaside holidays.)*

do is only used in this way when we want a simple present or past tense (i.e. when *do* would be the auxiliary verb). In other cases *be*, *have* or a modal is used. (*You haven't seen him,* **have** *you?*)

double

1   double: adjective

- for two; having two parts; the same thing repeated
double is the opposite of *single*:
   *The traffic police caught me parking on **double** yellow lines.* (= two lines painted on the side of the road where parking is forbidden)
   *Hello, nine one **double**-eight five* (i.e. the telephone number is 91885)
   *'How do you spell your name?' '/em d*ʌ*bl əʊ diː waɪ/, Moody.'*
   Also: *a **double** room . . . a **double** bed . . . a **double** garage . . . a **double**-decker bus* (= with two 'decks' or floors)

2   double: before determiners   ▶ Compare **twice**

double can come in front of *the* and some other determiners:
   *It's a bargain – it's worth **double** the price.*
   *We're selling the house for **double** what we paid for it.*

3   double: verb
   *Think of a number, **double** it . . .* (= multiply by 2)
   *Prices have **doubled** in the last few years.*

4   double: adverb
   *There's something wrong with my eyes – I'm seeing **double**.*

doubt; doubtful; doubtless; undoubtedly

1   doubt: verb (not usually in progressive)

- not trust
   *They seemed to **doubt** me/my honesty/my ability to pay.*

2   doubt: verb and noun and **doubtful**: adjective

a

I doubt There is considerable **doubt** There is some **doubt** It is **doubtful**	if whether (? that)	our team can win again. they can find the money in time.

When we *doubt* something, we are uncertain, just as we are when we ask questions. We are not sure. So the following clause begins with *if* or *whether*. Some people do use *that*, but many people consider this non-standard.

b

Few of us **doubt**	that	our team is going to work hard.
There is no **doubt**		
I am in no **doubt**		
We have no **doubt**		

On the other hand if we have no doubt about something, we are certain that something is a fact and so we can use *that*, because our meaning is affirmative.
doubt (noun) can also be followed by *wh*-clauses, and by *about*:
*There's no **doubt** what he ought to do.*
*I have a lot of **doubts** about his plans.*
*There is no **doubt** about it; we've all got to work harder.*

3 Sentence adverbs

a *no doubt* and *doubtless* usually mean 'probably, but not certainly':
*No **doubt**/**Doubtless**, you're tired after your long journey.*
*This will **no doubt** come as a great surprise to you.*

b *without doubt* and *undoubtedly* are much stronger (= it is absolutely certain that . . .):
*Without **doubt**/**Undoubtedly** there is great injustice in the world.*

---

down

1 **down**: adverb

a • in/to a lower position
*Come in and sit **down**.*
*Off we went over the hills and **down** into valleys over dreadfully rough rugged roads.*
Also: *fall **down**, get **down**, lie **down**, put (something) **down** . . .*

b *down* often follows a verb to show that something becomes less or smaller:
*It is very important that you keep your weight **down**.*
*The problem with her leg seems to have settled **down**.*
Also: prices and temperatures *go/come **down** . . .* you can *turn a heater/a cooker **down**.*

c With other verbs *down* can mean that something is destroyed or no longer exists:
*The scrap metal is melted **down** at the factory and re-used.* (= The old pieces of metal are melted . . .)
Also: houses can *burn **down**,* or *be pulled **down** . . .* trees can be *cut **down*** or

blown **down** . . . cars break **down** . . . tires may die **down** . . . if you are unlucky, you may be turned **down** for a job (= refused).

d   With verbs of fastening and fixing, *down* strengthens the verb:
>. . . you can *glue/stick/tie* something **down** . . .

e   With verbs of writing, you can:
>. . . *copy/note/put/take/write* something **down** on paper.

f   *down* can also mean towards the south:
>*Richard and I might come **down** to London on the 4th.* (i.e., from the north of England)

2 down: preposition

a   ● in/to a lower position
>*A guard made me reverse (the car) **down** the hill.*
>*Our boat got swept into the middle of the river and within a very short space of time we found ourselves about a mile **down** the river.*

b   ● to the far end of/along
>*You go right **down** the main road, till you get to the brick wall.*

dress

1 dress: verb

a   ● put clothes on
>*Wait a minute – I'm just **dressing** the baby.*
>*You're old enough to **dress** yourself now, Timmy.*

Often when *dressing oneself*, the verb *get dressed* is used:
>*Go and **get dressed** (Go and **dress**) – we're waiting to have breakfast.*
>*I've hurt my back and it takes me ages to **dress/get dressed**.*

b   *be dressed* means 'to be wearing (clothes)':
>*Why aren't you **dressed** – it's nine o'clock.*
>*She **was dressed** in black from head to foot.*

2 dress: noun (C, U)

a   ● an article of woman's clothing (C)
>*What a pretty **dress**!*
>*She's got dozens of **dresses** – but I'd rather wear a blouse and skirt.*

b   ● clothes of a particular kind, worn by men or women (U)
>*They were in/wearing evening **dress**/national **dress**.*

drink

1 drink, drank, drunk: verb

a   with an object, *drink* can be used with any liquid:
>*You haven't **drunk** your tea – it's going cold.*
>*Would you like something to **drink**?*

b without an object, *drink* usually means 'drink alcohol':
You shouldn't drink and drive.
John doesn't drink.

c drunk
The participle *drunk* is also used as an adjective and a noun to describe someone who has had too much alcohol:
They were so drunk they could hardly walk.
The drunk started shouting out in the middle of the street.

2 drink: noun

a By themselves *a drink* and *drinks* often mean alcohol, but *a cold drink* or *a hot drink* is probably non-alcoholic:
I need a drink. (probably alcohol)
It's my turn to pay for the drinks.
Could I have a drink of water/a hot drink?
Mum's bringing in some cold drinks.

b As an uncountable noun, *drink* usually means alcohol in general:
All this drink isn't good for you.
There was too much drink and not enough food.

drive

```
        —
drive + OBJECT
        O + ADJECTIVE
        O + to-INFINITIVE
```

1 drive, drove, driven: verb

drive is used with and without an object.
a ● control and move a vehicle
He drives a Rolls Royce/a lorry/a taxi/a train.
Do you drive? (= Do you know how to drive a car, etc.?)
We'll drive you home.
We drove 400 miles that day.

b ● move something or someone into a new position
The wind had driven the snow right across the path.
Two young boys were driving the sheep along the road.

c ● force someone into an unpleasant position or to do something unpleasant
▶ Compare **force**

Here *drive* + OBJECT can be followed, not only by an ADVERB PHRASE but also by an ADJECTIVE or a *to*-INFINITIVE:

*He was **driven** out of his mind by worry.*
*This noise is **driving** me mad.*
*Whatever **drove** him to commit suicide?*

2 **drive**: noun

a As a count noun, *drive* can mean a journey by car, or a path or place for a car at the front of a house:

*We've got a 400-mile **drive** ahead of us tomorrow.*
*You can leave your car in our **drive**.*

b As an uncountable noun, *drive* can mean energy, willingness to act:

*We want staff with **drive** and enthusiasm.*

due

1 **due**: adjective

a ● owing as a right or debt; proper

*My children always treated him with the respect which was **due** to such an old man.*
*With all **due** respect, I cannot agree with you.* (polite way of disagreeing)
*The police said he was driving without **due** care and attention.*

b ● expected; supposed

*The patient was **due** to be seen for a check-up today, but failed to appear.*
*The train is **due** at 11.35 a.m.*

2 **due to**: preposition ▶ Compare **because of**

● caused by

NOUN PHRASE (RESULT)	be		NOUN PHRASE (CAUSE)
The pain in her hands	was	**due to**	rheumatism.
A lot of her problems	are		worry. the fact (that) . . .

Strict grammarians and examiners say that *due* is always an adjective, and that *due to* should only be used as shown in the table (*be **due to** something*):

*A lot of her problems are **due to** the fact that she worries so much.*
*It was **due to** his kindness that I got the job.*

However *due to* is in fact also used with verbs (*Something happened **due** to . . .*) Such sentences are quite common, making *due to* grammatically like *because of* and *owing to*:

*She has never been absent **due to** illness.*
***Due to** the snow, I only got here on Friday, a day late.*
*There will be no meeting in June, **due to** the election.*

---

during: preposition   ▶ Compare **in**

a   • throughout (a stated period of time); from the beginning to the end
    *We're open from 10 o'clock until 6 o'clock **during** the week.*

b   • at some time or times between the beginning and the end of a period
    *I've sent him two letters **during** the course of this year.*
    *Only two trains left **during** the morning.*
    *I have been unable to contact him **during** the past week.*

---

each   ▶ Compare **every**

each refers to two or more things/people separately or individually

1 **each**: determiner and pronoun

A	**each** **every**	book student	(sing)
B	**each of** **every one of**	the these/those my/his . . .	books students (pl)
		these/those mine/hers . . . (pl) you/us/them	

a *each* can be an independent pronoun and is followed by a singular verb:
    *Various explanations are possible. **Each** depends upon a particular way of looking at history.*
    *Shall I take one of **each**?*
    *He could not manage more than two dozen patients, as he had to see **each** twice a week.*

b *each* is also a determiner used with singular count nouns (**A**):
    *She had a present for **each** member of her family.*
    *Mrs N had to lecture for about sixteen hours **each** week.*
    *It costs £29 **each** way for the car. (= £29 going and £29 coming back.)*

c *each* cannot be used with other determiners. We use *each of* + *the/these/my*
   . . . + PLURAL NOUNS, and with various pronouns (**B**):
   *They have failed in **each of** their three major attempts to reach the top.*
   *He tells **each of** us only what we have to know.*
   *She has more than twenty hats, **each of** which cost a small fortune!*

2 **each** and **every**

a *every* refers to three or more things/people, so it cannot be used if we are
   talking about only two:
   *Stand with your feet together and stretch **each arm** in turn.*

b *each* is a pronoun and a determiner; *every* is only a determiner. So only *each* is
   possible in the example sentences in **1a**. *Every* would be possible in the first
   two examples in **1b** (. . . ***every** member* . . . ***every** week*) though not of course in
   the third, where we are only talking about two ways. In **1c** we could use *every
   one of* . . . The meaning would change slightly: *each* sees things/people
   separately, *every* sees them as a group.

c Both *each* and *every* are meant to take singular verbs, but *each of* + plural
   noun is sometimes followed by a plural verb when the meaning is 'both' or
   'all':
   ***Each** of them knows/know what to do.*

3 nouns/pronouns + **each**

a SUBJECT + **each**

SUBJECT (+ **each**) and VERB			DIRECT OBJECT
The children We	**each**	gave have	some money.
	have	given	
	are	**each** giving	£5.
	can	give	a present.

When it refers to the plural subject of a sentence *each* (NEVER **every*) can come
after the subject, or after an auxiliary verb, as shown.
*The children **each** . . . We **each** . . .* are therefore alternatives to ***Each** of the
children . . . **Each** of us . . .* Plural verbs are used. If the object is some stated
amount, *each* can also come at the end, after the object:
*We have given £5 **each**.*
*We paid £50 **each** for a twelve-week course.*
*We had a couple of mouthfuls **each**, and then confessed we preferred Coca-
Cola.*

This is not possible with indefinite amounts as direct objects (NOT *We have given some money **each**).

b   INDIRECT OBJECT + **each**

He gave	INDIRECT OBJECT	**each**	OBJECT chocolate £5 a book some money
	them you us		
		OBJECT £5 two books	**each**

When *each* refers to an indirect object it can follow it (*them* **each** . . . *us* **each** . . .). But if the direct object is some definite number or amount, *each* can come after the direct object:

>   *He gave us two books **each**.* (But NOT *He gave us books **each**.*)

For *each other*   ▶   See   **other**

---

early, earlier, earliest   ▶   Compare   **late**

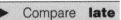

   ● near the beginning of some period of time or before the expected time

1   early, earlier, earliest: adverb

>   *If we go **early** in the week the place should be less crowded.*
>   *I hope to see him **early** next month.*
>   *We got there half an hour **early** and they weren't ready for us.*
>   *Two months **earlier** he had been almost dead, and now he was climbing like a young man.*
>   *I can't finish this before April at the **earliest**.*

2   early, earlier, earliest: adjective

>   *Even from an **early** age he was interested in planes.*
>   *Her **earlier** books were for children, really.*
>   *I need an **early** night.* (= to go to bed early)
>   *My **earliest** memory is sitting on my grandfather's knee.*
>   *in the **early** hours* (i.e. after midnight) . . . *in **early** January* . . .

---

easy and **easily**   ▶   Compare   **difficult; hard**

1   easy, easier, easiest: adjective

>   *easy* is the opposite of *difficult*

easy can come before nouns (*an easy exam*) and can be used predicatively (*The exam was easy*). Both patterns can be followed by a *to*-INFINITIVE:

> *Is English an easy language to learn?*
> *That's not an easy question to answer!*
> *It's easy for some people to learn perhaps.*
> *It would be easier if you had more people to practise with.*

2 easily: adverb

easy is used as an adverb in a few expressions:

> *You're working too hard – you must take it/things easy.* (= don't work so hard.)

But the usual adverb is *easily*:

> *He passed the exam easily.*
> *We got here very easily, with no traffic problems.*
> *I'm sorry you got the date wrong, but that sort of thing is very easily done.*

eat, ate, eaten: verb

eat can be used with and without an object:

> *What would you like to eat?*
> *I've already eaten, thank you.* (= I've had a meal.)

education: noun

education is usually uncountable, although it is possible to say *an education* of a particular type:

> *Only some of the children in these countries get secondary education at all.*
> *He had an expensive education, but doesn't seem to know much.*

effect and effective

1 effect: noun (C, U)

- result

effect is the noun that matches the verb *affect*:

> *The climate had a bad effect on her health.*
> *Nothing I say has much effect on him.*
> *The effects of this disaster will last for months.*

2 effect: verb   ▶ Compare **affect**

effect is a formal way of saying 'cause something to happen':

> *This law will effect major changes in the way criminals are treated.*

3 effective: adjective

- getting the required result

> *Their efforts were not effective.* (= had no results)

e.g.

- for example (actually two Latin words, *exempli gratia*)
  *They should grow green vegetables, **e.g.** cabbages or peas.*

  ▶ See *for example* at **example**

---

either ▶ Compare **neither**; **each**

either usually refers to one of two people/things. In British English *either* is pronounced /'aɪðə(r)/ or /'iːðə(r)/, in American English it is pronounced /'iːðə(r)/.

1 either: determiner and pronoun

either	man side (sing)	is . . .
either		
either of	the these/those ways my/your . . . men (pl)	is . . .
	these/those them/you/us (pl)	(are) . . .

a *either* can be a determiner:
   Either side could win.

   or an independent pronoun:
   *'There are two jugs here. Which do you want?' 'Oh, **either** will do.*

   When used as a determiner *either* cannot be used with another determiner (NOT *__either his car__*).
   either of can be used with plural nouns and pronouns as shown.

b *either* usually means 'one or the other', but not both:
   *Pass **Either Side**.* (traffic sign)
   *Would **either of** you care for a cup of tea?*
   *The result could go **either** way.*

   But *either* sometimes means 'both', though considered separately:
   *There he stood, a tray in **either** hand.*
   *That's where she met the traffic – traffic going into Windsor from **either** side.*

c Verbs following *either of* are usually singular, but are sometimes plural after *not . . . either* when the meaning is 'both . . . not':
> *I don't think **either** of my parents like/likes pop music.* (= Both of them dislike it.)

2 either . . . or: conjunctions

You		love him		hate him.
	either		**or**	
It was		faulty brakes		something wrong with the engine.

a *either . . . or* describes two alternatives. One is possible or true and the other is not:
> *You **either** love him or hate him.* (not both)
> ***Either** you pay for it, **or** you must send it back.*

b Theoretically, *either* and *or* must be followed by the same type of grammatical item (two verbs, two nouns, etc. as shown) but in practice this 'rule' is often broken:
> *It **either** goes **or** it doesn't.* (More correctly – ***Either** it goes or **it** doesn't.*)

c Theoretically too, *either . . . or* refers to only two things, but again this is not always so:
> *Dame Flora brought it to a halt* (= stopped the camel) *without damage **either** to herself, the camel or the pyramid.* (Notice also the 'wrong' position of *to*.)

3 either: adverb

either can come at the end of a clause containing a negative, following an earlier negative clause or sentence, and roughly means 'also . . . not':
> *When he arrived at Zurich they had no post for him, and when he went to Trieste there was no post for him there **either**.*
> *'I don't believe I have ever met her.' 'I don't think I have, **either**.'*
> (Compare the affirmative – *'I think I've met her.' 'I think I have **too**.'*)

---

elder, **eldest**: adjectives and nouns
▶ Compare **older**; **oldest**

elder and *eldest* mean older and oldest, but they are only used attributively or with *the* and only when talking about family relationships:
> *my **elder** sister . . . your **eldest** son . . . the **eldest** child . . . Who's the **elder** (of the two)?*
> *Life can be difficult for the **eldest** child* (in a family)
> *I am the **elder**/the **eldest**.* (But NOT **I am **elder**/He is **elder** than his sister*)

else

A			
	any-	-body	
	every-	-one	
	no-	-thing	
	some-	-where	**else**
B			
	who/what	(ever)	
	how/where/why		
C			
	little		
	much		

1 else: adverb

a *else*, roughly meaning 'other' can follow words beginning *any-*, *every-*, *no-* and *some-* words such as *anywhere, somebody* (A):
> *I want to do something **else** – I've done this job for ten years.*
> *Someone **else** wants me to marry him, and I don't want to.*
> *Everybody **else** was having a good time, but Henry was feeling awful.*
> *Fold up the bed and put it somewhere **else**.*
> *It's not mine. It's someone **else's**.*

b *else* can also follow various *wh*-words (but NOT *which*) (B):
> *What **else** does he do?*
> *Where **else** can he go if he doesn't go to university?*
> *How **else** could you do it?*

c *else* can also follow *little* and *much* (C):
> *Very lazy day. Didn't do much **else**, apart from washing my hair.*

2 or else

Sometimes *or else* is just an emphatic *or*, and sometimes it means 'otherwise':
> *He was either taking his time **or else** he didn't bother.* (= I don't know which he was doing.)
> *We need the money by Friday, **or else** she'll sell the house to another couple.*

By itself, with the alternative not mentioned, *or else* is often a threat:
> *Give that back to me at once, **or else**!* (= or else I will do something unpleasant.)

elsewhere: adverb

- at/in/to some other place
> *It was advertised in* The Times *and **elsewhere** last week.*
> *There was no rain – and no food. But **elsewhere** in Africa there had been almost too much rain.*

'em

'em is a very informal form of *them*:
> *If I hadn't known the facts of life before I began teaching, I'd know 'em now.*
> (from a personal letter)

end ▶ Compare **finish**

1 end: verb

a ● finish
> *Term ends on the 28th of the month.*
> *The war ended in 1946.*
> *The story ends with them getting married.*
> *She ended (her speech) by thanking us all for our help.*

b ● make (something) stop
> *There ought to be some way of ending this terrible war.*
> *The referee ended the fight in the fifth round.* (= stopped the boxing match)

2 end: noun

a *the end of the week/the year . . . the end of the road . . .*
> *You're holding the wrong end of the rope – hold it by the other end.*
> *The best part came at the end of the film.*

b **in the end** ▶ Compare **eventually; finally; at last**
● finally; after some delay or difficulty; after some earlier decision to do something different
> *You'll pass your driving test in the end – if you go on trying.*
> *I thought of buying a horse, but in the end I bought a bicycle.*

enjoy: verb

```
enjoy +   OBJECT
          -ing
```

enjoy must be followed by an OBJECT or and *-ing* phrase:
> *Most people enjoy parties.*
> *I enjoy my job, but I don't enjoy working as hard as this.* (NOT *enjoy to work)
> *Enjoy yourself!*

enough

A	
enough	cheques (pl) money (U)

B		
enough of	the these/those my/your . . .	books students (pl)
	the this/that my/your . . .	book (sing) money (U)
	this/these it/them you/us	

C	
good/quick well/quickly	**enough**

1   **enough**: determiner

• sufficient (**A** in table above)
enough normally comes before plural count nouns and uncountable nouns:
   *I'm not doing **enough** work nor **enough** interesting things.*

In formal language NOUN + *enough* is possible, but this is rare and a bit old-fashioned:
   *The service itself was reward **enough**.*

2   **enough**: pronoun   ▶ Compare   **plenty**

• a sufficient amount of something
   *I knew **enough** to survive on at the age of 10.*
   *They'll have to get **enough** to eat.*
   *I have **enough** on my mind. I don't want any more problems.*
   *I don't know **enough** about it – I just can't advise you.*
   *That's **enough** now – please be quiet!*

Like many pronouns *enough of* can join with several determiners + nouns or with certain pronouns (**B**):
   *. . . **enough** of these pens . . . **enough** of the others . . .*
   *There weren't **enough** of them to play football.*

We can also have *enough of* + *a* (SINGULAR NOUN):
   *This is **enough** of a problem without you making difficulties. (= a big **enough** problem)*

3 **enough**: adverb

- sufficiently (*C* in table)

a As an adverb *enough* follows an adjective or adverb:

Leo looks amazing since she's had her hair cut so short – it was bad enough before.

Right. Right. Yes, fair enough. (= All right.)

The proposals may not go far enough.

Strangely enough, his face reminded me of Miss Peters. (=although it is strange . . .)

b Notice the pattern ADJECTIVE/ADVERB + *enough* + *to* INFINITIVE

The youngest son was just old enough to serve in the First World War.

I don't know the others well enough to judge yet.

4 The word order when there are adjectives plus nouns is ADJECTIVE + *enough* (as in *C*) + NOUN:

Surely with six bedrooms, it'd be a big enough house. (= *a house that is big enough*)

Compare:

I'm not doing interesting enough things. (*enough* = adverb, talking about 'how interesting', so the meaning is 'The things I am doing are not very interesting')

and:

I'm not doing enough interesting things. (*enough* = determiner, talking about quantity. The meaning here is 'I'm perhaps doing some interesting things, but not *enough* things'.)

---

entire: adjective ▶ Compare **whole**

- whole

We spent the entire holiday on the beach.

They've painted the entire house white.

---

entirely: adverb

- wholly; completely

I entirely agree with you.

That's not entirely true, is it?

It's entirely up to you what we do.

---

especially: adverb ▶ See **specially**

---

etcetera

etcetera is usually shortened to *etc* – with or without a full stop.

- and so on; and things like that

He asked me all sorts of questions . . . what condition the snow was in, and if we used ropes, etc.

---

even

1 even: adverb

a *even* emphasises the fact that something is surprising. It usually comes just in front of the words being emphasised, but occasionally it comes right at the end:

> They don't **even** know I'm coming over.
> I'm so short-sighted, **even** with glasses on.
> I think that **even** Shakespeare could have learned something from some modern writers.
> Nobody will speak to him, not **even** the children.
> He won't see me, won't talk to me, won't answer my letters **even**.

b **even** + COMPARATIVES ▶ Compare **still**

even is often used to emphasise comparative adjectives, adverbs and determiners and pronouns:

> This is our greatest tourist attraction; this is **even** better than Stonehenge.
> These countries have an **even** more serious crime situation than we have.
> I think he knows **even** less about it than Tom does.

c **even if, even though**

even is often used to emphasise the conjunctions *if* and *though*:

> I think of you a lot, **even if** there's no time to write.
> We shall take whatever steps are necessary, **even if** they are unpopular.
> It would be tiring, I think, **even though** these trains are now said to be quite comfortable.

d **even so**

- although that is true
> It is probably more expensive than any of the others, but **even so** I think I shall buy it.

2 even: adjective

a *even* numbers are 2, 4, 6, 8, etc.
They contrast with *odd* numbers 1, 3, 5, etc.

b *The pavement was not **even*** (= not flat and smooth)
*. . . an **even** chance* (= a 50-50 chance)

---

evening: noun (C) ▶ See **morning**

---

eventually: adverb ▶ Compare **finally; in the end; at last**

- after a long time; happening as a natural event or after many other events
> Don't worry – I'm sure they'll get here **eventually**.
> He **eventually** stopped working at the age of 95.

---

ever: adverb

ever is usually used to add emphasis

a ● at any time
ever is normally used non-assertively, that is in questions, and with negatives (we sometimes use *never . . . ever* for special emphasis), and with near-negatives like *hardly*; also after *if* and *when*. It is usually used in mid-position:
*Do you **ever** look to see if your birthday's listed in* The Times?
*Nobody **ever** behaves quite the same in private as they do in public.*
*I've **never** heard her so excited about a holiday **ever**.*
*You will **never ever** see property at the price it is today.*
*I was trying to think when I'd **ever** driven a car on my own before.*
*I wonder if I shall **ever** learn.*
*We hardly **ever** hear from them now.*

b *ever* is used in sentences of comparison, after superlatives, and after *first, only*:
*The engineer was hotter than **ever**.* (= He had never been so hot before.)
*This is about as close as I **ever** get.*
*It was the best holiday I'd **ever** had.*
*It's the first heart attack he's **ever** had.*
*His brother was one of the nicest men I've **ever** known.*
*I've only **ever** seen him wear one jumper and two different shirts.*
*It's the only film I've **ever** walked out of in the middle.*

c ● always
ever only has this meaning in affirmative sentences and in a few limited expressions:
*His mother describes him as a chap who's been shy and nervous **ever** since he was a child of two.*
*I love it there, but I don't want to stay there for **ever**.*
*Thrilled, as **ever**, to have any news from you.*
*Take care, Yours **ever**, David* (or *Ever yours* – an informal phrase at the end of a letter)

d to emphasise question words and to express surprise:
*Why **ever** didn't you tell me? I could have helped you.*
*Who **ever**/What **ever** are you talking about?*
*How **ever** did you find that out?*

▶ See also **whatever**, **whoever**, **however** . . . written as single words.

2 ever so, ever such + ADJECTIVE/ADVERB

ever is used informally to add emphasis to *so* or *such*:
*I just think of you and I am being **ever** so good.*
*I think that families are **ever** such hard work.*

---

every: determiner   ▶ Compare **each**

1 *every* refers to at least three people/things

a *every* is used with singular count nouns to talk about all the members of a particular group:

---

*This is true of **every** single department in the shop.*
*She is excellent in **every** way.*
*Don't you find that you go out **every** night for about two weeks, and then you don't do anything for a month?*

b With some uncountable abstract nouns (nouns referring to things that exist as an idea but which we cannot touch or see: e.g. *crime*, *love*), *every* means 'total', 'complete', 'all possible':
*We have **every** confidence in the committee.*
*I have **every** sympathy for their claim.*

2

every	three few	days months
	now and again so often	
	other day	

every followed by various time expressions shows how often things happen:
*His blood should be checked once **every** three months.*
***Every** now and again/**Every** so often she suddenly decides to clean the house.*
(= at irregular intervals)
*We only eat meat **every** other day.* (e.g. on days 1, 3, 5 . . .)

3 every one and everyone

everyone (see next entry) only refers to people. *Every one* can refer to people or things:
*We invited twenty friends and **every one** of them came.*
*I bought a bag of oranges and **every one** of them was bad.*

For other phrases beginning *every one of . . .* and the differences between *each* and *every* ▶ See **each**

---

everybody, everyone: pronouns
▶ Compare **anybody; somebody**

● every person
everybody, *everyone* are the opposites of *nobody*, *no one*:

a There is little difference in meaning between *everybody* and *everyone* but *everyone* is more common. They can both refer to all the people in a group, even all the people in the world:
*Now, does **everybody** know what to do?*
*Not **everybody** liked the play, but most of us did.*

b Adjectives, relative clauses, *else* and other phrases can all follow *everybody*, *everyone*:

> **Everybody** *else knew exactly what he was talking about, but I didn't understand.*
>
> *. . . **everybody** sensible . . . **everybody** who has read this . . . **everyone** in the class . . .*

c everybody/everyone . . . they

everybody and *everyone* are singular and take singular verbs. But sentences often continue with plural possessives, pronouns and verbs:

> **Everybody** *is expected to help themselves.*
> **Everybody** *in the world knows Dr Sowerbarn, don't they?*
> **Everyone** *has to live their own lives.*
> **Everybody** *has made up their minds.*

For the difference between *everyone* and *every one* ▶ See **every**

---

everyday: adjective

- ordinary; suitable for every day
  *His delusions don't prevent him from living in the ordinary **everyday** world.*

Do not confuse with *every (single) day* (= *every* + noun).
> *I shall be in the office **every day** next week except Thursday.*

---

everything: pronoun   ▶ Compare **anything**; **something**

- all things, ideas, events, etc.
everything is the opposite of *nothing*:

a   **Everything** *in the garden's lovely.*
> *You must keep **everything** to yourself.* (= Don't tell anyone anything.)
> *One moment I seemed to be **everything** to him* (= all he wanted) *and then the next moment all he could think of was the child.*
> *Not **everything** can be done at once.*

b Adjectives, relative clauses, *else* and other phrases always follow everything:
> *The government will do **everything** possible to improve the position.*
> **Everything** *I can think of to say about him is in his favour.*
> *He told them **everything** I'd said – it was horrible.*
> *I was teaching **everything** but English there.*
> *I remembered **everything** else except his address.*

2 and everything

- etc.; and so on; and things like that
  *They put a lot of pressure on me to get a job and **everything**.*

---

everywhere: adverb

- all places in general
  *The car is taking a long time to repair and so we're walking **everywhere**.*

*They're a pleasant crowd of people here – except for the usual one or two awkward types one meets **everywhere**.*
*I've never been to the Lake District, though I've been **everywhere** else.* (= all the other places in Britain)
***Everywhere** you go you see new buildings.*

example ▶ Compare **instance**

1 **example**: noun
a • instance
*You say that some of the world's wildlife is in danger. Could you give us any **examples**/an **example**?*

b • a model
*You are setting a bad **example** to your children if you watch TV all day.*

2 **for example**: connector

*The situation is serious. **For example**, rhinos could disappear completely if people go on shooting them.*

For example is not shortened to **f.e.**

▶ See **e.g.**

except

1 **except (for)**: preposition

except (for) is used to mention something that the main part of the sentence does not refer to, and means 'apart from', 'excluding':
*There are not many other places to go – **except** Iceland.*
*All the meals **except** tea should have been at least an hour later than they were.*
*All the family liked the idea of going abroad for a holiday, **except for** Dad, who wanted to go to Scotland.*

2 **except (that)**: conjunction

• apart from the fact that
*There's nothing of interest to report **except that** Jim is a good nurse and looking after me well.*

except (not *except that*) can be followed by a bare infinitive:
*There's nothing we can do **except** wait.*

excuse

1 **excuse**: verb /ɪkˈskjuːz/

• forgive
a *You can't **excuse** that sort of behaviour.*
*I hope you'll **excuse** me/my saying so, but I don't think that hat suits you.*
***Excuse** me (for) interrupting you, but could I just say something?*
*Please would you **excuse** us, but we have to go now.* (= please would you let us leave)

b Excuse me!

We can say *Excuse me* to attract attention or to disagree with someone. In American English you can also say *Excuse me* if you annoy someone, but in British English we say *(I'm) sorry* to apologise:

'Excuse me, but actually that's my seat.' 'Oh, sorry.'
Excuse me, but is there a post-office near here?
Excuse me, Paul, but I did not say that.'

2 excuse: noun /ɪkˈskjuːs/

*There is no **excuse** for this sort of behaviour – these people must be stopped.*

---

expect: verb

<pre>
                OBJECT
expect +   (o) + to-INFINITIVE
            that-CLAUSE
            so/not
</pre>

a • believe/think/hope something will come or happen
*We're **expecting** friends to dinner.*
*I'm **expecting** a letter from Celia.*
*We **expect** to hear from her soon.*
*We were **expecting** you to telephone.*
*I was **expected** to pay all my own expenses.*

b When *expect* means 'think' or 'suppose' that something is true, we do not usually use a progressive:
*'Why isn't Tom here?' 'I **expect** he's forgotten.'*
*'Is Muriel coming?' 'I **expect** so'.*

c When we *expect* that something did not or will not happen, we often make *expect*, not the other part of the sentence, negative:
*I don't **expect** I'll get that job.*
*'Is Muriel coming?' 'I don't **expect** so.'*

▶ Compare **believe**; **imagine**; **suppose**; **think**

d • be pregnant
*She's **expecting** a baby in May.* (= The baby will be born in May.)

e • rely on someone to do something
*We **expect** the children to behave when we have visitors.*

---

experience: noun (C, U)

a • something that happens to you (C)
*We had a horrible **experience** in the storm.*
*Tell us about your **experiences** in the war.*

b • process of gaining knowledge; the knowledge gained by doing something (U)

*Nobody will give me a job because I've no **experience**, but I can't get **experience** without a job.*

NOTE: Do not confuse with *experiment* which is a test carried out to study something, especially by scientists.

explain: verb

$$
\begin{array}{l}
\text{OBJECT} \\
\textbf{explain} + \textit{that-}\text{CLAUSE} \\
\textit{wh-}\text{CLAUSE}
\end{array}
$$

explain can be followed by an OBJECT, a *that*-CLAUSE or a *wh*-CLAUSE.
Explain often has an indirect object, but we must always use *to* – you **explain** something *to* somebody:

*Can somebody **explain** this timetable to me?*
*I **explained** (to them) that I wanted to leave home.*
*I can't **explain** why I feel like this.*

fact

1 **fact**: noun

• something that happens, and is therefore true
*I don't want your opinions, I want hard **facts**.*

2 **in fact**: sentence adverb ▶ Compare **actually; really**

in fact emphasises what is said or adds some surprising or stronger details:

a *There's been a lot of rain – all day, **in fact**.*
*You know, I hadn't done this well. **In fact**, I'd done it badly.*
*I don't know whether they are **in fact** happy with these new rules or not.*
*He doesn't respect her for it – **in fact** he despises her.*
*He was not worse than when I saw him before, and **in fact** below the knees he was rather better.* (doctor's report)

b *in actual fact* and *as a matter of fact* are other ways of saying 'in fact':
*He said he never did any work, but **in actual fact** he is, I am told, very hardworking.*
*As **a matter of fact** I'd be glad if they didn't come till after next Thursday's party.*

3 The fact is ...   ▶ Compare *The thing is* at **thing**

We sometimes say *The fact is (that)* . . . when we are admitting something truthfully or pointing out that something is unfortunately true:

*I'm sorry I didn't telephone. **The fact is** I forgot.*

*I'm not surprised he didn't get the job – **the fact is** he's too old.*

4 the fact that ...

a We can use *the fact that* (*something happened/happens*, etc.) after verbs and prepositions which cannot grammatically be followed directly by a *that*-clause:

*Mary and I were discussing **the fact that** Donald is leaving.*

*In view of **the fact that** he seems very much better, there is no need for him to return to the hospital for another three months.*

b *the fact that*, rather than plain *that* . . . is usually used at the beginning of a sentence:

***The fact that** Mr Biggs resigned on the same day and then joined your company caused us to become suspicious.*

fail: verb

```
       –
fail + OBJECT
       to-INFINITIVE
```

fail (meaning 'be unsuccessful') can be used with and without an object:

a *Of course you're not going to **fail** (the exam) – you're going to pass.*

*I **failed** (in) the oral, and passed (in) the written papers.*

*If the crops **fail** again, thousands of people will starve.* (= If there are no crops . . .)

*Once again the rains have **failed** in Ethiopia.*

b If we *fail to do* something, we don't do something that was expected or that was necessary:

*He **failed** to let us know that he would be late, so we were very worried.*

fair, fairer, fairest: adjective

a ● just; reasonable

fair is the opposite of *unfair*:

*You're not being **fair** to her – it's really not her fault.*

*He's always a very **fair** person.*

*It would be **fairer** to everyone if we waited a bit longer.*

NOTE – *fair* is sometimes used as an adverb, but only in a few phrases:

*You must play **fair**.* (= by the rules)

b ● light in colour

fair is the opposite of *dark*:

***fair** hair . . . a **fair** complexion . . . **fair** skin . . .*

c *fair* also means 'quite good' and with this meaning it has no comparative or superlative:

> *It's a **fair** distance to walk.* (= quite a long way)
> *Her paintings are of a **fair** standard, but nothing special.*
> *'Look, I can't let you know until tomorrow.' 'O.K. **Fair** enough.'* (= All right)
> *I've got a **fair** idea now of what they want.*

fairly

1 fairly: adverb

- in a fair, just way
fairly is the opposite of *unfairly*:
> *You're not treating her at all **fairly**.*

2 fairly: emphasising adverb　　　　▶ Compare **quite; rather**

a *fairly* is used with positive adjectives and adverbs. It is not used with comparatives or superlatives. It means 'moderately' but is weaker than *quite* and *rather*. It sometimes means 'not quite good enough', so it is often used with words that suggest something good:

> *It's a big room and **fairly** cheap.*
> *He spent his first year at university doing French and is **fairly** fluent in the language.*
> *You can protect your plants **fairly** simply by leaving a heater near them on frosty nights.*

b *fairly* can be followed by an ADJECTIVE + NOUN:

> *We can talk about this when I see you, which I hope will be in the **fairly** near future.*

With a singular count noun the word order is always *a* + *fairly* + ADJECTIVE + NOUN:

> *a **fairly** successful course . . .*
> *We hope to meet on a **fairly** regular basis, say every 4–5 weeks.*

c *fairly* as an emphasizing adverb is not normally used with verbs, except informally, when it means 'to a great extent', 'absolutely':

> *He **fairly** screamed at us!*
> *She **fairly** raced down the stairs.*

fall

1 fall, fell, fallen: verb

a The general meaning is 'come or go down', often (but not always) as the result of an accident:

> *The temperature **falls** rapidly at night in the desert.*
> *Rain was **falling** as we arrived.*
> *He **fell** (over) and broke his leg.*
> *Your coat's **fallen** on the floor.*

*The lamp **fell** off the desk and broke.*
*The government **fell** as a result of 'people power'.*

b If you *fall for* someone, you *fall in love* with that person:
*We **fell for** each other – I can't explain why.*

c *fall* when followed by an adjective in a few phrases has the meaning of 'become':
*He was so tired he **fell** asleep during the concert.*

2 fall: noun

a *He had a nasty **fall** and had to go into hospital.*
Also: *a heavy **fall** of snow . . . a **fall** in prices . . .*

b In American English, *fall* is another word for autumn.

c *falls* (plural) means a waterfall:
*Niagara **Falls** . . . Iguassu **Falls***

---

family: noun

family is a collective noun that can take singular or plural verb according to the meaning:
*The **family** is the basis of most societies all over the world.*
*My **family** have always lived in the East End of London.*
*That **family** are always quarrelling.*

---

far, farther, farthest and further, furthest

1 far: adverb

- a long way; at/to a distance
a *far* on its own is usually non-assertive. In affirmative sentences *so far* and *too far* are possible, but *far* on its own sounds unusual and formal. *Far* on its own is perfectly normal in questions and negative sentences:
*'How **far** is it from London to Edinburgh?*
*I can't remember which tube station – but their house isn't very **far** away.*
*He knew if he got out unhurt he wouldn't have **far** to swim.*
*One day they had gone too **far** and demanded all her money.* (= what they asked for was excessive.)
*He seems to me a young man who could go **far** in his career.* (= be successful)
*A lot of what people thought about the north was based on ignorance, because it was **far** away.* (formal)

b In everyday English we prefer *a long way*, instead of *far*, in affirmative statements:
*A young man who could go **a long way** . . .*
*It was **a long way** away.*

---

2 far: adverb of degree ▶ Compare **much**

- very much

A	
far	better/nicer/quicker . . .
	preferable
	more/more money/more people/more often
	less/less expensive/less money/less often
	fewer/fewer people

B	
(by) far	the best/the nicest/the quickest way . . .
far and away	the most expensive

C	
far too	expensive
	much/much money
	little/little money
	many/many people
	few/few people

D		
I would		prefer + *to*-INFINITIVE
He'd		rather + BARE INFINITIVE
	far	sooner + BARE INFINITIVE
It		exceeded/surpassed . . .

far, meaning 'very much', is used to emphasise comparative and superlative words (*A* and *B*), *too* (*C*) and a small group of verbs (*D*):

A   *British industry must have **far** bigger markets.*
*The A281 is **far** preferable to the A25.* (These are both roads)
*I think one learns **far** more from people – if they're honest – than from books.*
*There are going to be **far** fewer factories in Ireland because of this.*
*The cost of shipping the food was **far** less than the cost of storage.*
*This happens **far** more often than we realise.*

B   *He's **far and away** the most awful chairman we've ever had.*
*He's **(by) far** the most forward-looking member of the Party.*

C   *I am spending **far too** much money.*
*People say we are **far too** highly paid.*

D   *I'd **far** rather spend two weeks on a beach than spend all our time in the car.*
*Sales rose steadily until demand **far** exceeded supply.*

3 far from

- not at all
  *The city is **far** from united in the view that the miners deserve any sympathy whatever.* (= Some citizens think the miners do not deserve sympathy.)
  *I am **far** from convinced.*

4 so far

- up to now; up to/until then
  *We haven't told anybody **so far** except you.*

5 as/so far as: conjunction

as/so far as is often used when we want to limit what we want to say:
*As **far** as I know, it's just a particular type of beer which the Irish developed.* (= but I'm not absolutely sure.)
*As **far** as the new pandas are concerned, we all welcome their arrival.* (= but there are other things we are not so happy about.)

6 far, farther, farthest: adjectives

- distant; a long way away; a greater distance away, etc.
  *The score is still nil-nil and the ball is on the **far** side of the field.* (describing a game of football)
  *They watched the rat appear from between the bars on the **farther** side of the cage.*

7 farther, farthest; further, furthest: adverbs

These are alternative forms for the comparative and superlative of *far*

a Both *farther* and *further* can mean 'a greater distance (away)', but some people think *farther* is more correct:
*I can't walk any **farther** – I'm exhausted.*
*Another rock, **farther** along the road, is the extraordinary Bird Rock.*
***farther** apart . . . **farther** back . . . **farther** south . . . even **farther** forward . . . some distance **farther** on . . . **farther** up the valley*

b Both *farther* and *further* are also possible when the meaning is more metaphorical:
*Mr Lopez went **farther/further** than the others in his support for the president.* (= He supported the president more than others.)

c The superlative forms are not used very much:
*Surprisingly, some of the oldest people walked (the) **farthest**.*

8 *further* (not *farther*) can be an adverb and an adjective meaning 'more':

a *The problem of water shortage is likely to increase **further**.*
*Taxes will rise **further** this year.*
*There is nothing **further** we can do.*
*I shall be pleased to supply any **further** information you may require.*
*a college of **further** education* (i.e. for education after leaving school) *. . . a **further** appointment* (= another additional appointment)

b *further to* (not *farther to*) is sometimes used in business letters, roughly meaning 'with reference to':

> *Further to my letter of 21st September, I am writing to inform you that we now . . .*

fast, faster, fastest: adjective and adverb

(There is no adverb **fastly*)

a • quick/quickly, but referring especially to speed
fast is the opposite of *slow/slowly*:

> *a fast car . . . a fast train . . . a fast film* (for a camera)
> That clock is ten minutes *fast*. (= ahead of the right time)
> *Don't drive so fast.*
> *You must try to work faster.*

b • firm; firmly

> *The ship was stuck fast in the mud.*
> *My shirt was supposed to be fast colours, but the colour all came out in the wash.*
> *fast asleep* (Contrast **wide awake**)

fear   ▶ Compare **afraid**

1 fear: verb

```
          that-CLAUSE
fear +    so/not
          OBJECT
```

(*fear* is not usually used in the progressive)

a If you *fear* that something unpleasant will happen, you probably expect that it will happen:

> *Doctors fear that this disease will spread all over the world.*
> *It is feared that the disease will spread.*
> *I fear that Philip will be in hospital for the rest of his life.*

fear + *that*-CLAUSE can also be used like *I am afraid (that)* to mean 'I am sorry to say that', but it is more formal:

> *I fear I can't help you.*
> *'Is there no chance of his recovering?' 'I fear not.'*

b **fear** + OBJECT

fear can be followed by an OBJECT, but it is more formal than *afraid*, and the meaning is not quite the same. When people talk about things that already frighten them now, *afraid* is more usual:

> *He's afraid of spiders/thunder/the dark.*

But we *fear* (or *are afraid of*) things that may happen to us in the future:

> *He fears old age and loneliness almost more than death.*
> *If they don't decide soon, I fear more delays.*

2 fear: noun (C, U)

a *The climbers should have returned two days ago and there are **fears** for their safety.*
*Have no **fear** – everything will be all right.*
*Their **fears** that the disease would spread have proved true.*
*trembling with **fear** . . . somebody totally without **fear** . . .*
*Many people have a great **fear** of spiders/flying/the dark.*

b *No **fear*** is informal and means 'certainly not':
*'You're not going to be stupid and lend him any more money, are you?' '**No fear**.'*

---

feel, felt, felt: verb

	OBJECT
	OBJECT + BARE INFINITIVE
	OBJECT + *-ing*
feel +	COMPLEMENT
	as if/as though
	that CLAUSE
	OBJECT + *to be* + COMPLEMENT

1 We use *feel* + OBJECT to mean touch something (to test it in some way):
***Feel** this. Is it silk?*
*'What are you doing?' 'I'm **feeling** Tim's forehead to see if he's got a temperature.'* ▶ Compare **smell**; **taste**

2 When *feel* means 'experience some physical sensation', *feel* can be followed by an OBJECT and then a PREPOSITIONAL PHRASE, by OBJECT + BARE INFINITIVE, or by OBJECT + *ing*. We do not usually use progressive tenses with this meaning:
*It's wonderful to **feel** the rain on one's face.*
*I **felt** a hand on my neck.*
*She **felt** someone put a hand on her arm.*
*He **felt** the bee sting him.*
*I could **feel** the tears pouring down my cheeks.*
*I **felt** myself falling.*

▶ Compare **hear**; **see**; **watch**

3 *feel* + COMPLEMENT; *feel as if/as though* . . .; *feel like* . . . (sometimes in the progressive) are used with two meanings: 'to experience a sensation' and 'to produce a sensation in somebody':

a *She **feels/is feeling** cold/ill/disappointed/happy/worried.*
*It **feels** hot in here.*
*My feet **feel/are feeling** sore. My shoes **feel** uncomfortable.*
*His forehead **feels** hot.*
*I **felt** a complete fool. (Note the noun complement.)*
*I **feel** sure/confident/certain (that) everything will be all right.*

b   *I felt as if/as though I was going to be sick.*
It felt as if/as though the plane was about to crash.
It feels as if we're going to have a storm.

c   *This doesn't feel like silk to me.*
Do you feel like (having) a drink? (= Would you like a drink?)

▶ Compare **look; seem**

4   • think (not usually used in the progressive)

a   *We felt (that) he was unsuitable for the job.*
We felt him to be unsuitable.

b   Both these patterns can be used in the passive:
It was felt (that) he was unsuitable.
He was felt to be unsuitable.

▶ *Compare* **believe; think; understand**

---

feet   ▶ See **foot**

---

few, fewer, fewest: determiners and pronouns
▶ Compare **little; less; least**

(a) **few** **fewer**	of	people apples (pl)		
		the these/those my/her . . .	friends apples (pl)	
		these/those. mine/hers. you/us/them.		

1   few, fewer, fewest

few, fewer, fewest are determiners used with plural count nouns. They are also pronouns referring to a number of people or things. We use *(a) few of* and *fewer of* before other determiners and before pronouns.

a   *few, how few, so few, too few* and *very few* all have the rather negative meaning 'almost none':
Few of us are capable of influencing more than a handful of young people.
Few except the very young and the rather old ever seem to use this pool.
Many travel, but few arrive. (saying)
Few people know this, do they?
There were too few tractors, and the result was a ruined harvest.
We've got all the advantages, with very few of the disadvantages.

b   *few*, by itself, is rather formal (*Few thought he could win.*). It would be more informal to say '*Not many of us . . .*'/'*Only a few of us . . .*'/'*Not many people . . .*' etc. Notice the positive question tag (*do they?*) which shows that '*Few people know this, do they?*' is negative in meaning.

2 a few

a few is affirmative in meaning (roughly meaning 'some'):

> *I may be **a few** minutes late.*
> *This will take quite **a few** moments.*
> ***A few** days ago I decided that I must be in love.*
> *There are **a few**, aren't there?* (negative question tag, showing the affirmative meaning of *a few*)

3

the last the first the next every	**few**	years months days

Several words, as shown in the table, can come in front of *few*:

> *Over the last **few** years our relationship got worse.*
> *The first **few** months of college are going to be extremely hard.*
> *A friend of mine spends two or three days every **few** months working on his accounts.*

4 fewer

fewer is the comparative form of *few* and can be followed by *than*. Various words, including *even*, *far* and *still* can come in front:

> *There are going to be far **fewer** factories in Ireland because of this.*
> *Only 18 per cent of the villagers, **fewer** than one in five, turned out to vote in the election.*
> *The **fewer** people know about this, the better.*

5 (the) fewest

(the) fewest is the superlative form, but is rarely used

> *Last year there were **the fewest** murders on record.*

final: adjective

- last; finishing

a   *That is my **final** offer – I'm not paying a penny more than £45.*
*The judge's decision is **final**. (= No discussion is allowed.)*
*Arsenal scored the winning goal in the **final** minutes of the game.*

b **final and last**

last can mean 'the last one up to now'; *final* means there cannot be any more because something has finished:

> *The **last** programme was very good – I'm looking forward to next week's.*
> *I'm so sad that that was the **final/last** programme – I've really enjoyed this TV series.*

finally

1 finally: adverb

a ● after a lot of other things have happened and perhaps after some delay or difficulty or uncertainty
Finally is often used in mid-position:
> *The car broke down, and then we lost our way and we **finally** arrived at midnight.*

b ● with no possibility of any further change
> *He hasn't **finally** decided whether to change his job or not.*

c **finally; in the end; eventually; at last**
Sometimes all four of these expressions are possible, but the meaning is not quite the same.
eventually means after a long time, after a series of events.
finally suggests after a long time, or after a lot of other happenings (perhaps after a delay).
in the end is similar to *finally*, but it can emphasise a delay. It may also emphasise that what happened was somehow different from what was expected earlier, so *in the end* can express surprise.
at last suggests a long wait or delay (but it does not suggest an earlier different decision):
> *They retired to Wales, where he **eventually** died.*
> *I wasn't going to lend him the money, but I **eventually/finally** changed my mind. (or but **in the end** I changed my mind.)*
> *The weather has turned warm **at last**./has **finally** turned warm.*
> *So you've **finally/at last** made up your mind, have you?*
> *I think they **eventually** got married/got married **in the end** – nobody ever thought they would.*

2 finally: connector

finally is used as a connector, meaning 'lastly' or 'as a final or last thing in a list':
> *First I want to say . . . And then . . . And **finally**, I'd like to thank my family . . .*

find, found, found: verb

```
        (IO) + OBJECT
find +  O + PARTICIPLE
        O + ADJECTIVE/NOUN
        that-CLAUSE
```

a When *find* means 'discover', either by looking or by chance, it can take one or two objects; also OBJECT + PARTICIPLE:
> *I thought I'd lost my keys, but I've **found** them.*
> *We **found** a marvellously cheap little restaurant.*

*I'd like to play more games, but I just can't **find** the time.*
*The agents have **found** us a perfect house./a perfect house for us.*
*I **found** my car damaged.*
*The old man was **found** lying on the floor.*

b When *find* means 'realise by experience', it can be followed by '*that*-CLAUSE and by OBJECT + ADJECTIVE/NOUN COMPLEMENT:

*I **find** (that) I spent too much money last month.*
*Derek's **finding** (that) he can't see as well as he used to.*
*I **find** Tom impossible to talk to.*
*Most people **find** him an odd person.*
*He's **finding** it difficult to save any money.*

c *find out* means discover facts, information etc., and the object does not always have to be mentioned:

*I'd like to **find** out (something) about the Welsh language.*

1 finish: verb

```
        —
finish + OBJECT
        -ing
```

a • end
   *The programme **finishes** at midnight. (ends is also possible)*

b • complete something
   *Haven't you **finished** in the bathroom yet? – I want a bath.*
   *Which horse **finished** first in the big race?*
   *If everybody's **finished** (dinner), we'll have coffee in the other room.*
   *Please let me **finish**. (= **finish** saying what I want to say)*
   *I've **finished** Midnight's Children – what shall I read now?*
   *Haven't you **finished** the washing up yet?*
   *Why don't we **finish** (up) the pudding? It won't keep till tomorrow.*
   *Give us the tools and we will **finish** the job.*
   *I've **finished** writing to Mother. (NEVER *finish + to-INFINITIVE)*

c **finish** and **end** and **complete**
   Sometimes we can use either *finish* or *end* but not always. In fact *end* is not possible in any of the examples in **b**, where *finish* partly means 'end' in time but also has a 'completing' meaning. *End* means *finish in time* plus 'add an end, add a conclusion'. Compare:

   *He's **finished/completed** his 3-year engineering course.*
   *I've **finished** this book. (= I've read it.)*
   *I've **finished/completed** my book. (= I've written it)*
   *I've **ended/completed** it with a chapter about gardens. (= that is the ending I wrote.)*
   *He **ended/finished** his letter 'Yours sincerely'.*
   *We must **end** the fighting.*
   *You must **finish/complete** your work.*

2 finish: noun

Much less common than the noun *end*:
*an exciting **finish** to the race . . .*

| **first** | ▶ Compare **last**; **second** |

1 first: number adjective

● coming before everything else
first is the opposite of *last* and *final*

a/the my/your . . . this	first	prize time
the my/your . . . these . . .		prizes

As a number, *first* is rather like an adjective and often needs a determiner in front of it:
*Our **first** aim is to run this country's affairs efficiently.*
*My **first** reaction was to be very angry, but then I realised that perhaps it wasn't their fault.*
*The hi-fi department is on the **first** floor.* (= in Britain, the floor above street level; in American English, the floor at street level.)
*the **First** World War* (in 1914–18) . . . *a/the **first** prize* (= chief, top prize)
. . . *your **first** name* (= personal, not family name).

2 the first: pronoun

*I want you to be the **first** to know.* (= the **first** person . . .)
*This was the **first** that he heard of the earthquake.* (= the **first** news . . .)
*The **factory** is the first of its type in the country.*
*the **first** of April/April the **first**/1st April . . .*
*Queen Elizabeth the **First** . . .*

3 first: adverb

a ● for the first time (often used in mid-position)
*When I **first** read it, I thought it was silly.*
*I **first** went to Rome in 1969.*

b ● before anything or anyone else
*May I just try and answer your question **first**?*

c *first* is usually used in front position when we are making a list:
***First** we heard that the royal visitors were to be 45 minutes late, and then this was extended to an hour.*
*Our plans are – **first**, we are going to . . ., second . . ., third . . .*

---

4 first of all

first of all is a strong way of saying *first* when it means 'before doing anything else':

First of all *make sure the water supply is turned off.*

5 at first

at first always suggests 'but later something different happened':

I did not think much of the idea **at first**, *but the more I talked to him, the more it seemed to me that he was probably right.*
The weather was beautiful **at first**, *but by lunchtime it was raining heavily.*
At first *everything seemed O.K., but we had terrible problems later.*

For *the first time* ▶ See **have** (present perfect).

firstly: connector

firstly never means 'first in time'. It is only used when listing reasons or ideas:

The college should stop the scheme. **Firstly/First**, *it hasn't been properly thought out, and secondly . . .*

follow: verb

a • come/go after or behind
The dog **follows** *her wherever she goes.*
We don't know the way, so we'll **follow** *you.*
Sometimes a cold wet winter is **followed** *by a hot dry summer.*

b *I don't* **follow** *you* (= don't understand what you are saying.)
Follow *the instructions on the box.* (= Do what they say.)

c *as follows* introduces a list (Notice – NEVER **as follow*):
Saturday's football results were as **follows** *– Charlton 1, Derby 1; Liverpool 4, Everton 1, . . .*

following

1 following: adjective and noun

a • next; next mentioned
They waited all the evening, but left early the **following** *day.*

(NOTICE – *the* is optional in *(the) next day*, but we must say *the following day/ week*)

b **the following**
the following means 'the things or people whose names follow':
Can you send me information about classes on any of **the following** *– keep fit, Chinese for beginners or home decorating.*
Will **the following** *(students) please report to the office – Abdulrahman, M; Calderon-Gonzalez, J; . . .*

2 **following**: preposition

• after; after and perhaps because of
Following the meeting, there will be coffee and biscuits.
Following our discussions, I would like to suggest some changes.

foot: (plural feet)

a • the part of a person's or animal's body at the end of the leg:
Please! You're standing on my foot.
It's very difficult when you've got big feet to find shoes to fit.
Surely you didn't come all this way on foot. (i.e. walking. NOT **by foot*)

b a unit of measuring length, slightly less than a third of a metre (1 foot = 0.3048 metre). There are twelve inches in one foot, and three feet in one yard:
We were flying at 40,000 feet.
The garden is about 90 feet long, and 40 feet wide, with a twelve-foot high wall all round.

When talking about people's height, we use *tall* (not *high*). With an exact number of feet, we can say:
He's six foot tall or *six feet tall.*

When we give the inches too, we say:
She's five foot seven (NOT **five feet . . .*)

for

1 **for**: preposition

a *for* can be used to express a purpose, or a reason:
What is this bill for?
I am sending you a stamped addressed envelope for the return of the documents.
Thanks again for your letter.
I do not have enough money for the course.
We need houses for rent as well as houses for sale.
We haven't got time for a holiday.
Charles has been having treatment for his back.
He's taking me to London for my birthday.
How can I apologise for something I didn't do?

b *for* can introduce the person/people who will receive something, or use it, or be helped by it:
What can I do for you?
I have got an electric frying pan for you.
The interview date is convenient for me.
Today the Minister went to a party for 120 guests at Government House.
A seaside holiday would be best for the children.
He now works for Barclays Bank.
We all felt sorry for my brother-in-law.

c *for* can introduce the object or destination of something:
> *When I left for home the weather was clear again.*
> *I caught the 8.46 (train) for London.* (= that is where the train was going)
> (Contrast – *I caught the 8.46 to London,* which emphasises that I actually went to London).
> *We waited ages for a bus.*
> *Why do we always have chicken for dinner?*
> *We need a new carpet for the bathroom.*

d ● in favour of
> *for* is the opposite of *against*:
> *Stand up for free speech.*
> *Millions of people voted for the Conservatives.*
> *Are you for this change in the law?*

e As a preposition of time *for* answers the question 'How long?':
> *I was interviewed for twenty minutes.*
> *I've hurt my ankle and shall be limping for a few days.*
> *Daddy has invited her for three weeks.*
> *They were worried I might drive away and leave them for ever.* (Contrast *forever.*)
> *I haven't seen Nigel for ages*
> *In the evening I went to Scottish dancing – I hadn't been for a year.*

f **for** or **since**?
> *for* refers to a length of time, and this period can be at any time in the past, present or future, and any tense is possible:
> *We lived there (for) twelve years.*
> *I'm only here (for) a week*
> *We'll be away (for) a month.*

for does not tell us when the period begins or ends. '*I'm only here for a week*' could be said by somebody who has just arrived, or by somebody who is leaving tomorrow. But of course a perfect tense with *for* can tell us when the period began:
> *We have been married for twenty-five years.* (now)
> *We had only known each other for a week when we got married.*

since mentions an actual starting point at some time in the past, and always relates this to another point later on – often now, the moment of speaking. This is why *since* usually occurs with a perfect tense. So *since* tells us the length of time without actually mentioning it:
> *I've only been here **since** Sunday/yesterday.* (until now).

Contrast also:
> *She has lived here for twelve years/for ages.*
> *She has lived here **since** 1970/her childhood/she was two.*

g **Preposition of distance**
> *We walked (for) miles/three miles.*
> *We walked very quickly for three miles.*

for can sometimes be omitted with phrases of time and distance, as shown in **e** and **f**.

h **Various other uses**
> *I enclose a cheque for £50.20p.*
> *What's another word for silly?*

2 for + OBJECT + to-INFINITIVE

The ways this structure is used are shown in **a** to **e** below. In meaning the word following *for* is the 'doer' of the verb, but grammatically the word is the object of *for*, so if we use a pronoun it must be an object pronoun (*me, him, her, us,* etc.).

a subject of a clause/sentence:
> *I'm afraid for me to come on Monday would be difficult.*
> *It is not possible for me to check my account.*
> *It is right for a man to set aside a sum each week.*
> *That is very difficult for me to do.*

b after *be:*
> *The plan was for us to go camping with them.*

c after certain verbs and adjectives:
> *I am arranging for her to have an up-to-date X-ray.*
> *We're all waiting for you to come.*
> *I'm very keen for them to have the opportunity.*

d after nouns, to give more details:
> *There is no need for you to be rude.*
> *There is still plenty of work for us to do.*
> *It was such an expensive place for them to stay.*
> *The arrival of the second bottle of wine seemed a signal for her to relax.*

e to express purpose:
> *Send it on to your mother for her to sign.*

3 for: conjunction ▶ Compare **because**

- because
Boiling water will often unfreeze a frozen pipe, though this method must be used with care, for a sudden raising of the temperature if there is already a leak in the pipe could make matters worse.

for is more formal than *because*. It is also more limited in use. *because*-clauses can come before or after their main clause (see *because*); *for*-clauses must follow.

4 for + -ing or to-INFINITIVE?

Both *for* + *-ing* (e.g. *for doing*) and the *to*-INFINITIVE (*to do*) are used to express purpose, but they are used in different ways.

a Both can be used to say what a thing is used for, what its purpose is:
> *What's a stapler for? It's for fastening papers together with.*
> *It's to fasten papers together with.*

b When we talk about the purpose of people's actions, we use a *to*-INFINITIVE:
> *We'll have to hurry to get there on time.*
> (NOT **for getting there . . .*)

To get tickets, you usually have to stand in a queue.
(NOT **for getting tickets . . .*)
She telephoned her father to tell him the news.
(NOT **for telling him . . .*)

Sometimes *for* + a NOUN is possible:
We queued two hours for tickets.
We queued to get tickets.

▶ See also *as for* at **as**; *except for* at **except**; *for all* at **all**; *for example* at **example**; *for instance* at **instance**.

---

forbid, forbade (or **forbad**), **forbidden**: verb

OBJECT
forbid + *-ing*
    O + *to*-INFINITIVE

• refuse to allow
forbid can be followed by an OBJECT (including an *-ing* form) and also by an OBJECT + *to*-INFINITIVE. However, it is rather formal to use *forbid* in the active, and these patterns are often used in the passive:
New regulations now forbid smoking on the London Underground.
They forbid you to smoke.
I forbid you to use that word again to your mother.
Smoking is forbidden on the platforms as well as in the trains.
You are forbidden to smoke.
It is forbidden to smoke.

---

force

1 force: verb   ▶ Compare **cause, make**

force + OBJECT
        O + *to*-INFINITIVE

a In the pattern *force* someone + *to*-INFINITIVE, the meaning is usually make the person do something that they do not want to do:
The guards forced the prisoners to sit on the floor.
I forced myself to remain silent.
He was forced to resign.

b *force* + OBJECT can also be followed by an adverb phrase:
The crowd forced their way in (= into the building).
He keeps trying to force his ideas on me. (= make me agree).

c *To force a door* or *a safe* means use strength to break it:
Someone had forced the lock on the back door.

---

2 force: noun (C, U)

a When the meaning is 'strength', *force* is usually uncountable:
*If you use **force** to open the lid, you'll break the case.*
*The **force** of gravity pulls things down to the earth.*

b *force* is a countable noun when the meaning is a more particular type of power:
*Alone in the South Pacific, he was up against the terrifying **forces** of nature.*
*Nationalism may not be a **force** for good.*

c *force* meaning 'a group of people working together' is a collective noun:
*The work **force**/The sales **force** has/have achieved excellent results.*
*The United Nations peace-keeping **forces** have been flown in.*

---

forever: adverb and **for ever**

a *forever* (or *for ever*) means 'for always', and is usually used in end-position:
*We shall remember these brave men **forever/for ever**.*

b In mid-position with a progressive tense, *forever* (never written as two words) means 'continually' or 'extremely often':
*They were **forever** complaining.*

---

forget, forgot, forgotten: verb ▶ Compare **remember**

	OBJECT
	about . . .
forget +	*that*-CLAUSE
	wh-CLAUSE
	to-INFINITIVE
	(o) + *-ing*

forget is the opposite of *remember*

a We use *forget* with a number of different patterns. We can *forget (about)* OBJECTS, and we can *forget that . . .*; *forget + wh*-CLAUSES/*wh*-WORDS + *to*-INFINITIVE:
*I **have forgotten** my keys again.*
*Please telephone on Friday evening – don't **forget**.*
*I just **forgot** . . . the time/(that) I had promised to meet him/what he wanted me to bring/where to go.*
*I had **forgotten** all about it until you reminded me.*

b We can also *forget* something that has already happened, using the pattern *forget + (OBJECT) + -ing*; and *forget that* we ought to do something later, using the pattern *forget + to*-INFINITIVE:
*I've completely **forgotten** saying that, but perhaps I did.*
*I've **forgotten** his/him saying that, but perhaps he did.*
*I'll never **forget** seeing the Himalayas for the first time.*
*Don't **forget** to telephone on Friday, will you?*
*Why didn't you tell me? Did you **forget** (to)?*

former

1 former: adjective

- earlier; previous; ex-
  They will examine the different attitudes to the remarriage of divorced people whose former partners are still alive. (= the people they used to be married to.)
  When *former* is used with another adjective it is often put after the other adjective to avoid any possible wrong meaning:
  a male former employee . . . his English former wife.

2 the former

- the first mentioned of two, contrasted with *the latter*
  *Soon he turned to the law, much at the same time as he discovered women. Though he is in fact better on **the former**, his readers may be more interested in the latter.* (= This author writes better about his career as a lawyer (*the former*), but readers may prefer to read what he says about women.)

forward

1 forward: adverb

- towards the front; towards the future
  *The Queen just steps a few steps **forward**.*
  *I look **forward** to seeing you in the near future.* (= I expect to see you and I am pleased about it.)

2 forward: verb

- send to someone's new address
  *She gave me her address, so that I could **forward** any mail.*

forwards: adverb

Dictionaries often give *forwards* as an alternative to *forward* (adverb) but it is rather unusual except in the phrase *backwards and forwards*:
  *He started rocking backwards and **forwards** on his heels.*

forwards cannot be used in the expression *look forward to*.

free

1 free, freer, freest: adjective and adverb

a
- not a prisoner or a slave; not controlled by another country or state
  *You cannot have a **free** society without a **free** press.*
  *The prisoners were set **free**.*
  *The lion had somehow got **free** and was wandering on the motorway.*
  *Now they are **free** to choose their own leaders.*

b • not costing any money
*I've been given **free** tickets for the play tonight.*
*Children under five travel **free**.*

c • not busy; not being used
*Are you **free**?* (a question you can ask a taxi-driver)
*Is this seat **free**?*
*I'm **free** this afternoon if you'd like to come and see me.*

d   free from, free of
free from suggests 'not hurt by', *free of* suggests 'without':
*She is at last **free from** pain/**free from** her money worries.*
*Foreign visitors can get these clothes **free of** tax.*

2   free: verb

• make someone (or something) free
*These people have done nothing wrong and should be **freed**.*
*After an hour he managed to **free** himself from the rope and telephone the police.*

friend: noun

• person one knows and likes a lot
*my **friends** . . . a **friend** of mine . . . an old/good **friend** . . .*
*I'd like to be **friends** with everyone in the class.*
*It's difficult to make **friends** in a big city.*

friendly: adjective

friendly is the opposite of *unfriendly*:
*I tried to be **friendly**, but some of them were rather unfriendly.*
*They usually behave in a very (un)**friendly** way.*
(Note: *friendly* is not an adverb. NOT *behave (un)friendly)

from: preposition

a   *from* can show the starting point in time or place:
*'Where are you **from**?' 'I'm **from** Brazil, actually.'*
*Shell put up their petrol prices by 2.3 p **from** today.*
*Is there anything I can get you **from** the library?*
*I was a teacher at a secondary school **from** September to December.*
*We went **from** Izmir back to Istanbul.*

b   *from* can show the origin, source or cause of something:
*Much love **from** Clare.*
***From** reading the exam papers of his students I have the impression that his opinions are very ordinary.*
*I look forward to hearing **from** you.*
*She was suffering **from** the after-effects of her illness.*

c   *from* can show separation, removal or difference:
> *He was released **from** hospital after blood tests.*
> *Hero Rescues Son **from** Fire Trap.* (newspaper headline)
> *It was slightly different **from** the previous attack.*
> *York is only two and a half hours by train **from** London.*

▶   See also   **apart from**

front

1   front: noun

front is the opposite of *back*:
> *They just painted the **front** of the house – and left the rest dirty.*
> *I don't mind at the cinema, but at the theatre I do like to sit near the **front**.*

2   in front of: preposition   ▶   Compare   **opposite**

a   • facing
> *This would only mean a few minutes **in front of** a fairly large group of doctors, and would be at 9.30 a.m.*
> *She was last seen sitting **in front of** a warm fire smoking a pipe.*
> *The students were shouting **in front of** the embassy.*
> *She held the spade out **in front of** her.*

b   • farther forward
in front of is the opposite of *behind*:
> *The woman **in front of** me had a large hat on and I just couldn't see a thing.*

3   in front: adverb

in front is the opposite of *behind*:
> *The children walked **in front**, and we came on behind.*
> *By the tenth minute Spurs were a goal **in front**.* (i.e. had scored one goal more than the other team.)

4   Compare:
> *There was a tree in the road right **in front of** our car.* (preposition)
> *There's more room for your legs if you sit **in front**.* (adverb)/. . . *if you sit in **the front** (of the car).* (noun)

5   front: adjective
> *the **front** page* (of a newspaper) . . . *the **front** row* (in a cinema) . . . *the **front** seats* (of a car) . . .

furniture: noun (U)

The word *furniture* is always uncountable:
> *There wasn't much **furniture** in the room.*
> *There were only two pieces of **furniture** in the room – a table and an old chair.*

further, furthest ▶ See **far**

future

1 future: noun

a the future
the period of time after the present:
*None of us knows what **the future** holds for us.*
*Maybe in **the distant future**/**the near future** people will take holidays on the moon.*

b As a countable noun, *future* can mean an individual person's future or career:
*These young people should be thinking about their **future(s)**.*

c With the meaning of 'probable success' we usually say *a (good) future* in the positive, but *no* or *not much future* in the negative:
*I think there's **a future** for small cars.* (= small cars could be a success)
*There's **not much future** for heavy industry in this country.*

d in future
in future is often used in warnings and means 'from now on':
*I expect you to be a bit politer **in future**.*

2 future: adjective
*I'm thinking of your **future** career/your **future** happiness.*
*Has English got a **future** tense?*

general

1 general: adjective

a ● affecting most people
*The **general** public is more interested in television than politics.*
*These three-wheel cars are not in **general** use.*
*Concern about the environment is now **general**.*

b ● not specialised; not detailed
*I could answer the **general** knowledge questions, but I was hopeless at the maths.*
*This book is too **general** to be useful.*

c ● chief   A *general manager* of a company is the most important manager. A *general* (NOUN) in the army is a very senior officer.

2 in general
● as a general rule, usually
In general, I don't enjoy rock concerts, but this one I did.
*You shouldn't, **in general**, give children everything they ask for.*

generally: adverb

a • usually
I generally have rolls and coffee for breakfast.

b • by most people
It was generally believed that there were secret tunnels under the city.

▶ See *generally speaking* at **speak**

get, got, got: verb

In American English the past participle is usually *gotten*, but *have got* or plain *have* is used (NEVER *have gotten) when the meaning is possession (*I have got two brothers*) and 'must' (*I have got to go now*). ▶ See **have**

1 get (+ INDIRECT OBJECT) + DIRECT OBJECT

get + a simple direct object means 'receive', 'fetch', 'obtain'. It can also have an indirect object:
I got some super presents for my birthday.
I'm going out to get a paper. (= buy)
Oh, get me the Times, please, will you?
We're getting a new car.
He started to get very bad pains in his leg.

2 get + COMPLEMENT

a *get* without an object, but followed by adjectives, adverb phrases etc. often means something like 'become'. There is sometimes a meaning of intention or 'managing to':
I'm going to lie in the sun and get brown.
I do hope you'll get better soon.
She never got over the shock of his disappearing.

b *get* is also used as a verb of movement. Again there is often a sense of 'managing to', perhaps despite difficulties:
How did he get on to the roof?
We didn't get away last year – we were too busy.
(Contrast – *I never go away – I hate travelling.*)
Audrey doesn't get out much now, because she finds walking difficult these days. (Contrast – *She's just going out to the shops.*)
What time will we get there? (= reach)
We got to the station far too early. (= reached) (Contrast – *Does this bus go to Trafalgar Square?*)

3 get + PAST PARTICIPLE

a *get* + PAST PARTICIPLE is rather like *be* + PAST PARTICIPLE, so it is a sort of passive tense. But while both are concerned with a state, *get* suggests that some action caused the state. (*be* is possible in the following examples, but lacks this extra meaning.):

*If we don't go to training at least once a week we **get** dropped from the team.*
*We seem to have **got** cut off.* (during a telephone conversation)
*I **got** walked on by a rather large and muddy dog.*
*I **got** given a nice book.*
*My mother has **gotten** stuck in the traffic.* (American English)

▶ See also *get married* at **marry**; *get used to* at **use**

b Sometimes there is a big difference of meaning between *get* and *be*. Compare:
*Michael and Susan have **got** engaged.* (recent action. They are now engaged.)
*Michael and Susan have **been** engaged.* (This suggests that they are not engaged any more.)
They have been engaged for over a year. (= a state)
Compare also:
*She is **getting** old.* (= she is growing old: action/process)
She is old. (= state)
*I **got** in(to) the car.* (= action)
My gloves were in the car. (= state)

c Only *get* (not *be*) is possible in:
*Go and **get** dressed.*
***Get** lost.* (= a rude way of telling someone to go away.)
(Contrast – *to be born.* NEVER **to **get** born*)

4 **get** + OBJECT + PAST PARTICIPLE

a This pattern is again concerned with reaching a new state. It means 'cause something to be done' or 'experience something being changed'. *Have* + OBJECT + PAST PARTICIPLE is used in a similar way, but the *get* pattern often suggests that the subject is in some way responsible for what happens even if accidentally:
*We really must **get**/**have** it finished by lunchtime.*
*We **get**/**have** the English papers delivered.*
*I always **get** them muddled up.* (NOT *****have***)
*He **got** his hair caught in the machine.* (NOT *****have***)

b There are similar patterns with *get* + OBJECT + ADJECTIVES, ADVERBS etc, meaning 'cause something to be in that state':
*How did you **get** your hands so dirty?*
*I'm **getting** the room ready for you.*
*Don't **get** me wrong.* (= Don't misunderstand me.) *They are the nicest people, but terribly lazy.*
*I'll have to **get** a man in to mend the cooker.*
*Celia couldn't **get** him out of her mind.*

c A less frequent pattern is *get* + OBJECT + PRESENT PARTICIPLE, which can also mean 'cause or experience':
*They had **got** the army digging enormous ditches.*
*You **get** people refusing to help, of course.*

5 get + OBJECT + *to*-INFINITIVE:

> *get* + OBJECT + INFINITIVE means 'to cause or persuade':
> *We should **get** Sapper to investigate this.*
> ***Get** somebody to do your shopping for you.*
> *I can't **get** him to understand my point of view.*

6 Other, far less frequent, patterns include:
> *You **get** to know people much better if you're living in the same place.*
> *I didn't manage to **get** to see your mother.*
> *I **got** to thinking about the problem.*
> *I **got** talking to this chap on the train the other night.*

▶ See also *have got* at **have**.

---

give, gave, given: verb   ▶ Compare **take**

> give + $\overset{-}{\text{(IO)}}$ + OBJECT

a The main meaning of *give* is 'offer' (as a present) or 'provide with' or 'cause somebody to have'. It usually needs a direct object, and can also have an indirect object:
> *I think you should **give** (him) money.*
> *Don't be mean – **give** me a chance.*
> ***Give** them my best wishes.*

b When *give* is used in the passive, the subject of the sentence is often what would be the personal indirect object in an active sentence. This is because we have probably mentioned the person before, and the new information is the 'gifts', which we want to put in the more important position nearer the end of the sentence:
> *I was **given** so much fruit, I couldn't eat it all.*
> *He was **given** only three days to live when he was born with a hole-in-the-heart condition.* (= They only expected him to live for three days.)

In a general way, often with the meaning of 'giving money', *give* is sometimes used without an object:
> *Of course we must **give** to the Third World, but we must help them to help themselves.*

c Often the meaning of *give* + OBJECT is about the same thing as using a verb related to the object noun:
> *She's always **giving** them advice.* (= She's always advising them.)
> *We'll have to **give** it a push.* (= We'll have to push the car.)
> *They didn't even **give** me an interview.* (= They didn't even interview me.)

But *give* + OBJECT emphasises the event. It also lets us describe it in more detail:
> *She **gives** such good advice/rather confusing advice.*

---

d *give up*, meaning 'stop', can be used with and without an object, and with the *-ing* form of a verb but never with an infinitive:
> *I don't know. You tell me. I give up.* (= I've stopped trying to work out the answer to this puzzle.)
> *He gave up games years ago; now he's practically given up walking.*

---

go, went, gone: verb ▶ Compare **come**

```
         –
go  +  -ing
   COMPLEMENT
```

1 go, went, gone: verb

a *go* expresses movement (often away from the speaker) or progress:
> *Don't go; stay a bit longer.*
> *Does this bus go to Victoria?*
> *We went there by car/by train.*
> *Go and tell the others (that) dinner's ready.*
> *What's going on?* (= happening)
> *Go on.* (= continue) *Why have you stopped?*
> *My watch doesn't go.* (= does not work/function)
> *I can't get this stupid machine to go.*

b **go** + *-ing*

go is often followed by the *-ing* form of other verbs – particularly *shopping* and various sporting activities, and by *for* + NOUN phrases:
> *Let's go shopping/riding/swimming . . .*

c **go** + COMPLEMENT

● become
> *Something's gone wrong with the phone.*
> *The meat has gone off/bad/green . . .*
> *You've let your coffee go cold.*
> *Your kindness hasn't gone unnoticed.*

d Various other uses
> *Three goes into twelve four times.*
> *The knives and forks go in this drawer.* (= belong in . . .)
> *I thought a black skirt would go with all my clothes.* (= match)
> *Prices always seem to go up – they don't often come down.*

2 going to

a We use *going* + *to*-INFINITIVE to talk about the future. This *going to* future has two main meanings:
i) somebody has already decided to do something:
> *Henry has bought some paint and he's going to paint his room.*
> *I'm not going to eat any more chocolate until I have lost some weight.*

ii) something is certain to happen, because the cause already exists:
> *It's terribly cold – it's **going to** snow.*
> *I feel awful – I'm **going to** be sick.*

b Compare the *going to* future (*going* + *to*-INFINITIVE), which stresses 'this is what somebody has decided' and *going* (+ *to* + NOUN), which like any other present progressive tense can be used for a fixed arrangement:
> *'We're **going** to the theatre this evening.'* (= we have the tickets. It is all fixed.) *'Oh, how nice. What are you **going to** see?'* (question about an earlier decision)
> *'I hear you're **going** on holiday next week. Where are you **going**?'* (= I assume that it is all fixed)' *'Oh, we're **going** to Spain.* (= it is fixed) *and while we're there we're **going to** try and visit my cousin in Madrid.* (= that is the plan)

3 been or gone?

Both *been* and *gone* are used to form the perfect tenses (present and past) of *go*. But the meaning is different – *gone* means 'gone away', 'left', 'not returned'. *been* means 'gone/come and returned', either to here or to some other starting place:
> *'Have you ever **been** to China?' 'No, but I've **been** to Japan.'*
> *'Stella's **gone** to Rome – she won't be back till next week.'*
> *The postman's already **been**, but there weren't any letters for me today.*

good

1 good: adjective
▶ See **better; best; well**

good is the opposite of *bad*.
a • right, pleasant, satisfactory, suitable
> *The Save the Children Fund is a **good** cause.*
> *Vegetables are **good** for you.*
> *We had a **good** time on holiday.*
> *Please be **good** children while Granny's here.*
> *Is this a **good** time for a chat?*
> *He's always been **good** (= kind, helpful) to me.*
> *'Pamela's coming to the party after all.' 'Oh **good**.'*
> *a **good** book . . . a **good** idea . . . a **good** kind person . . .*
> *. . . **good** weather . . . **good** news . . . a **good** chance . . . a **good** tennis player . . . **good** at languages . . .*

b **Good morning, Good afternoon, Good evening**
These are fairly formal expressions. People use them instead of 'Hello' and 'Goodbye'. *Goodnight* is only said when you or someone is leaving at the end of the evening. You can say *Goodbye* at any time that you or somebody else is leaving.

c **Good heavens! Good grief! Good lord!**
These phrases all express surprise:
> *'I'm getting a new car,. '**Good heavens** – I thought you only bought one last year.'*

d   *good* can mean 'considerable' in size in a few phrases:
> *It's caused a **good** deal of trouble.* (= a lot of trouble)
> *. . . a **good** few mistakes* (=quite a lot of mistakes)
> *. . . a **good** distance* (= quite a considerable/big distance)

2 good: noun (U)

a   • something that is morally right, or an advantage
> *Some people don't seem to know the difference between right and wrong,* ***good*** *and evil.*
> *I was trying to help, but I think I did more harm than **good**.*
> *I'm sorry if you don't like what I'm saying, but I'm telling you for your own* ***good***.
> *It won't do any **good**, but we can try.*

b   **no good, any good, what good**
> *good* is used in various expressions to discuss the use or purpose of something:
> *It's **no good** – I just can't do this exercise.* (= impossible)
> *It's **no good**/**not much good** just saying you're sorry – you shouldn't have borrowed my car in the first place.* (= useless/pointless)
> *Is this old timetable **any good**, or shall I throw it away?*
> ***What**'s the **good** of going now? – it's far too late.*
> ***What good** is money when you're dead?*

> ▶   See also   *no point* at **point**; *no use* at **use**

c   *for good* means 'for ever':
> *That pre-war style of life has gone **for good**.*

d   **goods** (plural only, but not countable)

> • articles for sale
> *There weren't many **goods** in the shops at all – just empty shelves.*

---

great, greater, greatest: adjective ▶ Compare **big**; **large**

a   • very big/large
> *great* is not usually only about size, but it is used for emphasis in some expression of quantity:
> *A **great many** people would agree with you.*
> *We wasted a **great** deal of time looking for the right road.*
> *There are **a great** (or large) **number** of reasons for this.*
> *They've collected **a great** (or large or big) **quantity** of rubbish.*
> *A **great** (or large or big) **quantity** of rubbish.*
> *A **great** (or large or big) **crowd** of people had gathered in the square.*

> *The great majority means 'almost everyone'. This contrasts with a big or large majority, which is not so many:*
> *The **great majority** of people were in favour of reforms.*

b • noticeable, impressive, having some special quality
*Nobody thought that this **great** ship could possibly sink.*
*She is one of the **greatest** tennis players in the world today.*
*Churchill was a **great** statesman/a **great** man.*
*We are **great** friends.* (= very close friends)

c *great*, meaning 'impressive' (and sometimes large in size too) forms part of several names:
*Alexander the **Great** . . . The **Great** War* (the old name for the First World War) *. . . the **Great** Lakes* (in North America) *. . . the **Great** Wall of China*
. . .

d Informally, *great* can mean 'wonderful':
*It's a **great** little car.*
*I hope you have a **great** time.*
*'We've got you a ticket for the show.' 'Oh, **great**!'*

e **great** or **big**?
great or *big* (rather than *large*) are used with abstract nouns:
*It was a **great** (or big) advantage/disappointment/improvement/mistake.*
*Having enough money will make a **great** (or big) difference to my life.*

Great, rather than *big*, is best for uncountable nouns:
*Do take **great** care!*

group: collective noun

• a number of people or things seen all together
*There is/are a **group** of trees on the top of the hill that can be seen for miles.*
*A **group** of people were standing around the animal and shouting.*

grow, grew, grown: verb

```
            −
grow  +  OBJECT
         ADJECTIVE
```

grow can be used with and without an object
a • become bigger; develop
*Goodness! You've **grown** since I last saw you.* (an adult speaking to a child)
*Oranges won't **grow** in a cold climate.*
*I wish the grass would stop **growing**.*
*It started as a small family business, and now it's **grown** into a world-wide company.*

b   We mainly *grow* plants, vegetables etc., but people can also *grow* their hair (long):
> *You can't **grow** oranges in a cold climate.*
> *Tom's **grown** a beard.*

c   *grow* meaning become, can be followed by an adjective:
> *I don't look forward to **growing** old.*
> *We **grew** fond of the old couple eventually.*

d   *grow up* means become adult:
> *Children **grow up** so fast these days.*

---

had

1   *had* is the past tense and past participle of *have* – See **have** and see *had better* at **better**.

2   Had I/we . . .

Conditional clauses containing a past perfect tense can begin with *had* + SUBJECT + VERB. In these cases we do not use *if*. This is rather formal:
> ***Had** I known you would be so upset, I wouldn't have told you.* (= If I had known . . .)

---

hair: noun (U, C)

a   *hair* is usually uncountable when we talk about a mass of hair:
> *I must wash my **hair**.*
> *Your **hair** is lovely.*
> *He scratched the **hair** on his chest.*

b   *hair* is used as a count noun when we talk about individual hairs:
> *There are **hairs** all over the chair.*

---

half

1   half: determiner/pronoun

● ½.
There are two common patterns when *half* is followed by a noun – *half a/an* + NOUN (**A**) and *half (of) the/my* + NOUN (**B**). With a pronoun the pattern is *half of* + PRONOUN (**C**). (NOT **Half it. *Half them.*) *Half* can be used by itself when we know what we are referring to. Following verbs are singular or plural according to meaning.

A	**Half**	a dozen/a mile/a loaf . . . an hour/an orange		(sing)
B	**Half (of)**	the this/that my/your/etc.	water book	(U) (sing)
		the these/those my/your/etc.	books horses	(Pl)
		this/these/etc. mine/yours/etc.		
C	**Half of**	it them/you/us		

A   *They had seen it first from a hill **half** a mile above.*
*I'm leaving in **half** an hour.*
***Half** a dozen copies, please.*

B   *Amazonia might be responsible for **half** (of) the oxygen produced in the world.*
***Half** (of) the water was wasted.* (= but half was used)
***Half** (of) the horses here are wild.* (= but half are all right).
***Half** (of) his socks have holes in them, and **half** (of) mine do too.*

C   ***Half** of us went because we weren't told that the whole thing was cancelled.*

2   half: adverb

- partly, not fully

  *It isn't **half** as good as it sounds.*
  *I must express my astonishment that you should put me only **half** in the picture.* (= only tell me some of the facts)
  *She **half** thinks it was a ghost.*
  *The cinema was only **half** full.*
  *It's **half** past six.* (= 6.30)
  *She's **half** Scottish and **half** French.*
  *You don't **half** like getting your own way.* (= you very much like)

3   half/halves: noun

  *We must rethink Britain's role in the second **half** of the twentieth century.*
  *The other **half** of her is not stupid, but she hasn't asked awkward questions.*
  (= the other part of her character)
  *It was impossible to join the two **halves** together again.*

*They tore the tickets in **half**.*
*Getting there took a day and a **half**.*
*One and two **halves** to Leeds, please.* (= half price tickets for children.)

4 half: adjective
*It took one and a **half** days to get there.* (Notice plural *days*).
*the last **half** century . . . **half** price*

hand

1 hand: noun (C, U)

a When *hand* means 'a part of the human body', *hand* is an ordinary count noun:
*What have you got in your **hand**?*
*It is fairly formal to shake **hands** with people when you're introduced to them.*
***Hands** off my drink!* (= Don't touch it.)
***Hands** up those of you who think the answer's No.*

b *a hand* can informally mean 'help':
*Could you give me a **hand**/lend me a **hand** with this luggage?*

c *hand* is used as an uncountable noun in many common phrases including *by hand*:
*These chocolates are expensive because they're made **by hand**.* (= hand-made, not machine-made)
*This letter came for you **by hand**.* (= not through the post)

2 hand: verb

hand meaning pass or give something with your *hands* is one of those verbs that can have an indirect object:
*The child was **handing** round the nuts.*
*Please **hand** me the newspaper.*
*I was **handed** a letter just as I was leaving the house.*

3 (on the one hand) . . . on the other hand
On the other hand is used to introduce an opposite point in a discussion. If you are making two opposite points yourself, you can introduce the first with *On the one hand*:
*'If I go to university I'll get a degree.' 'Yes, but **on the other hand** if you start work now, you'll get practical experience.'*

happen: verb   ▶ Compare **occur**

    —
happen + *to* . . .
        to-INFINITIVE

a • occur (by chance)
*What ever is **happening**? What has **happened**?*
*What will **happen** if your teacher finds out?*
*It so **happens** that/As it **happens**, I met her yesterday.*

b **happen to** + OBJECT
• have a result or effect on
*Something odd has **happened to** the television.*

c **happen** + **to**-INFINITIVE
• do something by chance
*I just **happened** to be passing, so I thought I'd call and see you.*
*Fortunately there **happened** to be a doctor at the meeting.*
*You don't **happen** to know Muriel's new address, do you?*

hard, harder, hardest

1 **hard, harder, hardest**: adjective

a • firm; strong
hard is the opposite of *soft*:
***hard** seats . . . **hard** rock . . .*
*The ground was frozen **hard**.*
*These biscuits are too **hard** for my teeth.*
*Give the door a **harder** push.*

b • difficult; using or needing a lot of effort
hard is the opposite of *easy*:
***hard** work . . . a **hard** worker . . . a **hard** life . . . a **hard** language to learn
. . . a long **hard** climb*
*It's **hard** to know how to answer that.*
*She's a **hard** person to get to know.*
*It was the **hardest** exam I have ever taken.*
*'I've failed.' 'Oh, **hard** luck!'* (= bad luck)

2 **hard, harder, hardest**: adverb

hard is also an adverb with similar meaning to the adjective. It is not the same
as *hardly*:
*You're working too **hard** – you'll make yourself ill.*
*You'll have to kick it **harder** than that.*
*It's raining **hard**.*

hardly: adverb ► Compare scarcely

hardly is used in mid-position with verbs (e.g. *I **hardly** know them.*) and with
non-assertive words like *ever* and *any* (e.g. *I've **hardly** done any work.*) We use
affirmative question tags (e.g. *There's **hardly** anything to do, is there?*) because
its meaning is almost negative – we are almost saying 'There is nothing to do'.
Notice that none of the meanings is connected with the adjective *hard*.

1 • almost not
*I only met them yesterday – I **hardly** know them.*

*She **hardly** went out at all last winter – it was so cold.*
*I've **hardly** done any work/I've done **hardly** any work.*
*This is **hardly** the best time to tell me, when I'm worried anyway.*
*So many people came we had **hardly** enough food/we **hardly** had enough food.*
***Hardly** anybody remembered me.*
*He **hardly** ever visits his mother these days.*
*There's **hardly** anything to do there, is there?*

2 With *can/could* the meaning is sometimes 'almost not' 'only just':
*I've got/I've had a terrible cold. I can/could **hardly** breathe.*

and sometimes the meaning is 'it is/was completely unrealistic or impossible to . . .':
*In the circumstances I can **hardly** insist on his paying me any more money. (=* I cannot/could not . . .)

3 hardly . . . when . . .   ▶ Compare   **scarcely; no sooner**

* only just
*I had **hardly** gone to bed when there was a knock at the door. (=* I had only just gone . . .)
***Hardly** had I gone to bed when . . .* (Note the word order.)

Than is sometimes used instead of *when*, but people dislike this.
Inversion of auxiliary and subject is also used when *Hardly ever* begins a sentence:
***Hardly** ever have I seen such terrible poverty.*

---

has   ▶ See **have**

---

hate: verb

> OBJECT
> **hate +** *-ing*
> *you/your . . . -ing*
> (o) + *to*-INFINITIVE

a *hate* can be followed by an OBJECT, an *-ing* PHRASE; by a *to*-INFINITIVE; and by an OBJECT + *to*-INFINITIVE:
*I **hate** cruelty to animals.*
*It was a horrible film – I **hated** every minute of it.*
*I **hate** seeing people drop litter (=* rubbish*) in the street.*
*I **hate** to see people drop litter.*
*I'd **hate** you to worry.*

b ***hate** you/your . . . ing*
If we *hate* somebody else doing something we can say:
*I **hate** you talking like that.*
*I **hate** your talking like that.*

Some people think a possessive form is better, but often a possessive form is not possible:

*He **hates** other people telling him what to do.*

c   *hate* is usually stative, not used in progressive tenses, but a progressive tense is possible when the meaning is 'not enjoy':

*We've just moved to London, and we're **hating** it.*

d   **hate** + *-ing* or **hate** + *to*-INFINITIVE?

Sometimes both *hate* + *-ing* and *hate* + *to*-INFINITIVE are possible:

*I **hate** doing nothing.*
*I **hate** to do nothing.*
*I **hate** seeing you unhappy.*
*I **hate** to see you unhappy.*

But the meaning of these two forms is not the same. If you *hate doing* something, this means you have done it, at least once, possibly many times, and you do not enjoy it. If you *hate to do* something you probably try not to do it if you can choose. If we refer to a single occasion, something we did once, or are doing now for the first time, or if we are talking about some sort of existing state, *hate* + *-ing* is usual:

*We **hate(d)** camping – we'll never do it again.* (NOT **to camp . . .*)
*I **hate** living here, but this is where my job is.* (NOT **to live here . . .*)

And only *hate* + *-ing* is possible if we are talking about an existing state where we have no choice:

*I **hate** being an only child.* (NOT **to be . . .*)
*She **hates** growing old.*

But after hypothetical *I would hate*, where we are not talking about an existing state or habit, then *to*-INFINITIVE is normal:

*I would **hate** to be an only child.*

Notice: *I hate to say this* or *I hate saying this, but I just don't believe you.* (= a polite way of introducing some unpleasant statement. – 'I don't want to say this but I am saying this'.)

have: verb

1   Forms

I/we/you/they	PRESENT **have**	PAST
		had
He/she/it	**has**	

INFINITIVE and IMPERATIVE	**have**
PRESENT PARTICIPLE	**having**
PAST PARTICIPLE	**had**

a **Present and past**
The verb *have* has four forms (*have, has, had, having*). Like *be* and *do*, it is used as an auxiliary verb and as a main verb. As an auxiliary (and sometimes as a main verb) *have* has short forms, and makes questions and negatives without *do*.

b **Short forms**

I/we/you/they	've	'd
he/she/it	's	

Both present and past tenses have short forms, which can be added to subjects – but only in unstressed positions:
> *'I've a lot to do.' 'I have too.'* (NOT **I've too.*)
> *He's no idea, has he?*
> *I have cornflakes for breakfast every day.* (NOT **I've*)
> *'Would you like to see the new film?' 'Oh, we've already seen it.'*
> *'Have you seen the new film?' 'Yes, we have already/already have, I'm afraid.'* (NOT **We've already.*)
> *We already had two children.* (NOT **we'd already . . .*)

c **Negatives**
Negatives are usually formed by adding *n't* (or more formally *not*) to the unshortened verb:
> *we haven't . . . he hasn't . . . she hadn't . . .*

and questions are formed by inversion:
> *Have you . . .? Has she? . . .*

Less usually we can add *not* to the short forms:
> *He's not . . . they'd not . . .*

In negative questions, where *have* is an auxiliary, instead of adding *n't* to *have*, we can put *not* after the subject, but this is very formal:
> *Have you not heard?* (formal)
> *Haven't you heard?* (usual)

d *have* is also sometimes used as an ordinary verb, with *do* for questions and negatives, and with progressive tenses. See sections **4** and **5** below.

e **Infinitives and participles**
have has infinitives and participles like other verbs:
> *It must be nice to have a twin sister.*
> *I would like to have had six brothers.*
> *They seem to have had a lot of problems with Tom when he was a baby.*
> *They still appear to be having problems with him.*
> *It's fun having a party.*
> *Having children changes your life.*
> *Having had such a bad experience there, I'm definitely never going again.*

2   **have**: auxiliary verb

a   *have* is used with the past participle of other verbs to make perfect tenses of these verbs. Short forms are common.
Present perfect simple:
> *I **have** seen great changes in my lifetime.*
> ***Has** Henry ever been to China?*
> *We've lived here for the last twenty years.*
> *She **hasn't** had a holiday since 1985.*

Past perfect simple:
> *They **had** only known each other a week when they got married.*

b   *have* + *been* + PRESENT PARTICIPLE of a verb makes the perfect progressive tenses:
Present perfect progressive:
> *I **have** been feeling rather ill lately.*

Past perfect progressive:
> *I **hadn't** been expecting to see them, so I was surprised when they arrived.*

▶ See also *be* for perfect passive tenses, and see individual modal verbs (*can, could*, etc.) for perfect tenses with modals.

3   The meaning of the perfect tenses

a   **Present perfect**
The present perfect (simple or progressive) shows a connection between the past and the present. It concerns a period that stretches from some time in the past to the present moment.
The state or action may continue into the future; but this is not part of the meaning of the tense:
> *Charles **has** worked/**has** been working at the bank since 1980.*
> *We've been married nearly twenty-five years.*
> *'How long **have** you known Margaret?' 'I've known her all my life.'*
> *You've been watching television all day – when are you going to do something useful?*

b   Sometimes the action or state happens shortly before the moment of speaking, and it has some effect or result now:
> *I've finished 'The Lord of the Flies'. What shall I read now?*
> *I've been wondering where you were.*
> *Don't look at my wet hair. I've been swimming.*
> *There **has** been a plane crash – I heard it on the news – they're still looking for survivors.*
> *I couldn't eat another thing – I've eaten too much already.*
> *Don't make excuses. You've said enough.*
> *I've passed my driving test, so now I'll be able to come and fetch you.*

c   The present perfect is also used for an action or actions happening at some indefinite time in the period before now, often with indefinite adverb phrases like *ever, never, twice, several times*:
> *'**Have** you ever been to Hong Kong?' 'Yes, once. And I've been to Singapore.'*
> *I've noticed that a cold winter is often followed by a hot summer.*

(Contrast past tenses with definite past times – *I went there/I was there . . . last month/three years ago/in 1985.*)

d In subordinate clauses of time and condition (*if . . ., when . . .*), the present perfect can refer to the future. It emphasises that an action must happen before the action of the main verb can happen:

*I'll lend you this book when I **have** finished it.* (= I'll finish it first, and then . . .)
*We'll telephone you next weekend if we**'ve** heard from James by then.*

But with *before* and *until*, the order of the actions is changed:

*We may leave before James **has** telephoned.* (We can say *before he telephones* – if we are sure that he will.)
*You mustn't drive before/until you **have** passed your driving test.* (or *before/until you pass . . .*)
*You must wait until you **have** passed.*

e **Past perfect**
The past perfect (simple or progressive) shows a similar connection between a past moment and an even earlier past period:

*By 1982 Charles **had** been working in the bank for two years.*
*We **had** always taken our holidays in August, so a holiday in December was a complete change.* (= in December that year)
*When I **had** done the ironing I went to the cinema.*

f With past reporting and thinking verbs (*He said/we thought*) a past perfect may be used for the earlier event:

*The man said the radios **had** fallen off the back of a lorry.*

and a past perfect is usually essential after words such as *already* and *since* and after *realised*:

*So we realised of course that he **had** stolen them.*
*He told us he **had** already sold several.*

But a past tense is usually all right:

He said the lorry was going too fast, and the radios fell off.

g As with the present perfect, *until* or *before* with a past perfect introduces a later action. When we know that this action did in fact happen, a simple past tense is possible if we simply wish to relate two events in time:

*We left before James (**had**) telephoned.*
*He drove the car before he (**had**) passed his test.*

Because the past perfect can emphasise the idea of one action in some way depending on the other action being completed first, sometimes the past perfect can mean that this action never happened:

*Some of the students started shouting before the speaker **had** said a word.* (= He was probably unable to make his speech.)
*He decided to wait until he **had** passed his test.* (= We do not know whether he ever passed it.)

This explains why the past perfect is used in various kinds of hypothetical and unreal situations – things that could have happened, but did not:

*If I **had** become a dancer, I would have had a much more exciting life.* (= I did not become a dancer.)
*I wish I **had** become a dancer.*

The past perfect is also used to emphasise that something is no longer the case:
*I **had** hoped that a solution to this problem would be possible.* (= I now realise that it is not possible.)

h the first time
The present perfect or past perfect (not simple present or past tenses) are used with action verbs after expressions like *This is the first time . . . the only time . . . the best/worst . . .*:
*This is at least the fourth time **I've** asked you to turn that television off.*
*It's the only time she **has** ever won a prize.*

i *have* is also used to make perfect infinitives and participles of other verbs:
*I'm sorry to **have** kept you waiting.* (= that I have kept . . .)
*We were hoping to **have** heard from Robert by now.* (but we haven't.)
*To **have** forgotten my birthday again is unforgivable.* (= It is unforgivable that he/you forgot . . .)
*It is rather foolish of you not to **have** checked the timetable.* (= It is foolish that you didn't check . . .)
*They appear to **have** been waiting for us to telephone them.*
***Having** said that, I must admit it wasn't entirely Tom's fault.*
*Fancy **having** made a million by the age of twenty-five.*

4 have as a main verb

As a main verb *have* has two sorts of meaning.
a We use *have* to talk about things that are ours, that we own (***have** a car*); to talk about relationships, within our families for example (***have** a sister*); and to talk about states such as ideas and illnesses (***have** a cold*). This meaning is often called 'possession'.
b We also use *have* to talk about actions – about doing and experiencing things (***have** a holiday/ a dream*).

5 Main verb have, have got: possession

a With *have* meaning 'possession' we have three choices
1) the auxiliary forms: inversion for questions, – ***Have** you a sister?*; *haven't* etc., for negatives, – *I **haven't** a sister*; and no *do*.
2) *have got*: inversion for questions – ***Have** you **got** a sister? haven't got* for negatives – *I **haven't got** a sister*; no *do*.
3) questions and negatives with *do*: Do you **have** a sister? He doesn't **have** one; and no *got*.
Progressive tenses are not used with any of these forms, because we are talking about states, not actions.

b have got
have/has got refers to the present, and *had got* refers to the past. Short replies are *I have*, etc. (NOT *I have got.*)

c In British English the auxiliary forms (1) are common in formal style, in the present tense, with (2) *have got* very frequent in spoken English. American English prefers (3) (*do have*), and this is becoming common in Britain:
*He **has (got)** two brothers and a sister, but he **hasn't (got)** any cousins.* (3: he **doesn't have** any cousins.)
*We **have (got)** a lot of problems. **Have** you **(got)** any suggestions?* (3: Do **you have** . . .?)

'Have you (got) any bananas?' 'No, sorry. We haven't. We haven't (got) any.'
(3: *Do you have . . .? No, we don't. We don't have any.*)
What have they got that we haven't (got)? (3: *What do they have that we don't?*)
Have you got your passport/anything to read? (3: *Do you have . . .?*)
We haven't (got) enough money.

d In the past tense, *had* and *had got* are both used, but *do* forms are common
with negatives:
I had (got) an awful cold last week, so I couldn't go to the meeting.
She had (got) blonde hair last time I saw her.
We hadn't (got) enough money for a holiday last year. (3: *We didn't
have . . .*)
I hadn't (got) a care in the world. (3: *I didn't have . . .*)
I only had/I had only got your office phone number.

do is usually used to make questions:
Did you have Monica's number? (NOT **Had you/Had you got Monica's
number?*)
Didn't you have my home phone number? (or *Hadn't you got my
number?* but NOT **Hadn't you my number?*)

6 Main verb have: actions

For the second meaning of *have* – taking something, experiencing something
etc. – we always use *have* like an ordinary verb. Questions and negatives are
formed with *do*; there are progressive tenses and imperatives; *got* and short
forms of *have* are not used:
They have dinner at 7 every day. (NOT **They've dinner . . .*)
Do you usually have cheese for breakfast?
Did you have a nice weekend?
I didn't have a very happy childhood.
The lights went out while I was having a bath/dinner.
Celia's having another baby in April. (Contrast: *Celia has a baby girl.*)
We're having a wonderful time.
Have another drink!
Don't have a row about it.

7 have + OBJECT + PARTICIPLES etc　　　　　　　▶ Compare **get**

a *have* can be followed by an OBJECT + PAST/PRESENT PARTICIPLE, and the
meaning is 'cause something to happen' or 'experience something happening'.
get is sometimes a possible alternative:
I must have/must get my eyes tested.
They had/(? They got . . .) their house broken into again.
You had/You got me worried for a moment.
I won't have you doing nothing. (= I won't allow it.)
Perhaps we could get/have everybody working.

b **have + OBJECT + BARE INFINITIVE is also possible:**
I'll have the plumber mend it.

have got to and (do) have to

a *have got to* and *(do) have to* both express an obligation, a duty to do something. When the meaning is a duty now to do something now or in the future, British English often uses *have got to*, while American English prefers *(do) have to*:

> *I **have (got) to** get a new passport.*
> *Why **have** you got to? Why **do** you **have to**?* (NOT **Why **have** you **to**?*)
> *Well, I suppose I **haven't got to**/I **don't have to**, but I want to just in case.*

b *(do) have to* is used in both British and American English for repeated duties that we are already doing:

> *'**Do** you always **have to** start work at 8 a.m.?' 'Yes, I **do**. No, I **don't**.'*

In the past *(do) have to* forms are more usual than *have got to*, because we are often talking about something that was necessary and did happen. *Had got to* sometimes sounds more like a future-in-the-past:

> *Tim **had to** work last weekend.* (And he did work)
> *Why **did** you **have to** tell her what I'd said?* (You told her . . .)
> *I couldn't sleep properly because I'**d got to** get up at 5 a.m. the next day.*

c With regular *(do) have to*, we can also form other tenses:

> *You will **have to** save up if you want to go to China next year.*
> *I've been **having to** work at night for the past two months.*
> *I'm going **to have to** finish my novel by Christmas.*

d **have got to, (do) have to** and **must**

All three verbs express obligation and are sometimes interchangeable. But the two *have* verbs express a more external obligation. With *have to*, the speaker is saying somebody else or some external circumstance makes some action necessary. But if something *must* happen, the speaker has decided that it is necessary:

> *This firedoor **must** be kept unlocked during working hours.* (= The authorities who put up this notice say this.)
> *I wonder why that door **has to** be kept unlocked.* (= What is the point of this rule?)
> *In my opinion children **must** be treated firmly.*
> *At some schools children **have to** obey all sorts of silly rules.* (I do not agree with the rules.)

e *have (got) to* is sometimes used, particularly in American English, with the same meaning of logical necessity as *must*:

> *It **has to** be true.* (= *It **must** be true.*)
> *This **has to** be the most expensive meal I've ever had.*

f *haven't got to, don't have to* (NOT **haven't to*) mean the absence of necessity. So the meaning is the opposite of *mustn't* and more like *needn't*:

> *He **hasn't got to**/**doesn't have** to write a long letter – just a few lines will do.*

---

he: pronoun ▶ See **him**; **himself**; **his**

Third person singular subject pronoun (masculine)

1 he: usage

a *he* is used as the subject of a finite verb:
> *He is a kind man.*
> *He and I are just good friends.*
> *Paul's wife is taller than he is.*
> *I don't play the guitar as well as he does.*

b If no verb follows *as* or *than* in comparisons, *he* is possible, but is very formal. *Him* is more usual. *He* is less formal if the pronoun is not at the end and we can see that a verb has been left out.
> *You're not as clever as him.*
> *Paul's wife is younger than him/he.*
> Nobody knew more than **he** *(did)* about the dangers.

c *he* is usual after *be* when a subject relative pronoun follows (although in very informal speech *him* is possible):
> *It was he who first told us about the bank.*

Otherwise *him* is more usual after *be*. ▶ See **him**

2 he: meaning

he, him, himself, his can have several meanings.

a *he, etc.* refers to individual men and boys. Babies are *he/him* when we know they are baby boys, but they can be *it*. Male animals are often *it* but can be *he/him* if we consider them as individuals:
> *Robert isn't usually late, is he?*
> *Jock is a wonderful house dog – he always barks at strangers.*
> *That bull looks dangerous – don't go near him.*

b Traditionally *he, etc.* can also refer to anyone (male or female) when we are not talking about any particular person:
> *If a person is injured in an accident, he should not be moved until medical help arrives.*

But some people object that this use of *he, etc.* is unfair to women and prefer to use an alternative:
> *he or she should not be moved . . .*
> *(s)he should not be moved . . .* (written only)
> *he/she should not be moved . . .* (written only)
> *they should not be moved . . .*

---

hear, heard, heard: verb ▶ Compare **listen**; **see**

hear +	— OBJECT O + BARE INFINITIVE O + -*ing* *that*-CLAUSE *wh*-CLAUSE

---

a   *hear* is used with and without an object. It is often used with *can*/*could* when
we are talking about hearing with our ears on a particular occasion:
*Richard is going deaf – he doesn't/can't **hear** very well now.*
*Please speak up. I can't **hear** (you).* (NOT **I don't **hear**.*)
This is a bad line (= telephone line). *Can you **hear** me?* (NOT **Do you **hear**
me?*)
We ***heard**/could **hear** thunder in the distance.*
*Have you **heard** from Peter lately?* (= Has he written, phoned, etc.?)

b   *hear* can be followed by OBJECT + BARE INFINITIVE (often for a complete action)
or OBJECT + *-ing* (when the emphasis is on the activity). OBJECT + PAST
PARTICIPLE is also possible:
*I **heard** somebody shout 'Fire!' and then I **heard** people running and
screaming.*
*I was surprised to **hear** my name mentioned.*

Passives are sometimes used, but a *to*-INFINITIVE (not BARE INFINITIVE) is
needed, and the structure is rather formal:
*He was **heard** to say that he didn't really like being an M.P.*

c   *hear* is not usually used in the progressive with the literal meaning of 'hearing
with one's ears', but progressive is possible when the meaning is 'get news':
*I've been **hearing** a lot of nice things about you lately.*

With this meaning *that*-CLAUSES and *wh*-CLAUSES are also used:
*Have you **heard** what's happened?*
*Well I **hear** that Vanessa's got a new job.*

---

height: noun   ▶ See   **high**

height corresponds to the adjectives *high* and *tall*.
● measurement of something from the bottom to the top, or of a person from
head to foot
*What's the **height** of the Eiffel Tower?* (or *How high is the Eiffel Tower?*)
*They wanted to know my age, weight and **height**.*
*The castle stands at a **height** of 300 feet above the town.*
*Caroline is afraid of **heights**, so she'll never go up a tower.*

---

help: verb

> **help** + OBJECT
> O + (*to*)INFINITIVE

1

a   *help* can be used with or without an object:
*Can I do anything to **help** (you)?*
*I need someone to **help** (me) in the garden/with the gardening.*
*Crying doesn't **help**. A bit more money would **help**.* (= would be useful)
'Could I have another biscuit, please?' 'Oh help yourself.' (= Take what you
want.)

b   *help* is grammatically an unusual verb because it can be followed by OBJECT + INFINITIVE (with or without *to*):
   *Henry is **helping** me (to) sort out my tax papers.*

2   can't/couldn't help

   If someone *can't help* something, or *doing something*, it is not their fault:
   *She **can't help** what she looks like.* (= it is not her fault)
   *I **couldn't help** it if the shops were shut.*
   *I **can't/couldn't help** wondering if she really meant what she said.* (= I had to wonder if . . .)

---

hence: connector

   a rather formal word with two meanings:

a   ● therefore
   *To what extent has rice agriculture in South India been converted successfully into a more modern (and **hence** more industrialised) system of food production.*
   *They had gone without permission, and **hence** at their own risk.*

b   ● from now; from here
   *Now he gets an invitation to the big match in Florida two weeks **hence**.*

---

her   ► See **she**; **hers**; **herself**

1   her: pronoun

   Third person singular object pronoun (feminine).
   For meaning   ► See **she**
a   *her* is used as the object of a verb or a preposition, and in other positions where it is not the subject, including short remarks without verbs:
   *Elizabeth loves being a flight attendant, but I don't think the uniform suits **her**.*
   *I must talk to **her**.*
   *Go and fetch Rachel, and tell **her** dinner's ready.*
   *They saw **her** win the race.*
   *We watched **her** climbing the tree.*
   *Ask **her** to come at once.*
   *Your mother says you are taller than **her** now.*
   *But are you as musical as **her**?*
   *He came, not **her**.*
   *Lucky **her**!*
   *God bless this ship and all who sail in **her**.*

b   *her* (NOT *she) is usual after *be*:
   *That's **her** over there in the blue dress.*
   *It"s **her** I really want to meet, not her sister.*

c   *her* is non-standard when used as a subject:
   *Diane and her discussed it.

2 **her**: possessive determiner

Third person singular (feminine):
For meaning ▶ See **she**
 *Have you met **her** new boyfriend?*
 *I don't even remember **her** mentioning him.*
 *The ship and **her**/its crew sailed quietly away yesterday.*
 *The brown hen always lays **her**/its eggs under the same bush.* (▶ See **its**)

here: adverb   ▶ Compare **there**

1 • the place where the speaker/writer is
 *Having a lovely time – wish you were **here**.* (message on a postcard)
 *Hello. What are you doing **here**? I thought you were still away.*

2 If we begin a sentence with *here* we usually do so because we want to stress the
 subject, so we put the subject at the end (*here* + VERB + SUBJECT), unless the
 subject is a pronoun (*here* + PRONOUN + VERB):
 *Oh good – **here** comes the bus. **Here** it is.*
 ***Here's** your umbrella. **Here** it is.*
 *And **here** are your gloves. **Here** they are.*

 Informally we can say *Here's* with a plural noun:
 ***Here's** your gloves.*

hers: pronoun   ▶ See **her**; **herself**; **she**

Third person singular possessive pronoun (feminine):
 *Have you seen those matching bathrobes for couples marked **His and Hers**?*
 *He takes quite nice photographs, but **hers** are much better.*
 *That's another of **hers**.*

herself: pronoun   ▶ See **her**; **hers**; **she**

Third person singular reflexive pronoun (feminine).

For meaning ▶ See **she**

1 **herself**: reflexive
 *Vanessa nearly killed **herself** by falling out of a train.*
 *She doesn't look after **herself** properly.*
 *Was she travelling by **herself**?* (= alone)

2 **herself**: emphatic
 *She **herself** said that she'd had a lucky escape.*
 *She says **herself** that she's been drinking.*

high, higher, highest: adjective and adverb ▶ Compare **low**

high is the opposite of *low*

a *high* is used to describe how far something reaches upwards:
  '*How **high** is Mount Kilimanjaro?*' '*It's 5888 metres **high**.*'
  '*Is it **higher** than Everest?*' '*No, but it's the **highest** mountain in Africa.*'
  *a **high** shelf . . . **high** tide*

b *high* is also used to describe other things:
  *a **high** voice . . . a **high** note* (in music) *. . . a **high** salary . . . **high** blood pressure . . . **high** prices . . .*

c high *or* tall

  high and *tall* relate to different meanings of the noun *height*
  Things are *high* because they extend a long way above the ground (*a **high** wall*), or above the floor (*a **high** shelf*) or above sea-level (***high** mountains*); or they are above the normal (***high** heels, a chair with a **high** back*).
  People are *tall*. So are buildings, or a few things that measure more upwards but are not very wide:
  *How **tall** is your son?*
  *The Empire State Building in New York used to be the **tallest** building in the world.*

high, highly: adverbs

high is the usual adverb connected with meanings of *height*:
  *We were flying **high** above the clouds.*
  *Feelings were running **high**.* (= people were getting angry)

highly means 'very' or 'very well':
  *It is **highly** unlikely that they will ever find out.*
  *Everybody speaks **highly** of you.*

him: pronoun ▶ See **he; himself; his**

Third person singular object pronoun (masculine).
For meaning ▶ See **he**

a *him* is used as the object of a verb or a preposition, and in other positions where it is not the subject, including short remarks without verbs:
  *I don't care what you say, I love **him**.*
  *Why don't you tell **him** the truth?*
  *Yes, I must talk to **him**.*
  *She's younger than **him**.*
  *She doesn't earn as much as **him**.*
  *I saw **him** leave.*
  *She came, not **him**.*
  *Lucky **him**!*

b *him* is often used before *-ing* in structures where *his* is formally correct:
   *Do you remember **him**/his telling the boss how to run the department?*

But only *him*, not *his*, is correct after verbs of the senses (e.g., *hear, see*), and after some other verbs, including *find, keep*:
   *We heard **him** telling the boss what to do.*
   *You mustn't keep **him** waiting.*
   *They found **him** hiding in a cupboard.*

c *him* (NOT *he) is usual after *be*:
   *That's **him**.*
   *It's **him** I want to see.*

d *him* is non-standard as a subject:
   *?**Him** and me went to the disco.*

---

himself: pronoun ▶ See **he; him; his**

Third person singular reflexive pronoun (masculine).
For meaning. ▶ See **he**

1 himself: reflexive
   *Tom takes **himself** too seriously.*
   *The old man was all **by himself** when they found him.* (= alone)
   *My grandfather sometimes talks to **himself**.*
   *Nobody wants to blame **himself**.* ▶ See **themselves**

2 himself: emphatic
   *I expected his secretary to ring, but he telephoned **himself**.*
   *Paul **himself** admitted he was wrong.*

---

his ▶ See **he; him; himself**

1 his: possessive determiner

Third person singular (masculine)
For meaning ▶ See **he**

a *Eric told us all about **his** plans.*
   *He hurt **his** neck in a car accident.*
   *That horse isn't eating **his**/its food.* (▶ See **its**)
   *The baby was crying for **his** mother.* (▶ **its**)

b *his* is formally and correctly used rather than *him* before some *-ing* patterns:
   *I remember **his**/him telling me all about his childhood.*
   ***His** saying that was very rude.*

2 his: possessive pronoun

Third person singular (masculine)
For meaning ▶ See **he**
   *I thought it was Eric's tennis racket, but he says it's not **his**.*
   *Robert has told everyone he's away, but a friend of **his** keeps telephoning.*

---

hold, held, held: verb

$$\text{hold} + \begin{array}{l} \text{OBJECT} \\ \text{O} + \text{COMPLEMENT} \end{array}$$

a When people *hold* things, they keep or support them in their arms or hands:
> *He **held** the child in his arms.*
> ***Hold** my hand while we cross the road.*
> *The man was **holding** a gun.*
> *She **held** the umbrella over my head.*

b *hold* can also mean 'keep something or someone in a particular place' and here
hold + OBJECT + COMPLEMENT is possible:
> *The prisoners were **held** in terrible conditions.*
> *Can you **hold** the door open for me, please?*
> *These men have been **held** hostage for three years.*
> *The old woman **held** out her hand for money.*

c *hold* also means 'be big enough to contain':
> *This jug **holds** two litres.*
> *We need a room that will **hold** at least 100 people.*

d **Various other meanings**
> *He **holds** strong views on education.* (= has)
> *We're **holding** a meeting next Wednesday.* (= having)
> *He **holds** the world 500 metres record.*
> *'Mr Lambert is on the other line. Will you **hold**?'* (i.e., Will you wait? – on the telephone.)
> *'**Hold** on a minute!'* (= Wait – an informal use)

home

- home is the place where we/our parents live permanently

1 **home**: adverb

home is used with verbs of movement without the preposition *to* (e.g. *arrive, come, drive, get, go, hurry, leave, return, walk* . . .):
> *We took a taxi **home**.*
> *We shall be **home** quite soon.*
> *Miss Smith gave me a lift **home**.*
> *I wrote **home**.* (= sent a letter . . .)
> *The children have all grown up and left **home** now.*

2 **home**: noun (C, U)

a uncountable noun
> *Charles had decided to stay at **home**.*
> *We left for **home** at 7.15.*

You will have to start out from **home** *very early.*
You cannot claim for the cost of travel between **home** *and work.*
He felt **at home** *even though he had never been to this place before.* (= he felt comfortable, relaxed)

b count noun
  • a house/place to live
    I felt that I simply had to give him a **home**.
    an old people's **home**

hope +	for . . . *to*-INFINITIVE *that*-CLAUSE *so/not*

1 hope: verb

a We can *hope for* something, *hope to do* something, hope *that*:
    I'm **hoping** *for a letter from Crispin.*
    We **hope**/*We're* **hoping** *to see him next week.*
    I **hope** *(that) he's all right.*

b When there is a negative idea, *not* is usually put with the verb following *hope*:
    I **hope** *(that) you haven't been waiting long?*
    'Has Paul changed his job?' 'I **hope** *so/not.'*
                         ▶ Compare: **believe, expect, suppose, think**

c **hope** and **wish**

We *hope* when we do not know the facts (past, present or future) and we use ordinary tenses:
    We **hope** *Alan wasn't/isn't/won't be tired.*
    I **hope** *Marie enjoyed/enjoys/will enjoy her holiday.*

We *wish* about past or present events which we would like to be different (though we know they cannot be changed), or about future events which seems very unlikely:
    I **wish** *Alan hadn't been so tired yesterday – it spoiled everything.*
    I **wish** *he weren't/wasn't always so tired.*
    I **wish** *Marie could come next week, but I don't think she'll be able to.*

2 hope: noun (C,U)

  • belief that something you want to happen may happen
    We all have high **hopes** *of Mary.* (= we believe she will do well)
    Tom hasn't a **hope** *of getting that job.* (= we don't think he will get it)
    Don't give up **hope**.
    There's little **hope** *that the firemen will find any one in there alive.*

how

1 how: question adverb

● in what way?

how asks questions about temporary things, things that change:

a *How are you? How are you keeping?* (questions about your health)
How did the interview go? Was it all right?
How was your holiday? (Was it good? did you enjoy it?)
How can/do I get to the station?
How on earth did you get here so soon? (***how on earth . . .?*** expresses surprise)

b *How do you do?* – is a formal greeting when people meet for the first time, and the reply is the same:
‘*How do you do?*’ ‘*How do you do?*’

Informally when we meet friends we can say:
How’s life? How are things? How’s it going? and the reply could be *Fine thanks*, or *Oh, not too bad.*

c *How can/could* may express criticism:
How can you be so rude!
How could he have forgotten – I reminded him on Sunday.

d With indirect questions, it is sometimes possible to use *how* + *to*-INFINITIVE as well as *how* + a FINITE CLAUSE:
She told me how to get there.
I asked how I could get to the station.

2 how: degree adverb   ▶ Compare **so**

a In questions, *how* + ADJECTIVE/ADVERB/DETERMINER/PRONOUN means ‘to what extent’, to what degree’, ‘to what amount’:
How old are your children?
How long is a piece of string? (No answer to this one!)
How soon will you be ready?
How much does this coat cost? (= what is the price?)
How many shopping days (are there) to Christmas?
I asked how old his children were. (Notice the word order for reported questions.)

b *how* + ADJECTIVE is often used in exclamations:
How nice!
How silly!
Compare: *It’s so nice/so silly.*

c In longer exclamations and other statements, *how* + ADJECTIVE/ADVERB, etc. means ‘to a large degree’ ‘very much’. These sentences are rather formal:
How pretty she is!
How pleased we were to hear she had won.
How hard you work.
How badly they behaved.
How I wish you were here!
I told her how pleased we were.
No amount of money can make up for how much we miss him.
                                                        ▶ See also **what** + NOUNS

3 **how**: subordinate conjunction

how explains the way that something happens or is done:
*I'll never forget **how** we first met in a thunderstorm.*
*I don't mind **how** you do it, as long as you do it.*
***How** you do it is up to you!*

4 **How about ...?**

How about + NOUN/*-ing* . . .? is an informal way of making a suggestion:
***How about** some more coffee?*
***How about** going to the cinema tonight?*

however

1 **however**: question word

however is an emphatic alternative to *how* in questions and shows surprise:
***However** did that happen?* (= I am surprised that it was possible.)
***However** many times have I got to tell you to leave the cat alone?*

2 **however**: conjunction

a **however** + SUBJECT + VERB
● it makes no difference which way . . .
***However** I do it, it just doesn't work.*
*You can pay in cash or by cheque . . . or **however** you like.*

b **however** + ADJECTIVE/ADVERB/DETERMINER/PRONOUN
● it makes no difference how good/well etc. . . .
*I'd better do some work now – **however** awful that seems.*
History is the record of what has happened in the past . . .
*however long ago or **however** recently.*
***However** many you have, I'm not taking one of yours.*
***However** much it cost, it was worth every penny.*

3 **however**: connector

● but, nevertheless
with this meaning, *however* expresses a surprise or contrast. It is usually in front or mid-position:
*To my extreme annoyance I have got horribly sunburnt. **However**, I love the warmth.*
*I think there is nothing more we can do for her. I have, **however**, given her a further follow-up appointment.*
*In general the car should be all right. You may still have a few minor problems, **however**.*

human

1 **human**: adjective

● referring to people, not animals
*The train crash was due to **human** error.*

*You can't change **human** nature.*
*I'm sorry. I'm only **human**.* (i.e., anyone can make a mistake)

2 human: noun

Although the word *human* is sometimes used as a noun, some people think it should only be used as an adjective, and they prefer the phrase *human being* for a noun:

Human beings/Humans *– unlike animals – know that they are going to die.*

hundred

- also written as 100

a For numbers between 100 and 199 we can say *a hundred and . . .* or *one hundred and . . .* When counting numbers from 200 and above we say *two hundred and . . .* NOT *two hundreds. In American English *and* is often left out:
*£150 = a/one **hundred** and fifty pounds*
*249 = two **hundred** and forty-nine*

b For numbers from 1000 upwards, we say:
1000 – a/one thousand
1001 – a/one thousand and one
1010 – a/one thousand and ten
1100 – one thousand one hundred
1201 – one thousand two hundred and one

For numbers from 1100 to 1900 it is also possible to count in hundreds:
*1100 – eleven **hundred***
*£1800 – eighteen **hundred** pounds*

c When we refer to years, round numbers may be said in the same way:
1000 BC – *one **thousand** BC*
500 AD – *five **hundred** AD*
1700 – *seventeen **hundred*** (NOT *one thousand seven hundred)
2000 – *two thousand*

But most dates are said in two parts, without mention of hundred or thousand
597 – five ninety seven
1989 – nineteen eighty-nine

d *hundreds* means 'a big number', 'lots':
*There were **hundreds** of people in the streets.*

hurt, hurt, hurt: verb

hurt can be used with and without an object
a - cause or feel physical pain; injure
*My feet are **hurting**. My feet **hurt**.*
*These shoes **hurt**. They **hurt** me/my feet.*
*Stop it – you're **hurting** me.*
*He was seriously/badly **hurt** when his car hit a tree.*
*Be careful – don't **hurt** yourself.*

hurt

b • cause mental pain; upset
  *I was deeply/rather/terribly/very **hurt** when you said I was stupid.*
  *Your remarks **hurt** me deeply.*

(Notice the different adverbs when the meaning is hurt feelings, rather than physical injury.)

I: pronoun ▶ See **me; mine; my; myself**

First person singular subject pronoun

1 I: usage

a *I* is used as the subject of a finite verb:
  I'm enjoying this.
  I was given some amazing presents for my birthday.
  Maria and I have known each other for years.
  My cousin's much taller than I am.
  She hasn't as much to do as I have.
  Nobody was as happy as I was that day.
  Who'd like to go swimming? I would.

b If no verb follows *as* or *than* in comparisons *I* is possible, but formal, and *me* is more usual. *I* is less formal if it is not at the end, and we can see that a verb has been left out:
  My cousin's much taller than me/I.
  She hasn't as much to do as me/I.
  Nobody was as happy as I (was) that day.

c After *be*, *I* is preferred when a subject relative pronoun follows (although informally *me* is possible):
  It was I who had to tell them the truth.

  Otherwise *me* is more usual after *be*.

d *I* is non-standard when used instead of *me* after verbs and prepositions:
  *They want my husband and I to join them.
  *Between you and I, he's made a mistake.
  *This is a matter for David and I.

2 I: meaning

  I, me, mine, myself refer to the speaker or writer:
  I'm sorry to hear that you aren't well.

---

idea: noun (C, U)

  idea is often followed by *of*, by *that*-CLAUSES and by *wh*-CLAUSES:
  *Have you any **idea** of the price?*
  *Have you any **idea** (of) what it's going to cost?*

188

*Give me an **idea** (of) how much we ought to pay.*
*I've an **idea** (that) it costs about £90.*
*The **idea** of paying £90 really upsets me.*

idea is not followed by a *to*-INFINITIVE (NOT **The **idea** to pay £90 . . .*).

---

if: conjunction   ► Compare **unless**

1 if: conjunction of condition

if can introduce both **(a)** open conditions – real events that happened in the past, happen now or are likely to happen in the future; and **(b)** imaginary or unreal conditions, where the events did not happen, do not happen now – although some could possibly happen later. Many different tenses are possible.

a Open conditions
   - on condition that; provided that; supposing that
   If you heat water to 100°C, it boils.
   If he was late, he always took a taxi. (= whenever/every time)
   I'll lend you the money if you let me know how much you need.
   If you see Crispin, give him my love.

   Sometimes the meaning is 'assuming it is true that':
   If you're going to be rude (which seems to be the case), *I'm leaving.*
   If you can believe that, you'll believe anything.
   I'm sorry if my letters have made you unhappy.
   If he was at home all the time, why didn't he answer the telephone?
   If you didn't have a holiday last year, you certainly should have one soon.
   If you're going to India in August, (remember that) it can be very hot.

b Imaginary conditions
   Imaginary conditions use the past tense to show that we are talking about something that is not true at the present time (*if she were here now*) and the past perfect for something that was not true in the past (*if she had been there*):
   If I knew the answer (now), *I wouldn't be asking, would I?* (now)
   If you loved me, you'd understand (= You don't love me and you don't understand!)
   What would he do if she left him? (at some time in the future).
   If I had known then what I know now, how different my life would have been!
   If you hadn't told her then, we wouldn't have this problem now.

c *will/would* are not used in *if*-CLAUSES when they simply refer to the future, but they can be used to mean that someone is willing or insists; or for politeness:
   If you will let me have this report back when you next come in, I shall be grateful.
   I would be grateful if you would kindly sign this.
   If you would like to come straight to the sixth floor, we can arrange for someone to take you over to our meeting.

d *if* does not have to be followed by a complete finite clause:
   If in doubt, say nothing. If forced, tell the truth. (= *If you are in doubt, . . . If you are forced to speak, . . .*)
   Well, I'll certainly come if possible.

---

*Write your full name – your full address – telephone number – number of children **if** any.* (= **if** you have any)
*Would you be interested in my writing an article for your magazine, and **if** so what length would you like it to be?* (= **if** you are interested).
*I think the door has a lock, but **if** not I'll buy one.* (**if** it doesn't have a lock . . .)
*The building is now nearing completion, **if** not already complete.* (= **if** it is not already . . .)

▶ See also **were**.

2 **if only**: expresses a wish or a regret:
*'**If only**', she said with sudden eagerness, 'I could be a full-time student for a year or two.'* (= I wish I could be . . .)
__If only__ I had known then what I know now.
__If only__ you hadn't told her! (= I wish you hadn't told her).

3 **even if**

● although
__Even if__ I don't want advice I do want someone I can talk to.
*I think of you a lot **even if** I have no time to write.*
*Further changes are necessary, **even if** they are going to be unpopular.*

▶ See also **as if**

4 **if**: conjunction, introducing indirect questions

Yes/no questions (i.e. questions beginning with *be*, *do*, *have* or a modal verb) need *if* (or *whether*) when they are reported:
*She's asked him **if** he'd like to go to South America with her.*
*But he doesn't seem to know **if** he wants to go or not.*
*I wonder **if** he's the right man for her.*
*Do you mind **if** I say something personal?* (= May I say . . .?)

▶ See also **whether**

ill: adjective ▶ Compare **sick**

a *ill* is mainly a predicative adjective meaning 'unwell', 'not healthy':
*I do hope this doesn't mean she's been **ill** again.*
*Sarah is unfortunately away from the office **ill**.*
*I feel rather **ill** – I hope I'm not going to get flu.*
*A lot of the children were taken **ill** and had to be sent home.*

b As an attributive adjective *ill* often means 'bad':
__ill__-feeling (= jealousy, annoyance), *__ill__ luck* (bad luck), *__ill__-health*

I'll

short for *I will*:
__I'll__ let you know.

imagine: verb

```
                OBJECT
                that-CLAUSE
imagine  +  wh-CLAUSE
                (o) + -ing
                so/not
```

a   When the meaning is roughly 'think', *imagine* is not used in the progressive. It can be followed by *that*-CLAUSES, *wh*-CLAUSES and *so/not*. When we *imagine* that something did not or will not happen, we often make *imagine* negative, not the other verb. (► Compare **believe**; **suppose**; **think**):
   *He **imagined** (that) I'd be angry, but I didn't mind.*
   *I **didn't** imagine that it was going to be easy.*
   *I can't **imagine** how I forgot the meeting, but I'm afraid I did.*
   *'Do you **imagine** that Sarah and James are in New York by now?' 'I **imagine** so/not.'* (or *I don't **imagine** so.*)

b   When the meaning is 'make a picture in one's mind', *imagine* can be followed by OBJECTS, by *that*-CLAUSES, *wh*-CLAUSES, and by (+ OBJECT) + *-ing*:
   ***Imagine** Tom's face when he hears this!*
   *Try to **imagine** that you are standing on the top of a mountain.*
   *You can **imagine** how I felt.*
   *'Can you **imagine** sailing round the world alone?' 'Well, I can't **imagine** myself doing it, but I can **imagine** some people enjoying it.'*

c   *imagine* can be used in the progressive when the meaning is 'have a mistaken idea':
   *He says people are following him around, but I'm sure he's **imagining** it.*

immediately

1   **immediately**: adverb

   ● at once
      *Turn the TV off **immediately**, and do your homework.*
      *It was **immediately** obvious that something was wrong.*

2   **immediately**: conjunction

   ● as soon as
      ***Immediately** I saw him I realised that something was wrong.*

important and importance

1   **important**: adjective

   important is the opposite of *unimportant*
   If something is *important*, it matters very much:
      *Money is much more **important** to her than love.*

*Well, maybe money is **important** to me too.*
It is important for people to decide what they really want.
*an **important** meeting . . . an **important** job . . . a very **important** person* (a
VIP)

2 importance: noun (U)
*The defence of this country is of the greatest **importance**.*
*I don't attach much **importance** to his complaints, because he is always
complaining.*

---

impossible   ▶ See **possible**

---

in   ▶ Compare **at; on**

1 in: preposition

in is a preposition of place and time. People/things can be *in* rooms or
containers and other three dimensional spaces. *In* contrasts with *at* (a point)
and *on* (surfaces and lines). *In* also contrasts with *at* and *on* with meanings of
time.
General meanings are 'contained by', 'not out', 'on the inside', 'at home' and
'surrounded by'. With these meanings, *in* often contrasts with *out* and *out of*.

a Place
in expresses position in a place without movement. To express movement we
use *into*:
  in a box/a car/a cupboard/a garden/a house/a room/a field/a wood
  in London/Britain/Europe/an island in the Pacific
  in Oxford Street (but American English *on Fifth Avenue*)
  in bed/church/hospital (without articles when these places are used for their
  main purpose – but American English *in the hospital*)
  in a mirror or *in a picture* (thought of as three dimensional even though they
  actually only have two dimensions.)
  Do you like sugar in your tea?
  There wasn't a cloud in the sky.
  I'd rather live in the country.
  Wrap it in paper.
  Madeleine was in a dark blue dress with matching shoes.

b Time
  in the morning/the afternoon/the evening (but *at night*)
  in the spring/January/1970/the 80's/the nineteenth century
  He wrote the play in three weeks. (= during the space of)
  I'll come in a day or two. (= from now)
  Jeremy will be here in a week. (= from now)
  I haven't been skiing in years. (= for years)

c Various other uses
  I read it in a book/a story/a newspaper.
  Write in ink.
  What's in the middle? (e.g. of a cake/a sandwich)

*Do you like walking **in** the rain?*
***In** reply to your letter . . .*
*She's only **in** her twenties.* (= aged between 20 and 30)
*She is **in** danger/difficulties/a hurry/love/tears.*
*The results are **in** doubt.*
*The gates are **in** use.* (= being used)
*We sat **in** a row/a circle.*
*They are **in** business/the army, etc.* (as a job)
*It was a chance **in** a million.*
*I spoke to her **in** public/private/confidence.*

d **in** + VERB-*ing*
***In** saying this I realised I was going to make myself unpopular.* (= I realised the result of saying this would be . . .)
(Contrast ***On** seeing me, they waved and rushed madly across the road.* = when they saw me . . .)

e Verbs often followed by *in* include:
*Do you believe **in** ghosts/life after death?*
*I eventually succeeded **in** solving the problem.*
*Divide it **in**(to) two.*

(Notice also: *I'm not interested **in** gossip.*)

2 **in**: adverb

in is the opposite of *out*
a • at home or in a building
*We stayed **in** and watched TV.*
*The poor dog is shut/locked **in** all day.*
*There was nobody **in** when I called.*
*We'll have the new season's styles **in** next week.* (= **in** the shop)

b • moving from the outside (with verbs of entering or causing something/somebody else to enter):
*Come **in**!* (= into a house or room)
*Please call **in**/drop **in**/look **in**.* (= visit us)
*I had lost my key and I couldn't get **in**.* (= into the house/room etc.)
*They won't let you **in** without a ticket.* (e.g. into the theatre)
*The sea's quite warm once you're **in**. Come on **in**!*
*He opened the car door and the children got **in**.*

c **Various other uses**
*Please give **in**/hand **in**/send **in** your application by Monday.* (= to our office)
*Please fill this form **in**.* (e.g. put your address, etc. in the spaces).
*You should write **in** to the manufacturers and complain.*
*The tide is coming **in**.* (= soon it will be high tide)
*The train was late **in**.* (= late arriving at the station)
*Let's hope the Conservatives get **in** again.* (= get into power/are elected)
*The roof suddenly fell **in**.* (= down into the house)
*Short skirts are **in** again.* (i.e. they are the new fashion)

▶ See also: *at* or *in* or *on* at **on**; *in case* at **case**; *at/in the end* at **end**; *in fact* at **fact**; *in front of* at **front**; *in order* at **order**; *in spite of* at **despite**; *in/on time* at **time**.

---

incidentally: connector　　　　　　► Compare **by the way**

incidentally is often used in spoken English to introduce a new topic of conversation – often something quite important:
Incidentally, *what happened to that book I lent you? I'd like it back.*

---

include: verb

a　When *include* means 'to contain something, as well as other things', *include* is not usually used in the progressive:
*The bill **includes** 15% VAT.* (= a tax)

b　But this 'rule' does not apply when the meaning is 'put in with':
*When I said 'family', I was **including** the dog.*

---

including: preposition

*It has got six rooms, **including** the kitchen and bathroom.* (= four rooms plus the kitchen and bathroom)
*That's £573 **including** VAT.* (= a tax)

---

indeed: adverb

1　very ... indeed

indeed is used in the pattern *very* + ADJECTIVE/ADVERB/DETERMINER + *indeed* to emphasise the words in the middle, so that *very . . . indeed* means 'extremely':
*It was **very** wet **indeed**, so Denis and I did the shopping on our own.*
*We should be **very** sorry **indeed** to lose her.*
***Very** few people **indeed** know this, of course.*
*Thank you **very** much **indeed** for your help.*

We sometimes have this pattern without *very*, but this is formal:
*We consider ourselves fortunate **indeed**.*

2　*indeed* is also used when we want to add some emphatic information to something we have already said. The meaning is a bit like 'in fact':
*He is willing to talk to her. **Indeed**, he loves not only to talk but to gossip.*
*The Bank does not think the position will be improved by waiting another three months. It is feared, **indeed**, the position may get worse.*
*'A wonderful place', said Kelly. And **indeed** it sounded wonderful the way he described it.*

3　In short replies to other people, *indeed* often means, 'yes, that's certainly true':
*'It's an awful problem.' 'It is **indeed**; it is **indeed** worrying.'*

It can also show surprise:
*'He says he'll make a million pounds before he's 21.' 'Does he, **indeed**?'*

---

information: noun (U)

information is always an uncountable noun:
> *Have you any **information** about/on boats to the Greek islands?*
> *I'm afraid there isn't much **information** available.*

inside

inside is the opposite of *outside*

1 inside: preposition

- to/on the inner side of
  > *Hateley kicked the ball magnificently just **inside** the far goal post.*
  > *Martin's toes curled up **inside** his socks.*

2 inside: adverb
> *Don't stand there in the rain . . . Do come **inside**. (in* is also possible.)
> *The church is very remarkable **inside**.*
> *If you shake it, you can find whether there's water **inside**.*

3 inside: noun
> *It would be rather nice if we could see the **inside** of the house, and not just the outside.*
> *The door had been fastened from the **inside** and we couldn't get in.*

4 inside: adjective
> *an **inside** pocket (= a pocket inside a coat)*
> *an **inside** lavatory (inside a house) . . .*

insist: verb

> insist + *on* . . .
> *that*-CLAUSE

When we *insist* we say that something is true or that something must be done whatever other people think. The usual patterns are *insist on* + NOUN/*-ing* or *insist (that)* . . .:
> *He **insisted** on paying. He absolutely **insisted**, so I let him.*
> *He's always **insisting** on his 'rights' – but what about my rights?*
> *You should **insist** on a cheque.*
> *You must **insist** that they give you one.*

instance ▶ Compare **example**

1 instance: noun
- a case of something happening; a single event
  *There have been many **instances**, I'm afraid, of the police failing to find a murderer.*

2 for instance: connector
- for example
  *Some TV programmes, Dallas **for instance**, run for years.*

instant

1 instant: noun (usually singular)
- moment
  *She didn't wait an **instant**, but rushed to help the injured man.*

2 the instant (that): conjunction ▶ Compare **the moment (that)**
the instant (that) can be used like a conjunction:
  *The **instant** she saw what had happened, she rushed to help.*

3 instant: adjective
- immediate; that happens or is made very quickly
  *an **instant** success . . . **instant** coffee . . .*

instead

1		PREPOSITION + NOUN	
	I'm daydreaming	**instead of**	working.
	Miss Brown is on the committee		Mr Green
2	She never works.	She day-dreams all day, **instead**.	
		Instead, she wastes her time day-dreaming.	

1 instead of: preposition
- in place of; as an alternative to
instead of is followed by a NOUN PHRASE or an *-ing* form of a verb as shown:
  *Miss Brown is on the committee now **instead of** Mr Green.*
  *I'm day-dreaming **instead of** working. (= I ought to be working!)*
  ***Instead of** taking the steep B4391 road for Bala, you can drive along the gentler B4401.*

2 instead: connector
  *It was much too late for mother to begin preparing lunch, so we all went down to the pub **instead**. (= **instead of** having lunch at home).*
  *There aren't any oranges – will you have an apple **instead**?*

intend and intention

1 intend: verb

- plan; mean

```
                 OBJECT
intend + (O) + to-INFINITIVE
         that-CLAUSE
```

a   *intend* can be followed by a noun phrase, by (OBJECT) + *to*-INFINITIVE and by a *that*-CLAUSE when it suggests great determination:
I didn't intend any harm.
We intend to leave next Tuesday.
My father intends me to join the army.
It was intended to be a surprise.
My father intends that I shall be a success.
The bomb was intended for the President.

b   *intend* + *-ing* is possible, but less common:
How long do you intend staying?

2 intention: noun (C, U)

Our *intentions* are things that we mean to do or want to happen:
I had no intention of upsetting them.
Pat has lots of good intentions, but she never seems to do anything.

interested and interesting

The difference between *interested* and *interesting* is the same as with most *-ed/-ing* pairs. (Compare   *a boring lesson . . . I was bored.*):

a   *I am interested in old furniture.*
I would be interested in joining a guitar class.
I was interested to hear (that) you have changed your job.
I would be most interested to meet your cousin. (. . . if I met)
I am *interested that you feel as I do about the Third World.*

b   *That museum of old furniture is interesting.*
an interesting book . . . an interesting fact . . . an interesting place . . .

into: preposition   ► Compare   in

into expresses movement to the inside of something

a   Particularly with verbs of movement
Your mother will have to go into hospital soon.
I must get into bed in a minute.
Charles dived straight into the water.
A lorry ran into the back of my car yesterday.

b With some verbs of change and result

*They've cut so many trees down, they're turning the land **into** a desert.*
*Her books have been translated **into** twenty languages.*
*Can I change this money **into** dollars?*

c Various other uses

*You should pay that money **into** your bank.*
*The plan for the city divides it **into** 68 districts.*

---

is ► See **be**

---

it: pronoun ► See **its**; **itself**

Third person singular subject and object pronoun (impersonal).

1 it: used for things and animals

a *it* is both a subject and object pronoun for a thing; an animal; and sometimes for a young child. It can refer to singular count nouns, uncountable nouns and collective nouns (► see also **he, she, they**):

*I can't find my case – I had **it**, but **it**'s disappeared.*
*This bread is stale – I can't eat **it**. (**it** for an uncountable noun)*
*Leave the cat alone; **it**'s not doing you any harm.*
*He ran into the blazing room, picked up the baby and carried **it** to safety.*
*The government says **it** is going to change the law. (**it** for a collective noun)*
► See **they**

b *it* is often used before *-ing* structures where *its* is formally correct:

*Move that glass. I'm frightened of **it**/**its** getting broken.*

Only *it* (NOT **its*) is correct after verbs of the senses and after other verbs, including *find*, *keep*:

*I saw **it** moving.*
*We found **it** lying on the floor.*

2 it: question tags

it is the pronoun used in question tags after *anything*, *everything*, *nothing* and *something*:

*Nothing ever stays the same, does **it**?*

3 it: empty subject or object

a Most English sentences need a subject, so with verbs that do not have any real doer we use an empty *it* – 'empty' because it does not refer to anything. We use this *it* when talking about the time, the weather, the temperature and often when making rather general comments:

*It is 8 o'clock. **It**'s still early but **it**'s already 28°C.*
It's going to be a nice day.

It's very quiet here, isn't it?
If it weren't for you, I don't know what I'd do. (= if you were not here . . .)
It will be good if you pass your driving test.
'Who's that? Who is it?' 'It's me.'
How's it going? (= How are things? How is your present situation?)

b Notice also *it* as an empty object:
I like it here.
Well, that's it for today; I'm going home. (= that's all . . .)
I hate it if/when you're unhappy.

4 it: introductory subject

a *to*-INFINITIVE CLAUSES and *that*-CLAUSES can be the subject of a sentence:
To miss Venice *would be a great pity.*
To put all the blame on Mr Pinner *is quite unfair.*
That you spent so much money *doesn't surprise me.*

But often this sort of clause contains some new or important information that we want to put at the end. So we use an introductory *it* as the grammatical subject and put the clause which contains this information later:
It would be a great pity to miss Venice.
It's quite unfair to put all the blame on Mr Pinner.
It doesn't surprise me (that) you spent so much money.

b Introductory *it* is used with various other types of subjects;
Is it all right for me to borrow the car?
It's been marvellous seeing you again.
It's no use expecting other people to solve all your problems for you.
It's a problem actually whether to tell my mother or not.
It's awful how many people don't get enough to eat.
It worries me what he might do next.
It's boring the way you complain all the time.
It's a long long way to Tipperary.

c *it* can also be used as the subject of a passive sentence with verbs of saying and thinking:
It is thought that the level of the sea is rising all over the world. (= People think that . . .)
It is not yet known how many people could be affected. (= We don't yet know . . .)

d *it* is used when a clause is the subject of *appears, looks, seems, happens, occurs*:
It appears that they just forgot to give us the message. (NEVER *That they just forgot appears . . .*)
It seems as if she doesn't care any more.
It occurred to me that she was probably pretending.

5 it: introductory object

it is also used as an introductory object when there is a clause as an object and this clause a complement. So the pattern is *it* + COMPLEMENT + CLAUSE. This introductory *it* is essential with *to*-INFINITIVES and *that*-CLAUSES:
We felt it necessary to point out his mistake.
They made it a rule not to eat meat on Fridays.
I find it rather surprising that you don't already know this.

But: Introductory *it* is optional with *-ing*-CLAUSES:
Do you find it fun learning English?
or:
Do you find learning English fun?

Notice also:
I leave it to you to choose.
I take it that you don't mind. (= I assume that you don't mind.)

6 **it**: introductory in CLEFT SENTENCES ▶ Compare **what**

Sometimes we use *it* to emphasise a particular part of a sentence by dividing the sentence into two (cleft means 'divided'). So instead of saying:
My little sister gave me a snake for my birthday.

we can say:
It was my little sister who gave me a snake for my birthday.
or:
It was a snake (that) my little sister gave me for my birthday.
or:
It was for my birthday (that) my little sister gave me a snake.
or:
It was me (that) my little sister gave a snake to.

Here are some more examples:
It was my parents who were shocked.
It was to meet some of the problems that I began making lists. (emphasis on the purpose)
It wasn't that long ago that I could still find wines like that. (emphasis on the time)
It was there that he suffered the worst defeat of his life. (emphasis on the place)
It's not what you say but the way you say it! (= The way you say it matters most!)

7 **it**: general reference to the text

it is also used in a rather general way to refer back or forwards to whole clauses or sentences:
Those who open their gardens to the public are not only doing it for the money. (doing *it* = opening their gardens to the public)
First they heard he was missing, and then came the news that he was dead. It was a terrible shock. (*It* = both these happenings together)
If it's at all possible, this coat should be dry-cleaned. (*It* = if dry-cleaning this coat is possible)
It's an awful nuisance, but I've got to write letters this evening. (*It* = the fact that I've got to write letters)

its: possessive determiner ▶ See **it**; **itself**

Third person singular (impersonal)
a *its* is the possessive of *it*, and usually refers to a thing, but sometimes to an animal or a small child, and sometimes to a collective noun for people:

I buy the Times for its foreign news.
That dog has got something wrong with its leg.
The government is proud of its record.
An army marches on its stomach. (= Soldiers need plenty of food.)
A baby often throws its toys on the floor.

b *its* is formally and correctly used, rather than *it*, in some patterns with *-ing*:
Put the milk back in the fridge – I don't like it/its being left on the table.

c *its* is not used as a pronoun. Do not confuse possessive *its* with *it's* (the short form of *it is* or *it has*). Compare these two in:
'Is your cat ill?' 'Well, it's (= it has) *got something wrong with its* (possessive) *ears, but of course it's* (= it is) *getting old'.*　　　▶　see **'s**

---

itself: pronoun　　　　　　　　　　　　▶　See　**it; its**

Third person singular reflexive pronoun (impersonal)

1　itself: reflexive
The committee has kept itself informed about the main problems.
I want to see our country with confidence in itself.

2　itself: emphatic
The house itself is three hundred years old, but the garden was entirely changed in the early years of this century.

---

job: noun (C)

a　● paid employment, work
The government has created thousands of new jobs.
She's got a part-time job as a tourist guide.

b　● task; work of various kinds
I had quite a job getting everything into one suitcase. (= a hard task)
Give the children little jobs to keep them busy.
It's not my job to look after your keys! (= duty)

c　*(It's) a good job . . .* is an informal comment meaning something is lucky or fortunate:
It's a good job your mother didn't know, or she'd have been terribly worried.

d　**job** or **work**?
The big difference is that *job* is a countable noun, and *work* in a similar sense is uncountable:
She had had six jobs by the time she was twenty-five, but they all involved the same sort of work.
He's found work/a job in a hospital.

just: adverb

1 We use *just* immediately before a particular word or phrase to focus attention on it.

a • only
> I've gone *just* a little pink from the sun.
> I'm being ever so good – *just* for you, darling.
> He was *just* a man on his own, and they were a family.
> Excuse me for *just* a moment, sir.
> I feel very proud of you. *Just* think what you might have turned out like.
> (=what you might have become – how awful you might have become).

b • merely; simply
> Sometimes I wish I could *just* go away and start again.
> There's nothing wrong with me. I *just* don't feel very well – that's all.
> I can't pay £30 *just* for bed and breakfast.

c • barely; almost not
> With this meaning we sometimes use *only just*:
> When he married the princess his wage was *just* over $5.
> She is *only just* able to walk around the house.
> We *only just* caught the train – by jumping on as it began to move.

d • exactly
> With this meaning *just* is used mainly in affirmative sentences:
> That is *just* right. (Contrast   That's not quite right.)
> You know what Tom's like – that's *just* what he would say. (Contrast That's
> not quite/not exactly what he said.)
> It's *just* the same as it always is. (Contrast   it's not quite the same.)
> You look *just* like your mother.

2 *just about* can mean 'almost', 'very nearly':
> I've *just about* had enough of your rudeness.
> Sorry. I'm *just about* ready.

▶ See also   *just about to* at **about**

3 Sometimes *just* is added to give emphasis, and the meaning is roughly 'absolutely', 'entirely':
> I *just* adore you. Aren't you *just* wonderful.
> It's *just* so amazing – it kind of blows my mind. (= it fills me with excitement and confusion).
> I *just* can't believe it – it's *just* impossible.
> That's *just* absurd/perfect . . .

4 *just* is used with various time meanings:

a • a very short time before
> With this meaning perfect tenses are usual in British English:
> I've only *just* got back to college.
> Daddy's train has *just* arrived.

The past tense is possible in American English – *His train just arrived.*

b With progressive tenses, *just* can mean 'a short time from now/then':
> *Wait for me. I'm just coming.*
> *I was just going to bed when they telephoned.*

c *just now* with a past tense can mean 'a short time ago':
> *Where on earth are my glasses? I had them just now.*

With a present tense *just now* means 'now', 'at this moment':
> *I'm sorry – I'm busy just now. Can I ring you back?*

d *just after/just before* mean 'only a moment after/before':
> *Cole arrived just after 6.*
> *just before Christmas . . . just before midnight . . . just before I left . . .*

e **just as**
- at the very moment that
> *Sir Henry Gillett rang just as I was leaving.*

▶ See also *just as well* at **well**

---

keep, kept, kept: verb

> OBJECT
> **keep** + (o) + COMPLEMENT
> (*on*)-*ing*

a - have and continue to have
In this sense, keep takes an object:
> *Can I keep this leaflet, or do you want it back?*
> *I'll keep this plastic bag. It might be useful.*
> *keep a diary* (= write a regular diary) . . . *keep a secret* (= not tell anybody)
> . . . *keep a promise* (= do what you promise)

b **keep** + OBJECT + COMPLEMENT

- cause something to be in a particular state or place
Adjective, adverb or participle complements are possible:
> *These boots will keep your feet dry.*
> *Why don't you keep the butter in the fridge?*
> *I didn't mean to keep you waiting.*
> *You should keep your arms covered.*

c **keep** + COMPLEMENT
- stay; remain
> *Keep calm. Please keep quiet.*
> *Keep off the grass . . . Keep left . . . Keep out.*

d **keep** + (*on*) + -*ing*
- continue doing
> *I keep (on) getting this wrong.*
> *Why do you keep (on) laughing at me?*
> *Listen! I can't keep (on) repeating things.*

keep is not followed by a *to*-INFINITIVE.

kind

1 kind: noun　　　　　　　　　　　　　　　　▶ Compare **sort**

• sort, type
kind is often followed by *of* + another noun:

a　*It's perfectly good toothpaste – but it's not the **kind** I buy.*
*There are many different **kinds** of bread.*
*I'm doing all **kinds** of exciting things.*
*'And what **kind** of (a) master is he?' 'Well he's a **kind** of (a) manager really.'*
*That was not the **kind** of Britain we wanted.*
*I'm not very keen on that **kind** of book.*

b　In informal English we can use *these/those kind of* + PLURAL NOUN + PLURAL
VERB:
*?These/those **kind** of people cause a lot of trouble.*

But it is safer to say:
*People of this/that **kind** cause . . .*
or:
*That **kind** of person causes . . .*

2 kind of: adverb　　　　　　　　　　　　　　▶ Compare **sort of**

In informal English we use *kind of* to mean 'a bit, but not very'; 'sort of':
*I feel **kind of** frightened.*
*The film was **kind of** silly.*
*I **kind of** hoped that you'd telephone.*

3 kind, kinder, kindest: adjective

kind is the opposite of *unkind*:

a　*I think it was cruel – it would have been much **kinder** not to have told her. The*
kindest *thing to do now is not to mention it again.*

b　*kind* is often used when thanking people, or when politely asking them to do
things:
*Oh Edwin, that is **kind**! Thank you.*
*How **kind** of you to invite me to come and see you.*
*Would you be **kind** enough to let me have this report back when you've
finished with it?*

know, knew, known: verb

```
                OBJECT
    know + that CLAUSE
            wh-CLAUSE
```

know is not usually used in the progressive
• to have knowledge or information

a *know* can be followed by OBJECTS, and by *that*-CLAUSES and *wh*-CLAUSES:
> *Do you **know** my friend Mary Radlett?*
> *How long have you **known** each other?*
> *What do you **know** about radio waves?*
> *I **know** (that) life isn't easy for you, but . . .*
> *I **know** what you're thinking, but you're wrong.*
> *Do you **know** how to use a computer* (NOT **Do you **know** to use . . .*)

b It is not always necessary to state the object of *know*:
> *I asked a man the way, but he didn't **know**.*
> *'There's a new airport in the City of London.' 'Yes, I **know**.'*

c *You know* – is sometimes used in conversation – either to emphasise what is being said:
> *It's very foolish of you, **you know**, to spend so much money on clothes.*

or with no real meaning while the speaker is thinking what to say:
> *I was just walking along the High Street, **you know**, when I suddenly saw Betty.*

lack and lacking

lack is a verb (not usually used in the progressive or in the passive); it is also a noun (singular only); and *lacking* is an adjective. The verb is followed by an OBJECT, but the noun needs *of*, and *lacking* is followed by *in*:
> *He's a nice chap but he **lacks** ambition.*
> *His wife is rather annoyed by his **lack** of ambition.*
> *There are worse things than a **lack** of ambition.*
> *He is **lacking** in ambition.*

large, larger, largest: adjective ▶ Compare big; great

large is the opposite of *small*

a • big in physical size
Often both *large* and *big* are possible (▶ See *big*), but *large* is more formal and is the preferred word to describe the size of things that are for sale:
> *A **large** brown loaf, please.*
> *The jumpers are available in small, medium, **large** and extra **large** sizes.*

b *large* (or *great*, but not usually *big*) is used in some expressions about quantities and numbers:
> *A **large**/great number of complaints were received.*
> *There is a **large**/great amount of work to be done.*

c *large* is much more concerned simply with size than *big* or *great* are. A *great man* is a man who is respected and admired for some achievement; a *big man* may be simply physically big, but he may be important; a *large man* is physically above average in size.

| last | ▶ Compare **first; latest** |

1 last: determiner/adjective

a • immediately before now; most recent   ▶ Compare **latest**

When we say *last week . . . last Friday . . . the week before last* (i.e. before *last week*) . . . *last December . . . last autumn . . . last year* etc. (without *the*), we are talking about the one immediately before now:
  I had a marvellous day in London last week.
Contrast: *this week/next week.*
If we mean *before* some other time, we can say *the week before . . . the Friday before.*

b When we say *the last* (+ lengths of time) we mean that length of time up till now:
  the last couple of weeks . . . the last fifteen months . . . the last few years . . .
  I've been to five parties in the last week. (= in the 7 days up until today).

Contrast: *I went to five parties last week* (i.e. between the Sunday and Saturday before this week)

c **last** or **past**?
In this usage (**b**) both *the last* and *the past* are possible:
  five parties in the last/the past week . . . the last/the past couple of weeks . . .
  the last/the past fifteen months.
(But NOT **I went to five parties past week* usage **a**).

d • final in a series
last is the opposite of *first*:
  It's the last house on the right before the traffic lights.
  We always take our holidays the last two weeks in June.
  . . . the last Monday in August.
  The last thing I wanted to do was upset you. (= I certainly did not want to upset you).

e • the only one remaining
  That's our last hope.
  I've drunk my last bottle of wine.

2 the last: pronoun

That was the last we heard of him. (= We never heard any news of him again).
I don't think Valerie wanted to come – she was the last to arrive and the first to leave. (= she arrived after everybody else . . .).

3 last: adverb

last is the opposite of *first*:

a • on the most recent occasion
In this sense *last* is often used in mid-position:

*It is some time since I **last** wrote to you.*
*The cottage was roofless when I **last** saw it.*

b ● at the end
In this sense *last* is used in end-position:
*It was a very fast race and poor Tom finished **last**.*

4 last: verb

● continue for some time
*The course **lasted** two years.*

5 at last   ▶ Compare *in the end* at **end; eventually; finally**

● after a long wait or delay

a *At last, after a lot of correspondence, we finally agreed on the figures.*
'So you've come at last, have you', said Alec, 'I've been waiting ages!'

b *at last* can be used as an exclamation:
At last! It's taken you a long time.

lastly: connector   ▶ Compare finally; firstly

● introducing the last thing in a list
. . . Secondly, the scheme would remove most of the traffic from Great John Street . . . Lastly, the planners could then make Upper Penny Street a pedestrians-only street.

late, later, latest   ▶ Compare early

1 late, later: adverbs

late/later are the opposites of *early/earlier*:
*Tom always arrives **late**.* (= after the proper time).
*I go to bed **late** but I try to get up early.*
*He **later** tried to get his money back* (= afterwards).
*I suppose you'll probably arrive **later**, will you?*
*We will get there sooner or **later**.* (= eventually)
Also: *I'm going **later** today . . . **later** this month . . . **later** this year . . .*
*a few days **later** . . . some time **later** . . . twenty years **later** . . .*

2 late, later, latest: adjectives

a *Don't be **late** for school!* (= after the proper time).
*I had a very **late** night so I'm tired this morning.* (= I went to bed very *late* last night).
*Perhaps we can arrange something at a **later** date.*
*What's the **latest** news of Charles?* (= the most recent news).

b **latest** or **last**?
Both *latest* and *last* can mean 'most recent', but *latest* also means 'newest, up to date', while *last* means 'final'.
Compare:
> *Lasky's have a department with all the **latest** car radios, car cassettes . . .*
> *There are some stories which may have no **last** chapters . . .*

the latter: pronoun and adjective

a   *the latter* is the opposite of *the former*. As a pronoun *the latter* means 'the second mentioned of two things/people':
> *Now I have the problem of deciding whether to take the job with the professor at college or the job in Scotland. I think it will be the **latter**.* (= the job in Scotland)

b   As an adjective *the latter* means 'the second (person/thing), not the first':
> *Interest rates rose in **the latter** half of 1973.* (= from July 1973 to December 1973)

lay (laying), **laid**, **laid**: verb   ▶ Compare **lie**

a   The verb *lay* normally needs an object. It means to set things out, to place things, to put something down, etc.:
> *I always **lay** my jumpers out flat to dry them when I've washed them.*
> *Have you **laid** the table for dinner?* (= put the knives and forks etc. out ready for a meal.)

b   When *lay* is used of birds to mean *lay an egg*, it can be used without an object:
> *That hen only **laid** two eggs last week, and she isn't **laying** at all now.*

c   Notice that *lay(s)* is the present tense of this verb, but the past tense of *lie*.

lead, **led**, **led**: verb

lead with the general meaning of 'go in front' or 'show the way' is used with and without an object:
> *If you **lead** (the way), we'll follow.*
> *Scotland was **leading** two goals to one at half time.* (= winning the match)
> *That sort of plan only **leads** to difficulties.* (= causes)
> *This path **leads** down to the river.*
> *She **led** us down a long corridor to a door marked 'Private'.*
> *Who is going to **lead** the expedition/the team?*

---

learn, learned (or learnt), learned (or learnt): verb
▶ Compare **teach**

```
              –
           OBJECT
learn +   that-CLAUSE
          wh-CLAUSE
          to-INFINITIVE
```

- gain knowledge or a skill; study

learn can be used with and without an object; we can *learn about* . . . and we can *learn that* . . ., *learn* can be followed by *that*-CLAUSES, *wh*-CLAUSES or by (*wh*-WORDS) + *to*-INFINITIVES:
*When will they ever **learn**?*
*You should **learn** from your mistakes.*
*The best way of **learning** is by doing.*
*We are **learning** Chinese/how computers work/how to use computers/what to do in an emergency . . .*
*I like **learning** about life two hundred years ago.*
*I think he's **learned** at last that it's no good shouting at people.*
*I've been **learning** (how) to cook/to drive/to fly.*

least

least is the superlative of *little*. The comparative is *less*, and the opposite is *most*. Determiners, pronouns and adverbs are all the same.

1 (the) least: determiner and pronoun ▶ Compare **fewest; most**

- the smallest in size or amount
a *least* is used mainly in a general sense or with uncountable nouns:
*You've given me far less than anybody else – I've definitely got **(the) least**.*
*It is hardly the place one wishes to go and sit in. The furniture is uncomfortable, to say **the least**, and the decorations are just awful.* (= We could be much ruder!)
*Please, there's nothing to thank me for – it was **the least** I could do.*

b Like *less*, *least* is sometimes used with count nouns where *least* would be more 'correct':
*?The Travel Show. How to pick the right place, the right beaches, the **least** noise, **the least** British, **the least** building work.* (i.e., the fewest British people – from a note about a TV programme)

c *least* can also be used with abstract count nouns with the meaning of 'smallest':
*Money is **the least** of my worries.* (= my smallest worry)
*The department never had **the least** complaint about his work.* (= the smallest complaint.)

---

2   least: adverb

- less than anything else
  *Perhaps the best thing to do would be to decide which of them I like **least** – and then marry him.*
  *That sort of thing always happens when you **least** expect it to.*
  *I believe that university teachers are the group **least** likely to be able to do this.*
  *We must certainly choose the **least** wasteful method.*

3   at least: adverb

a
- at any rate; if nothing else
  *He's stupid, but **at least** he's not rude.*
  *Gerald decided that he would **at least** allow himself the pleasure of staring at them.*
  *The score, 1-1, was about right – and Leeds **at least** would not complain about it.*
  *I revised all the afternoon to be ready for the test tomorrow – **at least**, I hope I am.*
  ***At least** you have got a man and some cows.* (= even if you have nothing else)
  *Tom's bought a new car. **At least** that's what I heard.*

b
- not less than and probably more (with a time or money phrase)
  *You must allow **at least** two days for letters to arrive.*
  *A new swimming pool in Essex is expected to be closed for **at least** a month after a fire in the boiler room yesterday.*
  *It'll cost you **at least** £50 to get there.*

4   not . . . in the least

- not . . . at all; not in any way
  *The treatment has **not**, I am afraid, helped **in the least**.*
  *I am **not in the least** convinced that he actually heard these noises at all.*
  *I don't find it **in the least** surprising that he does not remember more than that.*

---

leave, left, left: verb   ▶ See also **left**

```
         —
leave +  (IO) + OBJECT
         O + COMPLEMENT
         O + to-INFINITIVE
```

a
- go away from (with or without an object)
  *When does the next train **leave**?*
  *Simon is going to **leave** home/school/his job soon.*

b Like *give*, *leave* can be used with two objects, meaning 'put something for someone to get later':

> *Somebody telephoned and **left** you a message/**left** a message for you.*
> *Shakespeare left his 'second-best bed' to his wife/**left** his wife 'the second-best bed'.*

c We can also *leave* an object in a particular place or state:

> *You could **leave** the car at home and walk.*
> *Don't **leave** your car unlocked.*
> *Flu often **leaves** you feeling weak.*
> ***Leave** the cat alone – it's not hurting you.*

d *leave* + OBJECT + *to*-INFINITIVE means 'allow somebody else to be responsible for doing something':

> *Can I **leave** you to lock up the house?*
> *I **leave** you to choose.*

e *left* (past participle), is used after (not before) nouns and some pronouns, and means 'remaining', 'still there':

> *I can't go out this evening – I've no money **left**.*
> *'Is there anything **left** to eat?' 'There might be some cake **left**.'*

Contrast: *a **left**-luggage office*, a place at a station where you can leave luggage.

---

left: adjective, adverb, noun   ▶ Compare **right**

---

left is the opposite of *right*:

> *your **left** eye/hand/leg . . . Take a **left** turn . . .*
> *Keep **left** . . . Turn **left** . . .*
> *Our house is on the **left**.*
> *Take the second turning on the **left**.*

▶ See also **leave**

---

lend, lent, lent: verb   ▶ Compare **borrow**

> **lend** + (IO) + OBJECT

• give something to somebody for a short period of time
lend is the opposite of *borrow*:
lend like *give* can have one or two objects:

> *I don't like **lending** things.*
> *The library **lends** (out) records as well as books.*
> *Can you **lend** me your car this weekend?*
> *I'll **lend** it to you this time, but another time I might need it myself.*

length: noun ▶ See long

a *length* is the noun related to *long*, measuring things from end to end, in contrast to and *width* and *wide*:
> *What's the **length** of a football pitch?*
> *I can't read another book that **length**.*

b *length* can also refer to time:
> *He spoke at great **length**.* (= for a long time)

less

1 less: determiner and pronoun ▶ Compare **fewer; more**

- not so much; a smaller amount of

less is the comparative of *little*. The superlative is *least* and the opposite is *more*. Determiners, pronouns and adverbs are all the same. The comparison can be completed using *less . . . than . . .*

(a little) (a bit)			trouble money	(UNCOUNTABLE NOUNS)	
(much)			the/this/that . . . rice my/his . . . money	(UNCOUNTABLE NOUNS)	than
(a lot)	less	of	it/this/that. mine/yours . . .	(PRONOUNS)	
(even) (far) (rather)			than . . .		

a · *less* and *less of* are mainly used in a general sense or with uncountable nouns – in contrast to *fewer* and *fewer of* + PLURAL WORDS. After *less of* we use a determiner when a noun follows (*less of the rice* in contrast to *less rice*.) Various words as shown can come before *less*:
> *It's true I've lost weight. I must have been eating **less**.*
> *I'm sorry there's no rice left. There was **less** (of it) than I thought.*
> *We must plan more carefully and waste **less** money.*
> *I have nothing to do for an hour and even **less** if my ballpoint runs out.*
> *She's been having much **less** trouble since she's started these new pills.*
> *He has never done **less** than his best.*

b **less** + COUNT NOUNS (plural)
There is a rule that says we must only use *less* before uncountable nouns, and that we must use *fewer* with count nouns. But in fact this rule is not always followed:
>*?You have even **less** lectures than me.* (correct = *fewer*)
>*?They'll work **less** hours for the same money.* (or *fewer hours*)

c **less of** + COUNT NOUNS
less of is used with count nouns with several meanings:
>*I've read **less of** this book than I meant to* (= a smaller part of)
>*It was **less of** a success than we hoped.*
>*I shall see much **less of** my cousins now, because they'll be abroad.* (= see them less often)

Contrast:
>***Fewer of** my cousins ever visit me now – we're all too old.* (= not so many)

d **less than** + NUMBERS
With amounts of money, distances etc. that are treated as single units, *less* is normal (and *fewer* would be odd):
>*The two together came to a little **less than** £10.*
>*It's practically impossible for any student to buy the book for **less than** £3.*
>*We had walked rather **less than** two miles, when Claudia sat down and refused to go any further.*
>*There were only about 50 people or **less** at the meeting.*
>*There are **less than** 400 women members.*

e **no less than**
no less than often shows surprise at the large number. Notice the plural verbs:
>***No less than** 10% of the workers are involved in some kind of research.*
>*It appears that there are **no less than** five performances on Saturday.*

2 **less**: adverb ► Compare **more**

• to a smaller degree

less is the comparative of *little*. The superlative is *least* and the opposite is *more*.

A I was	(a little) (a bit) (much)		efficient		
B They come to see us	(a lot) (even)	**less**	often	(than) . . .	
C They talked	(far) (rather) (no) (any)				

As an adverb *less* is used with (*A*) adjectives (*less efficient*), (*B*) adverbs (*less often*) and (*C*) verbs (*talk less*). And again, it can have *a little*, *a bit*, etc. in front of it; and the comparison can be completed by *than*:

A   *I found that actually I was much less efficient when I knew exactly what I was supposed to be doing!*
This is no less true today than it was fifty years ago.
Today I felt less good than yesterday.
The chance of a home goal seemed even less likely.

B   *They come to see us far less often, now that they live so far away.*

C   *People talked much less about money in those days.*
I go to the theatre far less than I used to.

▶ See also **as . . . as . . .**

3   **less**: preposition

● minus
Total £2100 and £17, less payments already received of £1000. To pay £1117.

4   **less than** + ADJECTIVE

● not very
You are being less than honest/less than fair.

5   **The less . . . the less**

The less can form part of parallel structures with other comparative forms:
The less said about this unfortunate affair, the better. (= It will be worse if we discuss it.)
'A wise old owl lived in an oak,
The more he saw, the less he spoke,
The less he spoke, the more he heard!
Now wasn't he a wise old bird?'

6   **less and less**

less and less emphasises *less*:
I understand the modern world less and less.

▶ See   *more or less* at **more**

---

let, let, let: verb

let +	OBJECT
	O + BARE INFINITIVE
	O + COMPLEMENT
	go

---

1 • rent out a house, flat or room(s) to someone who pays regular rent for it
  *Flat to **let***
  *Mrs Green **lets** rooms to students.*

2 • allow, permit
let is used in various ways, including the pattern *let* + OBJECT + BARE INFINITIVE;
and *let* + OBJECT + COMPLEMENT. *Let* is not used in the passive, we use *allow* or
some other verb instead:
  *Please stop interrupting and **let** me speak (NOT *. . . to speak).*
  *My mother often **let** us watch TV when we were children.*
  *Please **let** me in/out/past.*
  ***Let** the dog alone.* (= stop annoying it)
  *Jim and I will meet you if you **let** us know what time your plane arrives.*

Notice also *let go* (= stop holding):
  ***Let go** (of my arm) – you're hurting me.*

3 let's

let's (sometimes *let us*) is used for making suggestions that include the speaker:
  ***Let's** go to the cinema tomorrow night.*
  *Don't **let's** quarrel any more.* (formally – ***let's** not.*)

(Notice that shortened *let's* is only used with this meaning.) Compare:
*Please **let us** watch TV, mummy!* (= allow us to watch)
***Let's** watch TV, shall we?* (a suggestion)

4 let alone

• even less; certainly not
let alone follows a negative statement, mentioning something even more
unlikely:
  *I can't even swim – **let alone** dive.*
  *I don't eat meat at all – **let alone** horsemeat!*

lie

1 lie, lay, lain: verb   ▶ Compare   **lay**

lie, lay, lain never has an object. It means 'to be in a flat or resting position':
  *The doctor says Rupert must **lie** flat on his back for a week.*
  *There were dirty coffee cups **lying** on his desk.*
  *The snow **lay** around for weeks.*
  *How long she had **lain** on the floor before they found her, I don't know.*

2 lie: regular verb and noun

• to tell lies (untruths)
  *Of course I didn't believe him – I knew he was **lying**.*

*She **lied** about her family and her money, because she wanted him to think she was rich.*
*Perhaps it is sometimes kinder to tell a **lie** than to tell/speak the truth.*

light

1 light: noun (C, U)

a *light* meaning the opposite of *darkness* is usually uncountable:
*There wasn't enough **light** for taking photographs.*
*She was reading by the **light** of the fire.*
*You're standing in my **light**.* (= preventing the light from a lamp, window etc. reaching me).

b *light* is countable when the meaning is a particular source of *light*, for example electric:
*The last person to leave the room, please turn off the **lights**.*
*Stop! The **lights** (i.e. the traffic lights) are red.*
Also: *Can you give me a **light**? (i.e. for my cigarette).*

2 light, lighter, lightest: adjective

As an adjective *light* has two main meanings.
a ● the opposite of *dark*
*We have long **light** evenings in the summer, but in winter it gets dark early in the afternoon.*
*The **light** blue shirt was nice, but I decided the dark blue (one) was more practical.*

b ● the opposite of *heavy*
*The case is **lighter** than it looks – the small one's much heavier.*
*We were only wearing **light** summer clothes.*

Also *a **light** meal* (= a small amount of food) . . . ***light** entertainment* (= easy to enjoy)

3 light, lit, lit (or **lighted, lighted**): verb

a If you *light* something you make it burn with a flame, so you can *light* a (coal) fire, or a candle, or a cigarette or possibly a gas fire, but you *turn on* or *switch on* an electric fire, central heating or electric lights. We can however *light* streets, buildings etc. with electricity:
*The streets were badly **lit**.*

b *light* can be used without an object:
*The wood was so damp, we couldn't get it to **light**.*

c *lit* is the usual past tense and past participle, except in front of a noun:
*The tragedy was probably caused by a **lighted** match.*

like

1 like: verb ▶ Compare **love**

> OBJECT
> **(would) like +** *-ing*
>   *you/your -ing*
>   (o) + *to* INFINITIVE . . .

a like + OBJECT, like + *-ing*
• to be fond of; to enjoy
If we *like* certain things or people, we are fond of them. If we *like* doing
something, we enjoy this.
American English sometimes uses *to*-INFINITIVE with this meaning:
> *I like him, but I don't love him.*
> *I like hard work, but I also like holidays.*
> *She likes getting letters, but she doesn't like having to answer them.*
> *Do you like talking about life?*
> *I don't like you/your laughing at me – please stop!*
> *I don't like it when you laugh at me.*

b like + *you/your -ing*
If we *(don't) like* somebody *doing* something we can say:
> *I don't like you/your laughing at me – please stop!*

Some people think the possessive is 'correct', but it is not always possible:
> *He doesn't like anyone using his things.* (NOT *anyone's)

c *like* is usually a stative verb, not used in progressive tenses, but with this
meaning of 'enjoy', a progressive tense is possible:
> *How are you liking your new school?*

d like (+ OBJECT) + *to*-INFINITIVE
If we *like to do* something we choose or prefer to do it, possibly as a regular
habit and perhaps because we think it is a good idea. If we *like* someone else to
do something, we want them to, we are pleased whenever they do it:
> *I like to have regular meals, if I possibly can.*
> *They like to keep the best jobs for themselves.*
> *She liked the children to be in bed by 7 o'clock.*
> *I like everything to be as comfortable as possible.*

e like doing or **like to do**?
Sometimes both *like + -ing* and *like + to*-INFINITIVE are possible, but the
meaning is never exactly the same:
> *I like swimming.* (= I swim and I enjoy it.)
> *I like to swim.* (= Perhaps I think it is good for my health – I choose to swim
> when it is possible.)

Both *I like to do* and *I liked to do* something suggest repeated actions or a
habit, and there may be no sense of enjoyment:
> *I like to go to the dentist twice a year.*

like + *-ing* can refer to a single occasion or several occasions, or to some permanent state:

> *We quite **liked** camping, but once was enough.* (NOT *to camp . . . in this sentence)
> *I always **liked** camping when I was young.*
> *Do you **like** living in London? – or do you just live there because you always have done?* (NOT **Do you **like** to live* . . .)

Negative *don't like* + *to*-INFINITIVE can refer to a single occasion, but the meaning can sometimes be very different:

> *I didn't **like** telling her.* (= but I had to)
> *I didn't **like** to tell her.* (perhaps I chose not to)

f *like* normally needs an object or a verb after it. So the answers to:

a. *Do you **like** talking about life?*
b. *Do you **like** to have regular meals?*

can be *Yes, I do*/*No, I don't* (a. and b.)
or *Yes, I **like** to*/*No, I don't **like** to* (b.)
but NOT **Yes, I **like**.*/*No, I don't **like**.*

However a few expressions do use *like* without a following word:

> *Come early if you **like**.*
> *Come when you **like**.*
> *Please do as you **like**.*

g **would/should like** (+ OBJECT) + *to*-INFINITIVE

As with other stative verbs, *like* in the simple present tense expresses a state now (*Oh I **like** your jacket. Where did you get it?*) or a state that has existed for some time (*I **like** rolls and coffee for breakfast, I **like** living in London, I **like** to have regular meals*).

Would often expresses a condition. So *I would like* is often a polite way of saying *I want* . . . *if* . . . , and *Would you like* . . .? or *Would you like (me) to* . . .? is a polite way of making an offer.

Would like (+ *to*-INFINITIVE) talks about the future and can refer to one occasion only:

> *What **would** you **like** for dinner, John?*
> *I **would like** a copy of the programme of language courses, please.* (request)
> *I **would like** to confirm that the 4th March is convenient for me.*
> *Perhaps you **would like** to come and watch a bit of parachuting?* (suggestion)
> *If you **would like** to telephone us when you have them we will call to collect them.* (request)
> *I **should (would) like** to have a bigger flat.* (= if it were possible)
> *I **should like** to have regular meals if I could.*
> *Would you **like** me to arrange this for you?* (offer)
> *I'd **like** this homework done by Friday, everybody!* (request. Notice *like* + OBJECT + PAST PARTICIPLE)

would like + *ing* is of course possible with the meaning of 'enjoy':

> *It's a super hotel. You'd **like** staying there.*

h **would like to have** + PAST PARTICIPLE/**would have liked** *to* + INFINITIVE

Both of these patterns express a wish about something not done in the past:

> *We had a long talk about certain things which I **would have liked** to say at an earlier date.* (OR . . . *which I **would like** to have said* . . .) (i.e., at last I said them. I wish I had said them before.)

2 like: preposition ▶ Compare **alike; as**

a • similar to; in the same way (as)
*His Mum looks more **like** his sister than his Mum.*
*He is 24 and behaves **like** a three-year-old.*
*She smokes, thought Madeleine, **like** a chimney.*
*It was **like** being under water – he felt he was drowning.*
***Like** me, you've had a lot of problems in your life.*
*There's no need to shout **like** that.* (= in the way you are shouting)
*It looks **like** rain.* (= The weather looks as if it is going to rain.)
*The next few days look **like** being as busy as the last few.* (= as if
they are going to be . . .)

b What is/are . . . like?
• Describe it/them . . .
*What is your father **like**?* (= What kind of man is he?)
*What is it **like** being at university?* (= Tell us about it.)

c • such as; for example
*This morning we were busy with routine affairs **like** going to the
bank, shopping and posting some parcels.*
*I'd like to do something exciting – **like** learning to fly or climbing
Mt Everest.*

d • typical of
*That's just **like** Crispin to send such beautiful flowers – he's always
so generous.*

e feel like
If people say they *feel like* something, or *feel like doing* something,
they mean they would like that:
*I **feel like** a nice evening, eating, drinking and dancing.*
*I don't **feel like** writing letters.*

f (not) anything/nothing like
anything like and *nothing like* are used in non-assertive contexts, with
the meaning, 'at all':
*It's **nothing like** as/so warm as it was yesterday.* (= not nearly as
warm)
*Was Cape Town **anything like** you had expected?*

▶ See also *anywhere like* at **anywhere**

g quite like/rather like
like is an unusual preposition and can have adverbs *quite* or *rather* in
front of it:
*It's **quite like** old times.*
*That's **rather like** saying Yes and No at the same time!*

3 like: conjunction

a • In the way that; how; as (informal)
Many people regard this use of *like* as non-standard, and prefer *as*. But
like is commonly used when we compare two (or more) people/things:
*He looks just **like** his father did at his age.*
*?Do it **like** I told you.*

*?If I played **like** he umpired, I'd be ranked 5,000th in the world.* (John McEnroe talking about a tennis umpire!)
*We should let our children behave **like** they want to.*

b • as if/as though
Using *like* instead of *as if/as though* is common, particularly in informal American English. But it is safer to use *as if*:
*?I felt **like** somebody had hit me on the head.*
*?It was **like** we were travelling through time.*

---

likely; unlikely ▶ Compare **bound**; **certain**; **sure**

1 likely: adjective

Frost (*A*)	is		
The situation (*B*)	appears looks	**likely** **unlikely**	to become more serious.
It (*C*)	seems		that . . .

a Predicative adjective
If something *is* (or *appears/looks/seems*) *likely*, it is probably going to happen. The opposite is *unlikely*. Notice we can say (*A*) something is *likely*, (*B*) something or somebody is *likely* + *to*-INFINITIVE and (*C*) It is *likely that* . . .:
(*A*) *Where severe frost is **likely**, you should protect the pipes to prevent freezing.*
   *The chance of a home goal seemed even less **likely**.*
(*B*) *What seems **likely** to happen?*
   *The action is not **likely** to be a popular one.*
   *The situation is serious and is **unlikely** to improve.*
   *The problem of the water supply is **likely** to increase further.*
(*C*) *It seems to me more than **likely** that a mental hospital really would send him mad.*
   *It does seem **likely** that the second suggestion was better.*

b Attributive adjective
• probable
   *What are the **likely** developments of such a movement?*
   *I think that your explanation is probably the more **likely** one.*

2 likely: adverb

• probably
As an adverb, likely is usually preceded by *very*, *most*, *quite*:
   *He will very **likely** hear from them before they hear from us.*
   *This is most **likely** the computer your children will be familiar with at school.*

---

listen (to): verb ▶ Compare **hear; look (at)**

The difference between *listen (to)* and *hear* is like the difference between *look (at)* and *see*. We *hear* simply because we have ears. But we can decide to *listen* or not *listen* (to sounds, to what people say, etc.). *Listen* is never followed by a direct object. It can be used alone or we use *listen to* + OBJECT:

Listen! *Is that thunder?*
*If you stopped talking and **listened** (to me), you might learn something.*
*I heard something about this on the radio, but I wasn't really **listening**.*

---

little

1 little: adjective ▶ Compare **small**

little is the opposite of *big*

a *little* does not mean quite the same as *small*, because it often expresses an emotional attitude (e.g., affection, amusement, dislike):

*You must let me break all the rules and give you a **little** kiss today.*
*I have a single room with my own **little** bed.*
*What a dear **little** girl! . . . such a silly **little** man . . .*

b *little* is usually used before a noun. (so? *He is little*, is odd.) Comparative and superlative *littler* and *littlest* are very rare and informal. It is usually better to use *smaller* and *smallest*.

2 (a) little: determiner and pronoun ▶ Compare **few**

● not much; a small amount (of)

The comparative is *less* and the superlative is *least*. *Little* is the opposite of much.

(a) (how)		food money	(UNCOUNTABLE NOUNS)	
(so) **little**	of	the/this/that my/his . . .	money work (UNCOUNTABLE NOUNS)	
((far) too) (very)		it this/that mine/yours . . .	(PRONOUNS)	

a *(a) little* is mainly used in a general sense (*I know **(a) little** about the problem*) or with uncountable nouns – in contrast to *few* + PLURAL NOUNS. *(A) little of* needs a determiner before a following noun (*(a) **little** of the money* in contrast to *(a) **little** money*). Various words – not only *a* – can come before *little* as shown.

b   *a little* has positive meaning, 'at least some':
> *I ought to do just a **little** work.*
> *She is now beginning to get a **little** pain in the right hip.*
> *I knew a **little** of his work before he arrived.*
> *I can only pay back a **little** of the money.*

c   *little* on its own is negative and has the meaning 'almost no', 'almost nothing'. It takes a positive tag:
> *For nearly an hour Simmons did **little** but watch and wait.*
> *There is **little** chance of his changing his mind, is there?*
> ***Little** effort was made to change things.*
> ***Little** of the money was ever found.*

It is rather formal. Less formally we could say:
> *There's **not much** chance of his changing his mind, is there?*

To emphasise negative *little*, we can use *how, so, very* and *(far) too* – meaning 'almost no/none, hardly enough, not enough':
> ***How little** we really know about our children!*
> *There is **so little** to do when you get here.*
> *In the flood plains . . . too much water is often as great a danger as **too little**.*
> ***Very little** heat is necessary.*
> *He was helpful, but he really knew **very little** himself.*

d   The pronoun *(a) little + of* can be used with singular and plural count nouns:
> *I read a **little of** my book and then watched TV.* (= a small part of . . .)
> *I see very **little of** my parents these days.* (= I do not often see them.)

3   a little/little: adverbs

● not much

The comparative is *less* and the superlative is *least*. *(A) little* is the opposite of *much* (and *a lot*). All these words are also determiners and pronouns.

(a) little	more/less more/less money nicer, colder . . . sooner, later . . . more/less expensive more/less frequently	(than . . .)

a   **With comparatives**   ► **Compare   a lot; lots; much**

As with the pronouns and determiners, the adverbial use of *a little* has a positive meaning 'a bit' – 'to some extent'. It is much commoner than *little*, which has a meaning that is almost negative – 'hardly', 'almost not'. *(a) little* is used with *more* and *less* and with comparative adjectives and adverbs:
> *Could I have a **little** more sugar, please?*
> *Bessie is feeling a **little** better than she was, though not much.*
> *He went into the station, where it was a **little** cooler.*
> *You're tired. You must take things a **little** easier.*

*When we look **a little** more closely, the situation seems quite different.*
*All left by 8.45, except Donald, who stayed **a little** later.*
*They did it **little** better the second time.* (= hardly any better)

b *a little* (but NOT **little*) – meaning 'slightly', 'a bit' – is also used with positive
(i.e., not comparative) adjectives and adverbs:
*All this may sound **a little** alarming.*
*It is **a little** inconvenient.*
*I've just gone **a little** pink from the sun.*
*They arrived **a little** late.*

c **little different**
   ● not very different; almost the same
   *The position was **little different** from what it is today.*

d **a little too**
   If something is *a little too* hard/soft, etc., it is a bit too hard/soft, etc.:
   *It was all a **little too** good to be true.*
   *I'm sorry if I took a **little too** much.*

4 (a) little: adverb (with verbs)

a With verbs, *a little* is much commoner than *little* by itself although *so/too/very
little* are possible with an almost negative meaning:
*She was self-conscious about her height; she stooped **a little** and wore flat
shoes.*
*A few people in the monastery do speak **a little** apparently.*
*Enlarge the hole **a little** with a nail.*
*I'm afraid I play tennis/so/too/very **little** now – I'm really out of practice.*

b *little* on its own is only used with a few verbs and comes in mid-position – rather
like *hardly*, and has roughly the same meaning (i.e., 'almost never'):
*I **little** knew/realized/thought how difficult it would be.*
*It was a method which never satisfied the best teachers, and it is **little** used
now.*

c If *little* comes at the very front, we need subject and auxiliary inversion, just as
we do with real negative adverbs:
***Little** did I realise how difficult it would be.*

live and life

1 live /lɪv/: verb
   *Where do you **live**?*
   *I'm **living** in Kensington at present, but I haven't **lived** there very long.*
   *She **lived** to be ninety.* (= until she was ninety)

2 live /laɪv/: adjective   ► See **alive**

3 life /laɪf/, **lives** /laɪvz/: noun (C, U)

   *You've only got one **life** – make the most of it.*
   *I'm reading the **life** of Lord Byron.* (= the story of his life)

*They say cats have nine **lives**.*
*Is there **life** on any other planet?* (= animals and plants)

'll ▶ See **will**

---

lone: lonely: adjectives Compare **alone**

Both *lone* and *lonely* mean 'without other people'. *Lone* has the meaning of being the only one in a place, *lonely* suggests that a person is unhappy because they are alone.

a *lone* is attributive only:

*The hotel was called **The Lone Pine** because it was near a single pine tree on the beach.*
***Lone** sailors often enjoy the experience of sailing alone.*

b *lonely* is both attributive and predicative:

*Simon felt **lonely**, even though there were other people there.*
*He was always a **lonely** child.*

---

long, longer, longest ▶ Compare **short**

---

1 long, longer, longest: adjective

The adjective *long* is used to measure the length of things and periods of time. It is often the opposite of *short*, but people are *tall* (NEVER **long*):

*How **long** is a piece of string?* (No answer to this one.)
*We were a **long** way from home – it took us a **long** time to walk back.*
*We need a table six feet **long** and three feet wide.*
*a **long** life . . . **long** hair . . . a **long** dress . . . **long** legs . . . **long**-sighted . . .*
*The days are getting shorter and the nights are getting **longer**.*
*If you live in the southern hemisphere 22nd December is the **longest** day.*

▶ See **far**

2 long, longer, longest: adverb

a As an adverb, *long* only refers to time. It is mainly used in questions and negative sentences and in end-position. For affirmative statements we prefer *a long time, a long while*:

*'Have you been waiting **long**?' 'No, not **long** – only five minutes.'*
*I can't stay **long**.*
*Although we have known each other **for a long time**, I still don't feel I know her very well.*

b no longer/not . . . any longer

We can use *no longer* or *not . . . any longer* to talk about time – something used to happen, but it has now stopped. *No longer* is more emphatic. Notice the different positions for the two phrases:

*This theory **no longer** convinces me.*
*Her hair **no longer** fell all over her face.*

---

*The children are grown up now and **no longer** need looking after.*
*My muscles **no longer** ache from all the riding.*
*I can **no longer** afford to run a car.*
*I am **not** going to wait **any longer**.*
*My muscles don't ache **any longer**.*

We can also use *not . . . any more*, with roughly the same meaning, but not
*no more:

*My muscles don't ache **any more**.* (NOT **My muscles **no more** ache.* **My
muscles ache **no more**.*)

c *long* on its own is sometimes used affirmatively in mid-position, but this is
rather formal:

*It has **long** been known that there is a close connection between food and
health.* (or *It has been known **for a long time** that . . .*)

long is also used in affirmative sentences in phrases like *long after, long before,
long ago*:

*They arrived home **long after/long before** midnight.*
*This all happened **long ago**.* (or *a **long time/while ago**.*)

d *long, longer, longest* can also be used affirmatively when they have various
other words in front of them as shown:

*Stay as **long** as you like.*
*Sorry I've kept you waiting so **long**.*
*This job is taking me (far/much) **longer** than I expected.*
*We'll just wait a bit/a few minutes **longer**.*
*The **longest** I've ever lived in one place is three years.*

3 **long**: noun

*I expect we'll hear from them before **long**.*

4 **as/so long as**: conjunction

as/so long as is not only used with reference to time (see **2d**), it can also mean
'provided/providing that' or 'on condition that':

*We won't worry **as long as** we know where you are.*

---

look: verb

	—
	at, for . . .
	what/where . . .
look +	
	ADJECTIVE
	NOUN
	like . . .
	as if, as though . . .

a One meaning of *look* is rather like '*see*' (but seeing because we decide to use our eyes.) Unlike *see*, *look* normally needs a preposition before a noun. However *look* without a preposition, particularly if it is an imperative, can be followed by some *wh*-CLAUSES:

*I'm just wrapping up your birthday present. Don't **look**.*
*'Can I help you?' 'No thanks. I'm just **looking**.*
*Why are you **looking at** me like that?*
*I'm **looking for** my glasses and I've **looked** everywhere.*
***Look** where you're walking!* (= be careful.)
***Look** what you've done.* (= You are careless.)

b *look* can also mean 'appear' or 'seem'. With this meaning *look* is followed by an ADJECTIVE/NOUN/*like*/*as if* or *as though*. (Compare *sound*, and notice that *look* is not used in all the patterns that *appear* and *seem* are):

*You **look** well – have you just had a holiday?*
*Maria **looks** annoyed/happy/pleased/worried.*
*The place **looked** dirty.*
*He **looks** a nice person.*
*It **looks** like rain.* (= I think it's going to rain.)
*She **looks** just like her mother.*
*She **looked** as if/as though she was going to cry.*
*It **looks** as if/as though we shall have to cancel the meeting.*

c look forward to   ▶ Compare **ahead**

When we *look forward to* something we expect it is going to happen, and we are pleased about it. The *to* here is a preposition, so it must be followed by a noun phrase or a verb in the *-ing* form; it is not part of a *to*-infinitive, and is never followed by an infinitive:

*They are all **looking forward to** the holiday.*
*I **look forward to** hearing from you soon.* (NOT **I **look forward to** hear from you soon.*)

loose and lose

1 loose /lu:s/: adjective

● not firm; not tight

All sorts of things can be *loose* – *a **loose** tooth* . . . ***loose**-fitting clothes* . . . *a **loose**-leaf book* (a file or book that you can fit loose pages into, for writing on). If a screw in something is *loose* you might tighten it up. If a button *comes loose*, it needs sewing on properly.

2 lose /lu:z/, **lost, lost**: verb

a *lose* is the opposite of *find*:

*I've **lost** my purse – I can't think what I've done with it.*

b *lose* is the opposite of *win*:

*Arsenal **lost** their match against Spurs.*
*No country wants to **lose** a war.*

c A more general meaning is 'no longer have' or 'have less of':

*He **lost** a leg in the war.*
*Valerie's **lost** her job.*

*Don't **lose** your temper* (= get angry)
*We **lost** our way and had to ask.*
*Thousands of working days are **lost** through illness.*
*I'm trying to **lose** weight.*

lost: adjective

If we are *lost* we do not know which way to go. If something is *lost* we cannot
find it:
*We were/We got **lost** and had to ask the way.*
***lost** property . . . a home for **lost** dogs . . .*

lot

Grammatically *lot* is a noun, but *a lot* and *lots* are used informally in some
rather special ways.

1 a lot (of), lots (of): determiners and pronouns ▶ Compare **many; much**

a *a lot (of)* and *lots (of)* are used with uncountable nouns to mean *much* (*a lot of
noise*) and with plural count nouns to mean *many* (*lots of toys*).
a lot (of) and *lots (of)* are particularly common with uncountable nouns in
affirmative statements (*I eat **a lot of** fish.*) because *much* is rather formal
(▶ See **much**). Verbs are singular or plural according to the noun they go
with (i.e., we can say *a lot of . . . is/are* and *lots of . . . is/are . . .*). *Lots of* is
more informal than *a lot of*:
*He makes **a lot of** noise, doesn't he? Yes **a lot**.*
*I want **lots of** money and a car and clothes.*
*There is always **lots** to do.* (Note: singular verb).
*Would he expect **a lot** to drink?*
***a lot of** good things have happened since then.* (Note: plural verb)
*A **lot of** people here are not well off.*
*I'm getting to know **lots of** people.*
*And darling, **lots and lots of** love.*

b With a singular count noun, the meaning is 'a large part of':
*I managed to read **a lot of** my book this morning.*

2 a lot (and **lots**): adverbs (with comparatives)

▶ Compare **a little; much**

a lot (lots)	more/less more/less money more people nicer, colder . . . sooner, later . . . more/less expensive more/less frequently	than . . .

a lot and sometimes *lots* are used as adverbs with comparatives, and mean 'very much', 'a great deal':

> *We've got some food in the house but we need **a lot** more for the weekend.*
> ***A lot** less noise please – I can't hear myself speak.*
> *I thought the exam was **a lot** more difficult than last year.*
> *You'd get here **a lot** quicker if you came by train.*
> *If they came on Saturday instead, it would be **lots** better.*

3 adverbs: with verbs

With verbs *a lot* and occasionally *lots* are also used with the meaning 'very much', 'a great deal'. They take end-position. Again, the usage is informal and *a lot* is more usual:

> *The problem is – I'm going round with Tony **a lot**, so I can't really 'flirt' with anyone.*
> *I think of you **lots**, even if I don't write.*

4 the lot: noun

- everything; all of it/them
  > *'Can I borrow some of these magazines?' 'Take **the lot** – I've read them.'*

love

1 love: verb ▶ Compare **like**

```
         OBJECT
love  +  -ing
         you/your . . . ing
         (o+) to-INFINITIVE
```

a **love** + OBJECT
- like very much; be very fond of
  > *I **love** my parents/my brother/my country/freedom.*
  > *I like him very much, but I don't **love** him.*
  > *Who do you really **love**?*

b We often say we *love* less important things:
> *I **love** my new job/chocolate cake/this warm weather/Venice/detective stories/ pop music.*
> *I **love** it when you laugh.*

Questions and negative statements about such things are not very usual with *love*; instead we often use *like*:
> *'Do you **like** this weather?' 'Oh I **love** this heat, but I don't **like** the rain.'*

c **love** + (*you/your* +) -*ing*
love + -*ing* usually means 'enjoy'. If we *love* somebody else doing something, we can say that we *love them* doing it or we *love their* doing it:
> *I **love** getting letters, but I don't like having to answer them.*
> *He **loves** reading/doing nothing/skiing/making things/walking in the rain.*
> *I **loved** you/your saying that – you were so right!*

d *love* is usually a stative verb, but progressive tenses are possible with the meaning of 'enjoy':
  *'How's Crispin getting on at college?' 'Oh, he's **loving** it.'*

e **love** + *to*-INFINITIVE
  If we *love to do something*, we very much like/prefer to do it, probably as a habit:
  *The family all **love to be** together at Christmas.*
  *I **love to see** the spring flowers, don't you?*

f **love doing** or **(would) love to do?**
  If you *love doing* something, the 'doing' verb refers to something that has already happened or is happening – though possibly only once – and you enjoy this. If you *love* (or *would love*) *to do* something, you choose (or would choose) to do this action – you decide you will do it. So there are differences between:
  *I **love being** busy. (When I am busy, I enjoy it.)*
  *I **love to be** busy. (I choose to be busy, whenever this is possible.)*

  Only *love* + *-ing* is possible when we refer to a single past or present occasion, or to something where we cannot choose:
  *We **loved** seeing you last weekend – you must come again.* (NOT *We **loved to** see you . . .*)
  *I **love** having four brothers.* (NOT *I **love to** have . . .*, because this is not something I can choose.)

g **would/should love** (+ OBJECT) *to*-INFINITIVE
  would love (+ o) + *to do* can refer to a single future occasion. It is often used for polite statements, offers and invitations:
  *We**'d love** to know what really happened. Wouldn't you?*
  *'Can you and Marie come to dinner on Saturday?' 'Oh, thank you, we**'d love** to'.*
  *We**'d love** you to come on holiday with us. Can you?*
  *I**'d love** to help, but I'm afraid I can't.*

  would love + *to*-INFINITIVE suggests choice:
  *My wife **would love** to meet you.* (I know because she has told me.) But:
  *?You **would love** to meet her.* (This is odd, because I do not know what you would choose to do.)

2 **love**: noun (usually U)
a **Love** *makes the world go round, they say.*
  Love *of money is the root of all evil.*
  *You don't show me much **love** and affection, do you?*
  *They were only sixteen when they fell in **love**.*
  *He has a great **love** for the old.*

b In social life we can *give* or *send love*, – which means friendly good wishes:
  *'I saw Muriel yesterday and she sends you her **love**.' 'Oh, how nice. Do give her my **love** when you see her.'*

c Letters to members of one's family or close friends often end:
  *(My) **love** to you all/to John and the children/to you and John.*
  *(With) **love** from . . .*

  love is not usually used by men writing to men.

low, lower, lowest: adjective and adverb ▶ Compare **high**

low is usually the opposite of *high* as an adjective and adverb

a   *It's an old cottage with **low** ceilings.*

Also ***low** hills . . . **low** pay . . . **low** prices . . . **low** temperatures . . .*

b   *The plane flew **low** over the house.*
*The **lowest** paid have a real problem.*
*It's too hot in here – can you turn the central heating down **lower**?*

'm ▶ See **am** (at **be**)

main: adjective

main means 'chief', 'most important'. It has no comparative or superlative forms:
*Be careful how you cross the **main** road.*
*The **main** thing is not to worry about the exam, but to do your best.*

make, made, made: verb

```
          (IO) + OBJECT
          O + COMPLEMENT
make +    O + BARE INFINITIVE
          certain, sure
```

1 • produce something that did not exist before ▶ Compare **do**

a   *Factories/people **make** cars/clothes/furniture . . . you can **make** sandwiches/a cake/a pot of tea . . . you can **make** an appointment/an arrangement/a decision/an effort/an excuse/a (good or bad) impression/a mistake/money (= earn money, become rich) /a noise/an offer/a phone call/a plan/a suggestion/ trouble . . . you can **make** use of something . . .*
*The students have to **make** their own beds. (= tidy them)*
***Make** love, not war!*
*Nothing I say **makes** any difference. (= nobody listens to my advice)*
*My jumper isn't **made** of wool – the label says it's acrylic.*
*Different wines are **made** from different sorts of grapes.*

b *make* can take two objects:
> *My mother's **making** me a jumper.* (or *She's **making** a jumper for me.*)
> *Shall I **make** you a nice cup of tea?*
> ***Make** me an offer!*

c **make** + OBJECT + COMPLEMENT
- cause something/somebody to be . . .
> *The news has **made** me angry/unhappy/ill.*
> *You are **making** things difficult for yourself.*
> *This medicine will **make** you better.*
> *They **made** it very clear that they did not agree with me.*
> *Why didn't they **make** James chairman?*

2 make + OBJECT + BARE INFINITIVE ▶ Compare **let**
- cause/force somebody to do something
When *make* is followed by an object plus verb we use the INFINITIVE without *to*. In the passive, however, we use the *to* + INFINITIVE:
> *They **made** us play football in the rain.*
> *We were **made to** play football in the rain.*

3 make certain/sure (that) . . .
> *Please **make** certain/sure that you have closed all the windows and turned off the lights before you leave the room.* (= be certain that . . .)

man (plural **men**): noun

a As well as meaning an adult male person, man has some more special meanings:
> *The women were waiting for news of their **men**.* (= their husbands and lovers)
> *All leave* (= holiday time) *has been cancelled for officers and **men**.* (= ordinary soldiers, sailors etc.)
> *I need a **man** to mend the taps.* (= a workman)

b Compound nouns that include the word *man* also make their plurals with *men* – *businessmen, chairmen, Frenchmen, milkmen, policemen, postmen, workmen* . . . Some of these nouns definitely mean men only, but do not cause problems of 'sexual bias' because there are corresponding feminine words (*a businesswoman, a Frenchwoman*) or neutral words that can be used in the plural (*business people, French people, the French, workers, (the) police*). *Chairman* has traditionally been used for either sex, but some people now object to this and use '*chairperson*' or even '*chair*'.

c *man* (without *a* or *the*) and sometimes *men* can mean 'people' (or both sexes), 'mankind':
> *Prehistoric **man** had a short, hard life.*
> ***Man** is the only creature with language.*
> *Peace on Earth, goodwill towards **men**.* (in the Bible)

This usage too annoys some people, who prefer words such as *people, human beings*.

| **many**: determiner and pronoun | ▶ Compare **much** |

- a great number of; a lot/lots of

The comparative is *more*, the superlative is *most*, and the opposite is *few*.

(how)	people advantages (pl)	
(so) ((far) too) **many**	of	the/these/those . . . books (pl) my/her . . . friends
(not(very))		these/those mine/ours . . . (PRONOUNS) you/us/them

a *many* and *many of* are used with plural count nouns and plural pronouns as shown. *Many of* needs a determiner before a following noun (e.g., *many of those people* in contrast to *many people*).

Many is common in questions and negatives, but formal in affirmative sentences, where we often prefer *a lot/lots of*. *How many* is used to talk about numbers. *Not (very) many* means 'only a few':

*How **many** readers remember his story?*
*Are there **many** lakes in your country?*
*There were not **many** at the meeting but we got quite a lot done.* (= *not **many** people*)
*The trouble is there are not **many** other places to go except Iceland.*
*I haven't had very **many** late nights, but all the same I'm tired.*
***Many** congratulations to you and Hattie on (the birth of) your new daughter.* (*a lot* would be too informal here)
*They would have **many** advantages to offer.*
*This is a problem that **many** of the small farmers have to face.*
*A few of the rivers are now overflowing, but **many** of them are no fuller than before.*
***Many** people don't know about this.*

b To emphasise *many*, we can use *so* and *(far) too*. *As many as . . .* emphasises a surprisingly large number:

*I never knew there were **so many** portable television sets on the market until I saw them in their very own department.*
*There are **far too many** characters in the book and it is impossible to remember who they all are.*
*As **many** as 80,000 visitors came in a single year.*

c *many* by itself is almost never used at the end, or near the end, of affirmative sentences (though *how many*, *so many*, *too many* are possible):

*(Have we got enough chairs? **How many** do we need? Do we need 500?)*

NEGATIVE: *There aren't **(very) many**.*
AFFIRMATIVE: *There are **a lot/lots** here.* (NOT *There are **many**.*)

---

*We need **a lot/lots**.* (NOT **We need **many**.*)
*I'll tell you in a minute **how many**.*
*We need **so many**.*
*500 would be far **too many**.*

marriage ▶ See **marry**

marry and marriage

1 marry: verb

- become somebody's husband or wife

marry can be used with or without a direct object:

a *Will you **marry** me?*
   *She dreams of **marrying** a tall dark handsome man.*
   *Alan has **married** that lovely Spanish girl he met on holiday.*
   *Clara didn't **marry** until she was 40.*
   *He'd like to **marry** and have a family.*

b *get married* is less formal and more usual than *marry* when grammatically
   there is no direct object. If there is an object *get married* is followed by *to*:
   *Clara didn't **get married** until she was 40.*
   *He'd like to **get married** and have a family.*
   *Michael and Lucy are **getting married** in June.*
   *When are you going to **get married**?*
   *I think he **got married** to someone much older than himself.*

c *be married* can refer to the actual wedding:
   *They **were married**/They **got married** in January 1980.*

   but *be married* often refers to the state, not the event:
   *My parents have **been married** (for) nearly thirty years.*
   *We **are married** now.*
   *She **is married** to a man much younger than herself.*

d *marry* can also mean 'officially perform a marriage':
   *Her uncle, the Bishop, **married** them.*

2 marriage: noun (C, U)

The noun *marriage* too can mean the event (the wedding), but often means the
state:
*Their **marriage** in Westminster Abbey was one of the biggest events of the
year.*
*Some feminists do not believe in **marriage**.*

matter

1 matter: noun (C)

a - a subject or situation of some importance
   *This is a **matter** of great importance to me.*

*Don't interfere – you're just making **matters** worse.* (= making things more difficult)
*He said it was a private **matter**, and he didn't want to discuss it.*
*Look, I'm not going to discuss business **matters** over dinner.*
*That is a **matter** of opinion – and I certainly do not agree.*

For *as a matter of fact* ▶ See **fact**

b the matter (with)   ▶ Compare **wrong**
the matter (with) is used with *what/anything/nothing/something* to ask if anything is wrong or to say that something is wrong:
*What's **the matter** with Geoffrey? He looks very upset. Something's **the matter** with him, but what?*
*Is anything/something **the matter**?*
*Stop worrying. There's nothing **the matter**./Nothing's **the matter**.*
We cannot begin a sentence with '*The matter is* . . .' in this meaning.

2 No matter + *wh-*CLAUSES
No matter is usually used as a conjunction, so it joins a clause to a main clause. It roughly means 'It doesn't matter', or 'it doesn't make any difference', but it is not used with just a single clause:
*She won't change her mind, **no matter what** you say.*
***No matter where** he is, he insists on reading the Times every day.*
NOT **No matter where* you sit – sit anywhere.*

(Compare *matter* as a verb as in *It doesn't **matter*** – below)

3 matter: verb (not usually in progressive)

If something *matters* (to us), it is important or it makes a difference. It is often used in questions and negative sentences:
*Nothing **matters** to me except your happiness.*
*Surely your family **matters** to you more than money?*
*Does it **matter** if I sign in red ink?*
*What does it **matter** if I break it? – I can buy another.*
*Of course it **matters**. You shouldn't break things.*
*It doesn't **matter** what I do/where I go/how hard I try – she won't change her mind.*
*'I'm sorry I'm late.' 'Oh, it doesn't **matter**'.*
*It doesn't **matter** where you sit – sit anywhere.*

---

may: modal verb   ▶ Compare **can**; **could**; **might**

may refers to the present and the future. The negative is *may not*, (*mayn't* is very rare).
may has two main meanings: (1) a practical meaning concerned with permission, and (2) a theoretical meaning – 'it is possible/that . . .' 'it is (perhaps) likely that . . .':

1 Permission now

a *may* is more formal than *can*:
*May I borrow your pen? Yes, of course you **may**.*

May I speak to Maria, please?
May we let you know later?
May I just interrupt you for a moment?
May I give you some advice? (an offer)

b *may* is usually connected with permission that can be given by the speaker:
*Ladies and gentlemen, you **may** smoke.*

Contrast a speaker describing a rule made by somebody else, where *can* is better:
*You **can** smoke in some cinemas, but in many theatres you **can't**/**you are not allowed to.***

c *may* cannot be replaced by *can* in the phrase, *If I **may** say so*:
*That's very attractive, **if I may say so**.* (= if you'll allow me to say so)

d *may not* means something is forbidden/not allowed. Again it is the speaker or writer who makes the rule:
*Food **may not** be brought into the library.* (Notice in a library.)

2 Possibility or likelihood (present or future) ▶ Compare **could; might**

a *may* is used to express possibility or likelihood in the present or future. It can refer to a single occasion:
*Paul **may** be in Hong Kong by now.*
*He **may** be 70 – I just don't know.*
*Bob **may** know the answer.*
*It **may** rain here tomorrow. It **may** already be raining in London.*
*Charles **may** arrive next week.*
*I **may** not be here. I **may** be leaving at the weekend.*

b When *may* expresses a possibility, it is not often used in direct questions:
NOT **May Bob know the answer?* (Say: *Do you think Bob knows . . .* or *Is Bob likely to know?* or *Could/Might Bob know?*)

c *may* expressing possibility is sometimes used with a meaning of concession, to admit that something is possibly true:
*Of course I **may** be wrong.* (= I agree it is possible, though I do not think that I am.)
*We **may** seem rich, but that's only because we're so generous.* (= We're not really rich.)
*They **may** be poor – but that is really no excuse.* (= I agree that they are probably poor, but . . .)
*They **may** have been poor, but that was no excuse.*

d When we are talking about a possibility *may not* means that there is in fact still a possibility that something may happen:
*It **may** not rain tomorrow.* (= but I think it probably will)
*Stop worrying – it **may** never happen.* (= though I agree that it could)

So this contrasts with the use of *may not* in its 'permission' sense (which means there is no permission). Contrast:
*These books **may not** be removed from the library.* (It is not allowed.)
*The book I want **may not** be in the library.* (But perhaps it is.)

3 Wishes

may is sometimes used in a rather formal way to express wishes. Notice the inversion of the subject and modal verb:

*She seems to have made a complete recovery. Long **may** it last.* (= Let's hope it lasts a long time.)

4 may as well ▶ Compare **might as well**

This phrase is used to make a rather unenthusiastic suggestion:

*We **may as well** pay now – we'll have to pay some time.* (= There is no point in not paying).

Do not confuse with *may well* (= probably):

*You **may well** be right.* (= You probably are.)

5 may have + PAST PARTICIPLE

a *may have* + PAST PARTICIPLE refers to possibility, not permission. (It is possible now that something happened or has happened.):

*Bob **may have arrived** by now.*
*The house **may have been burgled** while we've been away.*

In modern English there is a new tendency for *may have* + PAST PARTICIPLE sometimes to be used with the meaning 'it *was* possible that . . .':

*They **may have died** in the fire, but in fact they escaped without injury.*

This is still regarded as non-standard by many people. Use *could have died* or *might have died*.

b *may have* + PAST PARTICIPLE can also be used to say that it is possible that something will have happened in the future:

*I **may have finished** my work by tomorrow.*
*By AD 2002 they **may have changed** the rules again.*

maybe: adverb

- perhaps
  ***Maybe** it's because I'm a Londoner that I love London so.*
  Do not confuse with *may* (modal) + *be*. *Maybe* is an informal way of saying *perhaps*, and needs a verb. Compare:
  *I **may be** late home.*
  ***Maybe** I'll walk home.*

me: pronoun ▶ See **I**; **mine**; **my**; **myself**

First person singular object pronoun.
For meaning ▶ See **I**
a *me* is used as the object of a verb or a preposition, and in other positions where it is not the subject, including short remarks without verbs:
  *Do you still love **me**?*
  *Tell **me** the truth.*

*I haven't got my diary with **me**, I'm afraid.*
*Between you and **me**, he's made a mistake.*
*He's not as tall as **me**, but he's older than me.*
*You won't stop **me** going.*
*It's my mother who wants it, not **me**.*
*'Who said that?' '**Me**.'* (= I did.)
*They want Maria and **me** to join them.*
*'I wish I had more money!' '**Me** too.'* (= I wish I had too.)

b *me* is often used before *-ing* structures where *my* is formally correct:
*I don't know why they were annoyed at **me** asking questions.*

But only *me* (NOT **my*) is correct after verbs of the senses (e.g., *hear, see*) and after some other verbs, including *find, keep*:
*Please don't watch **me** cleaning my teeth.*

c *me* (NOT **I*) is usual after *be*:
*That's **me** in the back row, third from the left.*
*It **was me** they came to see.*
*Who's there?' 'It's only **me**.'*

d *me* is non-standard when used as subject:
****Me** and Kevin have known each other for years.*
Joanne and **me went on holiday together last year.*

---

mean

```
            OBJECT
            that-CLAUSE
mean +      -ing
            (O+) to-INFINITIVE
```

1 mean, meant, meant: verb (not usually in progressive)

a • represent; say in another way; be a sign of
*'What does daft **mean**?' 'It **means** silly, foolish.'*
*What does it **mean** – 'It's an ill wind that blows nobody any good'? 'It **means**
that something must be very bad indeed, if it doesn't have some advantages
for somebody.*
*Do you really **mean** that you can't tell the difference between butter and
margarine?*
*You **mean** everything to me.* (= you are very important to me)
*Going in for the exam will **mean** having to work very hard.* (= will make it
necessary to work hard)
*That red flag **means** danger.*

b I mean
People sometimes say *I mean* to explain something a bit more clearly:
*I thought it was all right – not marvellous, **I mean**, but O.K.*

c   *mean* is also used to emphasise that we are serious or to express what we want or intend to do. In this sense progressive tenses are possible and *mean* can be followed by (OBJECT +) *to*-INFINITIVE:

*Of course I'll willingly lend you the money – I really **mean** that.*
*When I said that, I **meant** (that) I'd come if I could.*
*I've been **meaning** to write to you for ages.*
*I didn't **mean** to hurt your feelings.*
*We didn't **mean** you to worry.*

d **be meant**
   • be supposed; be intended
     *This **was meant** to be a secret. How did you find out?*
     *You're **meant** to write in ink, I think.*
     *These seats **are meant** for elderly or handicapped persons.* (notice in buses)

e   *What do you mean?* is sometimes used when we are angry:
     What do you mean, you're not going to give me back my money?

2   mean: adjective
   • not wanting to spend any money; unkind
     *He's thoroughly **mean** and always lets other people pay.*
     *That was **mean** of you to tell my mother what I said – it upset her and me.*

means: noun (C, U)

1   • method:
Note that *means* is both the singular and plural form:
     *It is a **means** of using the Sun's heat to make energy.*
     *Is/Are there any **means** of finding out where Clara is?*
     *They somehow got across the river by **means** of a rope.*

2   by all means   ► Compare   **of course; certainly**

by all means is a polite way of giving permission:
     *'May I say something?' '**By all means**, do!'*

3   by no means/not by any means   ► Compare   **not at all**

   • definitely not; not at all
     *It is **by no means** clear whether he intended to return or not.*
     *This isn't the end of our problems **by any means**.*

meanwhile/in the meanwhile: adverb

   • while something else is happening, or until something else happens
     *Eric was working. **Meanwhile** Cynthia was busy spending money.*
     *Of course I'll be dead one day. (**In the) meanwhile** (= until I die), I intend to enjoy life.*

meet, met, met: verb

a When *meet* roughly means 'come face to face (with)' – whether by plan or by chance, *meet* can be used with and without an object:
*You'll be **met** at London (Victoria) by the tour guide.*
*Would you like to **meet** my boss?* (= be introduced to)
*We first **met** (= each other) in 1978.*
*Let's **meet** for lunch.*
*The History Society **meets** on Wednesdays.*

b *meet* needs an object when it means 'satisfy':
*All your conditions/demands/objections will be **met**.*
*They couldn't **meet** their bills.* (= pay)

c **meet (with)**
Both *meet* and *meet with* can mean 'experience' (especially something unpleasant):
*Five members of that family have **met (with)** violent deaths.*

meet with is used in American English with the meaning 'have a meeting with'
*I'm **meeting with** my advisers tomorrow.*

d *meet up (with someone)* is an informal alternative to *meet*:
*They went shopping while we visited the museum, and then we **met up (with them)** for dinner.*

meeting: noun

a As a count noun, *meeting* usually means people coming together for a particular purpose:
*political **meetings**, staff **meetings**, trade union **meetings**, etc.*
*The **meeting** was rather noisy and went on too long.*
*The chairman declared the **meeting** closed.*

b When the meaning is the people at a *meeting*, *meeting* is a collective noun:
*The **meeting** was/were angry with the government.*

mere, merest: attributive adjectives

There is no word **merer*, and *merest* is not used in a superlative way, but for emphasis. The meaning of *mere* is 'only a . . .' or 'nothing except'. *Merest* means 'smallest':
*A **mere** 7% of the population are in favour of the new law.*
*The **merest** suggestion that he might have to pay upset Tom.* (= the slightest suggestion/the faintest possibility)

merely: adverb ▶ Compare **just; simply**

- just; only; simply

We use *merely* in mid-position with verbs and immediately before other words we want to emphasise:

*I **merely** said that it was expensive, and she burst into tears.*
*There's no need to be angry – it's **merely** a suggestion.*
*It's not **merely** the expense I object to; I simply do not think we need another television set.*

might: modal verb ▶ Compare **may**

The negative is *might not/mightn't*

Like other modals, *might* is concerned with possibility and necessity. It is sometimes a tentative (less certain) alternative to *may* (**1–2**). It is less common than some of the other modals and is mainly used in its theoretical sense. It usually refers to the present and future. As a past tense it is hardly used except as the past of *may* in reported speech (**3**).

1 Permission

With its permission meaning, *might* is a more tentative and formal alternative to *may*, and is rather rare. Because *might* is tentative, it is very polite when asking for permission, but is not a polite way of giving permission:

***Might** I discuss this matter with you? (or May/Can/Could I . . .?)*
*If I **might** offer my advice, I think you should . . .*
*You **might** help with the washing-up sometimes. (criticism)*

2 Theoretical possibility

a *might* is less certain than *may*, so the meaning is 'It is possible (but not specially likely) that . . .':

*It **might** rain tomorrow. (but I don't think it will)*
*I **might/mightn't** be here next week – I just don't know.*
*If you need more money, you **might** try and get a holiday job. (suggestion)*

b Like *may*, *might* leaves the possibility open:

*It **might** – or **might not** – rain. (= We just don't know what to expect.)*
*Contrast: It **can't/couldn't** rain. (= I am sure it won't.)*

c As with *may* expressing possibility, *might* is not often used in direct questions. We do not normally say **Might it rain tomorrow?* We prefer to say *Do you think it will rain tomorrow?*

d Like *could*, *would* and *should*, *might* is used in the main clause of impossible or very unlikely conditions:

*If I were a fish, I **might** swim across the Pacific.*
*If I won a fortune, I **might** give up work.*

3 Past

Unlike *could* and *would*, which are sometimes used to talk about the past, *might* is very rare and old-fashioned as a past tense except in reported speech, where it can be the past of *may*. But even here there are usually alternatives:

*'May I borrow your dictionary?' He asked if he (**might**)/**could** borrow my dictionary.*

*'It may rain tomorrow, you know.' I thought it **might**/**could** rain the following day.*

*'He may not come.' She told me he **might** not come.*

4 might as well ▶ Compare **may as well**

a *might as well* is a rather unenthusiastic way of saying, 'I suppose we had better . . .':

*There's no point in staying – we **might as well** go.*

b *might as well* is also used to complain:

*The way you treat me – I **might as well** be a servant.*

5 might have + PAST PARTICIPLE

might have + PAST PARTICIPLE has two different meanings

a The possibility existed in the past for something to happen, but we know now that it did not happen:

*You were a fool to drive so fast – you **might have been** killed.*

*You **might have told** me!* (a complaint = you should have told me)

*I **might have** (told you), if you had asked me nicely.* (= but you did not ask me, and I didn't tell you)

may have + PAST PARTICIPLE should not be used here. ▶ See **may**.

b It is theoretically possible now (though not very likely) that something has happened/happened – or even that something will have happened by some future date. We are guessing. We do not know:

*They **might have got** lost.*

*They **might have forgotten** the date.*

*By this time next week, anything **might have happened**.*

*I **might have finished** my work by tomorrow* (though it is not very likely.)

may have + PAST PARTICIPLE is possible here.

mind

1 mind: verb

```
            —
          OBJECT
mind +  wh-CLAUSE
        that-CLAUSE
        (you/your)-ing
```

a   • be careful about; notice
> *You have to **mind** your head in some of these old cottages – the ceilings are quite low.*
> ***Mind** how you go – the path is slippery.*
> ***Mind** out! **Mind** what you're doing – you're dropping food on the floor!*
> ***Mind** (that) you remember to post my letters.*

Mind you adds an explanation or more information.
> *The seats were right at the back, but **mind you** we hadn't paid much for them.*

b   • dislike; object to (not usually in progressive)
With this meaning *mind* is usually used in questions and negative sentences:
> *'What shall we do?' 'Oh I don't **mind** – you decide.'*
> *'Terrible weather!' 'Oh, I don't **mind** the cold, actually.'*
> *I'm terribly tired – I wouldn't **mind** an early night.* (= I would like to go to bed early.)
> *They don't seem to **mind** what we do or how we do it, as long as it doesn't cost them anything.*
> *If you don't **mind** my/me saying so, that colour doesn't really suit you.*

(In this last example the possessive *my* is slightly more formal than the object *me*.)

c   *Do you mind . . .?* and *Would you mind . . .?* are often used for making requests and asking permission:
> *Do you **mind** if I open a window?*
> *Would you **mind** if I didn't come after all? I am rather busy.*
> *Would you **mind** making a bit less noise please?*

d   *Never mind!* means 'Don't worry – it doesn't matter':
> *'I'm afraid I can't come on Tuesday.' 'Oh well, **never mind**. Some other time!'*

e   • look after; take care of (progressive possible)
> *Would you **mind** my luggage for a moment? I've got to make a phone call.*
> *My mother **minded** the children while we were away.*
> ***Mind** your own business.* (usually a rather rude way of saying 'Don't ask me personal questions.')

2   **mind**: noun (C, U)

  • way of thinking; memory; brains
> *Please make up your **mind**.* (= decide) *You can't keep changing your **mind**.*
> *Keep your **mind** on your work.*
> *I'll bear in **mind** what you've said.* (= remember, consider)

---

mine: pronoun   ▶   See   **I**; **me**; **my**; **myself**

First person singular possessive pronoun.
> *'Whose is this umbrella?' 'It's **mine**.'*
> *'Is that bag yours too?' 'No, that's not one of **mine**.'*
> ***Mine** have all got red stripes on them.'*

minus: preposition

a *minus* is the opposite of *plus* and is shown by the sign (−):
  *Seven **minus** four is three (7−4=3)*

b ● below zero
  *The temperature was **minus** 20 degrees. (or 20 degrees below freezing).*

c Informally *minus* is used to mean 'without':
  *He came back **minus** his wallet.*

minute /mɪnɪt/: noun (C) ▶ Compare **moment**

1

a measure of time, equal to sixty seconds:
  *There are sixty **minutes** in an hour.*
  *It's seven **minutes** past five.*
  *I'll be back in ten **minutes**.*

b minute and moment

  minute and *moment* are often interchangeable when the meaning is 'a short time':
  *Tom always leaves everything till the last **minute**/the last **moment**.*
  *Wait a **minute**/a **moment** – I'm nearly ready.*
  *Stop worrying. They'll be here in a **minute**/in a **moment**.*

2 the minute/the moment (that): conjunction

  ● as soon as
  *The **minute**/the **moment** we saw the house, we knew that we wanted to live there.*

moment: noun (C) ▶ Compare **minute**

  moment (rather than *minute*) is used when the meaning is 'this/that point in time', 'now':
  *At that very **moment** the chimney fell through the roof.*
  *I'm not very busy at the (present) **moment**, but I shall be next week.*
  *There were **moments** when I felt that I couldn't continue.*
  *We both suddenly saw each other at the same **moment**.*

money: noun (U)

  As a word *money* is uncountable:
  *I haven't much **money**, and my brother has even less.*

more

1 **more**: determiner and pronoun ▶ Compare **fewer; less**

- a bigger number or amount

more is the comparative of *much* and *many*. The superlative is *most* and the opposite is *less* or *fewer*. The comparison can be completed using *more* . . . *than* . . .

a few		people/books . . . (pl)		
many two . . . three . . .			the/these/my books friends (pl)	
a lot/lots even far/rather some/any/no	**more**	of	them/you/us these/those mine/yours . . .	than . . .
a little		rice/money . . . (U)		
a bit much a lot/lots		of	the/this/my . . . money (U) book (SINGULAR)	
			it/this.	
			mine/yours . . .	
even far/rather some/any/no		than . . .		

As a determiner *more* is used with uncountable nouns (***more** rice*) (**a** below) and plural count nouns (***more** people*) (**b**).

Various words as shown can come in front of *more* (*of*). A comparison can be completed with *than*:

a *With a little **more** power and strength he might have won.*
*How much **more** green writing paper have you?*
*He must try to lose some **more** weight.*
*It uses **more** fuel than any other car.*

b *I can't afford to make any **more** mistakes.*
*This camera has even **more** uses than the old model.*
*I read a few **more** chapters and then fell asleep.*
*This method is being used in several research centres, and many **more** results can be expected.*
*I need three **more** stamps for these letters.*

Pronoun *more* is used in a general sense (*Tell me **more***) and also refers to uncountable nouns and plural count nouns (*any **more***, etc.) (**c**). *more of* (**d**) can also be used with both uncountable and count nouns, and with pronouns (***more** of it/them*) and even with a singular count noun – meaning 'a greater part of'.

After *more of* we use a determiner when a noun follows (***more** of your books*, in contrast to *more books*).

c   *Don't let's say any **more** about it.*
*Tell us **more** about Claudia.*
*The bill comes to a bit **more** than that.*
*I won't stay **more** than a few minutes.*
*I think one learns far **more** from people – if they're honest – than from books.*
*I can't stand much **more** of this.*
*I love your writing paper – do buy lots **more**.*
*This happened ten years or **more** ago.*

d   *We are ordering **more** T-shirts – particularly **more of** the small sizes.*
*Haven't you got any **more of** that paper?*
*I read a bit **more of** my book.*
*She liked my paintings and bought some **more of** them.*
*I enjoyed the wine but I don't want any **more of** it.*

e   *More of* is sometimes used with a meaning of time, rather than a greater quantity of something:
*After that we heard no **more of** this suggestion.* (= We did not hear about it again.)
*Perhaps we'll see a little **more of** you both now you have more free time.* (=See you both a little more often.)

2   more: adverb   ▶ Compare **less**

● to a greater degree
more is the comparative of *much*. The superlative is *most*. *More* is the opposite of *less*

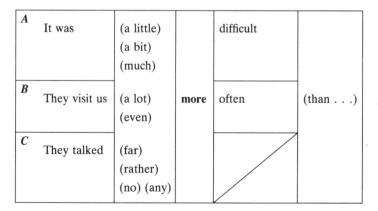

As an adverb *more* is used with adjectives (***more** difficult* (**A**) and adverbs (**more** *often* (**B**) to form comparatives – except with those words that add *-er* (e.g. *kinder*, *sooner*) or with exceptions (*bad*, *worse*). *more* is also used as an adverb with verbs (*talk more*) (*C*). Again, *more* can have *a little* etc. in front of it, and the comparison can be completed by *than*:

A   *I hope you are feeling a bit more lively and cheerful.*
The problem is much more difficult than I thought at first.
The position is no more encouraging today. (e.g., than it was before)
Men are much more generous than women.
I thought he was the more interesting man of the two.

B   *This happens more often than we realise.*
When we look a little more closely, these differences appear less important.

C   *I couldn't agree more.* (= I completely agree!)
If you smiled more, you'd be happier.
He really ought to work a bit more.
I don't know which I hate more – the heat or the cold.
Don't you love me any more? (= any longer).
I shan't do that any more. (= ever again).
I really like coffee more than tea.

3   more than + ADJECTIVE/ADVERB

more than + ADJECTIVE/ADVERB roughly means, 'very':
I was more than angry; I was absolutely furious.
It is more than probable that we shall go to the States next year. (= very probable)
I was more than a little upset. (= very upset)

4   more + (ADJECTIVE) than + (ADJECTIVE)

I was more amused than angry. This means '**I** was amused really; **I** wasn't angry' (though perhaps that is what people expected.)

5   the more . . . the more, etc., . . .

the more can form part of parallel structures with comparatives, e.g. to show something happening as the result of something else:
***The more** I talked to him **the more** it seemed to me that he possibly needs further treatment.*
***The more** noise and trouble it makes, **the more** quickly it will be noticed.*
***The more** we are together **the happier** I shall be!*

6   more and more

• an increasing number of; increasingly
This structure is often followed by a progressive tense:
***More and more** men, young men especially, are wearing their hair long.*
As that match wore on (= progressed), *success looked **more and more** likely.*

7   more or less

• roughly; approximately
*We have **more or less** decided to . . .*

*The rest of the time I was **more or less** unhappy.*
*She should know **more or less** what she'll be doing next year before Christmas comes.*

8 Because *more* can be a determiner (1) and an adverb (2), some sentences can have two meanings:
1   *I would like some **more** useful books.* (= more books that are useful)
2   *I would like some **more** useful books.* (= books that are more useful)

---

moreover: connector

a rather formal word meaning 'in addition', 'what is more':
*Changing the whole programme would be very expensive. It could, **moreover**, take up a great deal of time.*

---

morning, afternoon, evening: nouns (C, U)
▶ Compare **night**; **today**

a   *It was a hot **morning/afternoon/evening**.*
*I don't like working in/during the **morning**/the **afternoon**/the **evening**.*
(▶ Compare **at night**)
*We danced until 3 o'clock in the **morning**.* (= 3 a.m.)
*I can't do it today. I'll do it in the **morning**.* (= tomorrow morning)
*They are busy from **morning** till night.* (Note no articles.)

▶ See also *good morning* at **good**

b   Prepositions of time are frequently not used:
*She's got a job three **mornings/afternoons/evenings** a week.*
*Come and see us one **morning/afternoon/evening**.*
*The baby's been asleep all (the) **morning/afternoon/evening**.*
*I go jogging most **mornings/afternoons/evenings**.*
*He rests every **morning/afternoon/evening**.*

c

yesterday this tomorrow	**morning**
(on) Saturday	**afternoon**
last Tuesday next Friday	**evening**

Prepositions are not used with phrases like *yesterday afternoon* or *next Friday evening*, but with a phrase consisting of a day of the week + *morning* etc. *on* can be used:

*We saw them/We're seeing them (on) Sunday **morning**.*
*We saw them last Sunday **morning**.*

---

most ▶ Compare **fewest; least**

1 most: determiner and pronoun

• the biggest number or amount

most is the superlative of *much* and *many*. The comparative is *more* and the opposite is *least*:

A			
most	food		(UNCOUNTABLE NOUN)
	citizens		(PLURAL COUNT NOUN)

B			
	the/this/my	food	(UNCOUNTABLE NOUN)
		area	(SINGULAR NOUN)
most of	the/those/my students		(PLURAL COUNT NOUN)
	it/you/us/them		
	mine/yours . . .		

a As a determiner (*A*), *most* is used with uncountable nouns (***most** food*) and with plural count nouns (***most** citizens*):

*For grilling, **most** food should be brushed with fat.*
***Most** citizens of this country are likely to turn purple at the news. **Most** of them will be amazed.*

Pronoun *most of* (*B*) needs a determiner before a following noun, which can be uncountable or plural, and also singular, meaning 'the biggest part of' (***most** of the area*):

*At that time **most** of our students came for one year, and **most** enjoyed their stay.* (Here we do not need to repeat *of our students*.)
***Most** of the area within the Antarctic Circle remains frozen throughout the year.* (NOT **most area* . . .)

b *most* also has a superlative meaning (= *more than anything else*) when we make comparisons, and here we often need *the most*:

*We were all trying to see who could collect **(the) most**.* (= which of us could collect more than the others)
*I don't expect her to write – if she telephones us, that's **the most** we can expect.*

2 most: adverb

• to the greatest extent; more than anything else

most is the superlative of *much*. The comparative is *more* and the opposite is *least*.

---

a *the* (or sometimes *my/your* . . .) *most* is used with adjectives to form superlatives (except with those words that add *-est*: *kindest* . . .) in the pattern *the most* + ADJECTIVE + NOUN PHRASE:

*It was one of **the most** amazing matches I can recall.*
*I had **the most** awful pain in my stomach.*
*He would always stay in **the most** comfortable hotels.*
*Rachel was **the most** hardworking student in the class.*

Notice also *the most* + ADJECTIVE *of* . . .:
*She was definitely **the most** hardworking **of** our students that year.*

b *most* (without *the*) is possible when no noun follows:
*Which of them was (the) **most** hardworking?*
*What I'm **most** afraid of is that he will suddenly do something careless.*

c Sometimes *most* is used when we are not really comparing anything and the meaning is 'very'. The pattern is *most* + ADJECTIVE or ADVERB, always without *the*, (whether followed by a noun or not):

*I would be **most** grateful . . .*
*I've got a cold, but think it would be **most** boring to stay in bed.*
*Rachel was a **most** hardworking student.*
*They were **most** hardworking students.*
*This is **most** excellent work.*
*Seeing you **most** certainly made my weekend.* (= made my weekend enjoyable.)
***Most** unusually, he just arrived without telephoning.*

d Occasionally phrases with *most* are ambiguous. If we have no other clue, *most* can have either a superlative meaning or a 'very' meaning in:
*I'd like you to meet our **most** hardworking student.*

e *most* (or *the most*) is also used with verbs to make a comparison:
*The comments which you will value **(the) most** will come from Professor Hawkins.* (= more than anyone else's comments).
*It was a very good concert but I enjoyed the Mozart **(the) most**.*
*What I **most** fear/what I fear **(the) most** is loneliness.*
*I don't know which I dread **most** – seeing their holiday video or hearing about their airport experiences.*

3 at (the) most: adverb ▶ Compare **at (the) least**

- not more than
*It'll take you two hours **at (the) most**.* (= Perhaps it will take you less.)

---

mostly: adverb

mostly is a rather rare word. It does not mean *most*, but 'mainly' or 'usually':
*We **mostly** eat fresh vegetables, but just occasionally we buy frozen peas.*

much

1 much: determiner and pronoun ▶ Compare **little; lot; many**

- a big amount

The comparative is *more*, and the superlative is *most*. The opposite is *little*.

	How	**much**	is it?/are they? does it/do they cost?	
	how	**much**	food money (UNCOUNTABLE NOUNS)	
	so not very		of	the/this/that . . . money (UNCOUNTABLE NOUNS) my/his . . .
(far)	too			
(much)	too			it/this/that
(a bit)	too			mine/yours . . .

a *much* is mainly used in a general sense (*He doesn't know **much**.*) and with uncountable nouns. It refers to a quantity or amount, and contrasts with *many*, which is used with plural words. After *much of* we use a determiner when a noun follows (e.g., *not **much** of the food* in contrast to *not **much** food*). Various words can come before *much* as shown.

b how much

how much is used to talk about prices and quantities, (with singular and plural nouns) but not numbers:

  *How **much** do you spend a week on food?*
  *How **much** does this lamp cost? And how **much** are these cushions?*
  *Can you please tell me how **much** it would cost, including postage?*

c *much* by itself is common in questions and negative sentences:

  *Is there **much** to do there? Is (very) **much** happening?*
  *I don't know **much** about art, but I know what I like.*
  *There isn't **much** to tell you.*

d In affirmative statements, *much* by itself is fairly formal, both as subject and when it comes after the verb. It is very unusual at the end of an affirmative sentence unless we have *how, so, too* in front of it as shown. Instead of plain *much* we often use a *lot/lots (of)* or sometimes *plenty (of)*:

  *The fruit was thick and brown and **much** of it lay in the long grass.* (formal)
  *After a cloudy start, **much** of the south-east will have a dry day.* (BBC weather forecast)
  *So **much** depends on organization.*
  *They have so **much** to choose from.*

I am spending far too much money.
A lot of food today contains chemicals. (= More usual than ?*Much food today contains . . .*)
'Have you got enough?' 'Oh we've lots/plenty.' (NOT **We've **much**.*)

e   **much of** + COUNT NOUNS
   much of can be used with singular and plural count nouns, with a general sense of quantity. Again, in an affirmative sentence *much* is rather formal:
   ***Much of** the town had to be rebuilt after the war.* (= a large part of)
   *Sometimes you can have **too much of** a good thing.*
   *That's **not much of** an excuse.* (= not a very good excuse)
   *I didn't see **much of** Rome or Venice or of any of the big cities.* (= Maybe I only had a short time in them. Contrast: (*I didn't see **many of** the cities*).

2   much: adverb with comparatives and superlatives   ▶ Compare **far**

much means 'to a large extent'.

much	**A**	more/less more money/less money better/worse . . . nicer/more/less difficult sooner/more/less often	than . . .
	B the	better/worse/nicer, etc. more/less expensive	of (the two)
		best/worst nicest/quickest most difficult	of . . . in . . . (that) . . .
	C	the same	as . . .
	D	like	

A   *much* adds emphasis to *more* and *less* and other comparative forms. We can also make *much* stronger by saying *very much* or *so much*:
   *I can't take **much** more of this.*
   *It is a **much** less exciting book than her last one.*
   *You'll work **much** faster with your new typewriter, won't you?*
   *It is **much** more difficult to say what exactly happened.*
   *If the operation had not been done, her feet would have been very **much** worse by now.*
   *You could do the job so **much** quicker yourself.*

B much the better/best

When we are not making a comparison with some other, outside person or thing (as we do with *than . . .*) but among the people or things within a group, then we can use *much the +* COMPARATIVE/SUPERLATIVE, and sometimes a following phrase:

*Mr Roberts was so **much** the better leader.* (= of the two)
*Doing the index was **much** the most difficult part of the whole book.*
*It's **much** the best Italian restaurant in the area.*
*It was **much** the most expensive hotel (that) we've ever stayed in.*

C much the same

When *much* comes before *the same* it means 'roughly/almost the same':
*Here things are **much the same** as usual.*

D *much* also means 'roughly/almost' in the expression *much like*:
*Today has been **much like** yesterday.*

3 much too ▶ Compare **far**

much can also emphasise *too:*
*It's **much** too cold to go swimming.*

4 much: adverb with verbs

● greatly

a *much* when used as an adverb with verbs is mainly non-assertive (i.e. it is used in questions and negatives). In affirmative sentences we use *so much*, *too much*, *very much*, *as much*, etc. Notice that end position (i.e. after the verb) is usual:

*Do you go to the cinema **much**?*
*We don't go out in the evenings **(very) much** these days at all.*
*I love you **very much**.* (NOT **I love you much.*)
*Thank you **so much/very much** for the marvellous present.* (NOT **Thank you much.*)
*I'm astonished **how much** she's enjoyed the visits.*

b Mid-position with certain verbs

A				
I would	**much**	rather	do it now.	
They'd		sooner	they did it now.	
B				
I	**much**	appreciate/admire/enjoy/ prefer/regret		(very much)
C				
I/We don't	**much**	care/like/mind		(very much)
He doesn't				
D				
I	**very much**	agree/hope/like/ want/doubt/fear		(very much)

With certain verbs expressing likes, preferences, and with *rather/sooner* (as shown in the table) *much* can be used in mid-position. Notice (*C*): that it is *don't care* (not *care* in the affirmative) that is used in this way. Some other verbs (*D*) can use *very much* (not plain *much*) here. *Very much* can always come later in the sentence, except with *much rather/sooner* (*A*):

I would much rather/sooner you didn't tell anybody about this.
I should (very) much appreciate it if you would let me know where you obtained this information.
She says she doesn't much care what happens.
I very much doubt whether we shall get any positive results.
I doubt very much whether this is actually the case.

c Passive verbs
Plain *much* can come before the last part of the verb in passive sentences:
We have been (very) much helped in this work by Mr Andrews.
or
We have been helped very much in this work by Mr Andrews.

---

must: modal verb

must refers to the present and the future. The negative is *must not/mustn't*. *Must* has two main meanings, (1) a practical meaning concerned with obligations and duties – 'it is necessary to do something', and (2) a theoretical meaning concerned with deductions and logic – 'this is certainly true' or 'there are reasons why this is true'.

1 Obligation and duty   ▶ Compare **have to; ought to; should**

a *must* and *must not* often express very strong obligations to do (or not to do) something. We can also use *must* to emphasise our intentions or suggestions:
*Smokers **must** occupy rear seats.* (notice on some buses)
*You **must** be home by ten o'clock.*
*You **must not** tell anyone – it's a secret.*
*I **must** say, I think you were rather rude.*
*You **must** read this book – it's super.*

b *must/must not* usually means that the speaker agrees with the obligation. (Contrast – *It's ridiculous that smokers **have to** sit at the back.*)
Almost always the speaker is making the obligation, so with *I/we must* the speaker will probably carry out the obligation:
*I **mustn't** eat so much chocolate.*
*I **must** stay in and write letters this evening.*
NOT **I **must** stay in – but I'm going out.*
(Contrast – *I **ought to/should** stay in – but actually I'm going out.*)
*You **must** come to dinner with us.* (= I insist – a polite invitation)
Contrast: ?*You **should** come to dinner with us.* (which would be rather rude, meaning 'It is your duty to come!')

c Questions
Questions using *must* are usually asking about what the person spoken to wants to do or wants us to do. These questions usually suggest that the person spoken to has the power to decide that something is not necessary:
***Must** you really go so soon? Stay a bit longer.*

*Why **must** you always keep us waiting?* (= You could decide not to!)
__Must__ I go to school today, Mummy? Can I stay at home?

d Negatives ▶ Compare **needn't**
must not always means that something is not allowed:
*You **must not** drive at more than seventy miles per hour on the motorway – it's against the law.*

To say there is no obligation and that we can choose, we can use *needn't*:
*You **needn't** drive fast.* (= if you don't want to) ▶ See **need**

e *must* does not refer to the past, because we cannot make rules now for the past. But we can use *must* to report a past obligation, when using reported speech:
*They **said I mustn't** tell anybody.*
*I **said he must** be home by ten o'clock, and he was.*

2 must: deduction ▶ Compare **can; will**

a We can use **must** to show that we are certain that something is true; we are making a logical deduction now based on some clear cause or reasons:
*They always go to Brighton for their holidays – they **must** like it there.*
*You **must** be worried about her, if you still haven't had any news.*
*I **must** be getting old – I keep forgetting things.*
*It **must** be nice to have plenty of money.*

b Questions about theoretical possibilities usually use *can*. If we use *must* we are making a strong suggestion that something is quite certainly the case:
*What **must** they think of us?* (= They must think we are rude/unkind/stupid, etc.)
*'I must be getting old.' 'Why **must** you be getting old? – perhaps you're just tired.'*

3 must have + PAST PARTICIPLE ▶ See **can**
When we use *must have* + PAST PARTICIPLE we are making a deduction now that something happened or has happened. We are fairly sure:
*'Robert's just had two months travelling round Europe.' 'That **must** have been super.'*
*'That sounds like an ambulance.' 'Yes, there **must** have been an accident.'*

my: possessive determiner ▶ See **I**; **me**; **mine**; **myself**

First person singular.
For meaning ▶ See **I**
a *Please give me back **my** money.*
*I've got to get **my** eyes tested.*
***My** mother and father are coming to stay.*

b *my* is formally and correctly used rather than *me* before some *-ing* patterns:
*I hope you don't mind **my** asking.*

myself: pronoun ▶ See **I**; **me**; **mine**; **my**

First person singular reflexive pronoun.

1 myself: reflexive

I burnt myself when I was cooking.
I sometimes talk to myself.
I've lived by myself since my husband died.
I don't get much time to myself.

2 myself: emphatic

I won't post it – I'll bring it to you myself.
I myself believe in peace through security.

3 myself: subject or object pronoun

myself is sometimes used where *I* or *me* would be correct:
?My brother and myself are going to the States this week.
(My brother and I are going to the States this week.)

?They've invited my wife and myself to go with them.
(They've invited my wife and me to go with them.)

near, nearer, nearest
▶ Compare **close**; **closer**; **closest**

1 near, nearer, nearest: preposition

• close to, a short distance from in space or time
With the comparative and superlative forms we usually add *to*, but *near* is often used by itself:

I had parked the cars near the entrance to the block of flats.
A further year will bring us near to the time of the next General Election.
Could you please remind me nearer the time?
I was afraid to walk any nearer (to) the edge in case I fell over the cliff.
That's my car – the one nearest (to) the fence.

2 near, nearer, nearest: adverb

They walked together to the gate and looked once more, up, down, far and near.
Jane walked forward and stood at a little distance, near enough to see the strange object in the gateway.

3 near, nearer, nearest: adjective

> *The Watsons were **near** neighbours of ours for many years.*
> *Call into your **nearest** garage for a leaflet.*
> *Should you discover a fire, BREAK THE GLASS OF THE **NEAREST** FIRE ALARM.*

4 nearest or **next**?

Both *nearest* and *next* can be used to talk about space and time, but *nearest* means 'most near(to)' or 'closest to':

> *Where's the **nearest** bank?*
> *My nephew is my **nearest** living relative.* (= the most closely related member of my family still alive)
> *I couldn't get the biscuits you wanted – these are the **nearest**.* (= the most similar).

next refers to someone or something immediately following another in a series:

> *There's a post-office by the traffic-lights, and the **next** shop is a baker's.*
> *What's happening **next** week?*

or *next* can mean 'beside':

> *The baker's is **next** to the post-office.*

---

nearby: adjective and adverb

▶ Compare **near; nearer; nearest**

● near

nearby is less commonly used than *near*:

> *We suddenly saw some men on donkeys approaching from a **nearby** village.*
> *The reporter talked with the eight inhabitants of the island and the nine who lived on West Point Island **nearby**.*

---

nearly: adverb

▶ Compare **almost**

● almost, not quite

a *nearly* and *almost* are often interchangeable. With verbs, they are usually in mid-position:

> *I **nearly** went to see Charles today.*
> *I saw **nearly** everybody while I was there.*
> *She's **nearly** as tall as her mother.*
> *We were **nearly** late – I thought we were going to miss the train.*

b *nearly* (but not *almost*) can be made stronger by saying *very nearly* or *pretty nearly*:

> *We **very nearly** bought a boat.*
> *They **pretty nearly** didn't come.*

c not nearly

nearly (but not *almost*) can be used after *not* to express the idea 'the opposite is true', 'very far from':

*The weather is **not nearly** as good as last year.* (= It is much worse.)
*I **haven't nearly** finished.* (= I've hardly started.)
▶ Compare *nothing like* at **like**; *nowhere near* at **nowhere**

d *nearly* is connected with *near*, so *nearly* is not used when we talk about something which never could or never will happen, something we cannot get nearer to:
NOT **My dog can **nearly** talk.* (say – *He can almost talk.*)

nearly is not followed by negative words like *no, none, nobody*, etc.:
NOT **He saw **nearly** nobody.* (say – *He hardly saw anybody.*)
NOT **My grandmother **nearly** never goes out.* (say – *She hardly ever goes out.*)

necessary: adjective

● essential; needed
*Is it really **necessary** for us all to go to the passport office?* (= Do we all have to go . . .?)
*Couldn't just one of us go if they had the **necessary** papers?*
*Don't let's pay more than (is) **necessary**.*
*I'll walk if **necessary**, but I'm definitely going to be there.*

necessarily: adverb

The meaning of the adverb *necessarily* is rather like the logical deduction meaning of *have to*; it expresses the idea 'it must logically be a fact that' or 'reasoning proves that'. It is usually used with *not*:
*'Tom must have been telling lies!' 'Not **necessarily**. Perhaps he simply did not know what had really happened.'*

need: ordinary and modal verb

need is a rather strange verb, because it is sometimes an ordinary verb and sometimes a modal.
The ordinary verb is regular, so we can say *needs, needing, needed*. Questions and negatives are formed with *do*. We can use *need + OBJECT, need + -ing* and *need + to-INFINITIVE*.
The modal verb can only be followed by the bare infinitive. It refers to the present and future: it can refer to the past only in reported speech. It can only be used in the negative (*need not/needn't*), in sentences expressing a negative idea and in questions (*Need I/you . . .?*)

1 **need** + OBJECT, **need** + *-ing* (ordinary verb only)

need +	OBJECT *-ing*

When the meaning is require something because it is necessary', we use the ordinary, regular verb:

*'Do you **need** anything?' 'Yes, I **need** some string.'*
*With friends like that, who **needs** enemies?* (= it is unnecessary to have enemies, if your friends are so awful!)
*The windows **need** cleaning, don't they?*
*Oh I **needed** that cup of tea – I was thirsty.*

2 need + to-INFINITIVE (ordinary verb) **or need** + BARE INFINITIVE (modal verb)

I/we/you/they **need**		Need I/he . . .	
He/she/it **needs**		I/he . . . **needn't**	+ BARE INFINITIVE
Do I/Does he **need**	+ TO-INFINITIVE		
I don't/He doesn't **need**			

When *need* talks about the necessity for an action, both the ordinary and the modal verb can be used.

a affirmative sentences
Only ordinary regular *need* is used:
*You **need** to drive extra carefully in bad weather.*
*He really **needs** to be more careful.*
*Babies **need** to be fed frequently.*

b past tense
Only ordinary regular *need* is used:
*Did you really **need** to say that?*
*I **needed** to see my dentist.*
*You didn't **need** to wait, did you?*

c negatives, negative ideas and questions
Here both the ordinary verb and the modal verb are usually possible. The modal verb is rarely used in American English. In British English modal *need* is often used with negative words (e.g., *nobody*, *never*) and with nearly negative words like *hardly*:
*He doesn't **need** to write – he can telephone.*
*He **needn't** write – he can telephone.*
*I don't think he **needs** to tell anybody.*
*I don't think he **need** tell anybody.*
*Do we **need** to wait any longer?*
***Need** we wait any longer.*
*Nobody **need** ever know – if we both say nothing.*
*Nothing more **need** be said.*
*I **need** hardly say how sorry I am.* (= I am very sorry.)

d Short negative answers to the question *'Need you really go yet?'* or *'Do you really need to go yet?'* (i.e., do stay a bit longer) could be:
*'Well, perhaps I **needn't**'* or *'No I don't really **need** to.'* [NOT *I don't **need**.]

But in the affirmative, only the regular verb is possible:
Yes, I (do) **need** *to.* (NOT **Yes, I need.*)

Or another verb may be used:
Yes I must./Yes, I have to.

e   There is sometimes a difference of meaning between ordinary and modal *need*. Modal *need* is more personal. So *needn't* means the speaker has decided that something is not necessary, while questions with *Need . . .?* are often a way of asking the other person to decide that something is not necessary. With regular *need* there may be outside circumstances that affect whether something is necessary, and questions do not so clearly hope for a negative answer:
*You **needn't** apologise – I really don't mind.*
*You don't **need** to be clever to get a job.*
***Need** I eat this?* (= Please say 'No'.)
*Do we **need** to buy any more food?* (or *have we got enough?*)

3   Theoretical necessity

Modal *need* can be used in negative sentences and questions to talk about theoretical necessity. But this is very RARE.

4   needn't have + PAST PARTICIPLE

We use *needn't have* + PAST PARTICIPLE to say 'in our opinion now, something that has happened or happened was unnecessary':
*I **needn't have** telephoned them – they had already heard the news.* (= I telephoned them, but we know now that this was unnecessary.)
Contrast:
*She **did not need/didn't need** to telephone them.* (= It was unnecessary at the time. Out of context we are not saying what happened: perhaps she did, perhaps she didn't. Of course, in context it is usually clear what happened.)

5   needn't and mustn't

Do not confuse these two, because the meanings are different.
needn't means: It is not necessary for something to happen.
mustn't means: It is necessary that something does not happen:
*You **needn't** always speak the whole truth, but you certainly **mustn't** tell lies.*

Sometimes *needn't* is used to complain or criticise in sentences where *mustn't* would also be possible:
*You **needn't** be so rude!* (It is quite unnecessary.)

---

neither   ▶ Compare **either**

---

neither usually refers to one of two people/things.

1   neither: determiner and pronoun

a   ● not one and not the other (of two)

A				
Neither	man way	(SINGULAR NOUNS)		is . . .
B **Neither**				is/are . . .
C **Neither of**	the these/those my, etc.	men ways	(PLURAL)	is/are . . .
	these/those them/us/you	(PLURAL)		

A   *neither* can be a determiner:
   Neither *description is really adequate.*
   Mr Andrews switched on a light. **Neither** *man spoke.*

B   *neither* can be an independent pronoun:
   They both knew that **neither** *had been in any real danger.*

C   *neither of* can be joined to plural nouns when these have a determiner (*my/the/ these*, etc.) and pronouns, as shown:
   Neither of *the women saw me.*
   Neither of *them spoke.*

b   **Singular or plural verb?**
   neither + SINGULAR NOUN takes a singular verb. The strict rule is that *neither* always takes a singular verb but in fact *neither* by itself and *neither of* are sometimes followed by plural verbs, because the meaning is 'both not':
   Neither *candidate has enough experience for the job.*
   Neither *is suitable.* (or **Neither** *are suitable.*)
   Neither of them **was** *mentioned in the document.* (considered more correct)
   or:
   Neither of *them* **were** *mentioned in the document.*

2   neither . . . nor: conjunctions

   ● not this and not that
a   As with *either . . . or*, these two words are supposed to join similar grammatical items:
   It is something we can **neither** *explain* **nor** *control.*
   Neither *Bob* **nor** *Roger had enough money to pay for it.*
   I could **neither** *read what he was writing* **nor** *hear what he was saying.*

   But this does not always happen:
   A lecture like that would **neither** *be practical* **nor** *useful.* ('correct' English – *would be* **neither** *practical* **nor** *useful.*)

b   **Singular or plural verb?**
   The general rule is that *neither . . . nor* takes a singular verb, but particularly when the subjects are different persons, plural verbs are normal:

   Neither *Wendy* **nor** *I* **are** *talking about blame.* (*is* or *am* would be odd here)
   Neither *you* **nor** *he* **have** (**has**) *the right to say that.*

c   In general *neither . . . nor* must refer to only two people/things. But this rule too is sometimes broken:
   *I have **neither** pen, official writing paper **nor** a typist.*

3   neither: connector   ▶ Compare   **nor**

   ● nor
   neither is interchangeable with *nor* when it introduces a negative addition to an earlier negative clause or sentence. This *neither* must be followed by inversion (AUXILIARY VERB + SUBJECT . . .):
   *I don't know that, and **neither** do any of us.*
   *You don't believe what I write. I'll tell you something. **Neither** do I.*
   *Geoffrey had not ignored her. But **neither** had he encouraged her.*

never: adverb   ▶ Compare   **not**

   ● not ever, at no time
   never is the opposite of *always*
a   Mid-position is normal for *never*. We do not usually use *not* and *never* in the same sentence:
   *I **never** eat breakfast.*
   *Claudia's **never** been to America.*
   ***Never** do that again!*
   *It has **never** been done before.* (before participle with passive)
   But *never* usually comes after *is/are/was/were* when *be* is the main verb:
   *Tom is **never** on time.*
   *They were **never** at home in the evenings.*

b   If *never* begins a clause, then we use inversion of the auxiliary verb and the subject:
   ***Never** in my life have I heard such utter rubbish.*

c   **never mind**
   ● Don't bother; It doesn't matter . . .
   *Nothing has happened and there's nothing to write about. But **never mind**, I shall write and tell you about nothing.*

                                                       ▶ See   **mind**

nevertheless: connector

   ● however; in spite of that
   *These are difficult demands; **nevertheless** they must be faced.*
   or:
   *These are difficult demands; they must be faced, **nevertheless**.*
   *I don't suppose she'll agree. **Nevertheless**, I think you should ask her.*

new, newer, newest: adjective ▶ Compare **old; young**

a *new* is generally the opposite of *old* (except when referring to someone's age)
a **new** *book . . .* **new** *friends . . . a* **new** *house . . .* **new** *clothes . . .* **new**
potatoes
The **newest** *ideas are not always the best.*

b **new to**
The idea was **new to** *me.* (= I had not thought of such a thing.)
He's **new to** *the job.* (= He has only just started it.)

news: noun (U)

news is always uncountable:
There isn't much **news**.
That is good **news**.
I heard it on the **news**. (= on the radio or television)
Audrey told me an interesting piece of **news**.

next

1 **next**: determiner and adjective ▶ Compare **near**

a ● immediately following in space; nearest following in time
Take the **next** *turning on the left.*
What's the date of the **next** *meeting?*
The **next** *few days look like being as busy as the last few.*

b **the next** or **next**? ▶ Compare **last**
If we are looking ahead from now and using various time words, we say *next*
Tuesday, *next week*, *next weekend*, *the week after next*, *next month*, *next year*,
next January, *next spring*, – without *the*.
With the word *time* itself, *the* may be optional if we explain which time:
(The) Next time *you come, please remember your passport.*

If we are talking about some time in the past, we can say *next day* or *the next*
day:
So we went home and waited till **(the) next day.**

With other words we usually say *the following:*
He went **the following Tuesday.**
I saw her again **the following week.**

2 **next**: adverb

a ● after that
What happened **next**?
I think I'll wash my hair **next**, *and then write some letters.*
If you will let me have this when you **next** *come in, I shall be grateful.*

b We can use *next* in lists:
> *First boil the water, **next** heat the teapot, then . . .*
> ***Next**, I'd like to talk about . . .*

3 next to: preposition   ▶ Compare   ***near***

- beside
> *Come and sit **next to** me, and talk.*
> *We must go to that new shop **next to** the restaurant.*
> *I know **next to** nothing about snakes. (= almost nothing)*

---

next door and next-door

- in the next house, flat or building

1 next door: adverb phrase
> *Some new people have moved in **next door**.*
> *When Colin was in Derby there was a lady of about forty who did things like French lessons **next door**.*

2 next-door: adjective
> *Our **next-door** neighbours are very friendly.*

---

night: noun (C, U)   ▶ Compare **day; tonight**

- *night* is the opposite of *day*:

a *We spent six **nights** in New York.*
> *If you miss the last train, you can stay the **night** with us.*
> *The hotel charges £30 a **night**.*
> *one **night** . . . a **night** to remember . . . the **night** before last . . . the last **night** of our holiday . . . the other **night** (= a recent night)*
> *Did you hear the thunder during the **night**? (= last night)*
> *I kept hearing the dog in/during the **night**.*

b No article is used in the following expressions:
> *We met last **night**/last Saturday **night** . . . and we're meeting again tomorrow **night**/next Tuesday **night**.*
> *They slept by day and travelled by **night** when it was cooler.*
> *She's too frightened to go out at **night** alone. (This is night contrasted with day. But see **a** above for in/during the night seen as a long period of time.)*
> *I lie awake **night** after **night** unable to sleep.*

c Time prepositions are frequently not used:
> *I was awake all **night**.*
> *We met in a pub one **night**.*
> *There was a terrible storm here the **night** before last. (and see **b**)*
> *He works **nights**.*

---

no

no is used to deny, refuse, disagree etc.

1   no: the opposite of **yes**   ▶ Compare **yes**
'Would you like some more?' 'Oh, no thanks.'
'You've met my brother-in-law, haven't you? 'No, I haven't actually.'

Notice that we use *no* (not *yes*) when agreeing with a negative statement or question:
'You don't like milk, do you? 'No I'm afraid I don't.'
'It wouldn't take you long.' 'No, but I'm terribly busy.'

no is also used to show a negative reaction, like disappointment or surprise at bad news:
'I've just lost my job!' 'Oh, no!'

2   no: determiner   ▶ Compare   **none; not**

For the matching pronoun ▶ See **none**. ▶ See also   **nothing; nobody**, etc.

a   At the beginning of a sentence *no* + NOUN PHRASE is often used to make a completely negative sentence (i.e., 'not even one', 'not any at all'):
No stamp is required.
No other novelist gives such an accurate account.
No food is entirely non-fattening.
NO ENTRY/NO EXIT (i.e., Do not enter/There isn't a way out here.)

b   In other positions *no* + NOUN PHRASE is usually more formal and more emphatic than using a VERB + *not* + *a*/*any* + NOUN:
There had been no news whatever. (= There had not been any news.)
He has no backache now.
There should be no need for him to do that.
Honest citizens who have committed no crime . . .
I don't like hard work and there is no escaping from it here.
There is no time to waste.
We know of no way this could be done. (. . . there isn't any way.)

c   Sometimes *no* + NOUN PHRASE is so emphatic that the meaning is exactly the opposite:
This was no small achievement. (i.e., it was a very big achievement)
I have no hesitation in recommending her for the job. (= I positively do recommend her).
This is no time to be silly. (= This is a time to be sensible.)

3   no: adverb   ▶ Compare   **far; much**

● not at all; in no way
no is used before comparative forms and with *different* to mean that, surprisingly, something is not in any way better or worse or different, etc.

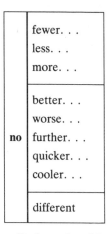

no	fewer. . . less. . . more. . .
	better. . . worse. . . further. . . quicker. . . cooler. . .
	different

No fewer than thirteen ministers supported the idea. (= Thirteen was a lot of ministers.)
*There are **no** less than five performances on Saturday.* (= Five is a lot of performances.)
No more than a dozen people attended the meeting. (= only a dozen)
*They pulled the curtains across, but the room felt **no** cooler.* (= it was just as hot)
*I'm sorry you're **no** better.* (= you're still ill)
*We have progressed **no** further with the work, I'm sorry to say.*
*I never manage to save any money. And this year has been **no** different.* (i.e., exactly the same – I have not saved any money at all)

▶ See also **no longer; no sooner**

4 no good, no use, no point

*It's really **no** use/**no** good worrying.* (= It is useless to worry.)
*There's **no point** in worrying.* (= It is useless to worry.)
*I am **no good** at mathematics.* (= I am very bad at . . .)

5 no way

no way is used informally for a very strong refusal:
*There's **no way** I'm going to tell lies just to get him out of trouble.*
*'You're coming to the disco, aren't you?' '**No way!**'*

6 no wonder: conjunction

● it's not surprising that
*No **wonder** you failed your exam if you didn't do any work.*

▶ See also **none; not; no doubt; no matter**

nobody, no one: pronouns

▶ Compare **anybody**; **somebody**

- not anybody; not even one person

nobody is the opposite of *everybody*, *everyone*:

a *nobody* and *no one* mean the same. Both refer to people (not things). Only
nobody/no one (NEVER – *Not anybody/anyone*) can be the subject of a verb,
but in other positions we can say either, but *nobody/no one* is more emphatic:
Nobody/No one *knows what is going to happen.*
There was **nobody/no one** *at home when I called.* (or *There wasn't anybody/
anyone . . .*)

b *nobody* or *a nobody* can mean an unimportant person:
Don't take any notice of him. He's (a) **nobody.**

c Adjectives, relative clauses, *else* and other phrases, can all follow:
no one *special . . .* **nobody** *you know . . .*
Nobody *in his right mind would pay that much.* (= Anybody who pays that
price must be mad.)
I've got **nobody** *to go with, and I can't go alone.*

d **nobody/no one . . . they**

nobody and *no one* are singular and take singular verbs. But sentences often
continue with plural possessives and pronouns:
Nobody *wants to lose* **their** *home, do* **they**?

none

▶ Compare **no**

- not one; not any; no part

none is the opposite of *all*:

1 none: pronoun

none of	the/these/my . . . neighbours letters (PLURAL NOUNS) them/you/us	is . . . are . . .
	the/this/my . . . paper (UNCOUNTABLE NOUN) town (SINGULAR NOUN) it/this	is . . .

a *none* and *none of* + PLURAL NOUN or PRONOUN refer to three or more people/
things. (See **neither (of)** . . . for two people/things).
Old-fashioned grammar says the verb here must be singular, but as the
meaning is roughly 'all . . . not', plural verbs are often used:

*Where are the envelopes? There are **none** left, I'm afraid.*
***None** of you are going to like this.* (Notice *are* here, with *you.*)
***None** of the **neighbours** know/knows that we're moving.*

b   With uncountable nouns and singular count nouns and pronouns, the meaning
is 'no part of'. Verbs of course are singular:
*'We haven't any writing paper, have we?' 'No, there's **none** here.'*
***None** of the city escaped the bombing.* (= No part of the city . . .)
***None** of this is true.*

2   **none**: adverb

none is used as an adverb in two types of expression.
a   *none too* + ADJECTIVE/ADVERB
  ● not at all
  *Poor old Charles is **none too** well.* (= He is not at all well – he is rather ill.)

b   *none the* + COMPARATIVE ADJECTIVE/ADVERB
  ● not . . . in any way
  *It was a nasty experience but she's **none the** worse for it.* (= She is not upset or
  injured.)

---

nonetheless: adverb

  ● nevertheless
  *It may be surprising, but it is **nonetheless** true that the company continue to
  produce about 8000 swords a year.*

---

nor   ▶ Compare **neither**

  ● and also not

1   **nor**: conjunction

a   *nor* is used as the second (or later) conjunction in negative statements
containing *neither*:
  *Neither Wendy **nor** I knew about it.*
  *We can neither explain **nor** control this.*

b   **Singular or plural verb?**   ▶ See   neither (2b)

2   **nor**: connector

nor can introduce a negative comment or addition to a previous negative
statement. *Nor* here must be followed by inversion (auxiliary verb + subject):
  *I don't know that, and **nor** do any of us.*
  *You don't believe it. **Nor** do I.*
  *There were no tickets left for Saturday, **nor** (were there any left) for Friday.*
  *'I don't like rock music'. '**Nor** me'.*

not

not is used to make sentences or parts of sentences negative.

1 *be*, *do*, *have* and MODAL VERBS + **not**

not (often shortened to *n't*) is added to *be*, *do*, *have* and modal verbs. This usually makes the whole sentence negative:

a   *I am **not** a medical man, he said crossly.*
*Do **not**/**Don't** expect too much.*
*You do **not** answer my questions.*
*I **haven't** a clue.*
*They **couldn't** agree, unfortunately.*

b   In questions there is a difference in the position of *n't* and *not*:
Wouldn't that be rather difficult?
*Would that **not** be rather difficult?* (formal)

not (usually *n't*) is used to make question-tags after positive statements:
*You are coming tomorrow, **aren't** you?*
(Contrast: *You **aren't** coming, are you?*)

Negative questions sometimes express surprise:
Haven't you had breakfast?
Aren't you ready?

or function as suggestions:
Couldn't we phone for tickets?
Why don't we phone for tickets?

2 *not* comes before *-ing* forms and *to*-INFINITIVES:
Not wanting to upset them, I kept quiet.
Not having heard from her for over a month, they were very worried.
*You were quite right **not** to say anything.*
*I told her **not** to waste her money.* (Contrast: *I **didn't** tell her to buy it.*)

3   **not**: negative clause   ▶ Compare **so**

A I assume/believe/expect/fear/guess/hear/ hope/imagine/suppose/think/understand I'm afraid It appears/seems	
B If/Or/Why	**not**
C Maybe/Perhaps/Possibly/Probably	
D Apparently/certainly/definitely/fortunately/ obviously/surely/of course	

not can be used for a whole clause (including the subject and verb) instead of repeating it in the negative.

A This can happen after various verbs of reporting and thinking, *to be afraid*, *it appears/seems . . .*:

'*I think it's going to rain.' 'Oh I hope not.'* (= I hope that it isn't going to rain.)
'*Did you give Charles my message?' 'No I'm afraid not – I forgot'.*
'*Is Henry coming tomorrow?' 'It appears/seems not.'*

B *if not* and *or not* are often used instead of repeating a clause:

I think the door has a lock, but if not, I'll buy one. (= if it has not got a lock)
Shall I telephone this evening, or not? (= or shall I not telephone?)
Why not? is used in the same way to question something:
'*I'm not going to the party'. 'Why not?'*

C+D Various sentence adverbs concerned with possibility, and some making general comments, can be followed by *not*:

'*Surely you don't need a new car?' 'Well, perhaps not, but it would be nice'.*
'*Did Celia get hurt?' 'Fortunately not.'*

Note: *not* can also be used to make short negative clauses which avoid repeating part of the previous clause, often the verb. It is often used in this way to make a correction or distinction:

The flags were flying for us, and not her. (= They were not flying for her.)
This may be a day late, not a fortnight I hope.
I was laughing, not crying.
He eventually found it on the floor, not on the shelf.
See you on the 25th, if not before.

4 not + think/want . . .

With some verbs, mostly of thinking, but also *want*, we often say *I don't think . . ./I don't want . . .* when logically the *not* belongs to the next clause:

I don't believe/think you love me at all. (= I believe/think that you don't love me).
I don't imagine/suppose you could lend me £10, could you? (Notice the positive *could you?* which goes with the meaning 'I suppose you couldn't'.)
He didn't want to go to the party. (Perhaps he definitely wanted not to go.)
It doesn't look as if Tom's coming now. (= It looks as if he isn't coming.)

Verbs like this include:
(I don't) *believe/expect/imagine/suppose/think* (that) . . .
It doesn't *appear/seem* that/as if . . .
It doesn't *look/seem/sound* as if . . .

▶ See also **so**

5 Negation of a word or phrase

Sometimes *not* makes just a word or phrase negative, but not the whole clause:

Not everybody can win first prize. (= Only one person can.)
Not all the Welsh speak Welsh. (= But some of them do.)
Not enough information was available. (= Some was.)
Not many people can speak 6 languages. (= Some people can.)

*He's the author of two **not** very good plays.* (= He is the author of two plays, although they're not very good.)
*The rate of pay is **not** less than £4 an hour.* (= It is at least £4 an hour.)

6 not and reasons

When we suggest two or more reasons for doing something and we say one of these was *not* the real reason, the *not* can come before the first verb:
*I **didn't** buy it because it was cheap, but because I liked it.* (= I bought it, not because it was cheap but because . . .)
*I do **not** drink to be happy; I drink **not** to be afraid.* (= I drink, not in order to be happy, but in order to be unafraid.)

7 not at all

- definitely not
*Tibet was **not at all** as we expected.*
*That's **not at all** funny.*

In conversation *not at all* can be used for politeness:
*'Do you mind if I leave this until tomorrow?' '**Not at all**.'* (= Of course I don't mind.)
*'That's terribly kind of you – thank you so much.' '**Not at all**.'* (= There's no need to thank me.)

8 not only . . . (but also)

a *not only* introduces two similar things. Usually they are both slightly surprising, but the second is more surprising. The second is sometimes introduced by *but* or *but also*:
*It's **not only** your mother who was upset, I was too.*
*I think you were **not only** rude, **but (also)** foolish.*

b If *not only* begins a sentence and belongs with the verb, we put the subject after the auxiliary verb:
***Not only** did he arrive late, **but** he came in the wrong clothes.*
***Not only** do these shops offer very good value, **but** they also provide an excellent after-sales service to their customers.*

9 'double negative'

a It is usually wrong in modern standard English to have a negative verb (with *not* or *never*) plus a negative word (e.g. *nobody*) in the same clause if our meaning is negative. So we say:
Nobody told me anything. (NOT **Nobody didn't tell me nothing.*)
You can't trust anyone these days. (NOT **You can't trust nobody.*)
Nothing ever happens to me. (NOT **Nothing doesn't ever . . .* **Nothing never . . .*)
I don't want any of this. (NOT **I don't want none . . .*)

Notice that we cannot begin a sentence with *Not anybody/Not anything*. (NOT ***Not** anybody knew. ***Not** anything happened.)

b We can however sometimes use two negative words, when our meaning is positive:

Nobody has no friends. (= Everybody has at least one or two friends.)
Not all of these people have nowhere to go. (= Some of them have somewhere to go).
The match was not unlike a battle. (= It was rather like a battle.)
They may not always do it for nothing. (= Sometimes they may want something in return).

nothing: pronoun ▶ Compare **anything; something**

nothing is the opposite of *everything*

a *nothing* is more emphatic than *not anything* but often both are possible. *Nothing* is preferred as the subject of a verb:

Nothing *ever goes right for me – I'm terribly unlucky.*
*There's **nothing** to do in a place like that.* (or *There isn't anything . . .*)

b *nothing* can be followed by adjectives, *else* and other phrases:

What's the matter with Paul? **Nothing** *serious, I hope.*
Nothing *else matters.*
*There was **nothing** much happening.*
*There's **nothing** I like better than an afternoon in the garden.*
*You have to tell the truth, the whole truth and **nothing** but the truth.*

For *nothing like* ▶ See **like**

notice

1 notice: verb ▶ Compare **see; watch**

  • look at; see

	OBJECT	
	that-CLAUSE	
notice +	*wh*-CLAUSE	
	O + BARE INFINITIVE	
	O + *-ing*	

a *notice* can be used with and without an object. It can also be followed by *that*-CLAUSES and *wh*-CLAUSES:

*They must have seen me, but they pretended not to **notice**.*
*I **noticed** that the cinema was shut, but I didn't **notice** whether the car park was empty.*

b Like *feel, hear, see*, etc., *notice* can be followed by OBJECT + BARE INFINITIVE and by OBJECT + *-ing*:

*I didn't **notice** the postman come this morning, but the post is here.*
*She **noticed** smoke rising from the chimney.*

c   Some passives are possible:
  *Your absence was **noticed**. Where were you?*

  (But NOT **The postman was **noticed** to come*.)

2   notice: noun

a   • written or printed information
  *Put a **notice** up on the wall/the notice board.*
  *There was a **notice** on the gate saying 'Beware of the dog'.*

b   • formal statement that somebody wants to do something, especially leave a job
  *I don't like my job – I'm going to hand in/give in my **notice**.*

c   take notice of
  • pay attention to
  *Don't **take any notice of**/**Take no notice of** what he says – he doesn't really know anything about it.*

---

now

1   now: adverb   ► Compare **then**

a   • at the present time; immediately; not then
  *I used to enjoy swimming, but **now** I don't.* (or *But I don't **now**.*)
  *I don't want to save up for it; I want to buy it **now**.*

b   When we are describing the past *now* can mean 'at that time (in the past)':
  ***Now** it was Maria's turn to say something, but she didn't know what to say.*

c   *now* can also be used rather like a noun, and even after prepositions:
  ***Now** is the time to do it.*
  *Come on – it's **now** or never.*
  *They ought to be here by **now** – wherever can they be?*
  *That's all for **now**.*
  *From **now** on . . .*
  *Up to/Until **now**.*
  *Before **now** . . .*

d   *just now* has two meanings:
  *I'm busy **just now**.* (= at this moment, at this present time)
  *I saw him **just now**.* (= a very short time ago)

e   any minute/any day/anytime now
  • very soon
  *They'll be here **any minute now**, and you're still not dressed.*

f   now and then/now and again
  • several times, but not regularly
  *I don't see my brother much these days – just **now and again**.*

2   now: connector

  now is often used in spoken English to keep the conversation moving:
  ***Now** what was I going to say?*

Now, where did I leave my glasses?
*Well **now** – what are we going to do?*

3 now (that): conjunction

now that often gives an explanation:
*Now **(that)** I'm older, I don't mind so much what people think.*

---

nowadays: adverb

- now; at the present time:
*I'm cooking more **nowadays** – especially for hungry and homeless friends.*
*They always expect people to have cars **nowadays**.*

---

nowhere: adverb
▶ Compare **anywhere**; **everywhere**; **somewhere**

a   • not anywhere; at no place

*It's hell driving a car round London – there's **nowhere** to park at all.*
*We arrived rather late at night, with **nowhere** to stay.*
*It's a place right out in the middle of **nowhere**.* (= far from other houses or a town)
Also: *nowhere else . . . nowhere cheap . . . nowhere (that) I know . . .*

b   **nowhere near**   ▶ Compare **nearly**
- not nearly
*Nelly is **nowhere near** old enough to go on her own.*
*£20 is **nowhere near** enough – you'll need £50 at least.*

▶ Compare *nothing like* at **like**

---

number

1 a number of   ▶ Compare **a lot of**

- several; many
a (large/great/small) number of – and sometimes *numbers of* – are used with count nouns only. (Contrast *a lot of/lots of*, which can also be used with uncountable nouns.) These expressions are used with plural verbs:
*A **large number of** people were injured in the accident.*
*There are **a number** of things I have to do.*
*Considerable **numbers** of animals have escaped.*

---

2 the number of

This phrase usually refers to the idea of an actual quantity, and here the verb is singular:

The number of people who complained was small. – where the verb is singular to agree with *The number*.

---

object (to) /ɒb'dʒekt/: verb

- be against; refuse to accept

object (to) is one of those verbs like *look forward to* where the *to* is a preposition, and any following verb must be an -*ing* form (never an infinitive):

*If you didn't want to pay, you should have **objected** before.*

*I don't **object to** paying £10, but I do **object to** the rude way the whole thing has been organised.*

---

occur: verb ▶ Compare **happen**

a We can use *occur* with the same meaning as 'happen', but *occur* is more formal:

*Something very strange **occurred/happened**.*

*The accident **occurred/happened** at a dangerous crossroads.*

occur is also rather more limited in use – we never say **What is **occurring** here?*

b occur to

occur to (somebody) is quite different from *happen to (somebody/something)*. It means an idea comes into somebody's mind:

*The idea that he could say 'No' apparently never **occurred to** him.*

*It **occurs**/It has **occurred to** me that Peter could probably help us.*

Contrast **happen to**:

*Something awful has **happened to** Peter.*

*Something has **happened to** my legs – I can't walk properly.*

---

of: preposition

of is one of the commonest words in the English language and sometimes does not seem to have very much meaning, except that it shows some sort of relationship between words.

---

1 Quantities

A

some, any, none many, more, most (a) few, fewer, fewest		the these/those . . . books (pl) my . . .
enough, several each, neither, either a lot, lots, one . . .	**of**	these/those you/us/them (pl) mine/yours . . .
some, any, none much, more, most (a) little, less, least enough a lot, lots, a bit . . .		the . . . book (sing) this/that . . . rice (U)
		this/that it (sing and U) mine/yours . . .

A We cannot usually use determiners with other determiners. So instead of joining *some, any, no,* etc. to *the, this, my,* etc. (**some the books, *no my pencils*) or to pronouns (**all them*) we use a PRONOUN + *of*. The pronoun is usually the same word, but notice *no* (determiner) but *none* (pronoun):

> *Some **of** the books are dirty.*
> *None **of** these pencils is sharp.*
> *All **of** them are broken.*
> *One **of** my friends has just gone to South America.*
> *Much **of** the time we were just waiting around.*

B

all/half	**(of)**	the/these/my . . . books (pl) the/this/my . . . book (sing) the/this/my . . . food (U)
		this/these . . . mine/yours/hers . . .
both		the/these/my . . . books these/those. (PLURAL) mine/yours/his/hers/ours/theirs.
all/half	**of**	it/you/us/them
both		you/us/them (PLURAL)

B With *all*, *half*, *both*, *of* is optional before *the*; before *this*, *those*, etc.; and before possessives (*my . . . mine . . .*). But we must use *of* before *it*, *you*, *us*, *them* (personal pronouns):

> *All (of) your friends came.*
> *Half (of) mine were ill.*
> *Both of us speak French.*

2   Measurements, units, containers . . .

of is used to join nouns referring to measurements, units and containers to another noun to show how much or how many there are:

> *a litre of wine . . . two spoonfuls of sugar . . . a piece of string . . . a pair of trousers . . . a group of children . . . a box of matches . . . a bottle of wine . . . a cup of coffee. . . . a book of problems . . . a list of students . . . a book of only 52 pages . . . a map of Britain* (the map shows Britain) *. . . a photograph of my parents* (the photograph shows my parents)

Also:

> *The diamond was the size of a bird's egg.* (= the same size as a bird's egg)
> *Her dress was the colour of grass.* (= the same colour as grass)

3   Possession, having   ▶ Compare   's

In this use the *of*-NOUN (the noun that follows *of*) shows what or who 'owns' something, and the first noun belongs to it or is part of it:

> *the days of the week* (= a week has seven days)
> *as a result of the storm* (= the storm had that result)
> *the 31st of December. . . . the University of London . . . the front of the house . . . the end of the affair . . . the beginning of the term . . . a member of the club . . . the length of the room . . . the events of the week . . . at the time of the disaster*

Notice that most of the 'owners' are things. This contrasts with possessive *'s*, which is mainly used for people (and animals). *The club's members, the week's events* are possible, but NOT **the week's days*, **the house's front*, etc. So it is safest to use NOUN *of* + NOUN when the 'owner' is a thing.

But if we refer to people as *the* + ADJECTIVE (for example, *the poor*), we must use *of*, and not *'s*:

> *the needs of the poor* (NOT **the poor's needs*)
> *the loneliness of the old*

4   of-NOUN as subject

Sometimes the *of*-NOUN is rather like the subject of a verb:

> *the arrival of the parcel* (the parcel arrived) *. . .*
> *the approval of your parents* (your parents approve) *. . .*
> (*your parent's approval* is also possible.)

Notice also ADJECTIVE + *of* + NOUN/PRONOUN + *to*-INFINITIVE, where the *of*-NOUN is also a kind of subject in meaning:

> *How kind of you to tell me.* (= You were kind to tell me.)
> *It was thoughtful of Roger to telephone.* (= Roger was thoughtful.)

5 Double possession

Sometimes two ways of showing possession – (1) *of*, plus (2) a POSSESSIVE WORD – are used together. This means that we can join an indefinite word (like *a* or *some*) to a definite word (like *mine* or *my mother's*):

Noah is a great friend of mine. (= Noah is one of my friends and he is a great friend.)
Some neighbours of my mother's told me that. (= Some of my mother's neighbours . . .)
I want a room of my own. (= a room that is my own room)

6 Of-NOUN as object

Sometimes the *of*-NOUN is rather like the object of a verb:

a change of plan (= somebody has changed the plan) . . . *the defeat of Arsenal* (= the other football team defeated Arsenal) . . . *a woman of courage* (= the woman shows courage) . . . *his love of life* (= he loves life) . . . *the Department of Education* (=the department that looks after education) . . . *my feeling of annoyance* (= I felt annoyed.)

7 adjectives followed by **of**

Some adjectives are normally followed by *of* plus a NOUN or an *-ing* form. Again, the *of*-NOUN (or *-ing* form) has a sort of object meaning:

I've always been afraid of the dark (= feared the dark)
But I'm fond of snakes. (= I like snakes.)
We were tired of waiting for something to happen. (= We disliked waiting.)
Similarly: *ashamed of . . . aware of . . . certain of . . . proud of . . . sure of . . .*

Notice also: *Suddenly the room was full of smoke.*

8 Causes, origins

Were Cinderella's shoes really made of glass?
His father has just died of cancer.

9 The two things joined by *of* are the same:

The City of London . . . the Isle of Wight (= the island called Wight) . . . *a gift of money . . . the age of 19 . . . a cost of £20,000*

10 VERB (+ NOUN) + **of**

Some verbs are regularly followed by *of*:

I wouldn't dream of telling you.
Celia's always talking of changing her job (or *talking about . . .*)
That tune reminds me of my childhood.
They robbed him of his wallet and then ran off.
Please don't accuse me of dishonesty.

▶ See *kind of* at **kind**; *sort of* at **sort**

off is a preposition and an adverb of place, particularly with verbs of movement. Things can come *off* surfaces and areas and *off* objects that we think of as two-dimensional. *Off* therefore contrasts with *out of* (3-dimensional spaces). For example, you take something *off a shelf*, but *out of a cupboard*. *Off* is also a sort of adjective.

off means 'not on', 'away from', 'separated from', and is the opposite of *on*.

1 **off**: preposition

*Another button has come **off** my coat.*
*I wanted to get **off** the bus at the bank but it didn't stop.*
*Keep **off** the grass.*
*How on earth did Tom manage to fall **off** the ladder?*
*Take that silly smile **off** your face.*
*You must turn **off** the motorway at junction 22.*
*Take your hands **off** me at once.*
*I was **off** work for two months last year with a bad back.*
*Celia's **off** her food.* (= not eating much)

2 **off**: adverb and adjective

*Well, I'm **off** now.* (= leaving) *See you tomorrow.*
*This coat isn't very well made. The buttons keep coming **off**.*
*Take **off** your muddy shoes.*
*Turn the hot water **off**.*
*Our plane takes **off** from Heathrow at 10.57.*
*We've had to put the meeting **off** until next week.* (= postpone)
*Everytime I telephoned her, we got cut **off**.* (= disconnected)
*He hurried/ran/drove **off**.*
*It's still too long. Cut a bit **off**.*
*I'm going to ask my boss for some time **off**.*
*The milk/meat is **off**. It's gone **off**.* (= it isn't fresh, it has gone bad)

3 **off** or **out (of)?**

a We can *switch/turn lights, heaters, radios, TV sets . . . off.*
We can also *turn* or *put lights out* (NOT **put off*).
The opposite is *put/switch/turn on*.

b We can *get off* or *out of* a *train . . .* (the opposite is *get on/in*)
We also *get off a bicycle, bus, horse . . .* (the opposite is *get on*)
But we *get out of a car . . .* (the opposite is *get in/into*)

c *I was **off** work.* (perhaps because I was ill)
*I was **out of** work.* (= without a job, unemployed)

offer

1 offer, offered, offered: verb

> —
> **offer** + (IO) + OBJECT
> *to*-INFINITIVE

a Like *give*, *offer* can have one or two objects:
> *They are **offering** a free trip to the West Indies as first prize.*
> *She didn't even **offer** me a cup of coffee.*
> *Why don't they **offer** Rosemary the job?/**offer** the job to Rosemary?*
> *Somebody else has been **offered** the job.*
> *The job has been **offered** to somebody else.*

b *offer* + *to*-INFINITIVE means 'be willing to do something':
> *They have **offered** to lend me the money, but I don't like borrowing.*

2 offer: noun (C)
> *I think we should accept their **offer**.*
> *Their **offer** to lend you the money was very kind.*
> *I made an **offer** of £500 for the picture, but he would not sell it.*
> *The supermarket has different special **offers** every week.* (= things at a special low price)

often: adverb

• frequently
often is usually used in mid-position:
> *I don't **often** get such pleasant opportunities.*
> *Boiling water will **often** cure the trouble.*
> *'How **often** do you water house plants?' 'Well, I don't water mine very **often**.'*

old, older, oldest: adjective ▶ Compare **elder, eldest**

1 *old* is the opposite of *young* (people) and *new* (things) and is the usual word when talking about people's ages:
> *'How **old** is the baby?' 'He's just three days **old**.'*
> *'Are you **older** or younger than your sister?' 'She's the **oldest**/eldest in the family and my brother's the youngest.'*
> *It's a very **old** house – at least 400 years **old**, but I suppose you'd rather live in a new house?*
> *We've known each other for ages; we are very **old** friends.*

2 *the old* can mean old people in general   (Compare *the poor, the young, the sick . . .*):
> *We must look after **the old** and the sick.*

on is first of all a preposition and an adverb of place. Things can be *on* a surface or *on* a line. *On* contrasts with *at* (a point) and *in* (a 3-dimensional space). It also contrasts with *at* and *in* with meanings of time.

The general meanings of *on* are: 'connection', 'touching', 'supported by' and also 'going forward', 'progress towards a destination.' With the meaning of 'connection', *on* often contrasts with *off* (separation).

1 on: preposition

a Place

As a preposition of place, *on* means 'connecting', 'touching'. The opposite is usually *off*:

*The food is **on** the table.*
*Let's sit **on** the grass/the sand/the beach.*
*I hate driving **on** the motorway.*
*Would you like to live **on** an island?*
*It tells you **on** page 51.*
*I wrote the address down **on** a bit of paper.*
*Put the lid **on** the biscuit tin, please.*
*She was sitting **on** the sofa.* (but: *in an armchair*).
*He was hit **on** the head.*
*He put his hand **on** my shoulder.*
*She lay **on** her back looking up at the sky.*
*He had a horrible look **on** his face.*
*Why don't you put a notice up **on** the wall.*
*She just dropped the empty packet **on** the ground.*
*I cut myself **on** a nail.*
*They live **on** a farm.*

b Time

on is used with times which are somewhere between a point (*at 6 o'clock*) and a long period (*in 1990*), usually days:

on Saturday . . . on Saturday afternoon . . . on 21st June . . . on my birthday . . . on New Year's Day . . .

Note: American English uses *on the weekend* but British English prefers *at the weekend*)

c Various other uses

*We came **on** a bus/**on** a train/**on** foot.* (▶ See **by**)
*I want a book **on** house plants.* (▶ See **about**)
*Whose side are you **on**?*
*Don't spend so much time **on** it.*
*He lives **on** £50 a week.*
*I saw it **on** television.*
*I heard it **on** the radio.*
*There's a cinema **on** the left/**on** the right.*
*This is **on** me.* (= I'm paying.)
*What **on** earth is the matter?*
*I couldn't answer the door – I was **on** the telephone.*

d **on** + *-ing* ▶ *Compare* **in** + *-ing*

on can introduce an *-ing* CLAUSE and means 'when':
   On *seeing me, they waved.* (= when they saw me)

e Some verbs are regularly followed by **on**:
   The success of the whole thing depends **on** *you.*
   We're relying **on** *you.*
   She insisted **on** *paying.*

2 **on**: adverb and adjective

a ● connection
The opposite is usually *off*:
   Switch/turn the radio/television **on**.
   Celia then tried to stick the notice **on** *with glue, but it fell off.*
   Hold **on** *a moment. Don't ring off.* (Telephone phrases).
   That jacket would suit you. Why don't you try it **on**?
   Put your shoes **on**. *Why have you taken them off?*
   What's **on** *at the cinema? 'The Living Daylights' was* **on** *last week, but it's come off now.'*
   'When does Harrods' sale start?' 'It's **on** *now.'*
   It's terribly hot in here. Is the heater **on**?

b ● continue, go forward
   Why are you waiting? Please go **on**.
   Keep **on** *walking. Don't stop.*
   The boys drove/hurried/walked/ran **on**.
   How are you getting **on** *with your work?* (= making progress)
   What's going **on** *here?* (= happening)
   I'm busy for the moment, but I'll be free later **on**.
   They said they were sorry, they wished they could have helped, they would help next time . . . and so **on**.

   ▶ See **onto**

once

1 **once**: adverb

once has two rather different meanings.

a ● On one single occasion, i.e., not twice or three times.
However if *once* is used with other words added like *once a week*), there can be a series of occasions. *Once* usually comes after the verb, and can refer to any time, past, present or future:
   To stop the bus, ring the bell **once**.
   I've only seen her **once** *since I heard this news.*
   This newspaper has argued more than **once** *that we can . . .*
   She does no teaching apart from the summer school **once** *a year.*
   I was thinking of writing to you **once** *a week.*
   I may have said the wrong thing **once** *too often.*
   The blood should be checked **once** *every three months.*
   ***Once** again, this is going to be the most perfect royal wedding.*

If you say that once more, I'll scream.
I wouldn't mind trying just once.
Dear Judith, . . . I am once again asking you to do something for me.

b • at some time in the past
With this meaning *once* is often in mid-position and NEVER refers to the present or future:
I once acted in 'Murder in the Cathedral'.
That once happened to me.
This house was once a boys' school.
Newtown is a lively place, once famous for its wool trade.

To talk about the future, we use *one day/some time*:
I'd like to act in a play some time.
I'm going to write a book one day.

2 once: conjunction

• as soon as; when
Once you've tried our coffee, you'll never want to drink any other brand.

3 at once

a • immediately
This at once solved the problem.
It's very urgent. Please come at once.

b • at the same time
One does not in all cases either love or hate. There are some cases where one does both at once.

one

1 one: determiner and pronoun

a • number
one, two, three . . . twenty-one
a/one hundred, a/one thousand, a/one dozen . . . a/one-fifth of a mile (1/5th)
. . . one and a half days . . .
It's one o'clock . . . one-thirty (1.30 a.m./p.m.)
Page one . . . one or two days (= a few days)

For the difference between *a/an* and *one* – See **a**.

b • a certain; some
One day my prince will come.
They woke up one morning and found their garden had fallen into the sea during the night.
Do come and see us one day. (= some day)

c • only; single
That's the one thing I'm afraid of.

d one . . . the other
one . . . the other are used to contrast two people or things:
One went east and the other went west.

One after the other . . .
She was holding a flag in **one** *hand and a chicken in* **the other**.

e   one of

one of is always followed by a plural noun or pronoun (or a possessive pronoun). A verb following the *one*-phrase is singular or plural depending on the meaning:

One of *my friends has just gone to Mexico.* (= A friend has . . .)
If you haven't got a case I'll lend you **one of** *mine.*
Any/each/every **one of** *these/them would be suitable.*
Not **one of** *these torches is any good.* (= none of them . . .)
He is **one of** *those awful people who are always late for everything.*

2   one, ones: pronouns

a   *one* and *ones* are used instead of repeating a singular or plural count noun (never an uncountable noun). The word *one* can be used alone, but with *ones* we have to give more information (*nice ones, the ones I like, ones with wooden handles*):

I haven't got an umbrella – I'll have to buy **one**.
Which **one/ones** *do you like?*
The **one/ones** *I like is/are too expensive. Anyway, I want a folding* **one** *and I don't like* **ones** *with wooden handles.*

b   *one, ones* are used instead of noun phrases, but they do not refer to the same actual things, where we use *it* or *them*:

Contrast:
Is that your umbrella? Can I borrow **it**? (= that umbrella)
Are these your gloves? Do you want **them**? (= these gloves)
I've come without an umbrella. Can I borrow **one**? (= an umbrella)
Have you any bright blue folding umbrellas? Yes, I think we have **one/some**.
(NOT *We have* **ones**.)
No, but we've got green **ones**. (= green folding umbrellas).
No, we've only got bright blue **ones** *with wooden handles.* (*ones* only replaces the word *umbrellas* here.)

c   *one, ones* can be used about people as well as things:
I'm not **one** *to waste money.* (= I'm not that sort of person.)
It's the quiet **ones** *who work hardest.*

d   these/those . . .

We can say *this/that one*, but we do not usually say **these/those ones*:
I like those umbrellas, but I prefer these. (NOT **these* **ones**) *I'm going to buy* **this one**.

We can omit *one/ones* after superlative adjectives and after colours:
The blue **(ones)** *are nice, but I think I'll buy a green* **(one)**.
You would like the most expensive **(ones)**.

3   one, one's, oneself: indefinite personal pronoun   ▶   Compare   you; they

a   *one* means 'anybody including the speaker' or 'people like the speaker'. It is fairly formal.

one's is the possessive form, and *oneself* the reflexive pronoun. (In American English, *one* is sometimes followed by *he/him/himself*):

One *shouldn't believe everything* **one** *reads in the papers.*
It's the kind of place where **one** *has to look after* **oneself**.

b Sometimes *one* is used when the speaker really means 'I/me'. This is considered very formal by some people:

People sometimes seem terrified of meeting us. I don't know quite what they consider **one** *to be.* (i.e., the speaker, and perhaps his wife too).
My parents are getting old, and so **one** *has to make sure they are properly cared for.*

c Except when *one* actually means the speaker (**b**), *one* is not used to refer to a particular person or people:

Somebody told me . . . (NOT **One told me . . .*)

▶ See *one another* at **another**

---

only

1 only: adverb

● just; merely

only emphasises the one thing that happens, that there is nothing else, nobody else.

a *only* can come almost anywhere in a sentence to emphasise a particular word or phrase:

Only *you can solve this problem.* (= Nobody else.)
We have **only** *just heard the news. Congratulations!*
It's **only** *natural to worry about the future.*
We have **only** *three days' holiday left.*
I was **only** *joking.*

The commonest position for *only*, however, is mid-position, before the main verb (as in the last example), even when *only* refers to some later words in the sentence:

Bob **only** *reads detective stories.*

As the most important part of a sentence normally comes at the end, this probably means *only detective stories* (i.e., no other sort of book). Rather improbably, it could also mean *only Bob reads them* (i.e., the rest of us don't) or *he only reads them* (i.e., at other times perhaps he writes them). When we talk we can make our meaning clear by our intonation, but in written English this sort of sentence can be ambiguous, so many people recommend rewriting this as:

Bob reads **only** *detective stories.*

– if that is the meaning. But sentences like this can sound formal and unnatural, and the context will often make the meaning clear. However there are real problems with some sentences:

Bob **only** *reads detective stories on holiday:*

could equally well mean:

He reads **only** *detective stories on holiday.*

or:
*He reads detective stories on holiday **only**.*

But again, both sentences sound formal, and it is usually better to reword them completely:
When he's on holiday he reads nothing but detective stories.
or:
*He reads detective stories **only** when he's on holiday.*

In practice the meaning of most sentences with *only* in mid-position is perfectly clear. *Only* could be moved in all the following, but the resulting sentences would be much more formal:
*I'm **only** here for the beer.* (= I'm here because I want to drink.)
*I **only** arrived here last night.* (= not before then)
*It **only** cost £10.* (= it was very cheap)
*I was **only** thinking the other day how nice it would be to see you again.* (= just the other day)
*Changes can **only** be made if all the banks agree.*

b Sometimes *only* is used to emphasise an affirmative sentence:
*I **only** hope you're right.* (= I very much hope . . .)
*I got to the station **only** to find I'd left my ticket at home.* (= I got there, but then I found . . .)

c *only* has a nearly negative meaning, so if we put it at the very beginning of a sentence as part of an adverb phrase, it needs inversion, like other negative adverbs in that position:
***Only** if the banks agree can changes be made.*
***Only** in China do you see such sights.*

2 **only**: adjective

- single
  *It's the **only** copy I have.* (= I have no other copy.)
  *I'd hate to be an **only** child.* (= without brothers and sisters)

3 **only**: conjunction

- but; except that (informal)
  *I would have telephoned – **only** I couldn't find your number.*

For *not only* ▶ See **not**
For *only too* ▶ See **too**
For *if only* ▶ See **if**

onto: preposition

Is it *onto* or *on to*?
Some people write *onto* as one word (just like *into*).
This is quite common when there is a meaning of actual movement resulting in a final 'position on':
*The man climbed **onto** the roof.* (= so he was on the roof)
*She pinned the badge **onto** her coat.* (= so it was on her coat)

But many people dislike this. It is always correct to use *on to*, and much safer when *on* has other meanings or belongs closely with the verb:

*?He is able to get **onto** good terms with students rapidly.*
*I have passed this information **on to** her.* (= I passed it on.)
*The dialogues in some of the TV plays was so thrilling I was holding **on to** my seat with excitement.* (= I was holding on.)
*He went **on to** say, 'We have a very high regard for this company.'* (= He continued, and said . . .)

---

onward(s): adverb

- from then; from that time

onwards is the usual form in British English and *onward* in American English. It is quite rare and is mostly used in phrases like *from tomorrow onwards* meaning 'from then and always after then':

*We drank everything you can think of from breakfast **onwards**.*
*The school itself opened more schools in Bristol, Belfast and Yorkshire from 1951 **onwards**.*

---

open   ▶ Compare **close**; **shut**

1 open: verb

open is a regular verb – often roughly opposite in meaning to *close* or *shut* and can be used with and without an object:

*Shut your eyes, and don't **open** them until I tell you.*
*The banks **open** at 9.30.*
*This window doesn't **open** – I can't **open** it.*

2 open: adjective

a *open* is an adjective without comparative or superlative forms:

*The banks won't be **open** tomorrow – it's a holiday.*
*The door was (wide) **open**, so I walked in.*
*Leave the window **open**, please.*

b open or **opened**?
Only the form *open* can be used as an adjective:

*Is the library **open** tomorrow?*
*The door was **open** so I walked in.*

opened is part of the verb:

*As soon as the door had been **opened**, I walked in.*

This contrasts with *shut* and *closed*, which are both used as adjectives and as parts of verbs:

*The banks are **closed/shut** tomorrow – it's a holiday.*
*The doors are **closed/shut** by a man in uniform.*

---

opportunity   ▶ See **possibility**

opposite

The word *opposite* has two rather different meanings – (1) 'facing', 'on the other side' and (2) 'completely different'. The adjective has both meanings.

1 opposite: adjective

a • facing; looking towards; on the other side of
The opposite side of the street is much sunnier than ours.
Budapest is really two cities, Buda and Pest, on opposite sides of the Danube.

b • completely different
Instead of leaving together, they drove off in opposite directions. (e.g., one went north, and the other went south)
I don't know why they married – they seem to have opposite views on everything.

2 opposite: preposition

• facing; on the other side
I sat opposite a man at dinner who didn't eat anything!
There's a small park just opposite the railway station.

3 opposite: adverb

• facing; on the other side
We are great friends with the people next door, but we don't know the people who live opposite. (= on the other side of the road)

4 opposite: noun

• a completely different thing
My sister's always happy and cheerful, but my brother's just the opposite. (= he is sad and miserable)
Plus is the opposite of minus.
Above and below are opposites.

or

1 or: conjunction

a *or* is used to mark a choice between words, phrases or clauses. If there is a choice between more than two things we often omit *or* except between the last two:
We could go in June or July. (= not both)
There's only tea, coffee or fruit juice, I'm afraid.
We could leave early and walk, or we could get a taxi.

b Notice that *or* is used with most types of negative statements. (▶ See **nor** for the special use of that word.):
Nobody saw or heard anything.
We can't go in either August or September.

c If *or* joins two singular nouns as subject, the verb is singular:
  *A headache **or** a bad cold always **makes** me very depressed.*

d *or* is sometimes used to correct or explain something we have just said:
  *Bob – **or** rather Robert as he prefers to be called – is giving another series of lectures.*
  *I'll come – **or** at any rate, at least I'll try to be there.*
  *Telephone your mother, **or** she'll worry about you.*

2 or so, or two

- or about that (number)
  *It'll only cost you a pound **or so**.*
  *I'm nearly ready – I'll only be a minute **or two**.*
  *There were already 40 **or so** people there when we arrived.*
  *Her blood pressure became quite normal until the last month **or so**.*
  ▶ See also *or else* at **else**; *either . . . or* at **either**; *or not* at **not**; *or other* at **other**; *or something* at **something**.

Notice the use of *or* with 'round' numbers (= numbers ending in -0) to mean 'about that number':
  *They were expecting 50 **or** 60 people.*

---

order

1 order: noun

order is both a count and an uncountable noun with a variety of meanings:
  *Why doesn't a waiter come and take our **order**?* (= We want to ask for something from the menu.)
  *You're to stay in bed – that's the doctor's **orders**.*
  *The government tries hard to maintain law and **order**.*
  *These names should be in alphabetical **order**.* (= A, B, C, etc.)
  *I couldn't ring you because the telephone was out of **order**.* (= not working)

2 in order (not) to/in order that/in order for (somebody to do something)

These three expressions all express purpose. They are more formal than *(so as)* to or *so that*:
  *I have given up work **in order to** return to full-time education for a year.*
  *He just kept quiet **in order not to** upset her.*
  ***In order that** everyone may have an equal chance, the numbers will be chosen by computer.*
  ***In order for** this to be fair, we're using a computer.*

3 order: verb

order +	(IO) + OBJECT
	O + ADVERB PHRASE
	O + *to*-INFINITIVE
	that-CLAUSE

a *order* can have one or two objects (like *give*):
   *We **ordered** steak, but the waiter brought chicken.*
   *I've **ordered** you a taxi/a taxi for you.*

b **order** + OBJECT + ADVERB PHRASE; **order** + O + *to*-INFINITIVE; **order** *that* . . .:
   *Stop **ordering** me around/about.*
   *He **ordered** the soldiers to shoot/that the prisoners should be shot.*

---

other, others: determiner and pronoun ▶ Compare **another**

- remaining; additional; different

some/any/no the/this/that my . . .	**other**	boy/chair/one (SINGULAR) food (UNCOUNTABLE)
some/any/no the/these/those		people/chairs/ones (PLURAL)
my . . . several/many	**others**	
	others	

1 *other* can be used with singular and plural count nouns and uncountable nouns, and can refer to people and things. *Other* is not used by itself as a pronoun (NOT **I saw **other***), and is not used by itself with a singular count noun. Instead we use *another*, e.g. **another boy**. (NOT **other boy*) *Other* can be used alone in front of an uncountable noun and a plural noun (**other** *work*, **other** *people*).
others is a plural pronoun only, and can be used by itself.
Various definite and indefinite determiners, as shown, can be used in front of *other/others*.
others can refer to people or things. In the singular (*the*) *other one* is sometimes used.

a **other**
   *He had left Hawton, where he had been so unhappy, and his future movements would be decided for him by **other** people in some **other** place.*
   *This woman, you see, could so easily do some **other** work and keep him.*
   *I think that I might come to fancy him if the **other** one doesn't do something interesting soon.*
   *If there is no **other** business, I declare the meeting closed.*
   *I thought I wasn't going to enjoy it at first, but I met some **other** young ones.*
   (= young people like me)

*I assume one of the photographs was of Marion and me, but the **other** must have been taken in Turkey?*
*Richard Herbert is buried here, the father of two famous sons: one was the clergyman, George; **the other** was the statesman Lord Herbert of Cherbury, who lived in Montgomery Castle.*
*She heard feet on the **other** side of the door.* (= the opposite side)
*She wrote 500-page romances which enjoyed a large public on **the other** side of the Atlantic.*
*I have one **other** suggestion to make.*

b   others
*You never think of **others**, only yourself all the time.*
*He spoke to Radcliffe and to a cameraman called Kelly, a friend of his brother's and to some **others**.*
*Only a few policemen now remain; all the **others** have gone home.*
*I brought the books you wanted; if you want any **others** let me know.*

2   the other day, the other night, the other week

● on a recent day, etc.
*I had a swim **the other day** and am just wondering if that will be the last.*
*I found him cutting his hair in my sitting-room **the other afternoon**.*

3   other than

a   After nouns, the meaning of *other than* is 'different from', 'except':
*For saucepans made of material **other than** aluminium, use a low heat.*
*. . . payments made by someone **other than** yourself . . .*
*If tax has been charged at a rate **other than** 30% . . .*

b   After a negative or near-negative the meaning is, 'except':
*There is nothing you can do **other than** take the exam again.*

4   somebody/someone/something or other
These phrases mean 'I'm not sure who/what':
***Somebody or other** was telling me . . .* (= I can't remember who.)
*They were planning to go to the States and then **something or other** happened that stopped them . . .* (= I can't remember what.)

5   every other day/week . . .

● one day, week . . . out of two
*I only have to take these pills **every other day**.* (= on the 1st, 3rd, 5th . . . or 2nd, 4th, 6th . . .)

6   each other, one another

each other and *one another* roughly mean the same thing, though *each other* is more informal. Both phrases are used mainly of people:
*We looked at **each other/one another** and everyone was silent.* (= Everyone in the group looked at everyone else in the group.)
*Paul and Henry were annoyed with **one another**.* (= Paul was annoyed with Henry, and Henry was annoyed with Paul.)

▶ Contrast: *Paul and Henry were annoyed with themselves.* (= Paul was annoyed with himself and possibly with Henry too, and Henry was annoyed with himself, etc. . . .)

Like *themselves*, *each other* and *one another* cannot be used in subject position, where we would have to say *Each/Both/All of them looked at each other . . .*
Notice where an apostrophe comes:
*They looked into **each other's** eyes.*

---

otherwise: adverb

• if not; except for that; differently, in some different way
*I hope Paul telephones. **Otherwise** we shall have to find his address and write.* (= if he does not . . .).
*Look, I don't think you're going to get the job: to pretend **otherwise** would be unfair to you.* (= to pretend differently . . .).
*Daddy still has a bit of a cold, but **otherwise** the family are all well.*

---

ought to: modal verb   ▶ Compare **should**; **had better**

The negative is *ought not to/oughtn't to* and is fairly rare.
ought to is similar to *should* in the way it is used to show (1) obligation and (2) theories about what is probable. But *ought to* usually includes some meaning of duty, and it is not used in the many other uses of *should* where the meaning is various kinds of possibility and probability.

1 Obligation

a   *You **ought to** write to your mother more often.*
*I know I **ought (to)**. But she **ought not to** treat me like a child.*
*Who **ought** my son **to** write to about a university place?*
*People **ought not to/oughtn't to** drink and drive.*

b   **ought to** and **should**
Although *ought to* and *should* are often interchangeable, there is a difference. *Should* often introduces personal advice. *Ought to* can suggest a more external law, or that the speaker has no power to get the thing done, or that he/she thinks it is unlikely to happen. Thus *ought to* is unlikely on printed instructions; because the writer is giving useful advice:
*This shirt **should** be ironed with a cool iron while still damp.* (NOT *****ought to** . . .).

2 Theories about probability

Like *should*, *ought to* makes pleasant or at least neutral guesses, mainly about the future:
*You **ought to** catch the train all right – you're in good time.*
*There **oughtn't to** be any difficulties.*
*Where **ought** Bob and Sue **to** be by now?*
*Oh they **ought to** be there by now.*

---

3 ought to have + PAST PARTICIPLE

a Obligation

This is used to say that somebody had a duty or obligation to do something, but did not do it:

*He **ought** to have let us know.* (= but he did not.)

b Theory

Ought to have is also used to say that it is reasonable now to assume that something has happened or happened:

*Bob and Sue **ought to have** arrived yesterday/by now.* (= They probably have, but we do not know.)

---

our: possessive determiner ▶ See **ours; ourselves; us; we**

First person plural
For meaning ▶ See **we**

a *Of course you can come and stay with us, but I warn you – **our** house isn't very large.*
*What sort of world will **our** grandchildren be living in in the twenty-first century?*

b *our* is formally and correctly used rather than *us* before some *-ing* patterns:
*They were cross about **our** asking for money.*
*Have you forgotten **our** telling you this?* ▶ See **us**

---

ours: pronoun ▶ See **our; ourselves; us; we**

First person plural possessive pronoun.
For meaning ▶ see **we**
***Ours** isn't the biggest house in the road, but I still think it's the nicest.*
*A friend of **ours** has offered to lend us the money.*
*'Is that your car?' 'No, that's **ours** over there.'*

---

ourselves: pronoun ▶ See **our; ours; us; we**

First person plural reflexive pronoun

1 ourselves: reflexive

*We hurt **ourselves** getting over the wall.*
*We've bought **ourselves** a tent.*
*It's very quiet having the house **to ourselves** when the children are away.* (= not having anyone else in it)
*In the end nobody else wanted to come, so we went **by ourselves**.* (= without anyone else)

---

2 ourselves: emphatic

*We built the garage **ourselves**.*
*We **ourselves** never watch television, but the children do.*

3 ourselves: as subject or object pronoun

ourselves is sometimes used where *we* or *us* would be correct:
*?My mother suggested the children and **ourselves** should go and stay with her.* (= *My mother suggested **we** and the children should go . . .*)
*?She's keen for the children and **ourselves** to go . . .* (= *She's keen for the children and **us** to go . . .*)

---

out ▶ Compare **in**

1 out: adverb

As an adverb of place, *out* means 'not in'; 'away from the inside'; 'away from home'. *Out* is the opposite of *in*. Other meanings include: 'appearing', 'distributing' and removing or disappearing'.

a *out* can mean 'not in':
*I'm afraid Mr Morrison's **out**; he'll be back about 3.*
*Keep **out**!* (= Don't enter.)
*Let's go **out** for dinner tomorrow.*
*I opened the parcel and some nails fell **out**.*

b *out* is used to say that something appears:
*The sun came **out** after the rain.*
*World War II broke **out** in 1939.*
*The roses are all **out** now.* (= flowering)
*Publishers seem to be bringing **out** more books than ever.*
*Don't stick your tongue **out** at me.*

c *out* can be used with verbs that suggest distributing things or spreading them in various directions:
You can *give **out**/hand **out**/send **out*** notices to people.
Contrast: *give **in**/hand **in*** your homework to the teacher.
*Open **out** the map on the table.*

d *out* can suggest that something is removed or disappears:
You can *rub/cross **out*** mistakes in something you have written. You can *turn **out*** lights, heaters, etc. (▶ See also **off**):
*There was something wrong with the electricity and the lights kept going **out**.*
*I've got a dirty mark on my coat and it won't come **out**.*
*It took the firemen six hours to put **out** the fire.*
*I shall have to look for another job when my money runs **out**.*

e *out* also emphasises a feeling of completeness with some verbs:
You can *call **out**, cry **out**, shout **out*** . . . (rather loudly). If your clothes are *worn **out*** they are too old to wear any more. If you are *tired **out*** you are very tired indeed.

2 **out of**: preposition

out of is the opposite of *in/into*

a   *out of* is often used to express movement away from the inside of a 3-dimensional space:

*He walked **out of** the room.*
*Some nails fell **out of** the parcel.*
*Someone's torn a page **out of** this book.*
*Tom hates getting **out of** bed.*
*I was too late to get my books **out of** the library.*
*Please get **out of** my way.* (= You are in the way.)
*Sorry I was only looking **out of** the window.*
*I've just taken £50 **out of** the bank.*

b   **Various other uses**

*We're **out of** sugar.* (= We haven't got any.)
*She made herself an extraordinary dress **out of** paper.*
*I don't often get 10 **out of** 10.* (= full marks)
*Is long hair for men **out of** fashion?* (= not in fashion, not the fashion)
*It's **out of** the question.* (= It cannot even be considered.)

outside

outside is the opposite of *inside*

1 **outside**: preposition

*We stood **outside** the restaurant for ages trying to decide whether to go in.*
*She left the tray just **outside** the door.*
*They live a few miles **outside** Aberdeen.*

2 **outside**: adverb

*The weather's marvellous – let's sit **outside**.* (= in the open air).
*He walked **outside** and took a look at the sky.*

3 **outside**: noun

*The house looks small from the **outside**, but actually it's quite large.*

4 **outside**: adjective

*My bedroom has three **outside** walls, so it's cold in the winter.*
*He's lived in hospital so long he doesn't know what's happening in the **outside** world.* (= the world outside the hospital)

over

1 **over**: preposition   ► Compare **above; across**

over is the opposite of *under*.

over (like *above*) means 'higher than', (*You could hang the picture over/above the fireplace.*)

For cases where both words are possible ▶ See **above**. *Over* also has the following extra meanings, where *above* is not possible.

a • from one side to the other

The plane flew low *over the house.*
The thief jumped *over the wall.*
There used to be a footbridge *over the river.*
He fell *over the dog.*
He tripped *over the step.*
I can't tell you *over the telephone.*
They never got *over the tragedy.* (= never recovered from it.)

b • on the far side of
My friend lives *over the road.*

c As a preposition of time, *over* means, 'during':
He told me *over dinner.*
We'll be at home *over the weekend.*

d *over* can mean that something is covering or touching something else:
He had a black patch *over his eye.*
She put her hand *over her mouth to stop herself laughing.*
I threw my coat *over the back of the chair.*
Claudia was wearing an orange jumper *over a purple shirt.*

e • more than
With this meaning *above* is possible for some speakers, but *over* is usual:
The house cost *over £100,000.*
Children of 14 and *over.* (= more than 14 years of age)

f *all over* emphasises the idea of 'covering':
Somebody has spilled wine **all over** the floor.
He's been **all over** the world. (= everywhere)

2 over: adverb   ▶ Compare **above; underneath**

a • from one side to the other
He walked *over to the door.* (= across the room)
The milk has boiled *over.* (= up over the side of the saucepan)
Please turn *over.* (= turn to the next page)
I kept turning *over in bed, but I couldn't sleep.*
Come *over here and sit by the fire. Don't stay over there by the door.*

b • down
I knocked the chair *over, and then somehow fell over myself.*
The little boy was knocked *over by a car.*

c • finished
You're too late – the party's *over.*

d • remaining
There was some food left *over after the party, but no drink.*

owe/owed/owed: regular verb

> **owe** + (IO) + OBJECT

owe can have one or two objects:

> If we **owe** *somebody money* we have borrowed it, and must pay it back.
> I **owed** *Pamela £5. I* **owe** *£5 to Pamela.*
> *Rupert hates* **owing** *people money/***owing** *money to people.*
> *The world doesn't* **owe** *you a living, you know – go and find yourself a job.*

owing to: preposition　　▶ Compare **because of**; **due to**

- because of
  > **Owing to** *the weather the plane is delayed.*
  > **Owing to** *some confusion over the phone you appear to think that my name is Lockward rather than Stevens . . .*
  > *I was extremely sorry that I was unable to get to your father's funeral* **owing to** *an attack of flu on Thursday evening.*

own

1　own: determiner

own as a determiner or pronoun cannot be used without a possessive determiner (e.g. *my* . . .) or the possessive form of a noun (*Celia's* . . .) in front of it. It means 'belonging to that person/those people and to nobody else'. *Very own* is used for even more emphasis.

my our your his her its their one's Celia's	(very)	**own**	shop

> *I'm never bored with my* **own** *company.* (= being alone)
> *They said they preferred to make their* **own** *amusement – they played games, watched football, went to the films . . .*
> *The village has its* **own** *toy shop.*
> *And I never knew there were so many colour and black and white portable televisions on the market until I saw them in their* **own** *department.*

2 own: pronoun

a In some sentences the noun after *own* can sometimes be left out if it has already been used once:

It may help if we think briefly about the history of one family, for example my ***own****.* (= *my* ***own*** *family*)

a room	of	my/our . . .	**own**
rooms		your . . .	
		etc.	
on			

b Instead of saying *a room that is mine*, *rooms that are mine*, we can say *a room/ rooms **of my own** . . .*:

*I left them with a sense of guilt, because I knew that I would return to a house **of my own**, with supper on the table.*
*They had gone in – certainly through no fault **of their own**, but without permission.*

c on one's own

- by oneself; alone

*I said I would go to the dance, but am a bit doubtful about going **on my own** – I hope Mrs Jay goes.*

3 own: verb (not usually in the progressive)   ▶ Compare **belong**

- possess

*70% of the population now **own** their own homes.*
*Why pay rent when you can **own**!*

---

part: noun (C, U)

- some, but not the whole of something

a *part* is often used quite regularly as a count noun:

*Which **part** of Scotland are you from?*
Parts *of the film were boring – the last **part** was the best.*
*Large **parts** of the country were flooded.*
*A large **part** of the country was flooded.*

b part of

When there is no adjective, *part of* is often used without *a*, rather like *half of*, *most of*:

Part of *the country was flooded.*
*I think **(a) part of** his trouble is that he is lazy.*
Part of *the time there's nothing for me to do.*
*They treat that animal as **(a) part of** the family.*

particular

1   particular: adjective

a   ● special; different from the others
In this meaning *particular* is attributive:
*Is there any **particular** kind of bread you want, or will an ordinary loaf do?*
*This film will be of **particular** interest to you because it was shot in Yugoslavia.*
*There's no **particular** advantage in driving there – we might just as well go by train.*

b   anyone/nothing, etc., **in particular**
After indefinite pronouns beginning with *any-* and *no-*, we often use *in particular*, rather than *particular*:
*It was a good holiday, but we didn't do **anything in particular**.*
*I might bring someone to the party, but there's **nobody in particular** I want to ask.*

c   As a predicative adjective, *particular* means 'very careful' or 'hard to please':
*He's terribly **particular** about the way his shirts are ironed.*

2   in particular

in particular is often used when we want to give examples of something we are talking about:
*My parents are both generous – my mother **in particular** is always giving me money.* (Notice the word order. NOT **in particular** *my mother*)
*My cousin has all sorts of plans. **In particular**, he wants to learn to fly.*

particularly: adverb

particularly means 'very' when it is followed by an adjective or an adverb, and 'very much' when it is followed by a verb. *In particular* is not used in this way:
*This cold weather is **particularly** difficult for old people.*
*I'm not **particularly** worried yet – but I shall be if we don't hear soon.*
*Henry **particularly** wanted to see the film and was annoyed that he had missed it.*

pass: verb   ▶ See also **past**

> pass + (IO) + OBJECT

a   ● succeed (at a test, exam, etc.)
In this sense *pass* can be used with or without an object.
*The exam was difficult – I hope I've **passed** (it).*

b   ● reach and go beyond
*He **passed** me in the street without saying hello.*

c • give something to somebody, especially by hand:
In this sense *pass* can be used with or without an indirect object:
*Please could you **pass** (me) the salt?*

d • go by; end; be over
*The pain has **passed**, but the unhappiness remains.*
*Time **passes** slowly, when you've nothing to do.*

past

1 past: noun

We usually say *the past* when we mean 'the time before the present':
*What alarms me even more than thinking about the future is looking back on
the past.*
*I think the organisers have thrown out my application because of my criticism
of them in **the past**.*

2 past: adjective ▶ Compare last

• earlier than the present; finished and over
*Many thanks to Fiona for all her work in the **past** two years.*
*This country knows from **past** experience that peace depends on strength.*

Also (in grammar), *past tenses* contrasted with *present tenses*.

3 past: preposition

a As a preposition of place, *past* means 'to/on the other side of', 'beyond', 'from
one side to the other', often when moving somewhere:
*Our house is just **past** the post-office.*
*They went out of the gate and took the lane that ran down **past** cottages, **past**
old farm buildings and **past** the church towards the river.*
*One route suggested for southbound traffic is to bring vehicles **past** the front
of the Kingsway Centre and into Parliament Street.*

b As a preposition of time, *past* means 'after', 'later than':
*It's half **past** eleven (11.30) and **past** my bedtime.* (American English: *half
past eleven* or *half **after** eleven*.)

4 past: adverb

• beyond in space or time
*We stood and watched the soldiers march **past**.*
*Minutes went **past** and nobody said a word.*

5 past or passed?

The verb *pass* is regular (*pass/passed/passed*) so *past* cannot be a verb. Notice
the difference between:
*This is all over and **past**.* (adjective)
*The pain has **passed** but the unhappiness remains.* (verb)
*He **passed** me in the street without saying hello.* (verb)
*He just walked **past** me.* (preposition)

pay, paid, paid: verb

```
        –
pay + (IO +) OBJECT
```

pay can take one or two objects. It can also be used without an object:
> We **pay** *sums of money, bills, rates, taxes . . . and we* **pay** *people* (e.g., builders, employees, taxi-drivers . . .)
> *Can I* **pay** *by cheque?*
> *They haven't* **paid** *me last month's salary yet.*
> *I haven't been* **paid** *last month's salary yet.* (note the passive)
> *I* **paid** *£100 for this picture.*
> *I lent him £50 and he hasn't* **paid** *me back/hasn't* **paid** *it back.*

people: noun

a   people: noun (plural only)   ▶ Compare **person**

people is a countable plural noun:
> *some/any/many/several/a lot of/lots of/these/those/ten . . .* **people**
> *Who were those* **people** *I saw you with yesterday?*
> *There were crowds of* **people** *everywhere.*
> **People** *hold strong views about defence.*
> *professional* **people** . . . *disabled* **people** . . .

b   the people

- the ordinary people in a state
  Sometimes the **people** *want one thing and their leaders decide another.*

c   people (C)

As a count noun, *people* roughly means 'a nation or a race' and can be singular or plural:
> *the different* **peoples** *in the Soviet Union . . .* **peoples** *of the South Pacific . . .*
> *One of Sir Winston Churchill's books was called 'A History of the English-speaking* **Peoples**'.
> *The Huns were an Asian* **people** *who invaded Europe in the fourth and fifth centuries.*

per: preposition

a   *per* is used with prices and measurements and means 'for each' or 'during each':
> *I remember when apples cost 5p* **per** *pound.*
> *No water and no cooking facilities but £15* **per** *week.*
> *The police said he was driving at 100 miles* **per** *hour.*

b   per cent
   • in every hundred
   Simple number phrases take a singular verb; phrases containing *of* + PLURAL
   NOUN take a plural verb:
   *30 **per cent** means a lot of money worth saving.*
   *99 **per cent** of workers now have four weeks holiday a year.*

perhaps: adverb   ▶ Compare **maybe**

   • maybe; possibly; it is possible that

a   *perhaps* is usually in front or mid-position when it refers to the whole
   sentence, but occasionally it comes at the end of the sentence:
   *'**Perhaps**, it would be a good idea if I went to see Herbert', she said.*
   *With regard to your remarks about the bank, I think **perhaps** we had better
   talk about this.*
   *I should **perhaps** add that I was not present at the interview.*
   *The key is always available so it wouldn't be too bad, **perhaps**.*

b   *perhaps* can also come elsewhere in a sentence to emphasise a single word or
   phrase:
   *Harcourt wrote to say he'd come down – **perhaps** next week – with Celia for a
   few days.*
   *Our company has contributed, **perhaps** more than any other, to the shaving
   comfort that men now expect.*
   *I waited for **perhaps** half an hour.*

c   *perhaps* is sometimes used to introduce a polite request or suggestion:
   ***Perhaps** you would be kind enough to give her a further prescription for these
   drugs.*
   *Professor Thomson knows more about her work than I do; and you may
   perhaps think of writing to him.*
   ***Perhaps** I should first explain what it is I want you to do.*

person: noun   ▶ Compare **people**

a   a/the *person* means an individual man, woman or child, and is a sort of singular
   for *people*:
   *He's a nice **person** but not a very good actor.*
   *There was only room for one more **person** in the lifeboat.*
   *She's a very important **person** – would you like to meet her?*
   *What sort of **person** do you think I am?*

b   *persons* (in the plural) is much more formal than *people*, and is used in official
   and legal language:
   *The police keep a list of missing **persons**.*
   *There are laws to control the employment of children and young **persons**.*
   *Capacity: 17 **persons** (Notice in a lift)*
   *These seats are meant for elderly or handicapped **persons** or for **people** with
   heavy shopping or young children. (Notice in London buses)*

place: noun

a *place* usually means 'a particular position in space' and is a count noun:
*You can't be in two **places** at once.*
*Venice is such a unique **place**.*
*There were several **places** in the book that I didn't understand.*
*The table is not the right **place** for your shoes!*
*Are there any **places** left on the tour?*
*Come round to my **place**.* (= my home)

b *take place* means 'happen', usually when something is planned:
*The prize-giving **took place** on 25th March.*

c **place** *or* **room**?
Both *place* and *room* can be used with a similar meaning, but *room* in the sense of 'space' is more general and uncountable; *place* is countable:
*Is there a spare **place**?*
*We'll keep you a **place**.*
*Is there **room** for one more?*
*Yes, I think we can make **room** for you.*

please, pleased

1 please: sentence adverb

We use *please* to make a request or an order more polite, and in polite questions:
***Please** don't tell Monica yet – it'll only worry her.*
***Please** forgive me for not typing.*
*Could you **please** note that my address has changed, and is now the one at the head of this letter.*
*May I **please** have your comments?*
*Come this way, **please**.*
*Is this the way to the station, **please**?*
*'Do you take sugar in your coffee?' 'Oh, yes **please**.'* (But to refuse we would say *No, thank you.*)

2 pleased: adjective

● glad/delighted
pleased is often followed by a *to*-INFINITIVE; or by a *that*-CLAUSE or by *about* or *with*:
*I was surprised to get a prize – but very **pleased** indeed.*
*She was **pleased** to be home.*
*I understand your views and shall be **pleased** to discuss them with you on Wednesday or Thursday.*
*I'm **pleased** that the flat seems quite satisfactory.*
*Sally did not seem **pleased** that we had got the money back.*
*She wasn't **pleased** about the money.*
*Mummy seemed quite **pleased** with her present.*

3 please: verb

a • make somebody happy
You're rather hard to please, aren't you?
Please *yourself! Do whatever you like!* (Often rather rude)
This news doesn't please me at all.

b *please* can mean 'want' or 'like', but not in a main clause:
She just lets the boy do as he pleases – I don't know why she doesn't control him.

---

plenty (of): pronoun ▶ Compare **enough**

• enough; lots; a lot
plenty and *plenty of* + NOUN are mainly used in affirmative sentences. In questions and particularly in negative sentences, we prefer *enough*. *Plenty (of)* is used with plural nouns and uncountable nouns, and the verb is plural or singular to agree:
Have we enough plates? Yes, there are plenty. (= of plates)
And there is plenty of food.
We need plenty to eat, but there is plenty more where this came from.
What you need is plenty of exercise, plenty of sleep and plenty of fresh air.

---

plus

1 plus: preposition

• with the addition of; and in addition
plus is the opposite of *minus* and is shown by the symbol (+):
Fifty-seven plus eleven is sixty-eight. (57 + 11 . . .)
The bill came to £25.80 plus VAT.
She always travelled with a lot of luggage, plus three dogs.

2 plus: connector

Informally *plus* can be used to mean 'also':
I haven't got time – plus I don't want to spend the money.

---

point

1 point: noun (C, U)

a • sharp end
the point of a needle/of a pin . . .
This pencil hasn't got a very good point. (Compare   *a ball-point pen*)

b • exact place; a small spot without any length or width
She showed us the point on the map.
The shortest distance between two points is a straight line.
There's a point on the road where you can see the sea from both sides.

---

c   In spoken English when we talk about numbers containing decimals we say
point for the mark (like a full-stop) that comes before the part that is less than
one. So 3.5 is said as 'three point five'. 'Nought point five' (0.5) is the same as
half.

d   ● exact moment in time; a stage at which something happens
boiling **point** (100°C); *freezing* **point** (0°C)
At one **point** *during the evening I thought I was going to faint.*
We were on the **point** *of leaving, when Donald suddenly arrived.*

e   ● main meaning or idea
I don't understand your **point**. *What are you trying to say?*
I thought the speaker made some important **points**.
He's got a **point** *there, you know.* (= he is saying something reasonable.)

f   **the point** (singular only) or **point** (U)
● meaning or purpose, or lack of it
What's **the point** *of inviting them? They never go to parties.*
That's not **the point** – *they'll be hurt if we don't ask them.*
There's no **point**/*not much* **point** *(in) arguing with him – he'll change his
mind.*

g   **point of view**
●   way of looking at a situation
Well that's an interesting **point of view**.
You never think of things from my **point of view**.
From the **point of view** *of cost, a camping holiday would be best.*

2   **point**: verb

● show where something is (especially with one's finger); aim (something) in
a particular direction.
point is used with and without a direct object
a   *Don't* **point** – *it's rude. Say which one you want.*
He **pointed** *to the clock* – *to remind me how late it was.*
The gun was **pointing** *at my stomach.*
He **pointed** *his gun at me.*

b   **point out**
● make (somebody) notice something
Our guide **pointed out** *Mount Everest, just visible in the distance through the
clouds.*
I would like to **point out** *that you already owe us £253.50.*

police: noun (plural only)

We usually use *the police*:
a   **The police** *are highly trained.*
There were **police** *everywhere, so obviously they were expecting trouble.*
Why didn't you tell **the police** *your car had disappeared?*

b   *police* is not normally countable. Instead we use *policeman/policewoman/
police officers*:
Two **policewomen** *came into the bank.*
I could only see one **police officer** *directing the traffic.*

poor; poorer; poorest: adjective

1

a • not good; not rich
*The people there are very **poor** – they are among the **poorest** in the world.*
*The hotel was fine, but the food was rather **poor**. The **poor** food spoilt the holiday.*
*We've had a very **poor** summer.* (= the weather has not been good)

b As an attributive adjective, *poor* can also mean 'unfortunate':
*The **poor** little boy said he was lost.*
***Poor** Mary is in hospital again.*

2 *the poor* can mean poor people in general:
*The **poor** need our help.*

possibility: noun and opportunity: noun

• chance; something that may happen:
*Is there any **possibility** of changing the date of the meeting?*
*There's a **possibility** that I'll have to go to New York next week.*
*Have you considered the other **possibilities**?*
Contrast: *opportunity*, which means 'a good moment for doing something':
*If I do go to the States I shall take the **opportunity** of visiting Washington. I had no **opportunity** to do any sight-seeing last time.*

possible: adjective

• that can happen; suitable
possible is the opposite of *impossible* and is mainly a predicative adjective:
*Is it **possible** (for me) to exchange this for a bigger size?*
*I'd really like my money back, if (that is) **possible**.*
*It is **possible** that George will still come, but I doubt it.*
*The doctors did everything **possible**, but they could not save his leg.*
*I can't manage Tuesday, but Wednesday would be **possible**.*
*Please let us know as soon as **possible** whether you need a ticket.*
*Wednesday is a **possible** date.*

possibly: adverb

possibly is used to say if or how things are possible:
*How could you **possibly** have forgotten my birthday?* (= How was it possible . . .?)
*'Are you free on Saturday?' 'Well, **possibly**. Why?'* (= perhaps)
*Could we **possibly** change the date – only, Tuesday is no good.*

prefer; **preferred**; **preferred**: verb

```
                OBJECT
    prefer  +  -ing
                (O+) to-INFINITIVE
```

* like (somebody/something) better than another
prefer is not usually used in the progressive. It can be followed by OBJECTS, by VERB + *ing*, by a *to*-INFINITIVE and by OBJECT + *to*-INFINITIVE. Notice that when the second person or thing is mentioned we use the preposition *to* (NOT **than*):
   *'Shall we go by train or bus? Which do you **prefer**?'*
   *'Oh, I much **prefer** train travel. I **prefer** trains to buses. I **prefer** travelling by train to sitting in a bus.'*
   *'Or would you **prefer** to go by road?' 'Yes, I would **prefer** to, actually. But I'd rather not drive. I'd **prefer** you to (drive)/I'd **prefer** it if you drove.'*

presence; **present**

1. **present** /'prezənt/: noun (C); **present** /prɪ'zent/: verb

   * gift; give
     *a birthday **present** . . . Christmas **presents** . . . wedding **presents** . . .*
     *Who's going to **present** the prizes?*
     *They've **presented** Charles with a clock.*
     *Charles was **presented** with a clock when he left the company.*
     *They **present** clocks to everyone.* (NOT **They **present** everyone a clock*)

2. **present** /'prezənt/: noun and adjective

   * now; existing now
   a *Do it now. There's no time like the **present**.*
      *I'm very busy at **present**, but I hope to have a holiday later.*

   b *at the **present** time . . . our **present** difficulties . . . past and **present** tenses of verbs . . .*

3. **present** /'prezənt/: adjective and **presence** /'prezəns/: noun

   As a mainly predicative adjective *present* /'prezənt/ is the opposite of *absent* and there is a noun *presence*:
   a *I'm afraid I can't be **present** at your lecture on Friday.*
      *There were over a hundred people **present** at the parents' meeting.*

   b *The **presence** of so many important people made me nervous.*
      *The show was given in the **presence** of the Prince and Princess of Wales.*

presently: adverb

a * later; soon
   *Wait for me, I'll be with you **presently**.*

b • now; at present
This is an American usage, also used in British English:
*He's **presently** out of the country on business.*

pretty

1 pretty/prettier/prettiest: adjective

• attractive to look at
pretty is not usually used of men or boys (where we could use *good-looking*):
*Not beautiful perhaps, but a very **pretty** girl.*

2 pretty: adverb

• rather, quite – but not completely (informal)
a *pretty* can be used with favourable and unfavourable words:
*I find that place **pretty** boring.*
*It makes it **pretty** awkward, doesn't it?*
*They know each other **pretty** well.*
*This chap was **pretty** impressed.*
*I'm **pretty** sure to remember again, now that I've written it.*
*That must have been a **pretty** useful one.*

b **pretty much/pretty nearly/pretty well**

These three phrases all mean 'almost', 'roughly':
*The hotels there are all **pretty much** the same.*
*I **pretty nearly** didn't go.*
*It rained **pretty well** all day.*
*He knows **pretty well** everything about me.*

prevent: verb ▶ Compare **stop**

• stop something happening (before it can happen)
prevent needs an OBJECT or OBJECT (+ *from*) + *-ing*:
*Quick action might have **prevented** this disaster.*
*The West must keep some nuclear weapons if it wants to **prevent** a third world war.*
*They should have **prevented** the fire (from) spreading.*

price ▶ See **cost**

probable: adjective ▶ Compare **likely**

• likely
This is a much less common adjective than *likely*, and the grammatical patterns are more limited. The opposite is *improbable*:
*Failure is/appears/looks/seems **probable** in the circumstances.*

It is/appears/looks/seems **probable** *that we shall fail.*
(But NOT **We are* **probable** *to fail.*)
The **probable** *result of the talks will be an arms agreement.*

- almost certainly

As an adverb *probably* is greatly preferred to *likely*, which is hardly used as an adverb:

We shall **probably** *fail.*
The talks will **probably** *result in some sort of arms agreement.*
'You think we will succeed?' 'Yes, **probably**.*'/'Oh* **probably** *not.'*

1 promise: verb

> IO + OBJECT
> **promise** + —
> (IO+) *that*-CLAUSE
> *to*-INFINITIVE

- say seriously, so that you can be trusted, that you will give somebody something or do something

a *promise* (like *give*) can have two objects:

I've **promised** *him a bird for his birthday.*
You **promised** *one to all of us!*

b *promise* + (IO+) *that*-CLAUSE; *promise* + *to*-INFINITIVE:

Promise *(me) that you won't tell anybody.*
Of course, I **promise**.
I **promise** *to keep this a secret.*
I **promised** *not to tell anybody.*

2 promise: noun

If you make a **promise**, *you must keep it, you must carry it out. You must not break a* **promise**.

- on condition that; if and only if

I said it would be far better if we kept the house – **providing** *we could get someone to look after it.*

*We were surrounded by wounded, worn out men, who were escaping
somewhere . . . anywhere . . . eastwards, **provided** it was far enough away
from the enemy.*

put, put, put: verb

put needs an object and usually it also needs some phrase showing where the
object is moved to:
Put *your luggage down on the floor./down./on the floor.*
*She **put** too much salt (on the potatoes).*
Put *a cross (in the right space) if you agree.*
*I'm **putting** you through.* (said on the telephone by the person connecting
you to the person you want to speak to)
*I'm going to take off my jumper and **put** on a shirt.*
*They've **put** the meeting off until next week.* (= postponed it)

question

1 question: noun

a • a sentence or phrase expecting an answer
*Don't ask (me) so many **questions**.*
*The history **questions** were the worst part of the exam.*
*I couldn't do the **question** about the First World War.* (in an examination)
*The **question** is what to do now.*
*The **question** whether unborn children should be killed was not even
discussed.*

b • problem; matter
*It's a **question** of trying to be fair to everybody.*
*There are some **questions** we should discuss.*
*I'm not talking about money – it is a **question** of principle.*

c **no question**
These are two tricky words because the meaning depends very much on the
rest of the phrase. If there is *no question of* (*something happening*), then there
is no possibility that it happened or will happen. It didn't; it won't:
*There was **no question of** her going alone.* (= the possibility was not even
discussed)
*There's **no question of** buying a new car this year.* (= it is impossible)
Compare:
*A new car is **out of the question** this year.*

But if *there is/was no question that* something will happen or did happen, then
the phrase is ambiguous. Strictly it means that the thing definitely did or will
happen, but people also use it to mean that it did not or will not happen:
*There is **no question that** the exam is going to be difficult.* (= It will be or it
won't be? We cannot be sure. To make the meaning clear we should say –
*There is **no question of** the exam being too difficult.* (= It will not be.) or
*There is **no question but that** the exam will be difficult.* (= It will be.)

question

2 question: verb

If you *question somebody*, you ask them very detailed and serious questions.
If you want ordinary information, you *ask (questions)*.
> *The police **questioned** the woman for several hours.*
> *They **questioned** her about the bombs.*

---

quick, quicker, quickest and quickly

1 quick: adjective

quick is the opposite of *slow*:
> *Be **quick**.* (= hurry)
> *You can see where you're going on the buses, but it's **quicker** by tube.*
> *Have we time for a **quick** drink?*

2 quick, quickly: adverbs

quick is sometimes used as an adverb with verbs of movement:
> *Come as **quick**/**quickly** as you can.*
> *They ran much **quicker**/much more **quickly** than we had expected.*

Notice also:
> *I want to get rich **quick**.*

But elsewhere *quickly* is preferred:
> *Goodness, you eat **quickly** – I've hardly started.*
> *He writes more **quickly** (? He writes **quicker**) than I do – but you can't read his writing.*

---

quite: adverb   ▶ Compare **rather**

quite has two different meanings, depending on what words it goes with.

1 ● moderately/more than usually (+ gradable words)

quite	nice/difficult
	easily/soon
	like (PREPOSITION)
	enjoy like (VERB)

With adjectives, adverbs and verbs that are gradable on a scale, *quite* means 'moderately' or 'more than usually' (but is less emphatic than *very* or *rather*). For example, *difficult*, *early* and the verb *like* are gradable, because things can be *more* (or *less*) *difficult*; something can happen *earlier* (or *later*); we can *like* something *more* (or *less*) than something else. (*Quite* is not used much in this way in American English):

*A boat of this kind can be **quite** difficult to control.*
*A lot of their ideas are **quite** similar, and they're all **quite** useful.*
*This can be done **quite** easily with a small piece of wood.*
*Well, it's hard work, but I do **quite** like it.*

We can also use *quite* with the gradable preposition *like*:
*It's lovely to be back – it's **quite** like old times!*

2 ● completely/entirely (+ extreme or absolute words)

quite	**A** clear/amazing clearly
	enough
	stopped (VERB) understand
	B the best the wrong thing

a With adjectives, adverbs and other words that can have an 'extreme' meaning (*amazing*, *ridiculous*, *terrible*) *quite* emphasises the meaning and means 'completely', 'absolutely'. *Quite* also means completely with words that have an absolute 'either . . . or . . .' meaning. (Either someone or something is or is not *alone*, *normal*, *right*; either there is or is not *enough*; either you *stop* or you do not (*A*):

*We have to be **quite** clear what this means.*
*Are you **quite** sure of your facts? It's **quite** useless if you're not.*
*Val has not changed at all – it is **quite** amazing, she will not wash her hair.*
*I don't agree at all – it's **quite** different.*
*Her blood pressure became **quite** normal.*
*There are **quite** clearly some actions which no one should forgive.*
*We've got some rolls and some cheese – but have we got **quite** enough?*
*Bedtime, children. You've stayed up **quite** long enough.*
*Of course I used to love the cinema, but I had **quite** stopped going.*
*Don't mention it. I **quite** understand.*

b *quite* cannot be used with comparative adjectives and adverbs. But it can be used with *better* in the sense of 'well in health' (▶ Contrast **rather**).

*I have seen him today and he is **quite** better.* (= completely well again)

quite meaning 'completely' is also used with superlatives: and with other definite phrases (*quite the . . .*). (*B*) These may sound formal:

*I thought his last novel was **quite** the best he's ever written.*
*That was **quite** the wrong thing to say.*
*Whatever I ask him to do he does **quite** the opposite.*

c As a reply, *quite* means, 'exactly', 'I entirely agree'. Again, this is rather formal:

*'Believe me, nowhere today is remote.' '**Quite**', Houston said.*

d not quite/not . . . quite

not quite or *not . . . quite* can mean 'not exactly' and is often used in phrases where we could not use *quite* in the affirmative:

*I **don't** quite know whether my mother will mention it to you.*
*Surely they can**not** make **quite** as many errors as they did last time.*
***Nobody** ever behaves **quite** the same in private as they do in public.*

not quite can also mean 'nearly':

*I'm **not quite** sure . . .*
*I'm **not quite** ready . . .*
*It is**n't** quite so hot as yesterday.*
*The water's **not quite** boiling.*

3 quite + (ADJECTIVE) + NOUN

a

quite	interesting	work (UNCOUNTABLE NOUN)
	remarkable	people (PLURAL NOUN)
quite a good	idea
	(SINGULAR NOUN)
a **quite** excellent	man

quite in both its meanings can come before an ADJECTIVE + NOUN:

*It was **quite** hard work.*
*I met some **quite** interesting people . . .* (= moderately)
*This is **quite** excellent work.*
*They are **quite** remarkable people . . .* (= completely)

But with an indefinite singular count noun the word order varies with the meaning. When *quite* means 'moderately' we use *quite* + *a/an* ADJECTIVE + NOUN:

***quite** a good idea . . . **quite** a pleasant party . . . **quite** an interesting man . . .*

When *quite* means 'completely', we prefer *a* + *quite* ADJECTIVE + NOUN:

*a **quite** excellent idea . . . a **quite** remarkable story . . . a **quite** horrible suggestion*

b

quite	a profit
	some time

quite + a singular NOUN (without an adjective) means 'rather a special or unusual one':
> *That cinema must make **quite** a profit – it is always crowded.* (= a large profit)
> *It was **quite** an achievement for a young woman in her very early twenties.* (= a great achievement)

quite some time means 'quite a long time':
> *I'm afraid he's going to take **quite some time** to get over this.*

4   quite a + DETERMINER/PRONOUN of quantity

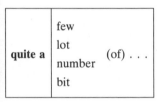

quite a	few	
	lot	
	number	(of) . . .
	bit	

quite a few/quite a bit etc. (as shown) mean 'a moderate number or amount':
> *At the time he knew **quite a few** people there.* (= actually a lot)
> *We've had **quite a bit** of rain this month.* (= a lot)

---

raise, raised, raised and rise, rose, risen: verbs

The difference between these two verbs is a bit like the difference between *lay* and *lie*.

1   raise needs an object:
> *Will all those in favour please **raise** their hands?* (= move them higher)
> *Have they **raised** the Titanic from the bottom of the sea?*
> *My rent has been **raised**.* (= increased)
> *There's another matter I want to **raise**.* (= mention for discussion)

2   rise, rose, risen never has an object: ▶ Compare **arise**
> *The sun **rises** in the east* (and sets in the west).
> *I wish prices wouldn't keep **rising**.*
> *The River Danube **rises** in the Black Forest in Germany.* (= begins to flow)
> *At the end of the ceremony the Queen **rose** from her seat and slowly walked out.* (= a formal way of saying 'got up')

rarely: adverb ▶ Compare **seldom**

- not often; almost never

rarely is a mid-position adverb, but it is also one of those words with an almost negative meaning that can begin a sentence when we want to emphasise this. In this case we invert the subject and the auxiliary verb. Notice also the positive question tag, which shows the negative meaning:

*The old lady **rarely** goes out these days, does she?*
***Rarely** have I been to such a wonderful concert.*

rather

1 rather: adverb

- considerably, to a great degree ▶ Compare **far; much**

	nice (er)
	stupidly
	more . . .
	less/fewer . . .
rather	too
	like (PREPOSITION)
	doubt . . .
	hope . . .
	like . . . (VERB)

rather is an emphasising adverb on a scale with *very*, *fairly* and *quite*. It is near the top of the scale, but below *very* or *too*. It is usually more emphatic than *fairly*. It is the only one of these words that can be used with comparative words or with *too*. It can also be used with *like* (preposition) and with a few gradable *verbs*:

*I sat around all day feeling **rather** miserable and taking cough mixture (= medicine).*
*Charlotte came around yesterday, I was **rather** rude to her.*
*'It would be **rather** nice if we could see the inside of the house as well.' 'Oh, that's **rather** more difficult', said Harry.*
*I **rather** stupidly made a hair appointment for Tuesday, so I shall have to be back here by then.*
*Sunday afternoon was sunny – but it was **rather** too windy for tennis.*
*He said something **rather** like that.*
*Anyhow, I (do) **rather** hope we may get to know each other.*
*I **rather** **doubt** this from what you tell me.*
*I **rather** liked Cynthia: I'd **rather** like to see her again.*

2 rather + NOUN; rather a lot ▶ Compare **quite**

A		
(some) rather interesting		work (UNCOUNTABLE) people (PLURAL)
rather an (a rather)	interesting	story (SINGULAR)
B rather a		shortage (SINGULAR)

a *rather* can come before an ADJECTIVE + NOUN (*A*), but with a singular noun the word order is often *rather a/an . . .*:

He's **rather** a good player.

b With a singular noun (without an adjective) the word order must be *rather a/ an + NOUN (B)*:

There is **rather** a shortage of space for meetings. (= *rather* a lack of space, definitely not enough space)

c We can also say *rather a lot*:

I can't come, because I've **rather a lot** of work to do. (= more than 'quite a lot')

3 would rather . . . (than) ▶ Compare **would sooner**

we'd	(much)	rather	go (than stay). not go.
he **would**	(far)		(that) you told us how. you didn't tell anyone.

If someone *would rather do something*, they would prefer to do it. They think it is nicer or better than something else:

I can go later, and I'd much **rather** have a weekend with you.

I suppose it's bad to go and listen to speakers, but I'd **rather** do that **than** watch TV.

He said he'd **rather** not drive.

Would you **rather** he was shy and shortsighted or smart and handsome?

I'd **much** rather it was your choice./I'd much **rather** you chose. (Notice that we use a past tense to express a hypothesis.)

4 rather than

● more than; instead of

Comparison of two things can be shown by *rather than*. It can join two nouns, two adverbs, two verbs, etc.:

The people bored him; they were Hugh's friends, **rather than** his own.

He adores his Mum, who looks like his sister **rather than** his Mum.

*Perhaps it would be better if the end came sooner, **rather than** later.*
*They must combine their efforts **rather than** fight each other.*
*'St Milo's?' repeated Isabel, breathing the words **rather than** saying them.*
*Increasingly, the farmers are seeing their land as a business **rather than** a way*
of life, and they prefer to keep their wives at home and send their sons away
*for education **rather than** employ them at home.*

5 or rather

- or to be more accurate

We use *or rather* to correct what we have said if we want to be more accurate:
*Barbers – **or rather** hairdressers, as they call themselves nowadays – say that*
long-haired men spend as much time and money on their hair as women.

're

're is the short form for *are*

read /riːd/, read, read /red/: verb

```
         –
read +   OBJECT
         IO + OBJECT
         that-CLAUSE
```

a When *read* means understand written or printed words, it is used with or
without an object:
*I can't **read** his writing – I wish he'd write more clearly.*
*She's only three, and her mother's teaching her to **read**.*

b - learn by reading

Here *read* can be used with or without an object or with a *that*-CLAUSE:
*I **read** in the paper last week that air fares are going up.*
*Did you **read** about that factory fire?*

c - say aloud to others something that is written

Here *read* can be used with one or two objects:
*She **read** the children a story.*
*She **read** the story to the whole class.*

real: adjective   ► Compare **actual**

a - not artificial or imagined; true
*It looks like **real** fur, and it's just as warm but much cheaper.*
*Drug-taking is a very **real** problem in today's world.*
***Real** life is more interesting than anything on TV.*
*Powdered coffee is very different from the **real** thing.*

b *real* is sometimes used informally to emphasise a word:
  *He's a **real** fool!*

---

1 really: adverb

a ● very/very much
With gradable adjectives and adverbs, *really* means 'very'; or 'very much' with gradable verbs:
  *The party on Friday was **really** enjoyable.*
  *I think you behaved **really** badly.*
  *To me it was a **really** big decision.*
  *I have got to do some **really** hard work.*
  *I **really** like their new house – it's wonderful.*

b When *really* is used with non-gradable words, it means 'actually', 'in fact', 'truly':
  *You are **really** very kind.*
  *I **really** mean this Charles.*
  *I have **really** given this a lot of thought.*

If we put *really* earlier in the sentence, it becomes more emphatic and means 'truly – I'm telling you':
  *You **really** are very kind.*
  *I **really** do mean this.*
  *I **really** have given this a lot of thought.*

With negatives there is a big difference in meaning between *not really* and *really . . . not*:
  *It doesn't **really** matter.* (= It doesn't matter much.)
  *It **really** doesn't matter.* (= It truly doesn't matter at all.)

2 really: sentence adverb

As a sentence adverb, *really* means, 'the fact is . . .' 'the truth is . . .':
  ***Really**, I sometimes wonder whether it is all worth it.*
  *There's probably some other reason entirely, **really**.*

As a short reply, *really* shows interest or surprise or sometimes annoyance:
  *'I work in a bookshop.' 'Do you **really**?'*
  *'It was an accident, I suppose?' 'No, I wanted to break it.' 'Oh, **really**! How stupid.'*

3 actually or **really**?

Sometimes both words are possible:
  *You don't **actually/really** want to give up your job, do you?*
  ***Actually/Really**, I don't know what I want.*

But the two words mean different things. *Actually* is closer to *in fact* or *as a matter of fact*. It often stresses 'This is a surprising fact' or even 'I admit . . .'; *really* suggests 'genuinely' or it adds emphasis. Compare:
*I don't **actually** know.* (= The fact is, I don't know at all.)
*I don't **really** know.* (= I don't know much about it.)
*He's **actually** lost weight.* (= Isn't that surprising?)
*He's **really** lost weight.* (= He is much thinner.)

Only *really* (NOT **actually*) is used in the sense of 'very' or 'very much':
*Do you **really** love me?*
*It was a **really** beautiful day.*
*You'll fail unless you try **really** hard.*

and only *really* (NOT **actually*) can be used as a question or exclamation:
'I love modern architecture.' 'Really?' (= I can't believe it.)

reason: noun (C, U)

reason, when it means an explanation or a cause, can be followed by *why*-CLAUSES, *that*-CLAUSES, *to*-INFINITIVES and *for*:
*I don't know the **reason** (why) they're going to live abroad.*
*Perhaps the **reason** (that) they're going is (that) they want to live somewhere warmer.*
*I had no **reason** to think she was lying.*
*They have (every/good) **reason** to believe he is still alive.*
*What is the **reason** for her leaving him?*
*I don't think she has any real **reasons** – you know what she's like.*

refuse: verb

> refuse + (IO+) OBJECT
> *to*-INFINITIVE

If you *refuse* you say 'no', or that you will not do something or accept something. *Refuse* can have people or things as objects, but it is not very usual for *refuse* to have two objects (like give). *Refuse* + *to*-INFINITIVE is common:
*I don't want to go, but I can't **refuse**.*
*Please don't **refuse** me/my request/the invitation/our offer.*
*We all thought she wanted to marry him, so why has she **refused** him?/**refused** to marry him?*
*We were **refused** permission/entry.*
*Closing Down Sale: No Reasonable Offer **Refused**.* (= people can offer the shop their own prices for things)
*They **refused** to say who had told them.*

regard

1 regard: verb (not usually in progressive)

If you *regard* someone/something as good, as a good person etc., you *consider* them to be good, a good person, etc.:
*We **regard** safe food as very important.*
*He didn't **regard** her as his mother, but as a friend.*
*He is **regarded** as (being) a very good teacher.*

2 regarding, as regards, with regard to: prepositions

* concerning; on the subject of; referring to
a These are all somewhat formal ways of referring to a particular topic, usually one that has been mentioned already. For example, a letter replying to a request for a grant might begin:
***With regard to/Regarding** your request for a grant, this will be considered at the next committee meeting.*
b *as regards* also introduces a particular topic, but could not introduce the first of a number of topics being discussed:
***As regards** the other matter you raise – your wish to move to a different course – I am afraid this is not possible at this stage.*

3 regard: noun (U), **regards** (pl)

regard (uncountable) is rather formal and means 'care', 'concern'; *regards* (always plural) means 'good wishes':
*You should show some **regard** for what other people think.*
*My **regards** to your mother and father.* (= give them my best wishes)

regret, regretted, regretted: verb

When we *regret* something we are sorry about it.

```
               OBJECT
               -ing
regret  +      that-CLAUSE
               to-INFINITIVE
```

a We can *regret* things, and we can *regret doing* something, and we can *regret that . . .*:
*We all **regret** your decision to leave the firm.*
*We **regret** that you have decided to leave us.*
*I don't **regret** buying a guitar – I wanted it at the time.*
b If we *regret to do* something, it is something that we are going to do. The verbs in this pattern are usually verbs of saying:
*We **regret** to say/to inform you/ (to have) to tell you . . . that Mr Andrews no longer wishes to buy your house.*
*We **regret** to announce that flight XYZ 123 to New York has been cancelled.*

remember: verb ▶ Compare **forget**; **remind**

```
                   OBJECT
                   that-CLAUSE
     remember  +   wh-CLAUSE
                   to-INFINITIVE
                   (o+)-ing
```

a *remember* can be followed by OBJECTS, by *that* and *wh*-CLAUSES, and by *to*-INFINITIVE and (OBJECT+)-*ing*. It is not usually used in the progressive:

> *You will **remember** your mother's birthday, won't you?*
> *You do **remember** that it's your mother's birthday next week?*
> *Have you **remembered** what I told you?*

b The difference between *remember doing* and *remember to do* is a question of time. The *-ing* form often refers to something that already exists or that has happened (Compare: *I enjoy swimming*), so the *-ing* action comes first and the *remembering* looks back to it:

> *I **remember** thinking that such happiness couldn't last.*
> *I can't/don't **remember** the name of the restaurant, but I **remember** the band playing our tune.*

The *to*-INFINITIVE often looks forward to the future (Compare: *I expect/hope/want to see you*), so the *remembering* comes first, and the *to do* action is what must be done later:

> *'Did you **remember** to send your mother a birthday card last week?'*
> *'Of course I **remembered** to.*

remind: verb ▶ Compare **remember**

● make somebody remember

```
                   of . . .
     remind  +  o  +  to-INFINITIVE
                   that-CLAUSE
```

remind needs a personal object:

> *He **reminds** me of my first boyfriend.* (= He looks or behaves like him.)
> *Please **remind** me to telephone my aunt tomorrow.*
> *I **reminded** him that he still had my library book.*
> *That **reminds** me – what happened to that snake you bought?*

reply ▶ Compare **answer**

reply, like *answer*, is a noun and a verb. But *answer* has more meanings and is the commoner word. A *reply* or *replying* means speaking or writing because somebody else has spoken or written. It does not mean solving a problem, and we can only *answer* (NOT **reply to*) the door or the telephone.

1 reply: noun

*I've written twice but I haven't had a **reply**/an **answer** to my letter.*
*I telephoned but there was no **reply**/**answer**.*

2 reply (to): verb

a *reply* cannot have an object. We use *reply to*:
*I asked her what she wanted, but she didn't **reply**/**answer**.*
*She **replied**/**answered** that she was feeling ill.*
*Have you **replied to**/**answered** her letter/your mother?*

b We *reply to* people and to what they say or write, but if there are questions and problems then we *answer* them. We *answer* exam questions.

right

right has several completely different meanings.

1 right: adjective, adverb, noun   ▶ Compare **wrong**

a *right* is the opposite of *wrong*. Its general meaning is 'correct', 'moral', 'fair':
*Is that the **right** time?*
*It's not **right** to keep a dog locked up in a flat all day.*
*You were quite **right** to speak to them about it.*
*'You spell Sylvia with a Y?' 'That's **right**.'*
*'You owe me £10. **Right**?'* (= Isn't that true?)
*I can't get this **right** – I keep making mistakes.*

b The nouns with this meaning are *right* (U) and *the right*:
*You don't seem to know the difference between **right** and wrong.*
*I'm in the **right** and I'm not going to apologise.*

c all right

all right is used as an adjective and an adverb, and means 'well', 'satisfactory', 'satisfactorily', 'acceptable'. But it does not usually mean 'very good' or 'very well'. The spelling *alright* is often used, but some people think it is incorrect:
*The flat's **all right**, but I'd like something smarter.*
*Their car went straight into a tree, but they were **all right**.* (= not hurt)
*'Are you feeling **all right**?' 'I'm **all right**, just a bit tired.'*
*'Sorry I forgot.' 'Oh, that's **all right**.'* (= it doesn't matter)
*Is it **all right** if I use your telephone?*
*I got to the station **all right** (= without any problems) – but Henry wasn't there.*
*Timothy's doing **all right** at school now.*
*'I'm very annoyed.' '**All right**, I've said I'm sorry.'*
*'Can I borrow the car?' 'Oh well, **all right** – I suppose so, but please be back by ten.'*

d right/all right

right or *all right* can be used at the beginning of a sentence to make people listen, or perhaps to show that the speaker is going to talk about something else:
*(**All**) **right**. Is everybody ready? Can we begin?*

or simply to agree with the previous speaker:
'Shall we go to the cinema tonight?' '(All) right. Let's.'
'They live just outside Cambridge.' 'Right!'

2 right: noun (C)

- a fair or legal claim
  *Do prisoners have the **right** to vote?*
  *I have a **right** to know. I must be told.*
  *People are always shouting about their **rights** these days – they aren't so keen about their duties to society.*

3 right: adjective, adverb, noun   ▶ Compare **left**

right is the opposite of *left*:
  *My **right** foot is bigger than my left.*
  *Turn **right** at the church.*
  *You want the third turning on the/your **right**.*
  *Keep (to the) **right**.*

4 right: adverb + (ADVERB or PREPOSITION)

- completely; exactly; directly
right is used before adverbs and prepositions to emphasise them:
  *Go **right** along this road as far as you can.*
  *We didn't get **right** to the top.*
  *She was wearing a skirt **right** down to her ankles.*
  *The house is **right** on the road and very noisy.*
  *If you wait for me **right** here, I'll be **right** back.* (= back very soon)
  *They came **right away** when I telephoned.* (= immediately)

rise   ▶ See **raise**

room: noun (C, U)   ▶ Compare **place**

a *room* is a count noun when it refers to one of the parts of a building:
  *There are four **rooms** – a living room and three bedrooms.*
  *The hotel had eighty double **rooms**, and only four single **rooms**.*

b *room* is uncountable when it means 'space':
  *The car's too small – there's no **room** to stretch my legs.*
  *The seats are all sold – it's standing **room** only.*
  Contrast:
  *I need **a room** where I can play my guitar.*
  *I need somewhere with **room** for all my animals.*

round   ▶ Compare **about; around**

1 round: preposition (usually **around** in American English)

a *round* refers to movement in circles:
*Imagine sailing **round** the world on your own.*
*He put his arms **round** her and kissed her.*
Also:
*sit **round** a table . . . sit **round** a fire . . .*

b *round* can refer to more general movement:
*We were walking **round** the centre of Istanbul.*
*We spent three days there looking **round** museums.*
*I walked **round** the corner.*

2 round: adverb (usually **around** in American English)

a with a circular movement:
*I feel as if my head's going **round** and **round**.*
*We had lost our way and were just walking **round** in circles.*
*Turn **round** and look at me – I don't want to talk to your back.*

b with more general movement:
*We didn't go anywhere special – we just wandered **round**.* (*about* is possible here)
*Will someone please hand **round** the nuts.*

c *round* is often used to mean 'to somebody's house':
*I'm so glad you came **round** that evening.*
*I went **round** to call on Tim this morning, but he'd gone out.*

3 round: adjective

● circular
*She has a **round** face and dark hair.*
*Meet me outside the shop with the big **round** sign outside.*

roundabout

1 roundabout: preposition

As a preposition, *roundabout* is quite rare and means 'about':
*I might be there **roundabout** sort of seven to half past.*

2 roundabout: adjective

● not direct
*He told her, in a **roundabout** way, that he loved her.*

rule

1 rule: noun

a *rule* is a count noun when it means a sort of law:
*What are the **rules** of American football?*
*There's a **rule** about not smoking in the canteen.*

b In a more general sense *rule* is uncountable:
*It's strange to think that America was once under British **rule**.*

2 as a (general) rule
- generally; usually
*I don't eat meat **as a rule**, but I did on this occasion.*

run, ran, run: verb

run is used with and without an object, and has a general meaning of movement.

a People and animals *run*, and they can *run a race/a distance*:
*The dog **ran** up to us.*
*Bannister was the first man to **run** a mile in under four minutes.*

b - move or travel in some general way
*The trains usually **run** on time.*
*The main line from London to Edinburgh **runs** through Newcastle.* (= the railway goes)
*We'll **run** you to the station.* (= in the car)
*The water will **run** hot if you wait a minute.* (= Turn on the tap and wait.)

c To *run* something means to organise it and keep it working:
*I **ran** the office while my boss was away ill.*
*This car **runs** on lead-free petrol.*

's

1 's: short form of **is**:
There's a lot to do.
It's much colder today.
Paul's expected to arrive on Saturday.

2 's: short form of **has**:
There's been a lot to do.
It's turned colder today.
He's expected this for a long time.

3 possessive ► Compare **of**

's is a sign of possession added to singular count nouns, and also plural count nouns that do not end in *-s*. Most 'possessors' are people (or groups of people) or animals:

> *the man's explanation . . . Janet's book . . . Mr and Mrs Smith's car . . . the class's decision . . . the dog's name . . . the children's room . . .*

's after words like *grocer, butcher* can mean that sort of shop:

> *I'm going to the grocer's. Is there a butcher's?*

's is also used with some phrases of place and time:

> *London's night life . . . the week's events . . . today's programme . . .*

's is also used with a sort of descriptive, not possessive, meaning:

> *men's shoes . . . children's clothes . . . a stone's throw . . .*

When singular names already end in *-s*, we often still add *'s*:

> *Mr Jones's job . . . Charles's wife . . .*

but with some older names we sometimes just add an apostrophe:

> *Socrates' death . . .*

With some place names, where the original meaning is in fact possession, we often today omit the apostrophe (*St Andrews* is a place in Scotland; *Harrods* is a big London store).

With regular plurals ending in *-s*, we simply add an apostrophe (') but not another *s*: *your parents' help*

sake

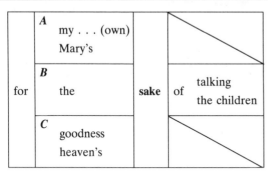

a *A* and *B* If we do something *for somebody's or something's sake*, or *for the sake of somebody/something* it means we do it to help them, or for that reason and no other:

> *Charles didn't want to go, but he went for Mary's **sake**/for the **sake** of the children.*
> *I was disgusted not only for his **sake**, but for my **sake**, you know.*
> *Tom was just talking for the **sake** of talking – he didn't have anything to say.*

For goodness sake/For heaven's sake (*C*) emphasises a remark, and sometimes show annoyance:

> *Don't let the dog lick your face **for heaven's sake**.*
> ***For goodness sake**, will you stop complaining!*

same

1 **same** (usually **the same**): adjective and pronoun

- that one and not another; exactly alike; not changed

a

the same (+ NOUN)   *as* . . .
                (that) . . .

same (usually *the same*) is often followed either by phrases beginning with *as* or by relative clauses beginning with *that*:

> *The novelist arrived at last, wearing **the same** brown suit (that) he had worn on the train.*
> *I have returned to the old hotel where I worked last year and here things are much **the same** as usual.*
> *A lighted match should be used to light the oven. Otherwise the instructions in this booklet remain **the same** as for the other cooker.*
> *Nobody ever behaves quite **the same** in private as they do in public.*
> *With this new shop, Tottenham Court Road will never be the **the same** again.*

2 **all the same**: sentence adverb

- nevertheless
  *The weather wasn't very good, but **all the same** we enjoyed ourselves.*

---

say, said, said: verb   ▶ Compare **tell**

that-CLAUSE
wh-CLAUSE
say + OBJECT
so/not

Like tell, say usually needs an object. (Contrast **speak** and **talk**.)

1 Direct and reported speech

a *say* is particularly used when quoting people's exact words – that is, when using direct speech, (– whether it is statements, exclamations, commands or questions):

> *I **said**, 'I'm very worried.' And he **said**, 'How awful for you!' and she **said** 'Stop talking about it.' So I **said**, 'Well, what can I do now?'*

If the words quoted come first, we can use *say* + a NOUN SUBJECT, but we do not usually use a PRONOUN SUBJECT at the end (so NOT *said she):

> *'Stop talking about it,' she **said**/Elizabeth **said** or **said** Elizabeth.*

b In 'reported speech' *say* (+ *that*) can be used to report statements and – in a slightly freer way – exclamations:

I said (that) I was very worried.
He said it was awful for me.
> ▶ See **ask** for reported questions and **tell** for commands

c   *say* can also be followed by *wh*-CLAUSES:
   He said how awful it was for me.
   He didn't say where they were going, what they wanted or how we could help . . .

d   Although *say* often refers to speaking, it can mean 'state' in a more general sense:
   This book says butter is good for you.
   There was a notice saying NO EXIT.

2   Passive   ▶ Compare **think; understand**

say can be used in two different passive patterns to report general opinions. Notice that the second one has no active equivalent:
   It is said he keeps all his money under his bed.
   (They say he keeps . . .)
   It was said that Noah lived to the age of 950.
   (= People said that Noah lived . . .)
   He is said to keep his money under his bed.
   (But NOT *People/They say him to keep . . .)
   He is said to have lived to be 950.
   *(But NOT *They say him to have lived . . .)*

3   say + OBJECT

a   The object of *say* may be the words that somebody has said (as with direct or reported speech in **1**) or the object may be some other noun or phrase:
   Say yes/no/sorry/hello/goodbye.
   They don't say much/a lot/anything.
   She has said very little/something about a horse/nothing to me.
   He said my name/a few words/something in Arabic . . .

b   *say* is sometimes used without an object, but the object is always understood:
   What do you want? Do say. (= say what you want)
   'How did it happen?' 'They didn't say.' (= say how it happened)
   Are they coming? Have they said? (= said if they are coming)

c   **say + so/not**
   'Do you think we're going to have a hard (= cold) winter?' 'They say so/not.'
   (= They say that we are/aren't . . .)
   'It's going to be a hard winter.' 'So they say.' (= Yes, that is what they say.)

d   *say* cannot have a personal indirect object like *tell*. We have to use *to*:
   That's what he said to me. (NOT *. . . what he said me.)

4   say or tell?

a   Both *say* and *tell* are used with reported speech. But *tell* usually needs an indirect object, the person who receives the information:
   She said (that) she could not come.
   She told us/him/her mother (that) she couldn't come.

b *say* is the usual verb to use when recording direct speech, or when suggesting what actual words were spoken:
> *'I can't come,' she said.*
> *He said goodbye/hello/sorry/no/yes.*

c *tell* is the usual word for reporting commands:
> *He told them to go away.*

Informally *say* is sometimes used like this (*He said to go away*), but some people find this odd.

d *say* can mean 'speak words'; *tell* suggests 'give information to':
> *You're very quiet. Say something.* (= Do speak).
> *Tell us the facts/a story.*

---

scarcely: adverb ▶ Compare **hardly**

scarcely is similar in meaning and usage to *hardly*, but *hardly* is more frequent. It is usually used in mid-position with verbs, and with non-assertive words like *ever* and *any*.
Positive question tags are used, showing the almost-negative meaning.

1 ● almost not
> *I scarcely know what to think about it – it's all so confusing.*
> *We scarcely ever go to the cinema these days, do we?*
> *They have scarcely done any work./They have done scarcely any work.*
> *Scarcely anyone remembers them now.*

2 With *can/could*, the meaning is sometimes 'almost not' and sometimes 'completely impossible':
> *I could scarcely believe my eyes!* (= but I did)
> *We can scarcely ask for our money back.* (= we will not)

3 **scarcely...when** ▶ Compare **hardly; no sooner**

● only just
> *He had scarcely started to speak when the audience walked out.*
> *Scarcely had he started to speak, when . . .* (notice the word order)

---

second

1 **second**: determiner and pronoun ▶ Compare **first**

● next after the first; another; the number corresponding to two (2)
> *Some people say Monday is the second day of the week, but others say it's the first.*
> *Their second child is only a year younger than the eldest boy.*
> *Surely you don't need a second car* (= another car for the same family).
> the *second of June* (2nd June) . . . Queen Elizabeth the *Second* . . . *the Second World War* . . .

b • not the best
Second-class post is cheaper but your letters will take longer.
a second prize . . . second best . . .

2 **second**: adverb and sentence adverb
He was hoping for a gold medal, but came second and got the silver.
First, I want to apologise, and second(ly) I want to explain what happened.

3 **second**: noun

• one sixtieth part of a minute; a very short time
'I was hoping to swim the distance in under 61 seconds,' the swimmer said.
Wait a moment – I won't be a second.

---

see, saw, seen: verb ▶ Compare **hear; look at; watch**

```
        –
        OBJECT
        O + BARE INFINITIVE
        O + -ing
see +   O + PAST PARTICIPLE
        O + as . . .
        that-CLAUSE
        wh-CLAUSE
```

a *see* is used with and without an object. It is often used with *can/could* when we are talking about actually *seeing* with our eyes – especially on a particular occasion:
Muriel's eyesight is not very good now – she doesn't/can't see too well these days.
'Is that Helen over there?' 'I don't know. I can't see. (NOT **I don't see.*)
But I can see Harold.' (NOT **I see Harold.*)
We could see the sea from the hotel.
I didn't see/couldn't see what was happening.

Progressive tenses are unusual, but possible:
There's something wrong with me – I'm seeing green spots in front of my eyes.

b *see* can be followed by OBJECT + BARE INFINITIVE (for a complete action) and by OBJECT + *-ing* (when the emphasis is on the activity); and also by OBJECT + PAST PARTICIPLE:
Diana actually saw the man pull a gun out of his pocket.
She also saw the crowd chasing him down the street.
She saw people knocked to the ground.

In the passive a *to*-INFINITIVE (not a BARE INFINITIVE) is needed:
The man was seen to pull a gun out of his pocket.
He was seen leaving the bank.

---

c *see* can also mean 'notice', 'understand', 'think (about it)' and here *wh-*
CLAUSES and *that*-CLAUSES are possible:
I see that 'Crocodile Dundee' is on at the cinema this week.
'You do see my point of view, don't you?' 'Well I do see what you mean.'
'I'm afraid I was too busy to do my homework.' 'I see.' (= The speaker
understands, but is not very pleased.)
'Why didn't you phone was me?' 'Well, you see, the phone box was broken.'
(you see = you do understand)
'There's a sale on at Harrods.' 'So I saw.'
'Can I have a bicycle for my birthday?' 'We'll see (about it).' (NOT *We'll see*
it/that.)
I don't see why you can't apologise.

d *see* can be used in progressive tenses with various other meanings:
'Whatever are you doing?' 'I'm seeing if this key fits this lock. (= trying to
find out)
We're seeing Paul on Saturday. (= meeting)

e *See you/Be seeing you* are informal ways of saying 'goodbye':
Well I must be off. See you!

f *see . . . as* ▶ Compare **regard**

If we *see* someone or something *as* something we consider them to be that
thing:
I see you as a very caring person, actually.
This remark was apparently seen as a threat.

---

seeing (that): conjunction

- as; since; in view of the fact that
Seeing you're so clever, why did you make such a silly mistake?

---

seem: verb ▶ Compare **appear**

seem +	(*to be*) + ADJECTIVE (*to be*) + NOUN *like* *to*-INFINITIVE *as if/as though*
It seems +	*that*-CLAUSE *so/not*

seem is often interchangeable with *appear* (as shown below), but *seem* is not
used with the meaning of 'suddenly arrive' or 'come into view'.
seem (not *appear*) is used for rather personal or private opinions – where we

are not judging from external appearances. *Seem* is not usually used in the progressive.

1 *seem* can be followed by an ADJECTIVE and by a NOUN.

a If the meaning is roughly 'Judging by what I am told or what I see, I believe the fact is that . . .', we can use *seem* or *seem to be* before an adjective, but we prefer *seem to be* before a noun (*appear* is possible here):
> *She **seems** (to be) ill/happy/successful/worried . . .*
> *He **seems** to be some sort of director/the new manager . . .*
> *There **seems** to have been a mistake.* (= I understand that there was a mistake.)

b But if the meaning is more like 'In my opinion . . .', then we do not need *to be*. (*Appear* is not used in this meaning.) We can also say something or somebody *seems like* something else:
> *It **seems** odd/extraordinary that/if nobody reported the fire.*
> *It **seemed** a pity/a mistake/a good idea . . . to do it twice.*
> *She **seems** an amateur/a fool/a hardworking person.*
> *It **seems** ages since we last saw you. How long is it?*
> *It **seems** like yesterday that we first came here. Do you realise it is actually ten years?*
> *She **seems** very like her mother.* (= I think she is.)

2 *seem* (like *appear*) can be followed by INFINITIVES. *appear* is possible in **a** and **b**:

a *You **seem** to think the world owes you a living.*
> *She **seems** to be having a good time in Japan.*
> *There **seems** to have been some argument about who should pay.*

b With a negative idea, we usually make *seem* negative, and not the second verb:
> *You don't **seem** to understand what I'm saying.*
> *You **seem** not to understand . . .* (formal)

c *seem* (not *appear*) is usual for expressing opinions about oneself:
> *I **seem** to forget people's names.*
> *I can't **seem** to concentrate these days.*
> *I **seem** to get one cold after another.*

Compare: *I **seem**/**appear** to have got the job.* (= I have been told that I probably have got it.)

3 seem . . . as if/as though, that, so/not ▶ Compare **appear; look**

a A personal or impersonal subject + *seem* can be followed by *as if/as though*. The meaning is roughly 'that is how it appears/looks':
> *He **seemed** as if/as though he was going to be sick.*
> *It **seemed** as if/as though he was going to be sick.*

b We can also follow *it seems* with *that*-CLAUSES and *so/not*. The meaning is roughly 'I understand that these are the facts':
> '*It **seems** that he is going to change his job.*' '*So it **seems**.*'
> '*Did you say train fares are going up again?*' '*It **seems** so/not.*'

seldom: adverb ▶ Compare **rarely**

- not often; almost never

seldom is a mid-position adverb with an almost negative meaning and takes a positive question tag. If used at the beginning of a sentence for emphasis, inversion of subject and auxiliary verb is needed:

*Things are **seldom** quite what they seem, are they?*
***Seldom** have I heard such utter rubbish.*

self, selves: noun

- a person's real character or nature

*Mr Roberts was his usual cheerful **self**.*
*People sometimes say things when they are upset and not their usual calm **selves** – and then they are sorry afterwards.*

▶ See also **myself**, **yourself**, etc.

send, sent, sent: verb

---

send + (IO) + OBJECT

---

a We can *send* things and sometimes people:

*I shall **send** all my books by sea – they're too heavy to **send** by air.*
*They **sent** the boy home from school because he was ill.*

b *send* is one of those verbs, like *give*, that can have two objects:

*Sarah **sends** (you) her love.*
*I must remember to **send** her a card.*
*We **sent** cards to the adults and presents to the children.*

set

1 set, set, set: verb

−

set + O + ADJECTIVE
IO + OBJECT

---

a *set* has a general meaning of 'put or place something in position', but is more formal:

*We ate the food that was **set** in front of us.*
*The story is **set** in Vienna.* (= takes place in)

b • cause something to be somewhere or to do something.
With this meaning, the object may be followed by an adjective:
When will they set the hostages free?
The man admitted setting the chairs on fire.

c • arrange or fix
I've set my alarm clock for 5am.
Who set these exams and these awful questions?
My mother has her hair washed and set every week.

d *set* can have an indirect object and then an object when the meaning is 'give some sort of task':
You should set the children a better example.
The teacher sets us too much homework.

e *set*, without an object, has various meanings connected with movement:
The sun rises in the east and sets in the west.
We ought to set out/set off early tomorrow. (= start on a journey)

2 **set**: adjective

One meaning is 'fixed':
set books (= for an exam) . . . *a set meal/a set menu* (= where the restaurant gives you very little choice)

3 **set**: noun

a • a group of things that are used together or that match in some way
a set of dining-room chairs . . . *a set of tools* . . . *a set of matching luggage* . . . *a complete set* of Shakespeare's plays . . .

b When the meaning is a 'group of people with the same interests' – *the jet set* (= rich people who travel a lot) . . . *the racing set* . . ., a plural verb may be used:
The jet set is/are too busy to stop and think.

c A woman can ask her hairdresser for a (*shampoo and*) *set*.

d *a television set/a TV set* is the piece of 'furniture' that people watch television programmes on.

several: determiner and pronoun ▶ Compare **many**; **some**

• quite a lot (but less than many)
several is only used with plural count nouns or pronouns.
Several of + the/these/my + NOUN, and *several of* + PLURAL PRONOUN are also possible:
He's written several books – actually I've seen his name around.
I've got several of them.
I've applied for several jobs, but I haven't been doing much about it.
Several of my friends came, but several more couldn't.

shall: modal verb ▶ Compare **will**

shall is fairly rare in current British English, and very rare in American English. The negative forms are *shall not/shan't* (*shan't* is very rare in American English).

We only use *shall* to talk about actions and events in the future.

1 shall I/we . . .?

shall (NOT *will) is used after *I* and *we* in offers and suggestions and in requests for advice in some varieties of British English:

*It's very hot. **Shall I** open a window?* (offer)
*What **shall** I do? I've lost my passport.*
*What **shall** we do tomorrow? **Shall** we go swimming?* (suggestion)
(In American English we could say *What should I/we . . . Should I/we . . .?*)

Notice the common use of *shall we* as a question tag after *Let's*:

*Let's forget it, **shall we?***

2 Plain future and promises

In older grammar, *shall* was used after *I* and *we* to express both a plain future (future as fact) and promises. But today *will* is often used for these meanings:

*I **shall/will** be 21 tomorrow.*
*This time next week I **shall/will** be in Singapore.*
***Shall/Will** we see you again before you leave?*
*Of course I **shall/will** write to you.*
*I **shan't/won't** know about my accommodation until I get there.*

3 Promises and orders

shall can be used with 2nd and 3rd person when the speaker is making promises or giving orders. But this is rather formal (as in legal language) and less formal alternatives are often preferred:

*You **shall** have my reply by Friday.* (= You will have my reply . . .)
*The gates **shall** be locked at midnight.* (= The gates must be locked . . .)

4 shall have + PAST PARTICIPLE

shall have + PAST PARTICIPLE is a possible alternative to *will have* + PAST PARTICIPLE after *I/we* when referring to the future:

*I **shall have** left school by this time next year.*

she: pronoun ▶ See **her; hers; herself**

Third person singular subject pronoun (feminine).

1 she: usage

a *she* is used as the subject of a finite verb:

*Is Susan there? **She's** wanted on the telephone.*

*Your mother tells me you are taller than **she** is now.*
*Are you as musical as **she** is?*

If no verb follows *as* or *than* in comparisons, (as in **a**) *she* is possible but formal, and *her* is more usual:
*I hear you are now taller than **her** (**she**).*
*Are you as musical as **her** (**she**)?*

c *she* is used after *be* when a subject relative pronoun follows, although informally *her* is possible:
*It was **she** who realised that something was wrong.* (Informally – *It was **her***).

Her is more usual after *be* in all other positions.

2 she: meaning

she, her, herself, hers can have several meanings.

a *she* and *her* usually refer to individual women and girls, but they can also refer to female animals if we consider them as individuals:
*That cow is really intelligent, isn't **she**?*
*Our cat is a very good mother to **her** kittens.*

b *she* and *her* can also be used (instead of *it*) for countries, and ships. Some people also use feminine terms for their cars and even for machinery, but this is not general:
*Japan has been exporting more than **she**'s been importing.*
*God bless this ship and all who sail in **her**.*
*HMS Belfast was once a fighting ship, but now **she**'s a sort of museum on the River Thames in London.*
*I love Concorde – there's no other plane like **her**.*
*You look at this North Sea Oil platform, and you wonder how well **she** is fixed to the seabed.* (= the bottom of the sea)

short, shorter, shortest: adjectives ▶ Compare **long**

a *short* is the opposite of *long* (for length in both space and time):
*Your hair's too long; it suits you **shorter**.*
*We can walk – it's only a **short** distance.*
*In the southern hemisphere the twenty-first of June is the **shortest** day.*
*'I'm' is **short** for 'I am'.*

b *short* is also the opposite of *tall* (for height):
*I think there's some rule about not having very **short** men in the police.*

c *short of* means 'not having enough':
*I'm **short of** money till next pay day.*

should: modal verb

The negative forms are *should not/shouldn't*.
In simple sentences, *should* refers to the present or the future. It is hardly used as an ordinary past tense (▶ See 4 below). It has various meanings connected with obligation or duty, and also more theoretical meanings (5–8).

1 Obligation ▶ Compare **ought to**

a *should* (like *ought to*) expresses obligation or duty. Often the speaker is giving advice or expressing a critical opinion. *Ought to* is possible in the following, though not very likely in the last one:

*You **should** write to your mother more often.*

*I know I **should**. But she **shouldn't** treat me like a small child.*

*Who **should** my son write to about a university place?* (asking for advice)

*We **should** explain that sodium chloride is the same as common salt.* (= we must, and do, explain)

b If the speaker/writer is in a position of authority, *should* is almost as strong as *must* and is not replaceable by *ought to*:

*Applications **should** reach the above address by 31st July.*

*This jacket **should** be drycleaned.*

2 Theory – probability ▶ Compare **ought to**

a *should* can mean that something is probably true now or will probably happen in the future. (Contrast *must*, which usually expresses certainty about the present, not the future). *Ought to* is also possible in the following:

*Bob **should** be in Sydney now if his plane was on time.* (*must* is also possible here)

*You **should** catch the train all right if you hurry.* (NOT **must*)

*There **shouldn't** be any difficulty over the ticket.* (NOT **must*)

b The theoretical meaning of *should* often contains some meaning of obligation as well, so *should* is mainly used to make pleasant guesses (NOT **You **should** miss the train if you don't hurry.* Say *You **may/might/will/could** . . .*).

3 *If*-CLAUSES

should (never *would* and never *ought to*) can be used in the *if*-clause of a conditional sentence about the future, to mean that the possibility is not very likely:

*If you **(should)** hear from Paul, do let us know.*

should + SUBJECT + VERB (without *if*) is a formal alternative:

***Should** you see Paul do let us know.*

***Should** you discover a fire, BREAK THE GLASS OF THE NEAREST FIRE ALARM.*

b *should* can also follow *in case*, to make something sound unlikely:

*I must get some more food **in case** Bob and Sue **should** call.*

4 Past of **shall**

should is not an ordinary past tense, but *should* is used as the past of *shall* in reported speech:

Shall I open a window? → *He asked if he **should** open a window.*

Shall we go swimming? → *They suggested we **should** go swimming.*

should or *would* can be used as the future-in-the-past after *I/we*:

*We were so happy. Soon, if all went well, we **should/would** have a house of our own.*

5 Politeness

should (compare *shall*) can be used in *I/we* questions to make a polite offer or a suggestion:
> **Should** *I open a window?* (or *shall*)
> **Should** *we wait another ten minutes to see if they come?* (or *shall*)

should (or *would*) can be used after *I/we* when accepting offers:
> '*Can/Could you come to a party next Saturday?*' '*Oh thank you, we* **should** *(would) love to come.* (NOT **I/we* **shall** *love to.*)

It is sometimes polite to speak as if we are not completely certain about something, and *should/would* are often used in this way after *I/we*:
> *I* **should/would** *imagine it is very expensive but I don't know.*
> *I* **should/would** *think there were a hundred people at the meeting.*
> *I* **should/would** *say/guess that he isn't very pleased.*

However, *I should hope so/not* often sounds rather cross:
> '*He says he'll pay you back everything he owes you*' '*I* **should/would** *hope so.*'

6 Hypothesis/condition ▶ Compare **would**

a *should* is an alternative to *would* after *I/we* in the main clause of a sentence about an unreal condition, one where we know that something is not true:
> *I* **should/would** *learn Chinese if I had the time.* (= but I haven't got the time)
> *If we were fish, we* **should/would** *hate these fishermen.*

b Even without an *if*-clause there is often an idea of condition.
Notice that in these examples *I should/would do something* is used as an informal way of giving advice.
> *I* **should/would** *keep quiet about that.* (i.e., if I were you)
> *I* **should** *write to your mother – she'll be so pleased if you do.*

c In *wh*-QUESTIONS, *should* (for all persons) suggests annoyance or surprise.
Notice also the example in the 3rd person and compare 'emotional' *should* (7):
> *How* **should** *I know?* (= I don't know and I'm not interested.)
> *Why* **should** *you care about it?* (= I don't believe you care.)
> *Why* **should** *anyone want to buy a ruin?* (= Surely nobody would want to.)

7 'Emotional' **should**

a *should* (not *would*) is widely used in subordinate clauses to give the speaker's emotional reaction to events:
> *It is natural (that) you* **should** *feel annoyed.* (or – *that you feel annoyed.*)
> *I was furious (that) they* **should** *believe those lies.*

Notice that ordinary tenses are possible here, because we are talking about facts; subjunctives are impossible. Other words and phrases that can be followed by *should*-clauses in this way include:
> *It is a pity . . . It is disgraceful/odd/strange/unfortunate . . .*
> *I am/was . . . annoyed/disappointed/glad/pleased/sorry/surprised . . .*

b *should* is also used after main clauses containing words saying that something is desirable or needs doing, (i.e., *it* **should** *be done*):
> *I suggest that everyone* **should** *try.*
> *They insisted that he* **should** *stay at school another year.*
> *It was essential/I was keen that everyone* **should** *be given a chance.*

Here subjunctives are a possible alternative, because we are not talking about facts. But ordinary tenses are also possible:

. . . that everyone try/tries . . .
. . . that he stay/stayed . . .
. . . that everyone be given/was given . . .

8 Purpose

should or *would* (and other modals) are used after *so that* to express purpose:
*We took it in turns so that everyone **should/would/could** have a chance.*

9 should have + PAST PARTICIPLE

a *I/we should have* + PAST PARTICIPLE is an alternative to *I/we would have* + PAST PARTICIPLE in the main clause of unreal past conditions:
*We **should/would** have gone if we had been invited.*
*I **shouldn't/wouldn't** have told them if I had realised it was a secret.* (= I did tell them.)

b *I should/would have expected/thought . . .* can be used with two rather different meanings:
*I **should/would have expected** him to like it.*

implies 'if you had asked me'. But it could be a comment meaning 'I am not surprised that he likes it', or it could mean 'I would have been quite wrong – he does not like it. I am surprised.'
I should/would have thought is also a polite way of giving an opinion (▶ See also **5**):
*I **should/would have thought** it would be expensive.* (= I think it would be expensive.)

c *should have* + PAST PARTICIPLE (with all persons) can express an obligation or a duty which existed in the past. So it is often used to criticise some past action or behaviour:
*He **should have** let us know his plans.* (= but he did not)
*He **should not have** just disappeared like that.* (= but he did)

d *should have* + PAST PARTICIPLE (with all persons) also has a theoretical meaning 'It is reasonable now to believe that something happened/has happened/will happen':
*Bob and Sue **should have** arrived home yesterday/by now – let's telephone and see if they're there.*
*Let's wait until the morning – they certainly **should have** arrived by then.*

This is not as certain as *must have* + PAST PARTICIPLE or *can't have* + PAST PARTICIPLE.

e Emotional meaning
should have done (for all persons) can be used in subordinate clauses like *should do* to express personal reactions:
*It is sad that he **should have** died only two months before his great book was published.* (or *that he died*)
*I was furious that they **shouldn't have** bothered to tell us.* (or *that they didn't bother*)

show, showed, shown (or showed): verb

The past participle is usually *shown*, but *showed* is sometimes used.

```
              —
           (IO+) OBJECT
show +     O + -ing
           O + PAST PARTICIPLE
           (IO+) that CLAUSE
           (IO+) wh-CLAUSE
```

a *show* has a general meaning of 'causing or allowing something to be seen'. It usually needs an object:
> The television news has been **showing** amazing pictures from Eastern Europe.
> A young man answered the door and **showed** us in/**showed** us into a large room. (= led us)
> A dark coat wouldn't **show** the dirt.

b *show* can have an indirect object and then an object:
> Do **show** me your new suit/what you've bought.
> '**Show** it to all of us.' 'I don't want to **show** you.'
> They've always **shown** me great kindness. (= been kind)
> You will be **shown** what to do/how the machine works.

c The direct object is sometimes followed by an *-ing* form or a past participle:
> The photos **show** my mother sitting in the garden.
> And this one **shows** the garden covered with snow.

d *show* is possible without an object:
> I've mended my coat, and I don't think the hole will **show** now.

e When the meaning is 'prove', *show* can be followed by a *that*-CLAUSE:
> The report **shows** that the accident was due to human error.

shut, shut, shut: verb　　　　　　　　　　　▶ Compare **close**

shut and *close* are often interchangeable, but we *shut people (up)* in places (NOT *close them up):
> He **shut** himself in his bedroom and refused to come out.
> Some criminals should be **shut up** for life. (= imprisoned)

Shut (not *close*) is used in such rude expressions as:
> **Shut** up! **Shut** your mouth! (both meaning 'Stop speaking')

sick: adjective　　　　　　　　　　　　　　　▶ Compare **ill**

1

a *sick* is used in front of nouns – i.e., it can be attributive, (which is unusual for *ill*):
> a hospital for **sick** children . . .

*My father is now a very **sick** man.*
*Miss Arrowsmith is off **sick**/is on **sick** leave.* (= she is away from work ill)

b   *sick* is also used as a predicative adjective – after *be, feel* . . ., but the meaning can be different. In British English, *be sick* here means to bring food up from the stomach (perhaps because the food was bad):

*I feel **sick** . . . I'm going to be **sick** . . . She was **sick** in the night.*
*. . . He's just been **sick** again . . . The dog's been **sick** on the carpet.*

Compare:
*Do you ever get/feel **airsick**/**carsick**/**seasick**?*

In American English, *be sick* is commonly used with the meaning 'be ill/be unwell' in general; but in British English it is clearer to use *be ill/be unwell* for this:

*'Why weren't you here yesterday?' 'I was **ill**./I wasn't feeling **well**.*

c   **be sick of** (informal)
If you are *sick of* something, you are 'fed up with' it, and you don't want it or don't do it any more:

*I'm **sick of** hearing how poor she is – she earns twice as much as I do.*

2   *The sick* can mean *sick* people in general:
*Winter is especially hard for the old and **the sick**.*

---

similar: adjective   ▶ Compare **(the) same**

● like; of the same sort
The opposite is *different*:

*They're a couple with very **similar** ideas about how to bring up children.*
*Well if the Hilton is fully booked, surely they can find us a **similar** hotel.*
*The shop had sold out of the suitcases I liked, and had nothing **similar**.*
*Your fridge is **similar** to ours, but it's not quite the same.*

---

since

since can be a preposition, a conjunction or an adverb of time. It always names the starting-point of a period. This period can either continue until now (a present perfect tense is usually used in the main clause), or end at some second point, also in the past (usually with a past perfect tense).

1   **since**: preposition
*We've been learning English **since** 1983.*
*They had only known each other **since** the previous winter.*
*We haven't seen Paul **since** the holidays.*
***Since** losing his job, he has been very depressed.*

2   **since**: adverb
*I began learning English in 1983 and have been learning ever **since**.*
*They sold the shop years ago, but they have **since** started another business.*

---

3 since: conjunction

> *I've been working very hard **since** I got back here on Sunday.*
> *Robin phoned yesterday – we hadn't heard from him **since** he went off to Australia two years ago.*

4 Non-perfect tenses and **since**

Present tenses in the main clause can be used with *since* with expressions involving *be* or some other stative verb, and with verbs describing present habits that depend on some past cause:

> *It is/It has been ages **since** we last saw you.*
> *It was/It had been a long time **since** he had felt so happy.*
> *I am much fatter **since** you last saw me.*
> *Leo looks amazing **since** she's had her hair cut so short.*
> *I'm feeling much better **since** I started taking these pills.*
> *Timothy goes for long walks every day **since** he bought the dog.*

5 since: conjunction of reason

When since means 'because' or 'as' (with little or no time meaning) any tense is possible. *Since*-CLAUSES usually come at the beginning:

> ***Since** so many people cannot come, I think we'd better cancel the meeting.*

---

sit, sat, sat: verb

> *Why are you **sitting** on the floor?*
> ***Sit** on this chair/in this armchair.*
> *I can't go on standing – I must **sit** (**down**).*
> *She was **sitting up** in bed reading.*

---

sleep ▶ See **asleep**

---

small, smaller, smallest ▶ Compare **little**

small is the opposite of *big*. It is also often the opposite of *large* (because *little* has emotional meanings), and of *great*.

a • not big, not large

> *a **small** box/family/house/room/town*
> *a **small** loaf . . . two **small** packets of peas*
> *Have you got this jumper in a **smaller** size? – this one's too large.*
> *There was only a **small** amount/quantity of food left after the party.*
> ***Small** children must be taught road safety.* (= young children)

b A *small farmer*, a *small shopkeeper*, etc. means someone with a *small farm*, or with just one shop, etc.

small

c   **small** or **little**?

Both *small* and *little* refer to size, but *small* is often more objective, while *little* suggests that the speakers like or dislike what they are talking about:

*   **Small** *houses are much cheaper to heat.*
*   *We only need a* **small** *flat – there's only two of us.*
*   *They have a dear* **little**/*a lovely* **little**/*an attractive* **little**/*a horrid* **little** *house.*

smell

	–
	ADJECTIVE
	of . . .
smell +	*like* . . .
	as if/as though
	OBJECT
	o + *-ing*

1   **smell, smelt** (or **smelled**), **smelt** (or **smelled**): verb   ▶ Compare **taste**

The meanings are connected with the sense of the nose.

a   If we simply say that something *smells*, we usually mean it is unpleasant. Progressive tenses are not usually used:

*   *His breath/armpits/feet/clothes* **smelt**.
*   *We'd better not eat this fish – it* **smells**.

b   But we can use *smell* + ADJECTIVE, *smell of* + NOUN, *smell like*, *smell as if/as though* . . . to say things are pleasant or unpleasant:

*   *Mm! you* **smell** *nice. What perfume are you using?*
*   *This soup* **smells** *delicious/good/meaty/odd/unusual* . . .
*   *The house* **smelt** *of roses/tobacco/warm new bread/wet clothes* . . .
*   *That* **smells** **like** *coffee/old boots* . . .
*   *This room* **smells** **as if** *nobody's opened a window for months.*

c   A personal subject (+ *can/could*) + *smell* (+ OBJECT) describes people's sensations – what they can sense with their noses:

*   *I can't* **smell** *(a thing). I've got a terrible cold.*
*   *The moment we got off the train we could* **smell** *the sea.*
*   *He opened the door and immediately* **smelt**/*could* **smell** *burning.*

d   We can also use *smell* + OBJECT + *-ing*:   ▶ Compare **hear; see**

*   *He* **smelt** *something burning.*
*   *We could* **smell** *dinner cooking.*

e   If we deliberately *smell* something – to find out what it *smells* of, or to see what state it is in, progressive tenses are possible:

*   *'What on earth are you doing?' 'I'm* **smelling** *this meat to see if it's all right for the cat.'*

2 smell: noun (C, U)

smells may be pleasant or unpleasant:
> *There's a smell of gas/of roses in this room.*
> *I like/dislike the smell of cheese/cigarettes/cooking/drains/fish/flowers/hamburgers . . .*
> *Cats have a very good sense of smell.*

SO

1 SO + ADJECTIVE/ADVERB/DETERMINER/VERB ▶ Compare **such**

so	bad oddly much/little . . . many/few . . .	(that) . . .
. . . **so**	annoyed me	

a Exclamations

With adjectives, adverbs etc. as shown, *so* (here an adverb) adds emphasis. It can be used in exclamations and in negative imperatives:
> *You are so kind!*
> *Was it really so difficult?*
> *Tom isn't so clever, after all.*
> *Don't be so rude.*
> *My suitcase is so heavy, as I have four bottles in it.*
> *He's behaving so oddly these days.*
> *I'm so awfully glad, Gerald, that you accepted the job.*
> *You're working far too hard – it does so worry me.* (= It worries me very much.)
> *Thank you so much.*
> *So many people try to do two jobs at once.*
> ▶ Contrast: *How kind you are* at **how.**

b so . . . that: result

that-CLAUSES after a clause with *so* + ADJECTIVE/ADVERB/VERB or *much/many* express result:
> *The roads are so bad that it will take nine days to get there.*
> *It's just so amazing (that) it kind of blows my mind.* (= I can hardly believe it.)
> *He behaves so oddly that nobody wants to see him any more.*
> *Played a ridiculous game of cricket on Saturday, which so annoyed me that I think I'll not play for this team again.*
> *There was an old woman*
> *who lived in a shoe;*
> *she had so many children (that)*
> *she didn't know what to do.* (children's verse)

c   **so . . . as to do**

This is a formal (and rare) alternative to *so . . . that*:

I am not so foolish as to imagine that we can improve the situation quickly.
(= I am not so foolish that I imagine . . .)

2   **so that/so as (not) to**: purpose

▶ Compare   **in order that; in order (not) to**

so that and *so as (not) to* express purpose. *So that* with this meaning is often followed by a modal verb (Contrast result clauses with *so* – at **1b** above – where ordinary tenses are usual):

Perhaps you could kindly let me have this information so that I can reply.
Please give me a ring whichever day you are coming so that I may be free to see you.
I wrote the number down so that I would not forget it.
She stood on a chair so as to reach the top shelf.

3   **so** (sometimes **so that**): connector

● therefore; for this reason
  I have a car now. So at last I can get about more.

4   **so** + ADJECTIVE/ADVERB etc. + **as**: comparison   ▶ Compare   **as . . . as**

	nearly		clever	
not	quite	so	well	as . . .
	anything like		much/many	

so . . . as can be used instead of *as . . . as* after *not* in comparisons. Various words can come before *so*, as shown:

Tom isn't so clever as his wife/as she is/as her.
He doesn't write anything like so well as she does.
There weren't quite so many mosquitoes as we expected.

5   **so**: clause   ▶ Compare   **not**

A	I assume/believe/expect/fear/guess/hear/ hope/imagine/say/suppose/think/understand I'm afraid It appears/seems	
B	I don't believe/expect/imagine/suppose/think	**so**
C	If/Even	
D	Maybe/Perhaps	

so can be used for a whole clause (including the subject and the verb) instead of repeating it.

A This happens after various verbs of reporting and thinking (but NOT **know*), *to be afraid*, *It appears/seems* . . .:

> '*Is Charles coming?*' '*I believe so/I hope so.*'
> *I think, and I have told her* **so**, *that she ought to work abroad for a few years.* (*so* = that she ought to work abroad)
> '*It's going to be a cold winter,*' '*Yes, they say* **so**.'
> '*Poor old Richard is going to lose his job.*' '*It appears/seems* **so**.'

B With a few of these verbs – mainly those shown in the table – instead of saying *I believe not*, etc., we often say *I don't believe so* (But NOT **I don't hope so* or **I'm not afraid so*):

> '*Are you going to get a rise?*' '*I don't suppose* **so**.'

C *If so* and *Even so* can stand for a whole clause meaning '(Even) if/though that is the case':

> *Are you free tomorrow? Because* **if so**, *we could go fishing.*
> *My father gives me an extra £100 a month, but* **even so** *I'm always short of money.*

D *so* can also follow a few sentence adverbs of possibility:

> '*My father is very strict.*' '**Maybe so**. *But you should listen to him all the same.*' (= that may be true, but . . .)
> '*Tom's such a nice person.*' '**Perhaps so** – *but he has some very silly ideas.*'

6 do so

The phrase *do so* is used instead of some other verb + a following phrase that has already been mentioned:

> *I sent the papers to Michael early last week and asked him to return them before the wedding, but unfortunately he forgot to* **do so**. (= return the papers before the wedding)
> '*I wish you'd tidy your room.*' '*I'm just* **doing so** *now.*'
> *She put the key in the lock, and as she* **did so** *she felt a hand on her neck.*

7 so + SUBJECT + VERB

a In short replies and comments *so* + SUBJECT + VERB can express agreement. This is possible with some of the verbs in **5A** (but NEVER **So I'm afraid*):

> '*Vanessa has changed her job again.*' '**So I heard**.' (= that is what I heard.)
> '*He'll come if we need him.*' '**So he says**.' (= that is what he says, but I'm not completely sure)

b *so* + SUBJECT + AUXILIARY usually expresses surprised agreement:

> '*You've dropped your purse.*' '**So I have**.' (NOT **So I have done.*)
> '*The kettle's boiling.*' '**So it is**.' (NOT **So it is boiling.*)

8 so + AUXILIARY VERB + SUBJECT

To add a statement that some second person does the same thing as the one who has already been mentioned, we can use *so* + AUXILIARY VERB + SUBJECT. Notice how this stresses the new different subject (which is the new information) by putting it at the end. The meaning is 'too'. Notice that we do not repeat the whole verb:

> *My father gives me money, and so does my mother.* (= my mother does too)
> *Vanessa's changed her job again. So have I.*
> *If lawyers are busy men, so are ministers.*
> *I missed the last two meetings, and so did Michael.*

▶ See also *or so* at **or**; *and so on* at **on**; *so far as* at **far**

---

some ▶ Compare **any**

some and words beginning *some* – (e.g. *somebody, somewhere*) are mainly used in affirmative sentences, and therefore contrast with *any* and *any*-words. *Some*-words can be used in questions if the answer is 'yes' is expected or hoped for:

> *'Will you have some coffee?' 'I'd love some. Thanks.'*

Some can even be used in negative questions if the speaker is suggesting that someone or something exists:

> *Wasn't there some talk of more money?*

some: determiner and pronoun

a ● indefinite quantity
some can refer to things and people. It is used with uncountable nouns and with plural nouns to mean 'a certain amount of' (e.g. *some money*) or 'a number of' (e.g. *some books*). With this meaning, *some* is usually unstressed (/səm/, or /sʌm/ in end position):

> *There is some bread. Of course there's some. Would you like some?*
> *We have some apples, but not enough. Could you buy some please?*
> *Some of these are bad.* (▶ See also the table at *any*)

b ● a particular person or thing
A second meaning of *some* is 'a particular person or thing' – though exactly what or which is not stated. With this meaning the pronunciation is usually stressed /sʌm/. This *some* can be used with singular count nouns as well as plural and uncountable nouns:

> *There must be some explanation for her behaviour.* (= though I don't know what)
> *I'd like to return there some day.* (= though I don't know when)
> *Some people love discos, but I hate them.* (= some, but not me: some but not others)
> *Some food is actually very bad for you.* (= some, but not all)

c **some of** ... can be followed by *the/this/these/my* ... + NOUN, and by PRONOUNS:

> *Some of her adventures were quite extraordinary.*
> *Some of us were rather worried.*
> *It was a long story, some of which I'd heard before.*

d **some more/some + NUMBERS** ...
Like *any, some* can be followed by *more*:

> *'Have some more coffee?' 'Oh, I'd love some more.'*
> *Some more students are arriving soon.*

---

some can also be followed by a number, and the meaning is then 'about' 'roughly':

Some *two hundred people attended the meeting.*

▶ for *some* or ZERO? see **any**

somebody, someone: pronouns
▶ Compare **anybody**; **everybody**; **nobody**

- some (indefinite) person
There is no difference between *somebody* and *someone*, but *someone* is more common.

a *somebody/someone* is used in affirmative contexts (that is statements and questions expecting the answer 'yes'):

She tells me it is the first time she has really loved **somebody**.
It's like kissing **someone** *for the first time.*
You mean there's **someone** *at the door?*

b *somebody* is also used with the meaning of 'an important person':

He seems to think he's **somebody**, *and doesn't want to know us any more.*

c *somebody* can be followed by ADJECTIVES, RELATIVE CLAUSES, NON-FINITE VERBS, PHRASES and *else*:

He sounds like **someone** *special.*
Only **somebody** *who doesn't understand would say a thing like that.*
It was already occupied by **someone** *called Sandra.*
Someone *with a funny hat was coming up the path.*
Isn't there **somebody** *else we could invite?*

d **somebody/someone . . . they**

Grammatically *somebody* and *someone* are singular and take singular verbs, but sentences often continue with plural possessives and pronouns:

Someone *brave has to lead the way, don't they?*
To **somebody** *who's not earning much, that could be 10% of* **their** *salary.*

somehow: adverb

- in some way; for some reason
Somehow *I doubt whether we'll be able to get up there.*
Very often the library copy has **somehow** *disappeared.*
It would be a bit unsuitable **somehow**.

something: pronoun
▶ Compare **anything**; **everything**; **nothing**

- a particular but indefinite thing, event, etc.

a *something* is used in affirmative contexts and contrasts with *anything* which is non-assertive:

He thinks Ella is worried about **something**.
Then the aircraft flew over – we knew **something** *was going to happen.*

b *something* can be followed by ADJECTIVES and other describing words:
> *We'll think of **something** exciting to do.*
> *He said **something** about going on holiday with his son.*
> *It's not his problem. It's not your problem. It's **something** that happens.*
> *Please send her back to me if you feel there is **something** else the hospital can
> do to help.*

c *or something* means 'or something like that':
> *He's twenty-four **or something** – and behaves like a three-year-old.*
> *We'll go out for a meal, then come back and have more wine **or something**.*

sometime or **some time**: adverb

- at some unstated time in the past or future
  > *It happened **sometime** last year – I'm not sure when exactly.*
  > *Come up and see me **sometime**.*
  > *Darling, please come to Cambridge **some time**.*
  > *Could you manage a day in London **some time**?*
  > ***Some time** in the 80's she and her young husband moved to the city.*

sometimes: adverb

- from time to time, but not very often
  > ***Sometimes** I wish I could just go away and start again in another town.*
  > *Womanly men have **sometimes** been foolish or thoughtless, but they have
  > never done much harm.*
  > *You certainly make a lot of noise **sometimes**.*

somewhat: adverb

- rather; to some degree; a bit
  > *She was tall and **somewhat** self-conscious about her height.*
  > *Our views are **somewhat** different.*
  > *Your house is **somewhat** bigger than theirs.*
  > *I was suffering **somewhat** from the effects of too many late nights.*

somewhere: adverb
▶ Compare **anywhere**; **everywhere**; **nowhere**

- in some place
  > *You should all go and live **somewhere** together.*
  > *You need **somewhere** to put them.*
  > *We'll go **somewhere** quiet.*
  > *Let's go to Venice or Florence or **somewhere** like that.*

somewhere is frequently followed by a PREPOSITION + a NOUN or name of a
place:
> ***somewhere** near King's Cross . . . **somewhere** outside New York . . .*
> ***somewhere** around Baker Street . . . **somewhere** along the river . . .*

soon, sooner, soonest

1 soon, sooner, soonest: adverb

a • in a short time from now
See you very **soon**, *darling. All my love – George.*
Perhaps we could meet **soon**.
How **soon** *could we meet? What about the 25th?*
Can't you make it **sooner** *than that?*
Well the 22nd would be the **soonest** *I could possibly manage.*

b When the meaning is 'a short time after some past time' or 'quickly', mid-position is usual:
Aunt Dot was at home when I got back, but **soon** *left.*
It **soon** *became clear that Mr Newton was much the better teacher of the two.*
We waited for a time – and **soon** *came the orders to move again.*
They were very hungry and **soon** *finished the food.*

2 as soon as: conjunction

If B happens *as soon as* A happens, then B happens very quickly after A:
As **soon as** *they were married, Ted forbade Maud ever to do any pole-vaulting again.*

as soon as possible and *as soon as (one) can* both mean 'very quickly':
Send the form off **as soon as possible**.
I'll ring again **as soon as I can**.

3 would sooner . . . (than) ▶ Compare **rather**

a If someone *would sooner* do something they would rather do it, they would prefer that thing to happen:
***I'd sooner** you didn't tell him.*
*We'**d** much **sooner** not go – but we've got to.*

b When we mention both possibilities, the meaning is often that both are unpleasant:
*He'**d sooner** die than admit he's wrong.*

4 no sooner . . . than: conjunction

No sooner has A happened than B happens means that B happens very soon after A. (▶ Compare **as soon as**.) The *no sooner* clause usually needs a perfect tense:
*They had **no sooner** got married **than** Ted forbade Maud ever to do any pole vaulting again.*
or *No sooner* *had they got married* ***than*** . . . (Note the inversion after the negative start.)

sorry

1 sorry: adjective

sorry is used to express sadness and sympathy or to apologise.

As an adjective *sorry* can be followed by various patterns:
*I'm **sorry** (that) Ian's in hospital again.*
*We were **sorry** to hear/to learn (that) Ian's in hospital.*
*I'm **sorry** to say this/to tell you, but you've failed.*
*I am/I feel **sorry** for Ian. He has terrible health.*
*(I am) **sorry** about the confusion – I thought you said Thursday, not Tuesday.*
*(I'm) **sorry** – but I think you are wrong.* (polite way of disagreeing)

2 sorry: exclamation

a As an exclamation, *sorry* can be used instead of *I am/I'm sorry* when we want to apologise:
*   **Sorry**. *I didn't mean to interrupt.*
*   *'That's my coffee you're drinking.' 'Oh, **sorry**. I thought it was mine.'*

b We can also use *sorry* if we don't hear or don't understand what somebody says and want them to repeat it:
*   *'It's not unlikely that he won't come.' '**Sorry?**' 'I mean, I don't think he'll come.'*

---

sort

1 sort: noun ▶ Compare **kind**

*   kind; type
    *It's perfectly good toothpaste, but it's not the **sort** I buy.*
    *What **sort** do you want? There are all different **sorts**.*
    *I'm not that **sort** of girl.*
    *We may soon sign some **sort** of agreement with them.*
    *Making this **sort** of money is terribly exhausting work.* (= this big amount of money)
    *This makes no **sort** of sense.*
    *It's a funny **sort** of day – is it going to rain or not?*
    *'Yes dear,' replied his mother, in a worried **sort** of way.*

2 sort of: adverb ▶ Compare **kind of**

*   a bit, but not very; kind of
    sort of is used informally and can be used with adjectives, adverbs, verbs . . . :
    *Some people think I'm **sort of** crazy.*
    *It's going to make everything so easy, it seems wrong and **sort of** unbelievable.*
    *I felt **sort of** in the way.*
    *He **sort of** tripped up and injured his ankle.*
    *It's bad when your money **sort of** disappears on nothing.*

---

sound: verb ▶ Compare **look**

sound can be used a bit like *look*, with the meaning 'from what I hear it seems that . . .' *Sound* can be followed by an ADJECTIVE, a NOUN, *like* (PREPOSITION) and *as if/as though*:

$$\text{sound} + \begin{array}{l} \text{ADJECTIVE} \\ \text{NOUN} \\ like \ldots \\ as \; if/as \; though \end{array}$$

*She **sounds** cross/happy/tired . . .*
*You don't **sound** very sure.*
*He **sounds** a nice person.*
*That **sounds** (like) a good idea.*
*He **sounded** as if/as though he didn't want to go after all.*
*It **sounds** as if/as though there's going to be trouble.*

---

speak, spoke, spoken: verb ▶ Compare **talk**

The general meaning is 'say words', 'talk'; and, like *talk*, *speak* usually has no object.

1 *speak* (not *talk*) is used when the meaning is simply saying words, and the content of the words is not important:
> *Basically her job is teaching deaf children to **speak**.*
> *He was in a state of shock and couldn't speak.*
> (On the telephone) '*Can I **speak** to Alan Watkins, please.*' '***Speaking***.'
> *(= This is Alan Watkins).*

In British English we usually *speak to* people. In American English *speak with* is preferred (*Can I **speak with** Alan Watkins?*)

2 *speak* is the word for making a formal speech:
> *Who is **speaking** in the debate next week?*

3 **speak** + OBJECT ▶ Compare **say; tell**

  speak can be followed by a rather limited number of objects.
a *speak* is the usual verb when the meaning is 'have knowledge of' a language, though *talk* is also possible when the meaning is 'actually using a language':
> *They **spoke** no English and I do not **speak** Swahili.*
> *Are those people over there **speaking** Chinese/**talking** Chinese/**talking** in Chinese?*

b Other objects
> *You've hardly **spoken** (or **said**) a word the whole evening.*
> *Always **speak** (or **tell**) the truth.*
> *I'm going to **speak** my mind! (= say exactly what I think)*

4 generally speaking

  generally speaking is used as a sentence adverb, meaning 'generally', 'usually':

> ***Generally speaking**, too many sweets are bad for you.*

---

5 speak or talk?

a *speak* and *talk* are often interchangeable, as both can be used when only one person or when more than one person is involved. But *speak* is more formal; *talk* suggests conversation:

> *The lecturer **spoke** (or **talked**) on the problems of pollution.*
> *My aunt **talked** to us (or **told us**) about her childhood.*
> *People were **talking** while the President was **speaking**.*

b If *speak* is used alone, without saying *to/with somebody*, or *about/on something*, (and the meaning is not 'saying words' as in **1**), then *speak* suggests that there is a particular topic, a special matter that is spoken about. Again this contrasts with *talk* (meaning 'giving information or taking part in conversation'):

> *The lecturer **spoke** without notes.*
> *My brother is always **talking**.*
> *We **talked** over dinner. (= There was conversation).*
> *We **spoke** over dinner. (= This sentence is odd unless the listener knows what problem or subject was discussed.)*

c *speak* (as with making a speech) may suggest that the people spoken to are not expected to reply:

> *Perhaps they don't realise their radio annoys you. Why don't you talk to them about it. (= discuss it with them)*
> *You should **speak** to them about it. (= complain to them)*

special: adjective

especial is possible, but very formal, and *special* is the commoner word.

- important for a particular reason
  > *Today's a **special** day for us – it's exactly a year since we met.*
  > *The film was all right – nothing **special**.*

(e)specially: adverb

a In many cases, when the meaning is 'particularly', both *especially* and *specially* are possible:

> *I've made this cake **(e)specially** for you.*
> *The exam wasn't **(e)specially** difficult.*
> *I don't **(e)specially** like coffee, actually.*

b *specially* is better when the meaning is 'in a special way' or 'for a special purpose':

> *These dogs are **specially** trained by the police.*
> *I made the cake **specially**.*

c *especially* is preferred when the meaning is 'above all':

> *It's a dangerous road – **especially** when it's icy.*
> *I love Scotland – **especially** the north-west.*

d When *especially* belongs with the subject, it comes after (not before), and is preferred to *specially*:

> *Old people especially should try to take regular exercise.*

speech: noun (C, U)   ▶ Compare **talk**

a ● a formal talk (C)

> *The Queen's Speech at the opening of Parliament is written for her by her Ministers.*
> *The trouble with these formal dinners is you get all these after-dinner speeches.*

b ● power or ability to speak (U)

> *Even the cleverest animals lack the power of speech.*
> *There's no freedom of speech if the newspapers are controlled by the government.*

spite, in spite of   ▶ See **despite**

stand, stood, stood: verb

1 ● be upright, on one's feet

> *Why are you standing? Do sit down.*
> *The train was crowded and we had to stand all the way.*
> *Everybody stood up when the Prime Minister entered.*
> *Stand clear of the doors!* (A common announcement at underground stations, telling people to stand well away from the train doors.)

2 can/could stand   ▶ Compare **bear**

(can)	OBJECT
stand + *-ing*	
(could)	*you/your -ing*

can/could + *stand* is used mainly in negatives and questions and roughly means 'can/could bear'. If you *cannot stand* something, you dislike it very much. It must be followed by an OBJECT or by (*you/your*)-*ing* verb. Unlike *bear* it is not followed by a *to*-INFINITIVE:

> *He can't stand classical music/discos/people who complain all the time . . .*
> *I can't stand being kept waiting/having to stand in a queue.*
> *She couldn't stand them/their interfering all the time.*

start

---

start: verb ▶ Compare **begin**

```
           —
         OBJECT
start +  -ing
         to-INFINITIVE
         o + -ing
```

1 *start* and *begin* are often interchangeable. Like *begin*, *start* can be used with or without an OBJECT, or be followed by *to*-INFINITIVE or *-ing*:
The war started in 1939.
Martin started (out) as a reporter on a local newspaper.
If they don't come soon, we'd better start (dinner) without them.
It's starting to rain.
Suddenly she started screaming.

2 Only *start* (NOT **begin*) is used with the meaning of 'begin a journey' or 'begin moving':
We must start (out) at 6 a.m., because it's a long drive.
They started (off) at great speed, but after a few miles they got slower and slower.
The car wouldn't start.
I didn't hear you come in – you made me start. (*start* = make a sudden surprised movement)

3 ● cause something to exist or make something work or move
People can start (up) a business/a club/a restaurant/a school . . .
You can start an argument/a fight/a fire/a quarrel/a rumour . . .
A couple can start a family. (= have their first baby)
It may be difficult to start a car if the weather is cold.
He blew his whistle to start the race.

Notice that all these involve fairly definite decisions. Contrast:
Queen Victoria began her long reign in 1837. (NOT **started*, because she became queen when the previous king died. She did not decide to become queen.)
In this meaning of causing, *start* can be followed by OBJECT + *-ing* (=causing somebody else to do something):
You've started me worrying.

4 to start with

to start with (like *to begin with*) usually means 'at first . . .', but suggests that something changed later on. It can also mean 'this is the first point I'd like to make':
He was worried about the job to start with, but then he realised he could do it.
To start with I haven't got the time – and anyhow I don't want to go.

354

5 for a start

for a start (PREPOSITION + NOUN) introduces a reason for something or an idea, usually with the suggestion that there are plenty more reasons or ideas:

*'Why haven't you brought your girlfriend?' 'Well, **for a start**, she isn't my girlfriend, and anyway . . .'*
'Who put the bomb there?' 'We don't know yet. Lots of people could have.'
*'Us, **for a start**!' said Bernard.*

still

1 still: adverb   ▶ Compare **already; yet**

a As an adverb of time *still* tells us about something continuing from some time in the past until now/then. It often shows surprise that something has continued so long or in spite of something. Usually it is in mid-position and mainly in affirmative statements and questions:

*We don't approve of what you did but we **still** love you very much.*
*She is **still** doing well.*
*'It was £50 and now it's only £40.' 'That's **still** expensive for a shirt.'* (= even at that lower price)
*Is Peter **still** in the States?*
*It's **still** a lot cheaper than flying.* (= although it is expensive)

b If we use *still* with *not*, we must be careful about word order. Usually we are saying that some negative state is continuing for a surprisingly long time or that some action has not happened yet:

*I **still** have not heard from Michael.*
*I **still** haven't got Michael's new address.*
*You **still** haven't written to your mother – you really ought to, you know.* (or *Have you **still** not written . . .?*)

But if we use AUXILIARY + NEGATIVE + *still* + VERB, then we are saying something used to be the case, but is not any more:

*I'm afraid I haven't **still** got his address.* (= I've lost it.)

Compare also:
*Nobody **still** believes the world is flat, surely?*

2 still: adverb with comparatives   ▶ Compare **even**

Used with comparatives *still* here roughly means 'even' and has an emphasising effect:

*It would be **still** worse if you hadn't told them.*
*We are **still** further behind with the work.*
*Surely you don't need a **still** larger television screen?*
*As the summer progressed she felt happier **still**.*
*I don't want my mother to know, and **still** less my father.*

3 still: connector

- however; despite this; all the same
  *The boat takes longer. **Still**, it's cheaper than flying.* (Compare the word order with the last example in **1a**.)
  *I wish I had more money. **Still**, life has been fun this term.*

stop

1 stop: verb ▶ Compare **end; finish; start**

```
            –
stop + OBJECT
      (o) + -ing
```

a *stop* is used with and without objects:
*The rain/the noise/the clock . . . has **stopped**.*
*The train **stopped** in a tunnel.*
*Let's **stop** for lunch. Let's **stop** and have lunch.*
***Stop** that thief!*
***Stop** the world – I want to get off!*

b **stop** + *-ing* and **stop** + o + *-ing*
If we *stop doing* something we no longer do it, and if we *stop somebody doing* something we prevent them from doing it:
***Stop** talking/worrying/making that noise.*
*We tried to **stop** her (from) making a fool of herself.*

c *stop* is not followed by a *to*-INFINITIVE, except when we mean 'stop (doing something else in order) to do a different thing':
*We **stopped** (walking) to **have** lunch in a village pub.*

2 stop: noun

• place where one stops; punctuation mark
*We must get off this bus at the next **stop**.*
*Put a full-**stop** (.) or a question mark (?) or an exclamation mark (!) at the end of every sentence.*

straight

1 straight: adjective
Comparative and superlative forms are rare.

• not curved; direct
*The shortest distance between two points is a **straight** line.*
*Why do so many people with **straight** hair wish it was curly?*
*Why can't you give me a **straight** answer?* (= direct, honest, truthful)

2 straight: adverb

• directly; without delay
straight is often followed by a PREPOSITION + a NOUN of place.
*Please come **straight** to the department on the sixth floor.*
*I came in so tired that I went **straight** to bed.*
*I've just come **straight** from the office.*
*We had somehow gone **straight** past the shop without seeing it.*
*I went into the army **straight** from school.*

I can't think straight – I'm too tired.
'Can you tell me the way to the station?' 'Yes, keep straight on.
It's straight ahead.'

straightaway (or straight away): adverb

- immediately
  I'll be with you straightaway.

such: determiner and pronoun ▶ Compare so

1 such + (ADJECTIVE) + NOUN

such	a long time fun friendly people a lot (of . . .)	(that) . . .

a Exclamations

such adds emphasis to an adjective before a noun (just as *so* does to plain adjectives, etc.). It is used for exclamations and in negative imperatives. With a plain noun it is only used in this way if the noun is gradable (e.g. *fun, a lot*). *Such* is only used when a noun phrase is indefinite (NOT *such. . . your/the/that lovely time*):

> *Eileen's forgotten, because it is **such** a long time since she lived in England.*
> *We must meet again soon – it was **such** fun.*
> *They are **such** friendly people.*
> *There's **such** a lot to do.*
> *Don't be **such** a bore.*

b such . . . that . . .: Result ▶ Compare so

A *that*-CLAUSE after a clause containing *such* expresses result:

> *It is **such** a long time since she was here **that** she's forgotten.*
> *It was all **such** fun **that** I quite forgot my worries.*
> *They're **such** friendly people **that** we really enjoyed ourselves.*
> *I had **such** a lot to do (**that**) I had to work all the evening.*

c The pronoun *such* can be used in the same way as *such* + ADJECTIVE + NOUN in b. It is rather formal:

> *His behaviour was **such that** they never invited him again.* (= His behaviour was such bad behaviour that . . .)

2 such + NOUN

- of that kind

a *such* + (*a/an* +) NOUN, often without an adjective, can refer back to something mentioned earlier, and means 'of that kind':

> *They wanted to build a round house, but **such** a house* (= a round house) *is more expensive than an ordinary one.*

*They are always protesting about something. I find **such** people rather a nuisance.* (= people who are always protesting)
*They said he was a liar and a thief. **Such** remarks are unforgivable.*

b DETERMINER + **such** + NOUN

some any many all no	**such**	place(s) person/people

such can follow *some* and various other determiners, as shown. Again, it refers to somebody or something mentioned elsewhere:
*Her boyfriend is called And or Art or some **such** peculiar name.* (= a peculiar name like And or Art)
*We were looking for this restaurant Bob had told us about, but there was no sign of any **such** place.* (= no place like Bob had mentioned.)
*Of course I have never seen a unicorn. There's no **such** animal.*

3 **such** (+ ADJECTIVE)+ NOUN + **as . . .**: Comparison

It wasn't Was it	nearly	**such**	a good idea fun	**as** . . .
They aren't Are they	quite anything like		difficult questions	

such (+ ADJECTIVE) + NOUN *as* . . . can be used after negatives and in questions to make comparisons. Various words as shown can come in front of *such*, particularly in negative statements:
*Was it really **such** a good idea (**as** you thought)?*
*The party wasn't nearly **such** fun **as** we expected it would be.*
*These are not quite **such** difficult questions **as** last time.*
*The examiners should not have set anything like **such** (difficult) questions **as** they did/**as** these.*

4 **such** + NOUN (without ADJECTIVES) + **as**-CLAUSE

This pattern often suggests that the *such*-NOUN is 'not very much' or 'not very good':
*I'll give you **such** help **as** I can – but I don't know much about it.* (= not much help)
***Such** news **as** we heard was always several days old.* (=We did not hear much news.)

5 such as (sometimes **such . . . as**)

- for example
  *The bank will lend you money for large purchases, **such as** cars, or a major home improvement.*
  *This is a problem in **such** areas **as** the Sahara Desert.*

6 as such

as such refers back to something/somebody already mentioned, and means that thing/person considered simply as that thing/person:
  *Protest **as such** can achieve some things, but not everything.*
  *'The house is yours, and will remain **as such**,' her lawyer told her.* (= would remain hers)

---

suggest: verb

> OBJECT
> **suggest** + *-ing*
> *that*-CLAUSE

a If we *suggest* something, we say that somebody might like it or like to do it. *suggest* can only take one object:
  *I **suggested** a skiing holiday (to them).* (But NOT **I suggested** them a skiing holiday.)*
  *They **suggested** going to Austria.*

b *suggest* can be followed by a *that*-CLAUSE containing *should* + VERB, an ordinary tense or a subjunctive:
  *I **suggested** (that) he should take/he took/he take a skiing holiday.*

suggest does not take (OBJECT +) + *to*-INFINITIVE:
NOT **They suggested** (us) to go to Austria.*

---

suppose

1 suppose: verb (not usually in progressive)

> **suppose** + *that* + CLAUSE
> *so/not*

a • imagine; guess
  *'What do you **suppose** Clare will do now?' 'Well, she'll have to stay with her mother, won't she?' 'Yes I **suppose** so.' 'I mean, she can't leave her mother, can she?' 'No, I **suppose** not.'*

When *suppose* is used with a negative idea, we often make *suppose*, not the other verb, negative. (▶ Compare **believe**, **think**):
  *I don't **suppose** you could/I **suppose** you couldn't lend me a pound, could you?* (= a polite request)

---

b *be supposed to* has two different meanings. The first is 'said to', 'believed to':
> *I want to see 'A Room with a View'. It's* **supposed to** *be a very good film.*
> *What are you doing here? I thought you* **were supposed to** *be ill in bed.*

The second meaning is a bit like 'should' or 'be meant to'. If people are *supposed to* do something, they have a duty to do it . . . But often they do the opposite:
> *We* **were supposed to** *do homework every night (but we didn't).*
> *You're not* **supposed to** *smoke on the London underground, but some people still do.*

2 suppose, supposing: conjunctions

a *suppose* and *supposing* both roughly mean 'if' or 'what if', but *suppose* is only used at the begining of a sentence:
> *'***Suppose/Supposing** *your father finds out – what on earth will you do?' 'Well, I'll have to pay, always* **supposing** (NOT *suppose) *I have enough money.'*

b *suppose* and *supposing* are also used to introduce suggestions:
> *'I can't find my gloves, Mummy.' '***Suppose/Supposing** *you have another look.'*

---

sure, unsure; surely

1 sure, unsure: adjectives   ▶ Compare **certain**

Like *certain*, *sure* is mainly used as a predicative adjective. There is a table at *certain*.

a **sure (that) . . . unsure/not sure if/whether** (or *wh*-word) . . .
If we are *sure* something is true, we are definitely certain that it is true. Like *certain/uncertain*, *sure* and *unsure* can be followed by clauses:
> *I am* **sure** *that I locked the door.*
> *I am* **unsure**/*not* **sure** *if/whether I locked it . . .*
> *We are* **unsure**/*not* **sure** *what we ought to do now.*

b **sure/unsure of/about . . .**:
> *If you are* **unsure** *of your facts, you should ask.*
> *I'm not too* **sure about** *Tuesday, but Monday's all right.*

c **sure to . . .** (NOT *unsure to):
If something is *sure to* happen, it means you are *sure* about it:
> *Crispin is* **sure to** *do well.* (= We are sure he will do well.)

d Notice that *sure* is different from *certain*, and is not used with an introductory *It* as subject (NOT *It is **sure** *he will do well.*) We can of course have an 'empty' *it* as subject:
> *It is* **sure to** *rain if we go on a picnic.*

2 sure, surer, surest: adjectives

sure (but not usually *unsure*) has comparative and superlative forms:
> *I felt* **surer** *than I'd ever felt before that he was the right man for me.*
> *Overconfidence is the* **surest** *recipe for disaster.*

3 **sure** and **surely**: adverbs

sure is used informally, especially in American English, with the meaning of 'of course'. (*Surely* is also used in American English with the same meaning.):
>   *'You will help, won't you?' 'Sure, I will/Surely.'*

4 **surely**: sentence adverb ▶ Compare **certainly**

a *surely* expresses disbelief or disagreement and the hope that the other person will now agree with the speaker:
>   ***Surely** you remember me?* (= You must remember me. I'm surprised if you don't.)
>   *Paul's **surely** not going to buy another car?* (= I cannot believe it. Tell me he isn't.)
>   *We should not feel guilty about what our grandparents did, **surely?***

b This contrasts with *certainly* and *definitely*
>   *We **certainly** should not feel guilty.* (= though perhaps we should behave differently ourselves)
>   ***Certainly**, we should not feel guilty.* (= I agree we should not . . .)
>   *We **definitely** should not feel guilty.* (= That is obvious/clear/certain.)

---

take, took, taken: verb ▶ Compare **bring**

> **take** + (IO +) OBJECT

---

a *take* often means move something to somewhere else (where neither the speaker nor the listener is at present). In this meaning take often contrasts with *bring*:
>   *I mustn't forget to **take** my camera with me next week.*
>   *She **takes** the dog for a walk every day.*
>   *Don't worry – we'll **take** you home in the car.*
>   *Somebody's **taken** my dictionary.* (= removed it without my permission)
>   *I didn't **take** my umbrella with me yesterday, so of course it rained.*

b *take* (like *bring*, *give* etc.) can have one or two objects:
>   *Let's **take** her some flowers.*
>   *They **took** presents to/for all the children and the old people.*

c Other meanings of *take* include accepting and getting possession of:
>   *Will you **take** a cheque?*
>   *Do you **take** sugar?* (e.g. in your coffee)
>   ***Take** my hand* (= hold it). ***Take** a seat.* (= sit down)

> *He **took** another piece of cake.*
> ***Take** your medicine*
> *I'll **take** this.* (= buy it)
> ***Take** my advice/this opportunity/a chance . . .*

d *take* + time words

There are several ways of using *take* to talk about the length of time needed for some work or a journey:

> *They **took** all day to travel ten miles.*
> *Getting across the mountains **took** all day.*
> *This letter has **taken** two weeks to get here.*
> *It **took** (them) all day to travel ten miles.*
> *It always **takes** ages to get across London.*
> *It has **taken** me all the evening to do my homework.*

e *take* is also used with some nouns to describe various actions:

> ***Take** care.* (= be careful)
> *He **took** a lot of trouble with/over . . .*
> *He **took** an interest in . . .*
> *You never **take** any notice of what I say.*
> ***Take** a look at this.*
> ***Take** a holiday/a photograph/a walk . . .*

Notice also that you ***take** a driving test* or *an examination*, which you hope you will *pass* (and not *fail*).

talk

1 **talk**: verb   ► Compare **speak**

The general meaning is 'speak', and like *speak*, *talk* usually has no object.

a *talk* suggests speaking with some meaning, giving some information:

> *The baby will soon be **talking**.*
> *Many people have tried to teach animals to **talk**.*
> *We can't **talk** here – it's too public.*
> *The secret police had horrible ways of making people **talk**.*

b *talk* often suggests conversation:

> *We sat and **talked** (to each other) all the evening.*
> *Look – if you're worried, why don't we **talk** about it?*
> *I think we should **talk**.* (= discuss some problem that is worrying us.)
> *If you behave like that, people will **talk**.* (= gossip)

c **talk** + OBJECTS   ► Compare *say; tell*

A few words are used after *talk*:

> *Please try and **talk** sense.*
> *He was **talking** nonsense/rubbish.*
> *Don't **talk** shop.* (= Don't discuss your work.)

2 talk: noun (C, U)

a • an informal speech or a discussion or conversation (C)
*She gave an interesting **talk** about her early life.*
*The management are going to have more **talks** with the unions.*
*I enjoyed our **talk** yesterday.*

b As an uncountable noun, *talk* often contrasts with action:
*There was **talk** of changing the timetable, but nothing has been done.*

taste

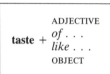

```
         ADJECTIVE
         of . . .
taste +  like . . .
         OBJECT
```

1 taste: verb   ► Compare **smell**

a We use *taste* to describe the sensation we get from food, drink, etc. In this sense *taste* is not normally used in the progressive.
Things can *taste* + ADJECTIVE, *taste of* or *like* something:
*This **tastes** delicious/good/meaty/odd/too salty/too sweet . . .*
*It **tastes** of beef/cheese/chocolate/curry/honey/lemon . . .*
*It doesn't **taste** of anything – it **tastes** like tap water.*

b A PERSONAL SUBJECT + *taste* + OBJECT describes people's sensations. In this sense *taste* is not used in the progressive. *Can/could* are often used:
*It's a beautiful pudding, but I can't actually **taste** the wine.*
*I've got a cold – I can't **taste** a thing.*

c *taste* + OBJECT can also mean 'eat':
*They hadn't tasted **meat** for a year, so the meal was a great treat.*

d If we *taste* something in order to try it, progressive tenses are possible:
*'Hi! So you're having a secret drink!' 'No, I'm just **tasting** it to see if it's OK.'*
*Why don't you **taste** it first before putting sauce all over it?*
*The room was full of people **tasting** dozens of different wines – and spitting them out.*

2 taste: noun

a *taste* as a noun can have similar meanings to the verb:
*I've no sense of **taste** with this awful cold.*
*The food has no **taste**/very little **taste**/a funny **taste** . . .*
*This is delicious – have a **taste**!*

b *taste* also means an ability to choose between good and bad art, design, etc. – or one's personal liking for such things:
*Their flat is full of horrible things – they've a lot of money, but no **taste**.*
*I admire her **taste** in clothes.*
*Unfortunately, I have expensive **tastes** as far as food and hotels are concerned.*

teach, taught, taught: verb　　　　　▶ Compare **learn**

```
              —
        (IO+) OBJECT
teach + o + that-CLAUSE
        o + wh-CLAUSE
        o + to-INFINITIVE
```

- help people to learn

a　*teach* can have two objects:
　*'What does your brother do?' 'He **teaches**.'* (= he is a teacher)
　*He **teaches** English/mathematics . . .*
　*She **teaches** the children/adults/foreigners . . .*
　*He **teaches** the children mathematics/English to foreigners.*

b　We can also *teach* people *that* . . .; *how* . . ., etc.:
　*Life **teaches** you (that) nothing is as simple as it seems.*

c　*teach* + OBJECT + *to*-INFINITIVE:

With an infinitive an object is essential:

My father is ***teaching*** *me to cook/to drive/to fly . . .*

Various passives are possible. Somebody or something can be taught:
*Latin is not **taught** in many schools now.*
*We were **taught** mathematics/that children should be polite to their parents/
(how) to swim . . .*

tell, told, told: verb　　　　　▶ Compare **say**

```
        (IO+) OBJECT
        o + that-CLAUSE
tell +  o + wh-CLAUSE
        o + about/of. . .
```

1　*tell* usually needs a personal indirect object as well as a direct object:
　*He **told** us his news/that he was getting married.*
　(NOT **He **told** his news/that he was getting married.*)

The main exceptions to this rule are some special expressions with *tell* +
OBJECT:
　*That child is eight, and she still can't **tell** the time.* (i.e., read the clock)
　*Surely you can **tell** the difference between butter and margarine?*
　People ***tell*** *jokes/various kinds of stories/lies/the truth . . .*

2 Direct and reported speech

a *tell* can be used when directly quoting statements and commands (not exclamations and not questions, which need *ask*), but usually only if *tell* comes after the quoted words:

'*I'm very tired,*' *I told them.*
'*Stop talking about it, and don't worry,*' *she told me.*
(But NOT **I told them, 'I'm very tired.'* etc.)

b With reported speech, we use *tell* + *that*-CLAUSES for statements, and *tell* + OBJECT + *to*-INFINITIVE for commands:

I told them (that) I was worried, but she told me to stop talking about it and (she told me) not to worry.

c *tell* can be followed by *wh*-CLAUSES and by *wh*-WORDS + *to*-INFINITIVE and by *about* and *of* phrases. Notice that *wh*-CLAUSES take normal subject – verb word order (not question inversion):

You have not told us where or when you are going/why you are leaving/what you want/how you found enough money . . .
I've told them how to get here, which bus to catch, where to get off . . .
Tell us about your holiday/your new job/your family . . .

tell of is more formal:
He told his audience of his experiences in the Sahara.

3 Passive

Most of the patterns in **2b** and **c** can be used in the passive with a personal subject:

They were told (that) he was worried.
I was told to stop talking and (I was told) not to worry.
We weren't told where he was going . . .
They've been told how to get here . . .
Nobody was told about the holiday . . .
They were told of the difficulties and dangers to expect.
We were told the news/the facts.

---

than: conjunction and preposition

1 Comparison

▶ Compare **as**

hotter/bigger . . . faster/sooner . . . farther/further . . . better/worse . . . fewer/less/more . . .	**than** . . .

a *than* follows comparative adjectives and adverbs, and other comparative words as shown, to join two parts of a comparison:

*It was far hotter there **than** we expected (it would be).*
*Well, it's better **than** doing nothing.*
*We walked much farther **than** we usually do/**than** usual.*
*This is a much more expensive watch **than** my last one (was).*
*More people own their own homes **than** ever before.*
*It's better to think first **than** (to) be sorry afterwards.*

b *than* clauses usually have some words missing which we 'understand'. Sometimes the *than*-CLAUSE is shortened to only one or two words. We cannot say **My sister is taller **than** I am tall.* Instead we say

*My sister is taller **than** I am.*
or ***than** I.*
or ***than** me.*

Of course we must use a subject pronoun (e.g. *I*) if we use a verb (*than I am*). But if we omit the verb we can say *than I* or *than me*. Some people think *than I* is better English, but most people today say *than me*. There can be another problem. What does the following mean?

*She loves her home more **than** her husband.*

It could mean either *She loves her home more **than** her husband loves it.* or *She loves her home more than she loves him.* It is best to make clear what we mean!

2 Preference

I would	rather	go by bus	**than**	waste money on a taxi.
We'd	sooner			go by train.
		buy apples		oranges.

would rather (and the less common *would sooner*) expresses a preference, and the *than*-phrase introduces the thing we don't want:

*I would rather go by bus **than** waste money on a taxi.* (= I would prefer to go by bus. I do not want to waste money . . .)

3 more than/less than + NUMBERS, AMOUNTS . . .

more than and *less than* are used with numbers and mean 'over' and 'under':

*I haven't had a holiday for **more than** a year.*
*You're not allowed to drive at **more than** 70 miles per hour.*
*I've got **less than** £10 to last me until Saturday.*

▶ See also *different than* at **different**; *less than* at **less**; *more than* at **more**; *other than* at **other**; *rather than* at **rather**; *sooner than* at **soon**.

thank and thanks

1 thank: verb

thank is actually a verb, even though we usually omit the subject *I* in the present tense. *Thank* needs a direct object:

> **Thank you** *so much/very much for your kind invitation/for your letter/for all your help/for asking me . . .*
> *I wrote and* **thanked** *him.*
> **Thank** *heaven it's pay day.*
> *Don't* **thank** *me,* **thank** *your mother.*

2 thanks: noun

a *thanks* is a plural noun. It cannot have an object. It is usually more informal than *Thank you*:

> **Thanks** *so much/very much/a lot/for all your help.*

But *(Very) many thanks* can be formal.

b *thanks to . . .* is used as a preposition, meaning 'because of'. It can refer to nice or nasty things:

> *We won 3-2,* **thanks to** *a brilliant goal by Edwards in the last five minutes.*
> **Thanks to** *Tom we missed the train – he had looked up the wrong timetable.*

3 *thank you* and *thanks* are often used in conversation when we accept things. If we want to refuse, we say *No thank you/No thanks*:

> *'Would you like some coffee?' 'Oh* **thank you**. *Black please.'*
> *'Sugar?' 'No* **thanks**. *I've given it up.'*

that

1 that: determiner and pronoun   ▶ See **this**

2 that: relative pronoun   ▶ Compare **what; which; who; whom; whose**

a As a relative pronoun *that* is only used in a defining relative clause. Compare:

> *I'm playing tennis tomorrow with that pretty girl* **who/that** *works in the library.*
> *I'm playing tennis tomorrow with Alison Walters,* **who** *works in the library.*

In the first sentence we need the relative clause *who/that works in the library* to identify (or 'define') which girl we are talking about. We can use *who* or *that* and we must not put a comma. This contrasts with the second sentence where *who works in the library* just gives us more information about Alison Walters. (It is a non-defining relative clause, we cannot use *that*, and we must put a comma.)

b *that* is used as a subject and an object pronoun for people and things (*who, whom, which* are possible but more formal). *That* can be left out when it is the object of a verb or preposition, but not when it is the subject of its clause, because most clauses need a subject:

> *The man* **that** *(or* **who***) came to mend the telephone said the public were always complaining.*

*The person (**that**) you need isn't here.*
*Are you the lady (**that**) I spoke to before?*
*I'm looking for a phone **that** (or **which**) works.*
*This is the third callbox (**that**) I've tried.*
*I've lost the bit of paper (**that**) I wrote the number down on.*

c *that* is preferred to *which* after indefinite pronouns like *all*, *everything* . . . and after superlatives:
*I'll do all (**that**) I can to help.* (NOT **all **which** I can . . .*)
*The worst thing **that** happened was we all got wet through.*
*I'd say that these are the best (**that**) money can buy.*

d *that* can also be used after various words of time, place and manner instead of the more formal phrases with *wh*-words:
*Is there somewhere (**that**) I could sit?* (or **where** *I could . . .*)
*The way (**that**) some children behave these days is quite awful.* (or *the way **in which** . . .*)
*The day (**that**) we left, it was snowing hard.* (or *the day **on which** . . .* or *the day **when** . . .*)

3   **that**: conjunction

that can introduce a subordinate clause giving facts, opinions, ideas and so on.
a *that* can usually be omitted when the *that*-CLAUSE follows a verb, adjective or noun as shown:
after verbs of speaking and reporting:
*He agreed/denied/said (**that**) he had always wanted a gun.*
*He told the police **that** it wasn't his.*
*I suggest (**that**) we need more gun laws.*
*They were told **that** he had no friends.*

after verbs of believing and thinking:
*He believes/He's decided/He knows **that** there is something wrong.*
*He realises/he understands (**that**) he needs to see a doctor.*
*I hope (**that**) I can help him.*
*I'd rather/sooner/I hope (**that**) you didn't tell anyone.*

after adjectives expressing emotions:
*I am afraid/sorry/sure (**that**) it is necessary.*

after nouns expressing opinions and emotions:
*There's no doubt (**that**) he is ill.*
*The idea (**that**) criminals cannot help it is popular with some people.*

b *that*-CLAUSES can also follow the verb *be*:
*The fact/truth is (**that**) this man is a danger to the public.*

c *that*-CLAUSES can also be the subject of a sentence. If they follow an introductory *it* (▶ See **it**), *that* is optional:
*It appears/seems (**that**) this man had no friends.*
*It's surprising (**that**) people aren't more worried.*
*It's a pity (**that**) this had to happen.*

But if a *that*-CLAUSE is the subject and begins the sentence we cannot omit *that* because the sentence would be too difficult to understand without:

That some people were content to go from Venice to Izmir and back without even leaving the ship is unbelievable – but true.

▶ See also *now (that)* at **now**; *in order that* at **order**; *provided/providing that* at **provided**; *seeing that* at **see**; *so that* at **so**; *such that* at **such**; *suppose/supposing that* at **suppose**.

4 that: adverb

Informally *that* can be used as an emphatic adverb:
'Did you have to wait long?' 'Well, not that long.' (= not very long)

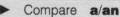

the: definite article　　　　　　　　　　　▶ Compare **a/an**

We can use *the* with all ordinary nouns – singular, plural and uncountable. It goes before adjectives, but follows *all*, *both*, and *half*. *The* has two main meanings – specific and general.

1 Definite specific reference

We use *the* when we are talking about actual, particular 'specific' things or people, which we think the listener (or reader) can definitely identify. This may be for different reasons.

a　the person/thing is unique – 'the only one', or at least we think of them as the only one – either in the world or in our situation:
the sun, the moon, the equator . . .
That's the telephone ringing, and there's someone at the front door.
Has the post come?
Shall we watch the news? (on TV)
You'd better tell the police.

NOTE: We talk about listening to *the radio*, but we can say *television* or *the television* when we are talking about broadcasting: *What's on the radio? There's nothing on (the) television.*

b　the thing/person has already been identified:
A train has arrived at platform 5. The train is crowded.

c　Sometimes even if the actual thing has not been mentioned before, we still clearly understand it from the general context:
We went on a camping holiday. The tents . . .

d　Sometimes there are other words in the noun phrase that identify the noun and make it definite:
The wildlife of East Africa is fascinating. (NOT wildlife in general)
The lions we saw in Kenya were huge.
The people in this photograph were Australians.

e　Sometimes there are other words (superlatives, or *only*, *same*, *first*, *last*) that mean there can only be one person or thing referred to:
For photographing animals the fastest film is the best.
It's the only film to use.
You don't get the same results with slower film.

2 Definite general reference

a We can also use *the* + SINGULAR COUNT NOUN to mean a whole class of things or people or that type of thing:

The elephant picks up food with its trunk.
Yehudi Menuhin plays the violin superbly.
The computer is changing our lives.
I love the cinema/the theatre. (= that type of entertainment)

the + PLURAL COUNT NOUNS (*the elephants, the violins*) and *the* + UNCOUNTABLE NOUNS (*the wildlife*) are not used in this way. They do not refer to a whole class, but are always specific and definite. See paragraph 1.

For plural nouns and uncountable nouns in a general sense, do not use articles:

Elephants are marvellous animals.
I play tennis.
I enjoy listening to music.
Life is hard!

b *the* + ADJECTIVE or *the* + PAST PARTICIPLE can sometimes mean a whole class of people or things:

The blind/The deaf/The poor . . . need our help.
The good ended happily, and the bad unhappily. That is what fiction means.
(= The good people were happy at the end of the book, but nasty things happened to the bad people.)
Sales rush for the unwanted and unneeded. (= newspaper headline about people buying things in sales)

But notice, we cannot make these phrases possessive – so NOT **the poor's problems*.

the + nationality adjectives (words with no plural form) can also be used like this:

The Welsh are great singers.
The Japanese are hard workers.

Nationality nouns (with plural forms) can be used with and without *the*:

(The) Brazilians enjoy Carnival in Rio.

3 Proper names

the is not usually used with proper names, but we use it with names of rivers, seas and oceans:

the Thames, the Black Sea, the Pacific Ocean

a few names of countries, and with plural islands and mountains:

The United States, the Soviet Union, the Netherlands, the Philippines, the Alps, the West Indies

b We can also sometimes use *the* with names of people:

the Browns (= Mr and Mrs Brown, or the Brown family)
a girl I know called Elizabeth Taylor, but not the Elizabeth Taylor (= not the famous one)

4 the . . . the . . .

There is a rather unusual kind of sentence where we use *the . . . the* plus two comparative words to talk about two parallel or related things:

The sooner we get this finished, the better. (= I'll be pleased.)
The more he drank, the less he moved.

▶ See also **less**; **more**

---

their: possessive determiner
▶ See **theirs**; **them**; **themselves**; **they**

Third person plural
For meaning ▶ See **they**

a   *Where are all the teachers? **Their** students are waiting.*
*The crowd were all waving **their** arms and shouting.* (Notice the collective subject.)
*Nobody had done **their** homework.* (Notice the singular subject.)

b   *their* is formally and correctly used rather than *them* before some *-ing* patterns:
*I don't like **their/them** borrowing things without asking.*

---

theirs: pronoun   ▶ See **their**; **them**; **themselves**; **they**

Third person plural possessive pronoun.
*The boys said our car was still there, but **theirs** had disappeared.*
*Paul's a friend of **theirs**, isn't he?*

---

them: pronoun   ▶ See **their**; **theirs**; **themselves**; **they**

Third person plural object pronoun
For meaning ▶ See **they**

a   *them* is used as the object of a verb or preposition and in other positions where it is not the subject, including short remarks without verbs.
Them can be followed by *all* and *both*:
*My parents don't want me to tell **them** everything.*
*How sensible of **them**!*
*I have better health than **them**.*
*I'll never be as clever as **them**.*
*We wanted **them all** to come with us.*
*We wanted **them both** to enjoy themselves.*

b   *them* is often used before *-ing* in structures where *their* is formally correct:
*I object to **them** arriving late for every meeting.*

But only *them* (NOT *their*) is correct after verbs of the senses and after *find* and *keep*:
*We could see **them** waving.*
*She found **them** sitting in the garden.*

c *them* is usual after *be:*
>*Here are some pictures of Liz and Jeff – that's **them** on holiday in Greece.*
>(NOT **that's they*)

d *them* is often used as a singular pronoun, especially after an indefinite pronoun like *someone/anyone:*
>*If you marry someone, you marry **them** them for better or worse.*

---

themselves: pronoun ▶ See **their; theirs; them; they**

Third person plural reflexive pronoun
For meaning ▶ See **they**

---

1 themselves: reflexive
>*People should help **themselves** – and not expect the State to do everything for them.*
>*I'm sorry for anyone who finds **themselves** in this position.*

2 themselves: emphatic
>*The animals **themselves** seem content, but then they were born in the zoo and know no other life.*

▶ *See also each other* at **other**

---

then

1 then: adverb ▶ Compare **now**

a ● at that time (either in the future or the past)
>*Before dinner Harriet said she could not be certain I had told her everything. I very nearly did **then**.*
>*Only a fortnight more and **then**, darling, we'll be together again.*

b We can use *then* like a noun and put prepositions in front of it:
>*I waited an hour and by **then** I was getting very annoyed.*
>*Until/Up till **then** I thought he was a nice person.*
>*We saw them in January, but we've heard nothing since **then**.*

c ● next; after that
>*Drive as far as the roundabout and **then** turn left.*
>*First I want to pass the exam, and **then** I shall think again about my future.*

2 then: connector

a *then* can mean 'in that case' and sometimes follows an *if*-CLAUSE or a *when*-CLAUSE:
>*'I left my bag here.' '**Then**, it must still be here.'*
>*If you didn't like it, **then** you should have said so.*
>***When** a cowboy has to sell his saddle, **then** you know times are hard.*
>*'I was going·to be a doctor, but I've changed my mind.' 'So what are you doing now **then**?'*
>*'Somebody told me the film isn't much good.' 'Oh, well, don't let's go, **then**.'*

---

b *but then* or *then again* adds another reason or more information to something that has been said:

> *I think she's beautiful – **but then** she's my sister.* (= so of course I do)
> *Well, it was a very expensive place, **but then** again they have to make money somehow.*
> *It was not a pleasant experience – **but then** life is never dull.*

c In conversation *then* can be used to get people to listen:

> *Now **then**, what are you children doing?*
> *Right **then**, are we ready? Let's go.*

then can also be used at the end of a conversation:

> *Goodbye, **then**.*

there

1 there is/there are . . .

a *there is* (often shortened to *there's*) and *there are* are used when we want to talk about something or somebody existing or not existing.
There is/there are is a kind of introductory subject that allows us to emphasise the thing or person we are talking about by putting it after the verb:

> ***There is** a man outside digging a hole in the road.*
> ***There's** nothing you can do about it, so **there's** no point in worrying.*
> *I think **there is** somebody at the door, but **there's** something wrong with the bell.*
> ***There are** several problems I want to discuss with you.*
> ***There are** some new people next door.*
> ***There is** hope for this mad world.*

b *there* and *be* change places for questions and *there* is used in question tags – just like ordinary subjects:

> ***Is there** life after death?*
> *Well, **there are** many religions that say so, **aren't there?***

c Any tense of *be* can be used. Modal verbs and *appears/seems* are also possible. A few other verbs (meaning 'being' and 'arriving') are also used:

> ***There have been** a lot of changes in my lifetime.*
> ***There were** over a hundred people at the meeting.*
> *I don't think **there can be** any other explanation.*
> *Once upon a time **there was** a beautiful princess . . .*
> *We are not expecting **there to be** many complaints.*
> ***There being** no more customers, we shut the shop.*
> ***There appears** to be some mistake, **doesn't there?***
> ***There came** a moment when he couldn't refuse any longer.*

d Because *there is/there are* tell us that somebody or something exists, they usually introduce a new and indefinite subject (*a man, several problems, some mistake* . . .) and not a known definite subject. But *there is/there are* can be followed by definite people or things if we want to remind ourselves that they exist:

> *'What else ought I to see in London?' 'Well, **there's** Buckingham Palace and the Houses of Parliament and the Tower . . .* (Notice here *there is . . .* followed by a list)

*'I don't care. I'm going to please myself.' 'Oh, but **there are** your mother and father to consider, you know.'*

e there's + PLURAL
there's can informally be followed by a plural subject in the kind of sentence shown in **a** above:
There's *two men at the door asking for you.*

2 there: adverb   ▶ Compare **here**

a *there* is the opposite of *here* and means 'at some place away from the speaker.'
With this meaning *there* can follow some prepositions of place:
*Hello. Is anybody **there**?* (perhaps said on the other side of a door)
*'Is Alison **there**?' 'No, I don't think she's here.'* (telephone conversation)
*I went to call on Mary, but she wasn't **there**.*
*She looked up and saw Bob standing **there**.*
*It's a wonderful place for a holiday, but I'm not sure I'd want to live **there**.*
*Your books are over **there** by the window.*

b *there* can come at the beginning of a sentence. Notice the word order:
*Look. **There**'s your father.* (*there* + *be* + NOUN)
*Look, **there** they are.* (*there* + PRONOUN + *be*)

Compare   *here*, and notice also the difference between this *there*, which is pronounced with some stress and means 'across there', 'in that place', and introductory *there* (as in **1** above) which is usually unstressed:
There's *your father to consider, you know.*

c Various other uses
*I would agree with you **there**.* (= on that point you are making)
There *you are, you see. Everything's all right.*
*Hello **there**!* (a casual greeting)
*Well, I'm sorry for her. But **there again**, it is partly her fault.* (*there again* introducing a reason or explanation. Compare   *then again*.)
*'Where did you go?' Oh **here and there**.'* (= different places, nowhere special)
*I'd like to go to Paris. Is it possible to go **there and back** in a day?*
*I got so fed up with the job that I just decided to leave **there and then**.* (= immediately)

therefore: connector

● so; for that reason
*The farmers were generally unable to find the necessary money and they were **therefore** obliged to continue with their traditional methods.*
*There is no reason for him to continue with these medicines. I have told him **therefore** to stop taking them.*

these and **those**: determiners and pronouns

1 *these* and *those* are the plural of *this* and *that*

a *these* and *those* refer to plural things and people, and contrast in meaning like *this* and *that*. *These* refers to things and people near the speaker, here and now; *those* refers to things and people farther away in space or time:

> *These pens are much better than **those** – they last longer.*
> *What do **those** people want? Why are they waving at us?*
> *I'm very busy **these** days.* (= now)
> *He was brought up in the thirties. In **those** days things were very different.* (= then)

b In informal English, people sometimes use *these* + NOUN when telling a story to make the listeners feel it is happening here and now (► Compare **this**):

> *We were just sitting there quietly and suddenly **these** young boys started a fight.*

c *these* and *those* are sometimes used to refer back to things or people or ideas already mentioned. *These* also points forwards:

> *The early years of the century were peaceful. **Those** were the days.* (= a good time to live)
> *Who's going to pay for it all? Where's the money going to come from? Will people be willing to pay more taxes? **These/those** are the questions we need to ask.*

2 **those**: people

The pronouns *these* and *those* usually mean things. But *those* can mean people if we add some identifying words:

> ***Those** who can, do. **Those** who cannot, teach.*
> ***Those** of you who are going on the coach tomorrow should meet in the hotel entrance at 8 a.m.*
> ***Those** familiar with the National Health Service know what to expect.*

---

they: pronoun ► See **their; theirs; them; themselves**

Third person plural subject pronoun

1 **they**: usage

a *they* is used as the subject of a finite verb. It can be followed by *all* and *both*:

> *It's a story about a lot of old friends pretending **they** don't know each other.*
> *We're richer than **they** are, but are we as happy as **they** are?*
> ***They all** arrived on time.*
> ***They both** enjoyed themselves.*

b If no verb follows *as* or *than* in comparisons, *they* is possible, but very formal. *Them* is more usual:

> *I've been waiting as long as **them**/(they).*
> *We work harder than **them**/(they).*

c *they* is used after *be* when a subject relative pronoun follows (although informally *them* is possible):

> *It **was they** who wanted it, not us.*

2 they: meaning

they, their, theirs, them, themselves can have several meanings.

a *they, etc.* can refer to people and animals (male and female) – so it is plural for *he* and *she*:

*I asked my parents, but **they** wouldn't tell me.*
*The lions were marvellous, weren't **they**?*

b *they* can also refer to things – so it is the plural of *it:*

*The cases were very cheap, because **they** were made of plastic.*

c As well as referring to people already mentioned, *they* can refer to some indefinite people. However, *they* is 3rd person, so usually excludes the speaker and listener (or writer and reader) and means other people – often people who have some control over our lives:

***They** say the world climate is changing.*
***They**'ve found that missing child.*
*When you're dead **they** can't tax you. So **they** tax your children instead!*

d *they* is often used as a singular pronoun, particularly after an indefinite pronoun like *anybody* or *everyone*. This avoids the problem of having to choose *he* or *she*, and is commonly found in both spoken and written English. Unfortunately some people still think this is ungrammatical:

*I don't know **any writer** who says **they** like it.*
***Everybody** wants to be loved, don't **they**?*
***Nobody** will read it, and **they** wouldn't understand it if **they** did.*

---

thing: noun

1

a *thing* is a very general word, and can refer to actual 'concrete' objects that we can see and touch, to ideas and events and even informally to people:

*What's that **thing** you're holding?*
*The **thing** I like about Maria is she's always willing to help.*
*There's just one **thing** I want to say.*
*A funny **thing** happened to me on my way to the station.*
*What's the best **thing** to do now, do you think?*
*Oh, you poor **thing**.*

b *things* can mean personal belongings:

*Please don't leave your **things** all over the floor.*

and also the general situation:

*How are **things** (with you)?*
***Things** were looking pretty bad until I suddenly got this job.*

2 The thing is . . .   ▶ Compare   **The fact is . . .**

We sometimes use *The thing is . . .* to introduce a reason or excuse:

*We meant to go, but **the thing was** we couldn't afford to.*
*I'm sorry to bother you, but **the thing is** I need your help.*

---

think, thought, thought: verb ▶ Compare **believe**

```
            —
         that-CLAUSE
         wh-CLAUSE
think + o + COMPLEMENT
         so/not
         of . . .
         about . . .
```

---

1 Without an object or a following clause, *think* means use one's reason/one's mind. With this meaning *think* can be used in progressive tenses:
> *I'm too tired to* **think**. *I just can't* **think** *straight.* (= think clearly)
> *'Well – yes or no?' 'Just a moment. I'm thinking.'*

2 *think* with meanings like 'believe', 'expect', 'have an opinion', can be followed by several patterns. With this meaning progressive tenses are not usual.

a **that**-CLAUSES
> *We all* **think** *(that) there will be an announcement soon.*
> *Everybody* **thinks** *(that) Tom told them.*
> *Experts* **think** *(that) the world's climate is changing.*
> *Do you* **think** *(that) you could telephone my mother for me?* (=a request)
> *It's going to rain, I* **think**.

When *think* introduces a negative idea, we usually make *think* negative:
> *I don't* **think** *it will rain.*

Although *think not* is possible, the more usual negative is *(I) don't think so*:
> *'Is that cinema open on Sundays?' 'I* **think** *so.' 'No, I* **don't think so**.'*

b **think** + OBJECT + COMPLEMENT
The complement can be either an ADJECTIVE or a NOUN:
> *We* **thought** *the hotel rather noisy.*
> *Everybody* **thought** *the Palace an expensive hotel.*
> *They'll* **think** *it rude if you don't reply.*
> *The Palace was* **thought** *(to be) too noisy.*

c In the passive there are two ways of reporting opinions:
> *It is/was . . .* **thought** *that . . .*
> *It is* **thought** *(that) there will be an announcement soon.*

and SUBJECT + *is/was thought* + *to*-INFINITIVE (usually *to be* or *to have*). (Notice that there is no active equivalent to this. NOT *They* **think** *him to have told them*):
> *Tom is* **thought** *to be in New York.*
> *Tom is* **thought** *to have told them.*
> *The world climate is* **thought** *to be changing.*

---

3 think + *wh*-WORDS

think is also followed by *wh*-CLAUSES and *wh*-WORDS + *to*-INFINITIVE:
*I can't **think** how I lost my bag.* (= imagine)
*Try to **think** where you last had it.* (= remember)
*We've got to **think** what to do now.* (= decide)
*I can't **think** how to get there.*

4 If we *do not think to do* something, we are not thoughtful or sensible enough to do it:
*I'm so sorry – I just **didn't think to** tell you.*

5 *think* is also followed by various prepositions

a If you *think of* something, you remember it or imagine it:
*I'm trying to **think of** their address.*
*Do you really want to climb Everest? Just **think of** the danger!*
*And **think of** the expense!*
*I couldn't **think of** anything to say.*

If you *think highly/nothing . . . of* something/somebody, that is your opinion of them:
*We all **think highly of** Miss Arrowsmith.*
*I didn't **think much of** that film – it was boring.*

If you *think of doing* something you definitely consider doing it. You may do it:
*I am **thinking of** changing my job.* (= I may change it.)

b If you *think about* something/somebody, you have that thing or person in your mind and keep your thought on them. (*think of* is sometimes also possible here):
*I keep **thinking about/of** my mother.*

If you *think about* doing something you may do it, but it is sometimes less certain than *think of*:
*Have you ever **thought about/of** changing your job? No? Well you ought to **think about** it.*

this and **that**: determiners and pronouns

this and *that* are the singular of *these* and *those*

1 *this* and *that* are determiners and pronouns used for and about singular count nouns and uncountable nouns. *This* refers to something or somebody near the speaker, here and now; *that* is used for things farther away in space or time, (there and then):
***This** tastes odd – I prefer **that** cheese we had the other day.*
*Don't take **that** orange – it doesn't look nice. Have **this** one.*
***This** is the BBC World Service. Here is the news.*

*Who's **that** man over there? What's he doing with **that** rabbit?*
*What happened to **that** girl you met on holiday?*
***This** is for you.* (e.g., a present, a gift)
*Come **this** way please.*
*I'm busy all **this** week, but could we meet **this** Sunday?* (= the Sunday after today.)
*She's the best Prime Minister **this** country has had since Churchill.*

2 In informal English people sometimes use *this* + NOUN when telling a story, to make the listener feel it is happening here and now:

*We were just standing there having a drink, and **this** chap comes in and . . .*

3 The pronouns *this* and *that* can be used to refer generally to events and situations:

*'What was **that**?'* (= that noise) *'Oh, just a door banging, I think.'*
*Goodness. What's going on here? What is all **this**?* (= all this muddle, or this party, that I can see)
*What's all **this** I hear about you getting engaged?* (= these stories)
*It's awful having to queue for tickets like **this**.* (= like we are doing now)

4 *this* and *that* are used to refer back to statements, opinions and ideas, and *this* is also used to refer forward, to introduce new information:

*'I told him I never wanted to see him again.' '**That** was foolish of you.'*
*I forgot to set my alarm clock and overslept. **That's** why I was so late.*
*'Any government must spend money on defence.' '**That's** true.'*
*'I'll pick you up at seven then.' 'Oh, **that's** very kind.'*
*Some cars go rusty rather quickly, and **this/that** is something we need to think about.*
*Listen to **this**. It says here butter isn't bad for you after all.*

5 this and **that**: people

Pronouns *this* and *that* can only refer to people when we introduce people or say who they are:

*Adam, **this** is my mother and father.* (NOTE *this* + PLURAL)
*Donald, **this** is Adam.*
*'Who's **that** over there?' 'Oh, isn't **that** Bob Geldof?'*

On the telephone, or if someone knocks on your door, you can say:

*Who's **that**? Is **that** John?*
***This** is James (here).*

But we cannot when we are referring to people, say **Look at **that** over there* or **Come and talk to **this***. We would have to say, for example:

*Look at **that** man/girl/child over there.*
*Come and talk to **this** lady/this friend of mine.*

those ▶ See **these**

though

1 though: conjunction ▶ Compare **although**

a • although; despite the fact that
though usually begins a complete clause, but it can also begin a clause where the verb is understood. For special emphasis we can use *even though* (▶ See **even**):
> **Though** *my mother lives quite near us, the children never go to see her.*
> *The children never go to see my mother,* **though** *she lives quite near us.*
> **Though** *quite fair, the exam was difficult.* (= **Though** *it was . . .*)
> *The exam was difficult,* **though** *quite fair.*

b Sometimes for a special effect a *though*-CLAUSE can have an unusual word order. (*although* is not used like this):
> *Incredible* **though** *this may seem, she has never been abroad.* (= **Although/** **Though** *this may seem incredible, . . .*)
> *Much* **though** *I like her, I do find her rather tiring.* (= **Although/Though** *I like her very much, . . .*)

▶ See *as though* at **as**

2 though: connector

• however; all the same
Only *though* (never *although*) is used in this second way as a connector. It is an informal usage, and *though* usually comes at the end or the middle of a clause. It adds something a bit surprising to what was said earlier:
> *I'm going to be busy for a bit. Perhaps we could meet soon,* **though**.
> *It's been a heavenly day. There's still a cold wind,* **though**.
> *'I should be delighted,' he said. 'I doubt if Robin will care for the idea much,* **though**.'
> *This kind of entertainment seemed,* **though**, *to be dying out.*

thousand ▶ See **hundred**

through

1 through: preposition ▶ Compare **across**

a Place
• in one side or end of something and out at the other
> *William came* **through** *the door/walked* **through** *the woods/climbed* **through** *a gap in the hedge.*
> *We* **drove** *through the city/the tunnel/France.*
> *Water was coming* **through** *the ceiling.*
> *I hope it doesn't take long getting* **through** *Customs.*

b Time
• from beginning to end
With this meaning we sometimes also say *all through* or *right through*.
> *She slept* **through** (or **right through**) *the thunderstorm.*
> *Halfway* **through** *dinner, Tom just stood up and left the room.*

*Douglas worked **(all) through** the night.* (or *throughout*)
*It was like that **all through** the 1970's.* (or *throughout*)

In American English we say:
*We'll be there Monday **through** Friday.*
In British English this would be *from Monday to Friday.*

c • because of
   *It was **through** him that I got the job.*
   *She had a terrible life **through** no fault of her own.*

d Various other uses
   *Did you get **through** your exam?* (= pass)
   *I'll never get **through** all my work.* (= finish)
   *I've looked **through** this catalogue, but there's nothing in it I want.*

2 through: adverb
   *The Orient Express train doesn't go **through** to Istanbul now – it only goes from Paris or somewhere to Venice.*
   *They won't let you **through** without your passport.*
   *Read the exam paper right **through** before you start answering any questions.*
   *'How was the exam?' 'I got **through**, thank goodness.'* (= I passed)
   *All the telephone lines were busy and I couldn't get **through**.*
   *I was wet **through**.* (= very wet)
   *My girlfriend's just told me we are **through**.* (= our relationship has finished)

throughout

1 throughout: preposition

a Place
   • in every part of
   *The new books are to be used **throughout** the school.*
   *We want peace and security **throughout** the world.*

b Time
   • during every part of; all through
   *He worked **throughout** the night.*
   *We had perfect weather **throughout** the holiday.*
   *My mother used to make enough jam to last us **throughout** the year.*

2 throughout: adverb

   • in every part of a place
   *We're having the house repainted **throughout**.*

thus: connector

   • therefore; as a result; hence; in this way
   Thus is a rather formal word:
   *I have made a special study of 16th century poetry and would **thus** feel able to lecture on this period.*

*Attempts have been made to control the flood water and **thus** to control the rivers more.*
*The harvest in 1955–56 was around 24 million tons, but by 1963 it was only 10.6, **thus** showing that state planning was most inefficient.*
*Column 2 shows the figures for the winter months. **Thus** comparisons are possible between summer and winter energy needs.*

till   ▶ See **until**

time: noun (C, U)

1 ● the measured length between moments in past, present or future (mainly uncountable):

a   *Time passes slowly when you're in hospital.*
*Learning English takes **time**.*
*I haven't much/a lot/any **time** for reading.*
*I simply haven't got (the) **time**.*
*He spends all his spare **time**/his free **time** watching TV.*

b   **all/half/most/some of . . . the time; the whole time**
We can use various quantity words with *time*:
*We had a disappointing holiday. It rained **all/half/most of . . . the time**.*
*And Tom complained **the whole time**.*

c   **in . . . time**
in . . . time and *in time* have several meanings:
*Donald is due to retire **in two years' time**/**in a few months' time**. (i.e., from now)*
*You'll forget about it **in time**. (= as time passes)*
*We arrived only (just) **in time** to catch our train. (= just early enough)*

d   **some time/a . . . time** (but never plural)   ▶ Compare **sometime**
● an amount of time
*This all happened **some time/a long time**/only **a short time** ago.*
*His leg is going to take **a time/some time** to heal.*
*We waited for quite **a time**, but there was no sign of him.*

2 ● hour, moment, occasion, period (mainly countable)

a   shown by the clock
*'What's the **time**, please? Have you the **time** (on you)?' 'It's half-past seven.'*
*You're a big boy now. You must learn to tell the **time**.*
*Can you tell me the **times** of trains to Oxford on weekdays, please?*

b   when something happens
*We both arrived at the same **time**.*
*By the **time** I got his message, he had already left.*
*This **time** last year I was in Cairo.*
*Now is the **time** to plant bulbs for the spring.*
*Every **time** (that) I try to telephone, the number is engaged.*

*How many **times** have I got to tell you to shut the door? Please remember next
time.*
*Did you have a good **time** at the party?*
*I didn't realise at the **time**, but he was in fact dying.*
*I do wonder at **times** (= sometimes) what I'm doing here.*
*This of course was in the **time** of Napoleon.*
*He was looking much better (the) last **time** I saw him.*
*(The) next **time** you come, could you remember my library book.*

c **It's (about) time** (uncountable)
It is time can be followed by *for* + NOUN, by a *to*-INFINITIVE or by a 'past' tense
with hypothetical meaning. (▶ Compare **wish**):
    ***It's time** for bed, children!*
    ***It's time** (for us) to go, I'm afraid.*
    ***It's time** we left. **It's time** we weren't here!*

It's about time often means that we are annoyed that something has not
already been done:
    ***It's about time** you could read a map.*

d **on time** (uncountable)
    ● not late
    *I hope the train will be **on time**.*

e **at a time/at one time**
at a time is used when counting:
    *Don't all answer at once – one **at a time** please.*
    *He ran up the steps two **at a time**.*

at one time means once, (in the past):
    ***At one time** all London taxis were black, but now you sometimes see other
    colours.*

f **. . . times**
times is used to say how much more, bigger, more expensive, etc. something
is:
    *I paid £80 for this coat, which is about ten **times** what I paid when I first
    bought my own clothes.*
    *Fives **times** four is twenty. (5 × 4 = 20)*

to

1 to: preposition

The general meaning is movement or direction towards, or actually reaching,
a 'goal' or destination.

a **Place**
sometimes the opposite of *from*:
    *We're going **to** London.*
    *Is this the way **to** the station?*
    *I'd rather sit with my back **to** the engine. (= in a train)*
    *He pointed **to** the door, but said nothing.*
    *We were wondering if you could come **to** dinner on the 17th?*
    *I've just received an invitation **to** a wedding.*

*The sea is **to** the north.* (= north of here)
*People go **to** bed/church/prison/school.*
*I've read the book from beginning **to** end.*

When we are talking about meeting or visiting people we can say:
*We're going **to** James and Barbara's.* (= to their home)
*We went **to** my mother* (or *my mother's*) *for Christmas.*
*You should go **to** your boss and explain.*
*Come **to** me if you have any problems.* (or *come **and** see me*)

But if we are thinking of movement in a very physical way we usually give more details and do not use plain *to*:
*I opened the door and went **across/over to** my mother, who was sitting by the window.*
*I saw my boss at the station, so I went **up to** him and explained.*

b   Time
*It's ten **to** six.* (= 5.50)
*The library's open from 9 a.m. **to** 8 p.m. Monday to Friday.*
*Only another 50 shopping days **to** Christmas!* (or *until*)
*The meeting's been put off **to** next month.* (or *until*)

c   Indirect object
We use *to* with people or things that receive something or are affected by an action. This includes the indirect object with verbs that have two objects if we put this object second:
*Remember to send a birthday card **to** your mother.* (or *Remember to send your mother a birthday card.*)
*Jane threw her coat **to** David, but he missed.* (▶ Compare   *at*.)
*Please explain the problem **to** me.*
*They're putting up a monument **to** the Royal Air Force.*
*I must write a letter **to** my aunt.*

to is used in a similar way after adjectives and nouns:
*Be kind **to** old people.* (= Show kindness to . . .)
*Don't be cruel **to** animals.* (cruelty to . . .)
*This sounds silly **to** me.*
*It doesn't make sense **to** me.*
*The storm caused a lot of damage **to** the crops.*

d • touching; joined; connected with
*The cloth is stuck **to** the table.*
*She's assistant **to** the chairman.*
*He's known **to** the police.*
*A very odd family lives next door **to** us.*
*Years ago she got engaged **to**/was engaged **to** a Norwegian, but now she's married **to** a Pole.* (But note – *she married a Pole.*)
*Where's the key **to** this cupboard?*
*There must be an answer/a solution **to** this problem.*
*Who does this umbrella belong **to**? It's similar **to** mine.*

▶ See also   *close to* at **close**; *next to* at **next**

e *to* can be followed by a noun to show a state that somebody or something reaches:
*She sang the baby **to** sleep.* (= She sang to the baby until it was asleep.)
*The policeman was kicked **to** death.*

To my amazement/surprise/relief they called out my name.
This is not to my liking. (= I don't like it.)
It would be to your advantage to reply.
Her rapid rise to fame/power has annoyed some people.

f We also use *to* in various expressions with numbers:
How many dollars are there to the pound?
Count from 1 to 20.
Add 9 to 107. (and you get 116)
This car only does 20 miles to the gallon.
I suppose he's 50 to 60. (= between 50 and 60 years old)

g Some verbs, because of their meaning, are usually followed by the preposition *to*. (*This belongs to me*). When this preposition *to* is itself followed by a verb, this verb must be in the *-ing* form. (▶ Contrast *to* + INFINITIVE below):
We look forward to seeing you.
They objected to (my) smoking.

2 to + INFINITIVE

a The word *to* is often used to mark a verb form as an infinitive. The simple *to*-INFINITIVE consists of *to* plus the base form of the verb (*to be*, *to do*, *to have*, *to want*). If we add *not*, this comes in front:
Promise not to tell anyone.
I pretended not to mind, but actually I was very upset.

Progressive, perfect and passives infinitives are also possible:
PROGRESSIVE: *We don't expect to be still living here in the year 2000.*
PERFECT: *You must be pleased to have sold your car.* (= pleased that you sold/have sold it.)
I hope to have finished this job by Thursday.
I'm sorry not to have telephoned.
PERFECT PROGRESSIVE: *He seems to have been waiting for somebody.*
PASSIVE: *Everybody wants to be loved.*
That door ought to be locked.

More complicated passives are also possible:
He appears to have been helped by a former policeman.

b VERBS + *to*-INFINITIVE
When verbs are followed by a simple *to*-INFINITIVE the action of the infinitive is usually later in time. This is true of those semi-modals that are always followed by a *to*-INFINITIVE:
We had to wait until the following day.
He is to start his new job next Monday.
She was later to become a world-famous singer.
You ought to listen.

Many verbs of agreeing and wanting also use a *to*-INFINITIVE with a future meaning:
They agreed to help.
Let's invite the Burnetts to come with us.
I hope to go to New York next year. (Contrast *I enjoy going to New York – I've been several times.*)

Newspaper headlines use *to*-INFINITIVES when reporting future plans:
*Prince **to** Visit Australia*

Sometimes instead of repeating a verb clause we just use *to*:
*'Are you going to New York next year,' 'Well, I'd like **to**.'*
*'Have you invited the Burnetts **to** go with you?'. 'No, we tried **to**, but we didn't get an answer.'*

c *to*-INFINITIVE CLAUSES as ADVERB CLAUSES
to-INFINITIVE clauses have various meanings but again many of them refer to the future:
PURPOSE:
*Tear here **to** open.*
*Please open that carefully so as not **to** spoil the stamps.*
RESULT:
*You'll live **to** regret this.*
*My grandmother lived **to** be a hundred.*
CONSEQUENCE:
*The police rushed to the building (only) **to** discover the criminals had fled.*
CONDITION:
***To** see him, you'd never think he was seventy.* (= If you saw him, . . .)
COMMENT:
***To** tell you the truth, I don't really like her.*
*I didn't think the play was much good, **to** be honest.*

d *to*-INFINITIVE CLAUSES used instead of NOUNS
to-INFINITIVE clauses can be used, rather like nouns, as subjects of sentences, after the verb *be* and so on:
***To** win the competition had always been his great ambition.*
***To** have thrown that opportunity away is an appalling achievement.*
*It isn't fair of people **to** change their minds like that.*
*For him **to** just take the money was very wrong.*
*The plan was **to** drive all through the night.*

wh-WORD + *to*-INFINITIVES are used in the same way:
*How **to** start is a problem.*
*We don't know what **to** do, where **to** go, who **to** ask, which **to** choose, or whether **to** do anything at all!*

e NOUNS + *to*-INFINITIVE
to-INFINITIVE after nouns are rather like relative clauses. They tell us more about the noun. Often they describe a purpose:
*a book **to** read . . . a house **to** let . . . something **to** open this parcel with . . .*
*What's the best way **to** do this?*

Sometimes, when there is an ADJECTIVE + NOUN + *to*-INFINITIVE, the *to*-INFINITIVE really belongs to the adjective:

*The first person **to** speak is a fool!* (= the first person who speaks . . .)
*This isn't an easy question **to** answer.* (= It isn't easy to answer this question.)

f ADJECTIVES + *to*-INFINITIVE
A lot of adjectives can be followed by *to*-INFINITIVES and there are various meanings:

*He is certain/likely/unlikely . . . **to** come.* (= It is certain, etc. that he will come. Note the future meaning.)
*They are bound/sure **to** forget.*
*I was afraid/keen/ready/determined **to** accept the job.* (Note the future meaning with all these.)
*The puzzle was easy/difficult/impossible **to** do.* (Compare *It was easy . . . to do the puzzle.*)

Sometimes the *to*-INFINITIVE is more like an *if-* or a *wh*-CLAUSE:
*We would be glad/happy/delighted . . . **to** see you.* (= if we saw you.)
*We were glad/happy/delighted . . . **to** see you.* (= when we saw you.)
*I was/would be pleased/sorry **to** hear that.*
*You were clever/kind/rude/sensible/silly (not) **to** tell them.*
*It would be clever of you (not) **to** tell them.*
Note the meaning of purpose also in the patterns *too/enough . . . to*-INFINITIVE:
*It is too cold **to** sit in the garden.*
*It is not warm enough **to** sit outside.*

▶   See also   *for . . . to*-INFINITIVE

3   **to**: adverb

This is a rare usage of this word:
*He pushed the door **to** (= shut), but he didn't shut it properly.*

---

today and **tonight**   ▶ Compare   **yesterday**; **tomorrow**

yesterday	today	tomorrow
yesterday morning	this morning	tomorrow morning
yesterday afternoon	this afternoon	tomorrow afternoon
yesterday evening	this evening	tomorrow evening
last night	tonight	tomorrow night

1   *today* and *tonight* refer to the day now, when we are speaking or writing. *Today* can sometimes refer generally to the present time:
*What are we going to do **today/tonight**?*
***Today's** my birthday, and we're having a party **tonight**.*
*I'll telephone her later **today**.*
*Christmas is a week **today/today** week.* (= a week from now)
***Today's** children have much more freedom than we did.*

2   To refer to various parts of *today* (except *tonight*) we use *this* + *morning/ afternoon/evening*:
*What are you doing **this evening**?*

3 *today* and *tonight* only relate to the present time. So in reporting what somebody else has said, unless their *today/tonight* is our *today/tonight* we must change the words:

*He said he would telephone her later **that day**/later **the same day**.*

*She said they were having a party **that night**.*

But –

*She said **today**'s children have much more freedom than we did.* (or *She said that children then/at the time when she was speaking had much more freedom than her generation had done.*)

together

1 together: adverb

- with each other; joined

  *Only a fortnight more and then, darling, we'll be **together** again.*

  *We simply decided to work **together**.*

  *We walked home **together**.*

  *They cut down small pieces of wood and nailed them **together**.*

  *I only get **together** with him when I've got something I want to talk to him about.* (= see him, meet him)

2 together with

- as well as

  *The £72 raised by the sale **together with** other gifts means we now have £86.*

tomorrow and yesterday   ▶ Compare today

- the day after, and the day before, today (or sometimes more generally the future or the past)

1   *The term doesn't start until **tomorrow**, so I haven't met the other students yet.*

*Look. **Yesterday** was Tuesday, and **tomorrow** is Thursday. You really are in a muddle.*

*I knew nothing about this until **yesterday**.*

*The problems we have today are quite different from **yesterday**'s, that's why the government is offering new solutions.*

2   We can use *tomorrow* and *yesterday* before **morning**, *afternoon* and *evening* (See **morning**), and as with *tomorrow* and *yesterday* we do not use in/on:

*We'll see you **tomorrow** morning/afternoon/evening/night.*

*We saw them **yesterday** morning/afternoon/evening* (but *last night.*)

3   *tomorrow* and *yesterday* only relate to now. So in reported speech, unless we are reporting what somebody has said earlier today (so that their *yesterday* and *tomorrow* are our *yesterday* and *tomorrow*) we cannot use these words.

Instead, we say *the day before/the previous day* . . . and *(the) next day/the following day*:

> *'What were you doing **yesterday**?' Marie asked, 'and where will you be **tomorrow**?'*
> *Marie asked (me) what I had been doing **the day before**, and where I would be **the following day**.*

tonight ▶ See **today**

too ▶ Compare **enough**

1 too: adverb

- excessively; more than enough

far rather		fat/thin . . .
much		quickly/soon/much . . .
(a bit) (a little) (a lot)	**too**	much (noise) little (money) (UNCOUNTABLE)
far (rather)		many (people) (PLURAL) few

a *too* is an emphasising adverb, used with adjectives, adverbs and determiners + nouns, or with pronouns, as shown. Various words can come in front of *too*, as shown:

> *She is much **too** thin. She doesn't eat enough.*
> *He is really a little bit **too** polite.*
> *Don't you think he's **too** young for her?*
> *She works herself **too** hard.*
> *I cannot speak **too** highly of him.* (= I cannot praise him enough, he is very good.)
> *Your are making much **too** much noise.*
> *I wouldn't be in **too** much of a hurry.*
> *Is there **too** much of the stuff or too little?*
> *They've invited far **too** many people.*

b *too* is sometimes used meaning 'very', 'extremely':

> *You are **too** kind.*
> *It's **too** ridiculous – I asked for two copies and they've sent twenty.*
> *His French remains fluent, if not **too** accurate.*
> *I'm not **too** sure.*
> *I wouldn't be **too** surprised.*

c If we add *too* to an adjective in front of a singular noun, the word order is *too* + ADJECTIVE + *a/an* + NOUN:
  *They charge me at **too** high a rate.*

d We do not use *too* with verbs, but we can use *too much*:
  *You're worrying **too much** – it'll be all right.*

e **too . . . (for . . .) . . . to**
  too is often used in the pattern *too* + ADJECTIVE/ADVERB (+ *for somebody*) *to* do something. The meaning is that the action probably does not or did not – or perhaps ought not to – happen:
  *It was much **too** cold to go swimming.* (= So we did not go.)
  *Everyone says we are **too** young to get married – but we're going to all the same!*
  *The Ramada Hotel is far **too** expensive for ordinary people to stay in.*

2 too: adverb and connector ▶ Compare **either** 3

  too is added after a word or at the end of a sentence, with the meaning of 'also':
  *'I hated that film.' 'Me **too**!'* (= So did I)
  *It was an amusing book, but violent **too**.*
  *You **too** could win a prize – other people do.*
  *That dictionary is very good for spelling mistakes **too**.*
  *I was only expecting Celia, but her mother came **too**.*
  *We **too** were pleased.*
  *Germaine's going on Thursday. I don't know whether Jake's going **too**.*

towards: preposition

  American English often uses *toward*.
  ● in the direction of
  *The new college is going to be miles out of town – right out **towards** the golf course.*
  *How can I apply for a grant **towards** fees?* (= a grant that will pay for part of my fees)
  *Do visit me – **towards** the end of the week is better, as I go out on Monday and Tuesday.*

true, **truer**, **truest**: adjective

a ● corresponding to the facts
  *Is it **true** (that) you've left your job?*
  *These are all **true** stories, though they are very strange.*

b ● real; faithful; loyal
  *They say **true** love lasts for ever.*
  *That was the act of a **true** friend.*

truth: noun

truth is usually uncountable

a **Truth** *is stranger than fiction.* (= Some things that really happen are stranger than things that happen in novels.)
'*Is there any* **truth** *in what he is saying about his neighbours?*' '*No, no* **truth** *at all.*'

b *the truth* is often used when the meaning is 'the true fact(s)':
I do try and tell **the truth**.
The truth *is, I'm sorry, but I don't want to lend you any more money.* (= The fact is . . .)
I'd like to know **the truth** *about his money. Where did it all come from?*

try, tried, tried: verb

1 *try* (+ *to*-INFINITIVE) means 'attempt to do something difficult', 'make an effort':
a *I know this work is difficult, but you must* **try**.
I **tried** *to telephone you, but the line was engaged.*
She's always **trying** *hard to lose weight – I hope she succeeds.*
I've been **trying** *to open this door – but it is stuck.*

b *try and do* something is also possible (but NOT *tries, tried, trying and . . .*)
They told him to **try and be** *his age.* (= **try** *to behave like an adult*)

2 *try* + *-ing* and *try* + OBJECT mean 'do something as an experiment', 'test something to see if it is suitable':
a **Try** *turning the key the other way – that might do it.*
I **tried** *going on the bus last time I went to Scotland, but it was much slower than the train.*

b *If the lock is stiff,* **try** *some oil on it.*
This chocolate isn't too sweet – **try** *it.*
Can I **try** *this coat on please?* (= to see if I want to buy it.)

turn: verb

turn is used without and with objects, and the general meaning is movement.

```
turn + ‾
       OBJECT
```

a without an object
The Earth **turns** *on its axis once every twenty-four hours.*
I **turned** *round because I heard a noise behind me.*

*I **turned** over in bed and went to sleep again.*
***Turn** right just past the post-office.*
*We've lost our way – we'd better **turn** back.*

b   with an object
*I **turned** the key in the lock, but the door wouldn't open.*
***Turn** the meat to brown it on the other side.*

c   *turn*, with or without an object can have a meaning of 'changing state'; and
with this meaning may be followed by an adjective:
***Turn** the light off/on.* (= switch it off/on)
*The tragedy has **turned** him into an old man.*
*The water in our water bottles **turned** into ice.*
*He **turned** white with fear.*

---

twice: adverb

- two times

a   *I've met them once or **twice**, but I don't know them very well.* (= a few times
but not often)
*He telephoned **twice** in the afternoon.*

b   *twice* is also used with measurements and time expressions:
***Twice** four is eight.* (2 × 4 = 8)
*A kilo is **twice** as much as we need – I wanted a pound.*
*About **twice** a year my brother takes his two children over to see her.*

---

unable: predicative adjective   ▶ Compare **able**

unable is only used after verbs (NOT **an unable person*):
*I am really **unable** to comment on these remarks.*
*I was extremely sorry that I was **unable** to get to your father's funeral owing to
being in bed with flu.*
*They seem **unable** to agree.*

---

uncertain   ▶ See **certain**

---

under: preposition ▶ Compare **below; beneath**

under is the opposite of *over*. *Under* (like *below*) can mean 'lower than'. For cases where both are possible (▶ See **below**). There are other meanings where *below* is not possible.

1 • from one side to the other
   *They're building a tunnel **under** the Channel.*
   *The dog ran **under** the table.*

2 • on the other side of
   *The baker's is just **under** the bridge on the left.* (= If you go under the bridge, it is on the other side.)

3 *under* can include the idea of 'covered' or 'touching':
   *The dog was asleep **under** the table.*
   *I was wearing a vest **under** my shirt.*
   *The road was **under** water.* (= flooded)
   *She read the letter again and put it **under** her pillow.*
   *I was sleeping in a room just **under** the roof.*
   *Hold the bucket **under** the tap.*
   *Come and stand **under** my umbrella.*
   *What's that you're holding **under** your arm?* (= between your arm and your body)

4 • less than
   *He's **under** thirty.*
   *There were **under** thirty people at the meeting.*
   *a meal for **under** £5 . . . **under** an hour . . . temperatures of **under** 5°C . . . children of five and **under** . . .*

5 We also use *under* (NOT **below*) to show who is in authority or power
   *the Soviet Union **under** Stalin . . . twelve teachers working **under** her . . .*

---

underneath

1 underneath: preposition

The meaning of *underneath* is similar to *under* or *beneath*, but it is mainly used referring to place:
   *The letter was pushed **underneath** the church door.*
   *The dog was asleep **underneath** the table.*

2 underneath: adverb

There is an adverb *under* but it is hardly used. So *underneath* is the adverb corresponding to the preposition *under*:
   *They've got the upper part of the house, and there's a garden flat **underneath**.*
   *He seems charming, but he's tough as hell **underneath**.*
   *She was only wearing a summer dress, but she probably had a lot on **underneath**.*

---

understand, understood, understood: verb

```
                    –
                    OBJECT
                    about . . .
    understand  +  you/your -ing
                    wh-CLAUSE
                    that-CLAUSE
                    O + to-INFINITIVE
```

understand is not usually used in the progressive.

1 ● know about; know the reason for; make sense of
understand can be followed by an OBJECT, or sometimes by *about* + NOUN.
It can also be followed by OBJECT + *you/your -ing . . .*, *wh*-CLAUSES, and
wh-WORDS + *to*-INFINITIVE:
    *I can't/don't **understand** this book/her/her accent/what you mean.*
    *My wife doesn't **understand** me.*
    *I **understand** you/your wanting more money, but I can't/don't **understand***
    why you took this job.
    *The film was very difficult to **understand**.*
    *I don't **understand** about the missing money – where has it gone?*
    *He didn't **understand** what to do.*

2 **understand** + *that*-CLAUSES, **understand** + OBJECT + *to*-INFINITIVE

a If we *understand* that something is true we realise or believe something
because we have been told:
    *We **understand** that the police wish to interview one of the car drivers/that the*
    police are working on the problem/that they have arrested two women.
    *The bank **understood** (that) he only needed a loan of £100.*

b *understand* + OBJECT + *to*-INFINITIVE has a similar meaning, but only a few
verbs are common in this pattern:
    *The bank **understood** him to say/to mean (that) he only needed £100.*

c In the passive, we can use an impersonal pattern with *it*:
    *It is **understood** that the police are working on the problem.*

We can also sometimes use personal subjects with the passive followed by a *to*-
INFINITIVE, but only a few verb forms are common. These are *to be*, *to be* +
PRESENT PARTICIPLE, *to have*, *to have* + PAST PARTICIPLE, *to say* and *to mean*:
    *The police are **understood** to be working on the problem.*
    *The driver is **understood** to be armed.*
    *The police are **understood** to have arrested two women.*
    *He was **understood** to mean/to say (that) he only needed £100.*

unless: conjunction   ▶ Compare **if**

unless means 'except if' and introduces a condition.

1 Open conditions

In open conditions, where we are talking about things that happened in the past or that happen now or are likely to happen in the future, *unless* can usually replace *if . . . not*. But they do not mean quite the same. *Unless* stresses that something is the only condition for something else happening; *if . . . not* refers to a possibility and result.
Contrast:

*I'll go **unless** it rains.* (= Rain is the only thing that will stop me going.)
*I'll certainly go **if** it doesn't rain.* (= But I might go even if it does rain!)

a Present and past conditions

Unless you're a twin, it's very difficult to understand what it's like. (= You can only understand if you are a twin.)
*You cannot treat a disease **unless** you know the cause.*
*He can't understand a word we say **unless** we shout at him.*
*Tom never went swimming **unless** the water was warm.*
*Hilda swam throughout the year **unless** the water was frozen.*

b Future conditions

*Don't marry him, **unless** you're sure.* (= Only marry him if you are sure.)
*Do not speak **unless** you can improve on the silence.*
*I'll telephone them **unless** they phone me first.*

2 Conditions using **would** or **could**

In conditions using *would* or *could* in the main clause, *unless* cannot always replace *if . . . not*.

a

unless often refers to something that happens that we think is good; *if . . . not* simply says 'if the facts were different.' Take the case of somebody who takes pills, and contrast:

*She would be in pain **if** she did **not** take these pills.*
*She would be in pain **unless** she took them.*
*She would be healthy **if** she did **not** take all these pills.*
But NOT **She would be healthy **unless** she took them.*

In the first two sentences, taking pills is a good thing with a good result. (she is not in pain) But being unhealthy because of pills is not good, and we do not use *unless*. Compare also:

*I'd starve **unless** my father gave me this allowance.* (= I do not starve because my father gives me this allowance.)
But NOT **You could afford a car **unless** you wasted money the way you do.*
and NOT **She would have more friends **unless** she argued so much.*

Similarly with past conditions – we can use *unless* when we think that what happened was good:

*He would have died **unless** the hospital had acted quickly.* (= He did not die because the hospital acted quickly.)
But NOT **They would have been all right **unless** the bus had hit them.*
and NOT **I would have remembered **unless** I had been so busy.*

b

unless can however introduce facts which are good or bad or neutral, when the main clause is negative. Here *unless* explains the condition or circumstance in which something does or did happen:

He wouldn't say silly things like that **unless** *he were stupid.* (= He says silly things because he is stupid.)

I couldn't afford this car **unless** *I had two jobs.*

I wouldn't have come **unless** *I loved you.*

He wouldn't have crashed the car **unless** *he had been drunk.*

You wouldn't be in this mess now **unless** *you had told all those lies.*

3 Hypothetical past and future

When *could* and *would* are used in the main clause, not to discuss actual facts, but something hypothetical (something imaginary and unreal), then *unless* is possible. Contrast:

You could afford a car **unless** *you wasted money on other things.* (= That would be the only thing that would stop you having a car. But I am not saying you waste money.)

But NOT **You could afford a car now* **unless** *you wasted your money now the way you do.*

Similarly contrast

I would have gone **unless** *I had been ill.* (= But the whole thing is hypothetical, because I was not invited, so it doesn't matter whether I was ill or not.)

But NOT **I would have gone* **unless** *I had been so ill.* (When the fact is that I did not go because I was ill.)

4 Emotional states

Only *if . . . not*, and never *unless*, is possible when we talk about emotional states (e.g., *amazed/glad if . . . not*) because the meaning here is 'If the fact is that something is not . . .':

I am amazed **if/that** *you cannot tell the difference.*

Will you be upset **if** *you don't get the job?*

Henry would be annoyed **if** *he wasn't/weren't asked.*

We were always surprised **if/when** *we didn't have to pay.*

They would have been pleased **if/that** *they hadn't had to go.*

▶ Contrast a real condition:

I'll be penniless **if** *I don't/***unless** *I get the job.* where we cannot say **I'll be penniless that . . .*

5 *Unless* cannot replace *if . . . not* when the meaning is 'whether . . . not' in indirect questions:

I asked him **if** *he wasn't ashamed.*

NOT *I asked him **unless** *. . .*

unlike: preposition

unlike is the opposite of *like*:

Unlike *her mother, who gave up her job when she got married, Pamela had always worked for her living.*

She's totally **unlike** the rest of her family.
Moscow, **unlike** London, has no area where the central government is concentrated.
It was a bright modern little flat, quite **unlike** his own.

unlikely: adjective

unlikely is the opposite of *likely* (see table at *likely*):
I think snow tomorrow is rather **unlikely**.
He is **unlikely** to come.
It is **unlikely** that he'll come.
He is a rather **unlikely** person for the job, but I suppose he might get it.
There is **unlikely** to be anyone else to look after him if Hilda leaves.
I suppose it is **unlikely** that they will ever quite succeed.

unsure ▶ See **sure**

until and till

Sometimes informally written as *'til*.
until and *till* both refer to a period that ends at a particular time. (Contrast *since* and *from*, which mention the time when some state or action begins.) *Until* occurs in written and spoken English; *till* is slightly more informal. Both words refer only to time, not place.

1 until: preposition

a   I'm going to stay over **until** Monday.
Well, cheerio **until** the weekend.
Some of the students were here **until** late – I mean 2 or 3 in the morning.
I cannot check my account **until** Monday at the earliest.
From 1980 **until** 1985 I worked at the Institute.
He wasn't free **until** after his exams.
He was here from 9 **till** nearly midnight.
I have bought a car without telling Mum and Dad **till** afterwards.

b   *until* is only possible when there is an idea of waiting:
Paul was coming today, but now he's not coming **until** next Wednesday.
He wasn't coming **until** next week, but his appointment has been changed to/brought forward to today. (NOT ***until** today)

2 until: conjunction

He'll stay there **till** I come out, she said.
He didn't wear glasses **until** he was ten.
I can't really finish **until** I've been through all the letters.
They were worried **until** they had found the will.

up is the opposite of *down*

1   up: preposition

a   ● in/to a higher place
*George climbed **up** the ladder and on to the roof.*
*I can't run **up** hills the way I did when I was young.*
*They sailed **up** the Amazon from the mouth as far as Manaus.* (= away from the sea)

b   When speaking of a level road it is usually possible to say ***up** the road/down the road* with no difference in meaning.

2   up: adverb

a   ● in/to a higher place; in or into the proper position
*We walked **up** and **up** for hours – I thought we'd never get to the top.*
*Looking **up**, he suddenly saw the new moon.*
*There was nowhere to hang my coat **up**, so I put it over a chair.*
*Sit **up** straight.*
*He was sitting **up** in bed looking much better.*
*Why have you got your umbrella **up**? It isn't raining.*
*Why don't you put a notice **up**?* (= on the wall)
*The children were supposed to put their hands **up** if they wanted to ask questions.*
Also: *climb **up**, get **up*** (= get out of bed. Contrast *lie **down***), *stay **up*** (= not go to bed), *stand **up*** (Contrast *sit **down***).

b   direction towards
With verbs of movement, *up* (*to*) often means 'close towards' somebody or something:
*A complete stranger came **up** (to me) and started asking personal questions.*
*I went **up** to the bar and ordered drinks.*
*You can drive right **up** to the house and park in front of the door.*
Also: *go **up**, run **up**, walk **up***

c   ● get or remain higher or bigger
*Prices are always going **up**.*

d   *up* often adds emphasis or a sense of completion to a verb:
*Eat **up** your vegetables, Tommy.* (= Eat them all.)
*There's no paper left – it's been used **up**.*
*I can't add these figures **up** – it's too difficult.*
Also: *clean **up**, clear **up**, cover **up**, drink **up**, finish **up**, hurry **up**, wash **up*** (the dirty dishes), *wipe **up***

e   up is also used with a sense of destruction:
*I tore **up** the letter and started again.*
*The terrorists said they would blow **up** the plane.* (= destroy it with a bomb)

upon: preposition

upon is a formal alternative to *on*:

a   *Have you any comment to make **upon** the kind of language this writer is using?*
*She looked **upon** this as absolutely impossible.* (= considered)
*He would sleep fully clothed **upon** the floor.*
*She is not dependent, for every penny, as some wives are, **upon** her husband.*
*Have you ever been to Richmond-**upon**-Thames?*

b Do not confuse with *up on*, as two separate words:
*Why don't you put those books **up on** the top shelf?*

upwards: adverb

- towards a higher place or level
  *There are no little children here – the children here are all twelve and **upwards**.*

us: pronoun   ▶ See **our; ours; ourselves; we**

First person plural object pronoun.
For meaning ▶ See **we**

a *us* is used as the object of a verb or preposition, and in other positions where it is not the subject, including short remarks without verbs. *Us* can be followed by a noun, a number, *all* and *both*:

*Come and see **us** on Sunday.*
*Paul's agreed to come with **us**.*
*They're not as lucky as **us**.*
*You've got more than **us**.*
*'Who's there?' 'Only **us**.*
*They want **us** nurses to work harder.*
*Is there room for **us** two?*
*Helen's invited **us** all/**us** both.*
*Helen and Nicholas want **us** to visit them.*

b *us* is often used before *-ing* in sentences where *our* is formally correct:
*He doesn't like **us**/**our** knowing about his private life.*

But only *us* (NOT **our*) is correct after verbs of the senses and after *find* and *keep*:
*He saw **us** crossing the road.*
*They kept **us** waiting.*

c *us* is usual after *be*:
*'Someone telephoned last night.' 'Oh it wasn't **us**.'*

d Sometimes, in very informal speech, *us* is used with singular meaning, instead of *me*:
*I was alone with the girl . . . 'Lift **us** up on that wall, come on,' she said.*

1 used to + infinitive

▶ Compare **would**

I/we/he/she/it/you/they	**used** (not) didn't **use**	
		to do . . .
Did(n't) you . . . **Used(n't)** you . . .	**use**	

a *used to* is a verb followed by an infinitive. It only has this past simple tense. It is a way of talking about past habits and states that have changed and so do not happen now. The pronunciation is /juːstuː/ before vowel sounds and finally, and /juːstə/ before consonants:
*I **used to** eat three meals a day.* (= But I don't now.)
*He always **used to** make the most horrible noises.*
*We **used to** be told to give up our seats to women on the tube, but now we just let them stand.*

b Negative sentences and questions can be made in the modal way (*used not to . . . usedn't you to . . ?*) but many people find this formal, and *didn't use to* and *Did(n't) you use to . . .?* are common:
*The traffic **used not to** be/**didn't use to** be as bad as this.*
***Didn't you use** to wear glasses? Yes, I did. Yes I **used to**.*
*How **did you use to**/**used you to** go to school?*
*Did you **use to** walk?*

c *used to* always refers to a past habit or state, but we do not use it when we mention the total number of times we did something:
*We **used to** go to the seaside every summer when we were children.*
*I always **used to** have a cheap secondhand car.*
But NOT **We **used to** go ten times.*

There is no corresponding **use to* for present habits, where we just use a present simple:
We always go by bus.

d **used to** or **would**?
Both *used to* and *would* talk about past habits and repeated happenings:
*When I was young I often **used to** go/I **would** often go swimming before breakfast.*
*It often **used to** be cold/**would** often we cold but we didn't mind.*

But only *used to* (not *would*) talks about permanent past states:
*There **used to** be a post office in the village, but they've closed it now.*
*I **used to** love him.* (= but now I don't)
*I **used to** have good eyesight when I was young, but I have to wear reading glasses now.*

2 be/get used to

be become get	used to	something doing it

To *be* or *get used to* something or *to doing* something means one has become very familiar with it. One has seen it or done it so many times that it is well known, one is accustomed to it. *Used* (pronounced / juːst/) is an adjective here and *to* is a preposition, so this *used to* is never followed by an infinitive:

*You'll have to **get used to** driving on the left when you come to London* (NOT **to drive*)
*Isabel was **used to** having her children always with her.* (NOT **to have*)
*He couldn't **get used to** how ill Margaret looked.*
*We were **used to** unheated bedrooms and thought nothing of it – but today everyone expects central heating.*

3 use, used, used: verb

There is also a regular verb *use* (pronounced /juːz/, with *used* /juːzd/) that is followed by a direct object:

*How many times have I got to tell you to **use** a knife and fork and not your fingers?*
*Pictures are **used** to explain the meanings of difficult words.*

4 use: noun

As a noun *use*, *uses* are pronounced /juːs, juːsɪz/:

*You'll find lots of **uses** for this paper, and wonder how you ever managed without it.*
*What's the **use** of telling you anything? You never listen.*
*It's no **use** crying over spilt milk.* (= There is no point in getting upset over something when it is too late to change it.)

usual and usually

1 *usual* is an adjective and *usually* is an adverb (often used in mid-position):
*11 o'clock is my **usual** bedtime.*
*I **usually** go to bed at 11.*

2 *as usual* is an adverb:
*Last night I went to bed at 11, **as usual**.* (= as I usually do.)

've ▶ See **have**

1 very: adverb

very	good/quick	(indeed)
	well/quickly/much	
	much/little (money)	
	many/few (people)	
the **very**	best/first/last/next . . .	

a   *very* is used to emphasise adjectives and adverbs, and also *much, little, many, few* as shown. These phrases can be followed by *indeed*, which makes the *very* even stronger:

*The film was **very** good; and we got in **very** cheaply too.*
*Actually, doctors know **very** little about this disease.*
*Not **very** many people realise this.*
*The film was **very** good indeed – I don't know when I've seen anything I enjoyed more.*

b   *very* can be used with superlative words (but not with comparatives):

*She always dresses in the **very** latest fashions.*
*I want the **very** best for my children.*
*I only decided at the **very** last moment.*

For *very much* with comparatives, ▶ see **much**.

c   *very* is not used with verbs. We can use *very* with past participles that have become adjectives:

*I was **very** annoyed/pleased/surprised/worried.*

But with verbs we must use *much* or *very much*:

*He is **much** criticized/**much** loved.*
*I love you **very much**.*

2 very: adjective

When we talk about *the very thing* or *the very person* we mean exactly the same thing or person we were already thinking about:

*That is **the very thing** I wanted.*

view

1 view: noun (C, U)

a   ● something you can see or the ability to see something
*We had a marvellous **view** of the mountains from the hotel.*
*They undressed on the beach in full **view** of everybody.*

b ● opinion; idea
*What are your **views** on drunken drivers?*
*political/religious **views** . . .*
*Many people share the **view** that strong defence is the best way of preventing war.*
*In my **view** (= in my opinion) money spent on national defence is money well spent.*

▶ See also *point of view* at **point**

2 in view of; preposition
● considering
*In **view of** her excellent record, it was unfair to sack her.*

3 view: verb

a *view* can be used formally to mean 'look at'. You *view* a house or flat if you think you might rent it or buy it. And you can *view* (but you usually *watch*) television:
*Some programmes can only be **viewed** late at night.*
*The island was extraordinary when **viewed** from the air.*

b *view* can also mean 'consider':
*They **viewed** my education as an investment for the future.*

---

wait: verb ▶ Compare **expect**

> **wait** + (*for* + OBJECT) *to*-INFINITIVE

If you *wait* you stay somewhere (perhaps not doing anything) because you are hoping something is going to happen soon.

a *wait* does not usually take a direct object (except in the phrase 'wait one's turn'). Instead, we must use *wait for*:
*Don't be so impatient. Just **wait**.*
*I'm sorry if I've kept you **waiting**.*
*If you **wait** here with the luggage, I'll go and get the tickets.*
*We **waited** all day/(for) an hour/(for) ages – but nobody came.*
*'What have you got me for Christmas?' '**Wait** and see!'*
*You'll have to **wait** until you're older – then you'll be able to do what you like.*
*Please **wait** for me. I'm just coming.*
*I'm afraid the doctor's busy. You'll have to **wait** your turn.*

b *wait* is also used with a *to*-INFINITIVE and with *for* + OBJECT + *to*-INFINITIVE:
*We are still **waiting** to hear from Peter.*
*I'm **waiting** for him to say what he wants to do.*
*There was a crowd on the pavement **waiting** for the shop to open.*

---

wake, waken ▶ See **awake**

---

want: verb ▶ Compare **wish**

> OBJECT
> **want** + (O) + *to*-INFINITIVE
> O + PAST PARTICIPLE
> O + ADJECTIVE

1 ● wish for; desire

a *want* can be followed by a direct object, by a *to*-INFINITIVE and by OBJECT + *to*-INFINITIVE, by OBJECT + PAST PARTICIPLE or OBJECT + ADJECTIVE:
*He **wants** a computer for his birthday.*
*Do you **want** anything/something to eat?* (= would you like . . .?)
*The Director of Studies **wants** (to see) you.*
*'Well, what do you **want** to do. Do you **want** to go out?' 'No, I don't really **want** to.'*
*They **want** us to meet them in London.*
*I **want** six copies made.*
*They **want** the house (to be) ready to move into by January.*

b When there is a negative with *want* + (OBJECT+) + *to*-INFINITIVE, we usually put the negative with *want* and not with the second verb:
*I don't **want** to tell my mother, and I don't **want** her to find out.*

It is possible to put *not* with the second verb, but the meaning is then much stronger:
*I definitely **want** her not to know!*

c *want* is never followed by a *that*-CLAUSE (NOT *They **want** that we meet them.*)

d *want* + OBJECT + -*ing* is sometimes possible, but the meaning is 'want something/someone to be doing something':
*She **wanted** the children all sitting round in a circle on the floor.*
*I don't **want** you worrying.*
(But NOT *They **want** us meeting them.*)

e If someone is *wanted*, it often means somebody is looking for them or wants to talk to them:
*You're **wanted** on the telephone.*
WANTED FOR MURDER! (often the heading of a police notice)

---

2 *want* + OBJECT and *want* + *-ing* can mean 'need', but they are less usual than *need*:

> *These shoes **want** a clean.*
> *All my shirts **want** washing.*

3 *want* + *to*-INFINITIVE can mean 'ought' or 'must':

> *You **want** to get that window mended – it's dangerous.*

---

was ▶ See **be**

---

watch: verb ▶ Compare **hear**; **look at**; **see**

```
                 –
watch +   OBJECT
          O + BARE INFINITIVE
          o + -ing
```

- look (at) carefully

a *watch* is used with and without an OBJECT, and can also be followed by *wh*-CLAUSES:

> ***Watch** carefully and you'll see how he does it.*
> *He should **watch** his weight – he's getting really quite a tummy.*
> *We spent the afternoon **watching** football/tennis/television . . .*
> ***Watch** what he does/how he does it/where he puts the ring . . .*

b *watch* can be followed by OBJECT + BARE INFINITIVE (for a complete action) and by OBJECT + *-ing* (when the emphasis is on an activity in progress):

> *We **watched** the parade go past.* (= we watched it all)
> *We **watched** the parade going past.* (= maybe only part of it)

These two patterns are not used in the passive.

---

way: noun

1 • right road or path; distance (in space or time) of a journey

a *Which **way** is it to the station?*
> *Can you tell me the **way** to the station?*
> *Oh, it's a long **way**/quite a **way** from here.*
> *I wish Granny didn't live such a long **way** away.*
> ***WAY OUT*** (= a notice meaning Exit)
> *Come this **way**, please.*
> *We kept losing our **way** and having to ask.*
> *The train was crowded and we had to stand the whole **way**.*
> *I suddenly realised I was driving the wrong **way** down a one-way street.*

*I was half **way** home before I realised I had left my bag in the shop.*
*A funny thing happened to me on the **way** to school.*

b   in/out of the way
If something is *in the way* it is blocking the way:
*'Please don't leave your suitcase by the stairs like that – it is **in the way**/in everybody's **way**.' 'Sorry. I'll get/move it **out of the way** in a moment.'*

2   • method; manner
*Let's do it my **way**.*
*My grandparents are far too old to change their **ways***
*What's the best **way** to clean/of cleaning jewellery?*
*She's always thinking up new **ways** of saving/to save money.*
*There are two **ways** of looking/to look at this problem.*
*He has an odd **way** of scratching his right ear when he's thinking.*
*That's no **way** to speak to your mother.* (= not the right way)
*The **way** (that) he talks, you'd think he was the boss.*
*It isn't what you say (that matters), it's the **way** you say it.*

3   one's own way

• what one wants to do
*He's a nasty child who screams if he can't get his own **way**.*

4   by the way: connector   ▶ Compare **incidentally**

by the way is often used in conversation to introduce a new topic. It sounds as if the topic is not important, but in fact it often is:
*By the **way** – I meant to tell you – Toby and I are engaged.*

5   in a way/in every way/in some ways

These expressions are used to show how much something is true:
*I enjoyed the play **in a way**/in some **ways**, but it was a silly story.* (= I partly enjoyed it.)
*But Paul thought it was marvellous **in every way**.* (= completely)
                    ▶ See also *no way* at **no**

we: pronoun   ▶ See **our; ours; ourselves; us**

First person plural subject pronoun

1   we: usage

a   *we* is used as the subject of a finite verb. It can be followed by a noun, a number, *all* and *both*:
We like it here.
We are being so well looked after.
*Our parents didn't have nearly as many foreign holidays as **we** do.*
*He is much more enthusiastic about the idea than **we** are.*
*'Who's coming swimming?' '**We** are.'*

We nurses must help each other. (NOT **Us nurses*)
You go on, and we two will wait for Joan.
We all agreed that it was a good idea.
We both know it isn't true.

b If no verb follows *as* or *than* in comparisons (See **a** above), *we* is possible but formal. *Us* is more usual:
Our parents didn't have nearly as many holidays as us/we.
But they were much more contented than us/we.

c We is used after *be* when a subject relative pronoun follows (although informally *us* is possible):
The trouble was – it was we who had to pay.

2 we: meaning
we, our, ours, ourselves, us can have several meanings.

a *we, etc.* can refer to the speaker and the person or people spoken to – or the writer and the readers:
Let's go and see Crocodile Dundee, shall we?
I can hardly wait until we see each other again. All my love, George. (in a letter)

b *we*, etc. can refer to the speaker/writer and another person/other people, but not the listener(s)/reader(s):
We will call for you at 8 o'clock.
Please let us stay – we're not hurting you.

c *we, etc.* can refer to 'mankind', 'our country' or 'our world':
We shall ruin our environment if we go on destroying the rain forests.
Common sense tells us that we need more international co-operation.

d There is also an author's *we*, which some writers feel is less personal than *I*:
As we shall show in the next chapter . . .

well

1 well: adverb

well is the adverb corresponding to the adjective *good*. It is the opposite of *badly*. The comparative form is *better* and the superlative is *best*.

a • in a good way; in the right way
Some people work well on their own, but others need a lot of help.
So you passed the exam. Well done!
I don't think you behaved very well.
'How's the job going?' 'Oh, very well, thank you.'

b • with good reason; properly
Notice that *well* is used here in mid-position:
You may well wonder why I didn't mention this before.
I couldn't very well ask him for money, could I? (= It would not have been a good idea.) (NOT **well ask*)

c • thoroughly:
*He's nice, but I don't know him (very) **well**.*

d **well** + ADVERB/PREPOSITION .
well is used to emphasise adverbs and prepositions:
*Profits are **well** up on last year.*
*The party went on until **well** after midnight.*
*The temperature's been **well** below freezing all day.*

2 well: adjective

• in good health
The opposite is *unwell*. *Well* is mainly a predicative adjective:
*'How's your mother? Is she keeping **well**?' 'Yes, she's fine now, thanks, though she wasn't at all **well** earlier this year.'*

3 well: exclamation

well is used in various ways in conversation, often when not quite agreeing with the other person:
*'How about going to the cinema?' '**Well**, I really ought to wash my hair.'*
*'I'm right you know.' '**Well**, you may be, but I doubt it.'*
*'I've decided not to go after all.' '**Well**, if that's how you feel, it's much bettter if you don't.'*

well can be used when continuing a story:
***Well**, what I was trying to say was . . .*

or when encouraging the other person to continue:
***Well**? So what did you do?*

▶ See *as well (as)* at **as**

---

went ▶ See **go**

---

were ▶ See **be**

1 In the ordinary past tense of *be*, *were* is only used after *we/you/they*, and the other pronouns use *was*. But we can use *were* (or *was*) after *I/he/she/it* in unreal hypothetical sentences. (We must of course still use *were* after *we/you/they*). The reference is to the present or future:
*If I **were** a dog, I wouldn't want to be kept on a lead all the time.*
*I wish she **were** on the telephone; it would be so much easier.*
*If we **were** to announce that there was no Loch Ness monster, on that day somebody would see it.*
*A married couple together can ask for separate taxation of the wife's earnings as if she **were** a single person.*

2 if I were you

if I were you is used to give advice:
*If I **were** you, I'd tell your father.* (= my advice is that you should tell your father)

what

1   what: pronoun and determiner used in questions

a   *what* is used in asking rather general questions. When *what* is the subject of a question the word order is *what* + VERB, but when *what* is the object we need the pattern *what* + AUXILIARY + SUBJECT + VERB:

>   ***What** happened?* (subject)
>   ***What** did you say?* (object)
>   ***What** does this word mean?* (object)
>   ***What** have you been telling them about me?* (object)
>   ***What** are you talking about?* (object of preposition)
>   *To **what** are you referring?* (formal)

b   In indirect questions we use the ordinary word order SUBJECT (+ AUXILIARY) + VERB:

>   *I asked her **what** she had said.* (NOT **asked . . . **what** had she said; *asked **what** did she say*)

c   In indirect questions we can also use *what* + *to*-INFINITIVE:

>   *(What shall I do next?) He asked **what** to do next.*

d   As a pronoun, *what* refers to things (not people) or asks questions in a general way:

>   ***What** happened?* (Contrast: ***Who** told you?*)
>   ***What** did you say?* (Contrast: ***Who** did you talk to?*)

But as a determiner we can use *what* with people or things:

>   ***What** food have we got in the house?*
>   ***What** time is it?*
>   ***What** news? **What**'s the matter?*
>   ***What** authors have you studied?*
>   ***What** visitor(s) were you expecting?*

e   Some *what* questions have rather special meanings:

>   ***What** does your sister do?/**What** is your sister?* (= What is her job?)
>   ***What** is she like?* (Pretty? Hardworking?)
>   ***What** are you doing all this **for**?* (*what . . . for?* = why?)
>   ***What** is this switch for?* (= What is its purpose?)
>   ***What** about having a holiday?* (= a suggestion)
>   ***What** about your mother?* (= what are you going to do about her?)

Notice also *What size* + NOUN for talking about clothes:

>   ***What** size shirt/shoes do you want?*

f   what or which?

We can use both *what* and *which* to ask questions, but *what* suggests that the answer could be almost anything, *which* suggests that the choice is more limited:

>   ***What** shall we do this evening?*
>   ***Which** do you prefer – radio or television?*
>   ***Which** of these bicycles is yours?*

With questions about people however, *which* is sometimes used even when there are several possibilities:

>   ***What/Which** famous person do you most admire?*
>   ***Which** members of his family haven't you met yet?*

2 what: relative pronoun

a *what* is used as a sort of relative pronoun meaning 'that which' or 'the thing which/that'. *What* can be followed by a *to*-INFINITIVE as well as by a CLAUSE. Notice that the resulting *what* CLAUSES are noun clauses. They can be subjects, objects and so on of sentences:

*The real question is **what** to do now.* (= what we ought to do now)
***What** you say does not surprise me.*
*I can't think **what** she sees in him.*
*I'm afraid I don't believe **what** he's saying.*
*I'm not sure **what** I can do to help.*
*From **what** I've heard about the company, it's just as well you left.*

Notice that *what* is a sort of double word and these sentences are all incomplete without the *what*-clause. We do not use another pronoun with *what*. Compare:

*I don't believe **what** he is saying.* (*what* = that which)
and:
*I don't believe the story **(that)** he told us.* (*that* = ordinary relative pronoun)

b *what* in CLEFT SENTENCES   ▶ Compare **it**
what is used in a special kind of sentence called a cleft sentence. Cleft means divided. The effect is to emphasise two parts of a sentence instead of just one:

***What** you need is a wife.* (= You need something. And that something is a wife.)
***What** I would like would be to start again.* (= There is something that I would like. And that is to start again.)

c *what* CLAUSES usually take a singular verb:
***What** you say does not surprise me.*

but if the two parts of the sentence are reversible, a plural verb is possible:
***What** I'm looking for is/are some cheap chairs.*
*Cheap chairs are **what** I'm looking for.*

A plural verb is necessary in the following:
*He made **what** I thought **were** very silly excuses.* (= he made excuses that were . . .)

3 what: relative determiner   ▶ Compare **such**

This is fairly unusual:
*I'll show you **what** maps I have.* (= all the maps I have, but I haven't got many – or they are not very good)

4 what: exclamations   ▶ Compare **how**

what is used in exclamations. With a singular count noun we need *a/an*:
***What** a shame you missed the party.*
***What** a lovely idea!*
***What** terrible weather we're having.*
***What** incredible prices!*

5   *what* is used in various ways in conversation.

a   to ask someone to repeat what they have said:
  'We'll be there about ten fifty.' 'What? Speak up. This is a bad line.' 'Sorry.
  We'll be arriving about ten fifty.'

b   to talk about surprising information:
  *'Rupert has just got a job in Timbuctoo.' 'He's **what**?'*
  *Guess **what**! Do you know **what**? James has won £5000.*

c   to make a suggestion:
  *I'll tell you **what**/I know **what** – why don't we go fishing?*
  ***What** about going fishing?*

d   *What if . . .* means 'What will happen if . . .?':
  ***What if** your wife finds out?*

---

whatever: determiner and pronoun   ▶   Compare   **whichever**

---

1   *whatever* can be used as an emphatic form of the *what* used in questions. It
usually suggests some criticism or surprise. This *whatever* is sometimes written
as two words – '**what ever**':
  ***Whatever**'s the time? (Heaven! It's very late.)*
  ***Whatever** are you tying string round your finger for?*

2   *whatever* (very formally *whatsoever*) is also used – like *what* – both as a
pronoun and a determiner. The meaning is 'any(thing) that':
  *I'll do **whatever** I can to help.*
  ***Whatever** I say seems to annoy her.*
  *We'll show you **whatever** maps we have. (= but we haven't many)*

3   ● it doesn't matter what . . .; no matter what . . .
  whatever is also used in separate clauses with the meaning of 'It doesn't matter
  what . . .' 'It doesn't make any difference what . . .':
  ***Whatever** you may say, something has got to be done about foxes.*
  ***Whatever** suggestions I make, you tell me I'm wrong.*
  ***Whatever** else you do, don't forget to feed the cat.*

4   *whatever* can also mean 'I don't know exactly what (and I don't care)':
  *She says he looks like a terrorist – **whatever** that means.*

5   after negatives, *whatever* is used to emphasise the negative and means 'at all':
  *There is no need **whatever** to be rude.*
  *It's got nothing **whatever** to do with you.*

when

- at what/which time

1 when: question word

a *When are you taking your holiday?*
When will you know your results?
When did you last see your father?
When do you need this by?
Since when has Patricia been a blonde?

b In indirect questions, ordinary SUBJECT-VERB word order is used:
She wants to know when I am taking my holiday.
They asked the boy when he last saw/he had last seen his father.
I was wondering when you need/needed this by.

c In indirect questions we can also use *when* + *to*-INFINITIVE:
(When shall I go?) *She asked when to go.*
(You should go in May.) *I advised her when to go.*

2 when: adverb/conjunction

a *when*-CLAUSES can tell us the time that something happened or will happen.
Notice (first example) that 'present' tenses are used for ordinary future
reference in this sort of 'time-clause':
Do come and see us when you're next in London.
I'll lend you this book when I've finished with it.
When I was a child we didn't have central heating.
We were all amazed when Hugh walked through the door.
How can you be in love, when you've only known him a week?
(=considering that you have only . . .)
The light suddenly went out when I was reading in bed.

b In the examples in **a** (above) the action in the *when*-CLAUSE happens first,
before the main-clause action. But with different tenses this is not always so:
We were having breakfast when Hugh walked through the door.
When the light went out, I was reading in bed.
I'd just gone to bed when the telephone rang.

c Shortened *when*-CLAUSES are also possible:
When in doubt, say nothing.
You must have a lamp on your bicycle when riding at night.

d *when*-CLAUSES can be subjects of sentences, and be used in other places where
simple nouns are possible:
When they will arrive is anybody's guess.
I'm not sure when I shall go. I'm not sure when to go.
When I'm going is none of their business.
We were talking about when to tell them.

e *when*-CLAUSES can also be used rather like relative clauses to describe a noun:
Do you remember that holiday when it rained every day?
You've only got until 3.30, when the banks shut.

whenever: adverb and conjunction

1 *whenever* can be used as an emphatic form of the *when* used in questions. It usually suggests some criticism or surprise. This *whenever* is sometimes written as two words – *when ever*:

> **Whenever** *did you learn to fly? I'd no idea you could.*

2 *whenever* can also mean 'at any time that' or 'at every time that':

> *I visit my mother **whenever** I can.*
> *Come **whenever** you like – I'll be here the whole weekend.*

3 *whenever* can also be used in separate clauses, and means 'It doesn't matter when . . .':

> **Whenever** *I see Hilda, she's wearing a different hat.*

4 *whenever* can also mean 'I don't know exactly when . . .':

> *In March, or **whenever** it was (that) I last saw her, she said she was going abroad.* (*when* is not possible here.)

where

- to/at/in what place

1 **where**: question adverb

a
> **Where** *do you live?*
> **Where** *are you going for your holidays?*
> **Where** *are you from?*
> *Have you read much of that book?* **Where** *have you got to?*

b In indirect questions ordinary SUBJECT-VERB word order is used:

> *They wanted to know **where** I live/lived.*
> *I asked her **where** she had got to with her book.*

c We can also use *where* + *to*-INFINITIVE in indirect questions:

> (*Where shall we go?*) *We are wondering **where** to go.*
> *Oh Julia will advise you **where** to go.*

2 **where**: adverb and conjunction

a *where*-CLAUSES tell us about the place of some action or state:

> *Look **where** you are going!*
> *Please sit **where** you like.*
> *We always had to live **where** my father's job was.*
> **Where** *there's a will, there's a way.* (= If you have really got the will and the intention to do something, you'll find a way of doing it.)

b *where*-CLAUSES can also replace simple nouns as subjects, etc. of sentences:
*It's a secret **where** they're going for their honeymoon.*
*I couldn't see a thing from **where** I was sitting.*
***Where** to look next is the big problem.*
*That is **where** you are wrong.*

c *where*-CLAUSES can also be used like relative clauses to describe nouns:
*Let's go to that Greek restaurant **where** we had dinner before.* (= that we had dinner at before)
*Highgate, **where** I live, is in north London.*
*I've reached the stage **where** I don't want to work as hard as I have been doing.* (the stage = the time in my life)

whereas: conjunction

- while; but
  *But then to me this decision is important, **whereas** everybody else seems to think nothing of it.*

wherever: adverb and conjunction

1 *wherever* is used as an emphatic form of *where*. It usually suggests some criticism or surprise. This *wherever* can be written as two words – *where ever*:
***Wherever** have you been? I've been waiting absolutely hours.*
***Wherever** does she get those hats?* (= They are awful.)

2 *wherever* can also mean 'at/to any place':
*I'll go **wherever** you want.*

3 *wherever* is used in separate clauses with the meaning 'It doesn't matter where':

***Wherever** you live, there are some disadvantages.*

4 *wherever* can also mean 'I don't know exactly where (and I don't much care')':
*They live in Cleveland, **wherever** that is.*

whether: conjunction   ▶ Compare **if**

1 ● if
whether is used like *if* (and is interchangeable with *if*) in reporting questions, doubts and so on:
*Really sometimes I wonder **whether** it is all worth it.*
*I only asked **whether** you could make less noise.*
*I doubt **whether** a letter will reach him in time.*
*It isn't very clear **whether** Cynthia actually wants to come or not.*
*If you shake it, you can find **whether** there's water inside.*

2 *whether* (but NOT **if*) can be used before an infinitive clause and after prepositions. Notice that sometimes prepositions can be omitted:

*We were discussing **whether** to invite her again.*
*It's a question (of) **whether** she needs to come.*
*There was a perfectly suitable bathroom and nobody cared to speculate (as to) **whether** he used it.*
*The problem **whether** you should borrow money is something only you can decide.*

whether-CLAUSES can also be used as the subject of a sentence and after the verb *be*:

***Whether** you should ever borrow money is a difficult question.*
*The problem is **whether** you should ever borrow money.*

3 *whether . . . or* introduces two alternatives. It means 'It doesn't matter if . . . or . . .':

***Whether** you're old **or** young you'd love it.*
*Politics is a funny old game – **whether** 'funny peculiar' **or** 'funny ha-ha' is a matter of opinion of course.* (= whether 'funny meaning strange' or 'funny meaning something to laugh at . . .')

▶ See also **be 2e**

4 whether or not

Although 'if . . . or not' is possible (▶ See **1** above), only *whether* can immediately be followed by *or not*:

*Could you tell me **whether or not** this recording is available as a cassette tape?*
*Therefore, **whether or not** it was true in fact, a large number of people claimed that the rising costs were caused by government policy.*

which

1 which: pronoun and determiner used in questions   ▶ Compare **what**

a *which* is used in asking questions about limited choices.
When *which* is the subject of a question the word order is *which* + VERB, but when it is the object we need the pattern *which* + AUXILIARY + SUBJECT + VERB:

***Which** influences you most – television or newpapers, or books?*
***Which** teacher told you that? I didn't!*
***Which** of these do you prefer?*
***Which** course books are we using – the blue or the red?*

b In indirect questions, ordinary SUBJECT-VERB word order is used:
*I asked her **which** of the books she preferred.*

c We can also use *which* + *to*-INFINITIVE in indirect questions:

(Which one shall I take?) *She asked me **which** one to take.*

d The usual question pronoun on its own for people is *who* (See **who**). But *which* is used in various ways to refer to people. This is particularly so when the choice is limited.

So, if someone is showing you a photograph of several people, you could say:

Which (one) is you? (NOT **Who is you?*)

We also, in modern English, say *Which of . . .* (NOT **Who of . . .*):
Which of *you knows the answer?*
Which of *your friends have you invited?*

2 which: relative pronoun ▶ Compare **who; that**

a As a relative pronoun, *which* usually refers to things, not people. In defining clauses, it is a formal alternative to *that*:
I'm looking for a phone box **which/that** *works.*
This is the third phone box (**which/that**) *I've tried.*
I've lost the bit of paper (**which/that**) *I wrote the number down on.*

b PREPOSITION + *which*
In a relative clause with a preposition we must use *which* (not *that*) if we put the preposition at the beginning of the clause. We can also use *which* in the pattern PRONOUN (or NUMBER) + *of which*:
I've lost the bit of paper **on which** *I wrote down the number.* (NOT **on that I wrote . . .*)
A soldier was jailed for thirty years yesterday for shooting three of his friends in a bank robbery – a crime **from which** *they had no chance of escaping alive.*
She's got 5000 stamps, some **of which** *are really valuable.*

c *which* is sometimes used (instead of *who*) when talking about small children:
Babies **which** (or *that*) *are born early are at risk.*

d In non-defining relative clauses about things – clauses that add extra information – *which* (NOT *that) is used. We cannot leave *which* out, even when it is an object, and we must use commas to show where the clause is:
British Telecom, **which** *runs the telephones in Britain, is not a government department.*
My number, **which** *I'll give you, is not in the phone book.*
Here's a copy of today's Times, **which** *you asked me for.* (very formally – *. . .* **for which** *you asked me*)

e Sometimes in rather formal English, the *which*-CLAUSE contains a new noun:
I suppose they may have missed the plane, **in which case** *they won't be here until tomorrow.* (= . . . and in that case . . .)
It is a serious political book, the anger **behind which** *is very real.* (= and the anger behind the book is . . .)
Elvedon, the house in Suffolk, the contents **of which** *Lord Iveagh is selling this week, was not a very comfortable place.* (▶ Compare **whose**)

f SENTENCE RELATIVE PRONOUN
Sometimes a relative clause refers not to just the previous noun, but to the whole sentence. *Which* is essential here (never *that*). Compare these sentences:
James lent me his guidebook, **which** *was torn but still usable.* (= the book)
James lent me his guidebook, **which** *was very kind of him.* (= his action)
He had an adoring mother, **who** *absolutely spoilt him.* (= his mother)
He had an adoring mother, **which** *was not good for his character.* (= having such a mother)

3 Grammatically, *which*-CLAUSES in indirect questions (**1b** and **c**) are noun clauses as objects. *Which*-CLAUSES and *which* + *to*-INFINITIVE can also be subjects of sentences and replace simple nouns in other ways. (▶ Compare **what**):

> **Which** *course books to use is not my problem.*
> *We were talking about* **which** *books you would prefer.*
> *It's really a question of* **which** *would be more useful.*

---

whichever: determiner and pronoun ▶ Compare **whatever**

1 *whichever* is used as an emphatic form of *which*. It usually suggests some criticism or surprise:

> *They both sound horrible.* **Whichever** *did you choose?*

2 *whichever* is also used with the meaning 'any one – out of a limited number':

> *I'm free all next week – come* **whichever** *day suits you best.*

3 *whichever* is also used in separate clauses that mean 'It doesn't matter which . . .' 'It doesn't make any difference which . . .':

> **Whichever** *school you go to, you'll make friends.*
> *Cynthia always wants something different,* **whichever** *programme I choose.*

4 whichever or **whatever**?

The difference between these two is the same as the difference between *which* and *what*. *Whichever* suggests a limited choice; *whatever* is unlimited:

> *Readers of* **whatever** *age, or* **whichever** *sex, will be caused to think about the experience.*

---

while

1 while: conjunction

The form *whilst* is also used but is rare and formal.

a *while/whilst* refers to states or actions that last some time. It is not used (▶ Contrast *when*) for very short actions:

> *I did what I could for him* **while** *he was in prison.*
> **While** *he was asleep with his head on the driving wheel, a policeman noticed him at 3.30 in the morning.*
> *Harry came to coffee* **while** *Dulcie had her hair set.*
> *Somebody always telephones* **while/whilst** *I'm having a bath.*
> **While** *you were enjoying yourself, I was slaving over a hot stove.*
> *They tried/were trying to do their homework* **while** *the others watched/were watching TV.*
> *She and Lady Hayward collected some things on Sunday* **while/whilst** *James was away.*

b *while/whilst* can also mean 'although', but with this meaning the *while/whilst*-CLAUSE cannot follow its main clause:
While everybody says litter is a problem, few people do anything about it.
The distinction between the old and the new, while/whilst it cannot be absolute, seems to be firm enough to be useful.

c • but on the other hand; whereas
You seem to think we need more government spending, while many of us think we need lower taxes.

d *while/whilst* can be used with shortened clauses:
She told me that whilst on holiday she had hardly any trouble with her knee.
Reports indicated that, while lacking professional knowledge and experience, he showed considerable ability. (= although)

2 while: noun

• a period of time
I've waited a long while/quite a while/some while for this.
A while back (= some time ago) *Peugeot exhibited in Paris a bike designed by Courrèges.*

who, whom: pronouns

Strictly speaking, and in formal English, *who* is only a subject pronoun, and *whom* should be used as the object of a verb or preposition. But in fact *who* is frequently used in these positions, and *whom* is becoming rare.

1 who, whom: pronouns in questions ▶ Compare **what; which**

• what person/people

a When *who* is the subject of the verb, the word order is *who* + VERB, but if *who/whom* is object then we need *who(m)* + AUXILIARY + SUBJECT + VERB:
Who was that on the phone? Who was it?
Who told you that?
Who are those people over there?
Who(m) do you mean?
Who(m) are you talking about?
Who(m) does that birdcage belong to?

b In indirect questions, the word order is SUBJECT + VERB:
I asked her who had told her.
I asked her who(m) she meant.

c In indirect questions we can use *who(m)* + *to*-INFINITIVE:
I wish I knew who(m) to ask.

d *whom*, not *who*, must be used if we put a preposition in front of the pronoun:
Who(m) are you talking to?
To whom are you referring?
It is difficult to know to whom one should talk.

2 who, whom: relative pronouns ▶ Compare **that; which**

a In defining clauses about people, *who/whom* are formal alternatives to *that*:
> *The man **who/that** came to mend the telephone said the public were always complaining.*
> *The person **(who/whom/that)** you need is not here.*
> *Are you the lady **(who/whom/that)** I spoke to before?*

b In non-defining relative clauses about people, – clauses that add extra information about people we already know about – *who/whom* (NOT **that*) are used. We cannot omit *who/whom*, and we must use commas:
> *Damages of £332,000 (= payment for injury) were paid to the family of Mr Paul Turner, **who** was killed in a car crash.*
> *The poet Sir John Betjeman, **who** died in 1984 at the age of 77, was known to millions through his television appearances.*
> *Alfred Austen, **who/whom** few people now remember, was a popular poet in his day.*

c PREPOSITION + **whom**
If we put a preposition before the relative pronoun, we need *whom* (NOT *who* or *that*) – whether in defining or non-defining clauses. We can also use a PRONOUN (or NUMBER) + *of whom*:
> *Are you the lady **to whom** I was speaking before?*
> *There were a lot of people in the hotel, some **of whom** had been coming for many years.*

d *who* can be used with words referring to groups of people if we are thinking of the people as individuals. This is true of defining and non-defining clauses. Notice the plural verbs, etc.:
> *Only a government **who** listen to their people are really democratic.*
> *The government, **who** are anxious to reduce unemployment, have several new training schemes.*

Compare:
> *The government, **which** was elected last year, intends to make some major changes.*

who can also be used of animals if we think of them as individuals:
> *Our neighbour's parrot, **who** is actually quite friendly, says some very rude things.*

e Wrong use of *whom*
Some people try too hard to use *who* and *whom* correctly, and in fact use *whom* when *who* would be more correct:
> **Like many novelists she disliked critics, **whom** she felt didn't understand her books. (= **who** . . . didn't understand . . .)*

3 who, whom

who and *whom*-clauses can be used as subjects of sentences and in other noun-like positions:
> ***Who(m)** you marry is for you to decide.*
> *We were talking about **who(m)** to invite.*
> *It's a secret **who** gave the money.*

whoever: pronoun

1. *whoever* can be used as an emphatic form of the *who* (or *whom*) used in questions, and in this sense is sometimes written as two words. It usually suggests criticism or surprise:
   Whoever/Who ever *would want to live at the South Pole?*
   Whoever/Who ever *do you mean?*

2. *whoever* is also used with the meaning 'anyone that' 'whatever person':
   Bring **whoever** *you like to the party.*
   Whoever *told you that had got it all wrong.*

3. *whoever* is also used in separate clauses with the meaning 'no matter who . . .', 'it doesn't make any difference who . . .':
   I wouldn't go to that sort of concert, **whoever** *asked me.*

whole

1. **whole**: adjective and noun   ▶ Compare **all**

A			
the this/that our . . .	**whole**	committee/family/school . . . experience/idea/plan . . . house/day . . . (SINGULAR NOUNS) time/truth . . .
B			
a/one	**whole**	day . . . tin of beans (SINGULAR NOUNS) sheep
(two . . .)		days, . . . tins of beans . . . (PLURAL NOUNS) sheep
C			
the **whole** of		Africa/London/October . . . last year . . . the family . . . (SINGULAR NOUNS) that day . . . our house . . .

a. *whole* is an adjective (not a determiner like *all*), although the meaning is sometimes similar. It is mainly used with singular count nouns, and is used in the pattern DETERMINER + *whole* + NOUN, as shown (**A**):

*The **whole** committee agreed.*
*Our **whole** idea was to hire camels and explore the desert. (= our one idea)*
*It rained the **whole** time we were on holiday. (Compare the word order in It rained **all** the time.)*
*You have to speak the truth, the **whole** truth and nothing but the truth.*

b We can use *a/one* + *whole* + SINGULAR COUNT NOUN or NUMBER + *whole* + PLURAL NOUN (**B**). These nouns are often units of time (e.g., days) or for 'concrete' things that we can see and touch. The meaning is 'complete and not divided up':
*We hadn't eaten for three **whole** days.*
*They cooked a **whole** sheep for us.*

Compare *They cooked **all** (of) the sheep* – which means every bit of it, but probably cut up first. *Sheep* could also be plural here of course, so *all the sheep* could actually also mean all three (or some other number of) sheep.
Whole + PLURAL NOUN (with no determiner or number) means complete or entire:
***Whole** books have been written on this one little subject.*
***Whole** pages were missing from my library book.*

c *the whole of . . .* can be used before SINGULAR COUNT NOUNS (**C**). We must use this before proper names:
*The **whole** of Europe is industrialised. (NOT *(The) **whole** Europe . . .)*
*It rained (for) the **whole** of October.*

With nouns that already have a determiner that makes them definite (*the*, *this . . . my . . .*) it is possible to say:
*the **whole** of the family . . . the **whole** of that day . . . the **whole** of our house*
or:
*the **whole** family . . . that **whole** day . . . our **whole** house*

2 on the whole

on the whole means 'generally', 'mostly, but not entirely':
***On the whole** I don't like his books, but I enjoyed his last novel.*

3 whole: adverb

*If you swallow these pills **whole**, you won't notice the taste.*

whom ▶ See **who**

whose

● of whom; of which

1 whose: question word

As a question word, both in direct and in indirect questions, *whose* usually refers to people who own things:
***Whose** is this umbrella? **Whose** umbrella is this?*
*I'm wondering **whose** coat this is.*
***Whose** life is it anyway?*

2 whose: possessive relative pronoun and determiner

a As a relative pronoun or determiner, *whose* can be used in both defining and non-defining clauses:
*Someone **whose** health is as bad as that can't be expected to do a full-time job.*
*Rutherford, **whose** discoveries about atoms changed twentieth century science, was a New Zealander by birth.*

b PREPOSITION + **whose**
We can put a preposition in front of *whose*, and we can use it in the pattern PRONOUN (or NUMBER) *of whose*:
*Neil Harrison, a twenty-five year-old law student at the University, three of **whose** uncles were killed in the war, said . . .*
(***whose** three uncles* would mean he only had three uncles; *three of **whose*** . . . means he had more than three)

c Some people dislike the use of *whose* with things, but this is quite common:
*This is an idea **whose** time has come, Mr Aitken added.* (= it is now the time to act on this idea)
*Malta, **whose** waters a recent survey showed to be the cleanest in the Mediterranean, . . .* (waters = the sea. From an advertisement for a Maltese hotel.)

d **whose** or **who's**?
These sound the same, but are quite different. *Who's* means 'who is' or 'who has'. Compare:
***Whose** is this bag? **Whose** bag is this?*
***Who's** left a bag on the floor?*
***Who's** asking?*

3 *whose* clauses can be subjects and objects:
*I was wondering **whose** umbrella I could borrow/**whose** umbrella to borrow.*
*Exactly **whose** story we should believe is a problem.*

why

1 why: question word

We use *why* to ask the reason for something:
a * **Why** are you worried? It's not serious.*
*   **Why** don't you like this rice pudding? What's wrong with it?*
*   **Why** don't you invite her out?* (a suggestion)
*   **Why** can't a woman be more like a man?*
*   **Why** are we waiting?*
*   **Why** do you ask?*

b Sometimes *why* (+ *not*) + INFINITIVE is used to make a suggestion:
*'I'm going to ask him for the money.' 'Oh, **why** bother? **Why** not just forget it?'* (= why do you bother? I suggest that you forget it.)

2 why: adverb/conjunction

a Ordinary SUBJECT-VERB word order is used in indirect questions:
*(**Why** do you like rats?) He asked me **why** I like(d) rats.*

b   why-CLAUSES (like other wh-CLAUSES) can also be subjects of verbs, objects of prepositions and so on:
 Why she ever married him is a mystery.
 We were talking about why some people stick pins through their ears.

c   why-CLAUSES can also sometimes describe nouns, rather like relative clauses:
 The reason why this furniture is expensive is that it is entirely made by hand.

3   why: exclamation

a   *why* is used as a sort of surprised exclamation:
 Why! It's Marie Scott, isn't it? What are you doing here? You remember me . . .

b   There is no word **whyever*, but we can use *why ever* as an emphatic surprised question:
 Why ever did she marry that horrid little man?

---

wide, wider, widest: adjective and adverb ▶ Compare long

- measuring from side to side, or to a great distance from one side to the other
  A football field is 110 metres long and 73 metres wide.
  The garage was only wide enough for a small car.
  The path was only two feet across at the widest point.
  I couldn't open my mouth any wider, so my dentist had rather a job.
  I was wide awake all night. (= completely awake)

---

wife: noun

wife belongs to a small group of words ending in *-fe* where the plural ends in *-ves*:
 The wives were all discussing their husbands.

Other words with *-ves* plurals include:
 half, knife, leaf, life, loaf, self, shelf, thief, wolf.

---

will: modal verb   ▶ Compare shall; would

The short form is *'ll* and the negative is *will not/won't*
will refers to present or future time, and has two main kinds of meaning – some practical (**1–3**) and others theoretical (**4–6**). Some uses partly combine both meanings. Practical meanings are concerned with people's will power, how hard they try to do things.

1   Willingness

will is often used in requests, orders, invitations and offers:
 Will you help me with the shopping? (request)
 I'll do it. Of course I will. (offer)
 Will you please make less noise? (order)

> *Will you have some more tea?* (invitation)
> *If you will just fill in this form . . .* (request)
> *Let us know how you get on, won't you?* (request)
> *Don't worry about it, will you?*

2 Intention

will is also used for promises and threats:

> *I'll go immediately. I won't wait.*
> *What will you do now?*
> *I'll never forgive you!*
> *I'll murder you.* (threat)

3 Strong insistence

With the word *will* stressed, and never shortened to *'ll*, this use of *will* focuses mainly on present time:

> *If you will go to discos every night, I'm not surprised you're always tired.*
> *He won't listen to reason – he just does whatever he wants.*

4 Theory

a This is the future meaning familiar from old grammar books:

> *She'll be thirty in the year 2000.*
> *It will be a pity if you don't see them.* (a future condition)
> *What will you do if your mother finds out?*
> *We won't know until the end of the month.*
> *This time next week, I'll be skiing.* (Note the progressive tense here. The future is an already arranged fact. *I'll ski* could mean a sudden decision now to ski next week.)

b This *will* is also used to give very firm orders, using 2nd and 3rd person:

> *You will do as you are told – don't argue.*
> *The last person to leave will lock the door.*

5 Habit

will is used with a present or 'timeless' meaning when we can safely 'predict' something – we can be certain about it – because it is always true or because it is somebody's habit:

> *This bottle won't hold more than a litre.*
> *Glass will often break if you pour boiling water on to it.*
> *A dog will usually find its way home.*
> *Boys will be boys!* (= you must expect boys to behave like boys)

6 Deduction about the present

will can also be used for a deduction (an opinion based on reason) about something now – we are nearly certain, even though we cannot see whatever it is:

> *That will be Paul – he said he was going to ring.* (= a remark on hearing the telephone)
> *He'll be ringing from a call-box, I expect.*

7 will have + PAST PARTICIPLE

a *will have* + PAST PARTICIPLE is called the 'future perfect tense' in some grammar books:

> *I/He* **will have** *left school by this time next year.*

But other modals can of course be used in this way to talk about the future with greater or lesser degrees of certainty (*I/you/he* etc. . . . *may/might/could . . . and I/we shall/should . . . have left . . .*)

b We can also use *will have* + PAST PARTICIPLE to make rather confident guesses about present or even past time:

> *Don't telephone yet – they* **won't have** *finished dinner.*
> *That house* **will have** *been pulled down years ago – it was empty and falling to pieces when I last saw it in 1950.*

---

wish: verb ▶ Compare **hope; want**

---

wish +	*that*-CLAUSE (o+) *to*-INFINITIVE IO + OBJECT *for . . .*

wish is not often used in the progressive

1

a *that*-CLAUSES after *wish* use 'past' tenses with a hypothetical meaning, because when we wish we are imagining things being different, just as we do in imaginary conditional sentences. (See **if**). Examples:

THE FACTS	THE WISHES
I didn't have a holiday last year.	*I* **wish** *I had had one.*
I couldn't have one.	*I* **wish** *I could have (had one.)*
I haven't finished my homework.	*I* **wish** *I had (finished it.)*
I spent/have spent all my money.	*I* **wish** *I hadn't (spent it).*
You can't remember Bob's address.	*You* **wish** *you could (remember it.)*
You don't know what to do.	*You* **wish** *you knew . . .*
You feel sick.	*You* **wish** *you didn't (feel sick.)*
He's got a headache.	*He* **wishes** *he hadn't (got one.)*
He's too fat.	*He* **wishes** *he weren't/wasn't.*
It's snowing.	*We* **wish** *it wasn't/weren't snowing.*
Her leg is going to take a long time to heal.	*She* **wishes** *it wasn't/weren't going to (take a long time.)*

b To describe past wishes, we also use past simple for something that was not true at the time of the wish; past perfect for something earlier, and *would* for a 'future-in-the-past':

FACT: Her father was dead. WISHES: *She* **wished** *her father was still alive.*
She **wished** *her father had not died.*
She **wished** *something nice would happen.*

c *Would* is not used with wishes about states:

FACT: WISHES:
You don't like it.   *I **wish** you liked it.* (NOT **I **wish** you would like it.*)
She will be 50 next year.   *She **wishes** she wasn't/weren't going to be.* (NOT **She **wishes** she wouldn't be.*)

Would can however be used in wishes where the meaning is willingness or insistence, and in wishes about future actions:

FACT   WISHES:
He keeps/will keep saying every-   *I **wish** he didn't/wouldn't (keep*
thing twice.   *saying everything twice.)*
Will you come and visit us soon?   *We **wish** you would (come and visit us soon).*
It is snowing.   *I **wish** it would stop snowing.*

Note that we cannot *wish* about our own willingness to do something now or in the future:

FACT: I make mistakes.
WISHES: *I **wish** I didn't make so many mistakes.* (now)
          *My teacher **wishes** I would stop making them.* (in the future)
          But NOT **I **wish** I would stop making them.*

Compare:
I hope I don't/won't make so many mistakes next time.

d *wish* (+ OBJECT) + *to*-INFINITIVE is similar to *want* (+ OBJECT) + *to*-INFINITIVE, but more formal:

*We **wish** to inform our customers that we shall be closed from 7th to 21st August for our annual holidays.*
*'Do you **wish** me to put this in writing?' 'Oh, do whatever you **wish**. Please do as you **wish**.'*

e *wish* can take two objects, but mainly in a few fixed phrases:

*We **wish** you a merry Christmas and a happy New Year.*
***Wish** me luck – I've an exam tomorrow.*

f Unlike *want*, *wish* does not take a single object, but *wish* + *for* is possible, though not very usual:

*The princess had everything she could possible **wish for** – except a handsome prince!*

g *wish* can also be used without any object or following phrase:

*Shut your eyes and **wish**!*
***Wishing** won't change your life – do something!*

2 wish: noun (C)

a • hope; desire
*We understand your **wish** to help, but . . .*

*The princess made a **wish**, and soon her **wish** came true – a tall, dark handsome prince arrived at the castle.*

b At the end of a friendly letter people often write:
*Best **wishes**, Yours (Sylvia)*
or
*Best **wishes** to all the family/to Peter/to you both/ . . .*
*Give your father my best **wishes**.*

1
a ● having

The opposite of *with* is *without*:
*a house **with** two bathrooms . . . a couple **with** five children . . .*
*a room **with** a view . . . a book **with** lots of pictures . . .*

b ● accompanying; together
*She's now living **with** her daughter.*
*Bring your passport **with** you.*
*Come and have dinner **with** us.*
*You can't do business **with** dishonest people.*
*I can't keep up **with** the others – they are too quick.*
*I'm **with** you there. (= I agree with you).*
*Are you **with** me or against me?*

c ● using (a particular thing); because of; in a particular manner
*Cut it open **with** a knife.*
*The table was covered **with** a sheet.*
*They were shivering **with** cold.*
*They were blue **with** cold.*
*Fill the jug **with** water.*
*Don't eat **with** your fingers.*
*I bought this **with** my prize money.*
*You have to mix these paints **with** water.*
*Treat this **with** care. (= carefully)*

d ● concerning; regarding; in connection with
*I'm pleased/annoyed/cross **with** him.*
*I agree/disagree **with** you.*
*Do keep in touch **with** us, and write regularly.*
*What's the matter **with** you?*
*That's got nothing to do **with** you.*
*How are you getting on **with** your new neighbours?*
*Are you in love **with** her?*

e Sometimes *with* introduces a sort of clause, and has a 'because' meaning:
***With** Charles at home ill, I can't get out much. (= because Charles is at home ill . . .)*
*It is difficult to get to sleep **with** crowds of people dancing in the street outside your window.*

2 with and by

with refers to the thing we use for doing something. *By* is used – when we use a passive verb – for the agent of an action, including non-personal agents:

*When a reporter said, 'Mr Hattersley, you were hit over the head **by** a chair.' Mr Hattersley replied, 'No, I was hit over the head **with** a chair **by** a demonstrator.'* (newspaper report)

Compare also:

*The fire was probably started **by** a cigarette.* (= a carelessly thrown away cigarette probably caused the accident.)
*The fire was probably started **with** a lighted cigarette.* (= Somebody who wanted to start a fire probably used a lighted cigarette.)
*The cyclist was struck **by** lightning.* (= a non-human agent)
*The cyclist was attacked **with** a hammer.* (= an unnamed human agent used a hammer)

within: preposition

a • in less than; inside

*He said there would be mass unemployment **within** fifteen years unless the education system was adapted to the computer age.*
*Anyway, I hope to hear from you **within** the not too distant future.* (= soon)
*Why did romance escape from me, always slipping away just when I thought it was **within** my grasp?* (= when I thought I could reach it.)
*His blood pressure was **within** normal limits.*

b *within* is a more formal word than *inside*, and when talking of actual places it is usually only used for large places:

*I was then working as a teacher at the Lubivi Senior School **within** the palace grounds.*

c within + NOUN + of . . .

Notice this pattern:

*The book was sold out **within** three weeks of publication.* (= less than three weeks after publication)
*The rabbit stayed until they came **within** a few feet of it, before running away.*
*I'd need a house **within** walking distance of a station and a church.* (= near enough for me to walk to these places)

without: preposition and adverb

a • not having something

*a house **without** a garage . . . people **without** children . . . a book **without** an index . . .*
*I can't cut this meat **without** a knife.*
***Without** doubt, this is the most important step in his career.* (= There is no doubt that . . .)
*You mustn't travel **without** a ticket.*
*We couldn't have managed **without** Wendy.* (= without Wendy's help)

b • alone; not together
*Please wait. Don't go **without** me.*
*If I can't afford a new coat, I shall have to do **without**/go **without** (one).*

c *without* is often followed by an *-ing* CLAUSE:
*It's wrong to travel **without** paying your fare.*
*I can't give you an answer **without** checking the figures. (= unless I check . . .)*

---

woman (plural **women**): noun   ▶ Compare **man**

The word *woman*, and other nouns that include the ending *-woman*, make their plurals *-women*:
*There were crowds of **women** and children waiting at the station.*
*There should be more **women** doctors.*

Also ***Englishwomen* . . . *policewomen* . . . *sportswomen* . . .**

---

won't   ▶ See **will**

---

work

1 work: verb

work is used without and with objects

a When people *work* they use some effort, particularly at a job:
*I'd like to stop **working** and retire.*
*He's **worked** as a bus-driver, a teacher and a tourist guide.*
*She **worked** for the government/in a factory/until she was sixty.*
*If you don't **work** hard at school, you won't pass your exams.*

b When things *work* they function properly, they succeed:
*The lift wasn't **working** and we had to walk up five floors.*
*Your plan is rather difficult, but it might **work**.*
*They've decided that communism does not **work**.*

c **work** + OBJECT
• make something (or someone) work
*These old machines were **worked** by water power.*
*Tim **works** his staff far too hard.*

2 work: noun   ▶ Compare **job**

work is usually uncountable

a • employment; occupation; a person's job, usually for money
*What time do you go to **work**?/leave **work**?*
*He's looking for **work**, but he's still out of **work**.*
*She even takes **work** on holiday.*
*They don't do much **work** in that class.*

b • effort, contrasted with rest or leisure
*You'll never get anywhere in life without hard **work**.*
*There's a lot of **work** going on in cancer research.*

c • things produced, results of actions
*The pictures were her own **work**. (= nobody helped her)*
*These crimes are the **work** of terrorists.*

d As a count noun, a work is a book, a painting, etc.:
*'The Sunflowers' is perhaps Van Gogh's most famous **work**. (= his most famous painting)*
*He claims to have read the complete **works** of Shakespeare. (= all his plays and poems)*

worse, worst

worse and *worst* are the opposites of *better* and *best*

1 worse, worst: adjectives

a comparative and superlative of *bad*:
*Her pain has become **worse** over the last few months.*
*In the new edition the bad jokes have been replaced by **worse** ones.*
*It was the **worst** earthquake in San Francisco for many years – though it could have been (much/far/even) **worse**.*
*What a boring book – quite the **worst** he's ever written.*

b comparative and superlative of *ill* or *bad* (relating to health):
*I'm feeling terrible – much **worse** than yesterday. I'll have to go back to bed.*

2 worse, worst: adverbs

comparative and superlative of *badly*:
*People who behave **worse** than animals will not be stopped by these notices.*
*I've done some work and hope that everyone else has done less and does **worse** in the exams.*

3 worse, worst: nouns

*Everything seemed to go wrong for him that first year in America, but **worse** was to follow.*
*If **the worst** comes to **the worst**, he knew he could always teach. (= if he could find no other job)*
*They do say exams bring out **the worst** in people. (= exams make people behave badly)*

worth

1 worth: preposition

If we say something is *worth* an amount, we think somebody would pay that much for it. If we say something is *worth doing* or *worth it*, we mean that it is a good thing to do.

a   *They were amazed how much the picture was **worth**.*
*My car isn't **worth** more than £100 or so now; it's simply not **worth** repairing.*
*His promises aren't **worth** the paper they're written on. (= they are **worth** nothing.)*
*I don't suppose there are any tickets left for tonight's show – but it's **worth** asking just in case.*
*We worked hard decorating the flat, and the results were **worth** it. (= It was **worth** working hard.)*
*'He's awfully badly educated', she said, 'and doesn't know anything **worth** knowing about.'*

b   **worth (somebody's) while**
   ● worth the time, effort, etc
   *It isn't **worth (my) while** going because I'd only have two hours there.*
   *It would be **worth while** admitting her to hospital.*

   Do not confuse with *worthwhile*, a one-word adjective:
   *Was your journey **worthwhile**?*
   *Yes, the whole thing was a **worthwhile** project.*

2   **worth**: noun

   ● value
   *First prize is a holiday for two in the West Indies, and there are £5000 **worth** of other prizes.*
   *The company believes it will lose between £4 and £5 million pounds' **worth** of business this year – a 20% drop from last year's figures.*
   *He bought a pound's **worth** of chocolates and ate the lot.*

would: modal verb

   The short form of *would* is *'d* and the negative is *would not/wouldn't*.
   Like *will*, *would* has practical meanings concerned with people's willpower, their intentions, and also theoretical meanings concerned with 'predicting', with using one's reason to guess that something is so. Some uses combine more than one meaning. *Would* has present and future meaning (**1, 2, 4**) as well as past (**3, 4**).

1   Willingness, intention, insistence   ▶ Compare   **will**

   would is sometimes a more polite alternative to *will* in requests:
   ***Would** you help me with the shopping?*
   ***Would** you wait a moment, please?*
   *If you **would** just fill in this form . . .*
   *Please help, **would** you? (a polite order)*

2   Theory

a   **Deduction**
   would is sometimes an alternative to *will* in making a deduction, a reasonable guess, about the present:
   *That **wouldn't** be Paul telephoning – he'd be away now, surely.*

b **Hypothesis/condition** ▶ Compare **should**

would is widely used in the main clause of a sentence about unreal conditions:

*It **would** be a pity if you didn't see them tomorrow.*
*You **would** learn more if you listened.*
*If I were a fish, I **would** swim away from here.*
*I'**d** be amazed if I ever became famous.*
*I **wouldn't** go parachuting even if you paid me.*

c Frequently a condition is suggested, even without an *if*-clause:

*'Why don't you marry a millionaire?' 'Where **would** I find a millionaire?'*
(i.e., 'even if I wanted one'. Where **will** I find one? suggests I do want one.)

d *would* is also used after *If only* and the verb *wish* to express wishes about the present or future:

*I wish you **wouldn't** shout.*
*If only you **would** lend me some money.*

e **Politeness** ▶ Compare **should**; **could**

The sense of condition can make *would* rather polite:

*I **would/should** keep quiet about it.* (advice)
*I **would/should** guess it's expensive.* (a polite opinion)
*I **would/should** hope/imagine that . . .*

Would you like . . . is often used in invitations and replies:

***Would** you like a drink?* (or *Will you have a drink?*)
*Oh, I'**d** love one. Thanks.*

3 Past ▶ Compare **used to**

a *would* often refers to a past habit. If you wanted to do something, and insisted on doing it, then you probably often did it:

*When we were children we **would** often walk to school and spend our bus money on sweets.*
*My mother **would** get cross when she found out, but she **wouldn't** tell my father.*

b *would* can also have more definite meanings of willingness, intention or insistence in the past – possibly on one single occasion:

*They **would** insist on driving me home after the party. They **wouldn't** hear of me getting a taxi.* (= refused to let me get a taxi)
*I wanted somebody to explain everything, but nobody **would** tell me anything.*
*If he **would** go to discos, no wonder he was tired.*
*You **would** go and forget when I specially asked you to remember.* (= that was typical of you)

c *would* is used in indirect speech as the past of *will*:

('Will/**Would** you help me?') *He asked if I **would** help him.*
('Tom won't listen to reason.') *She told me Tom **wouldn't** listen to reason.*

d **Prediction**

would is used for the future-in-the-past, that is looking from some past time to what was then the future:

*It was a long cold winter, but eventually the spring **would** come with the flowers and the longer days.*

For me this journey in the heat of the summer served as an apprenticeship (= a period of training) *to the five years I **would** later spend in Africa.* (and which the writer later did spend there)

4 would have + PAST PARTICIPLE

a   *would have* + PAST PARTICIPLE is often used in the main clause of unreal past conditions:
   *If he had been invited he **would** certainly **have** gone.* (= he was not invited and so did not go)
   Sometimes the condition is only suggested and *would have* + PAST PARTICIPLE is used to express an opinion:
   *I **would have** told your mother.* (= That is what you should have done.)

b   A less usual meaning is that probably something did happen or has happened:
   *Bob and Sue **would have** arrived by now, surely?*
   *I suppose so. They **wouldn't have** missed the plane, surely?*

   These are less certain guesses than *must have arrived* or *will have missed.*
   ▶   See also   *would rather* at **rather**; *would sooner* at **soon**

---

wrong and wrongly   ▶ Compare   right

1   wrong: adjective and adverb

   ● not right; bad(ly); unsatisfactory/unsatisfactorily

a   *That's the **wrong** answer.*
   *This is the **wrong** time of year to plant roses.*
   *We're on the **wrong** road. Can't you read the map?*
   *Every time I try and telephone her, I get a **wrong** number.*
   *It's **wrong** of her not to repay the money.*
   *You were **wrong** to tell her about her husband.*
   *They were **wrong** about the weather – we had a storm.*

b   *wrong* is used with *what/anything/nothing/something* in sentences like the following to ask if there is, or to say that there is a problem:
   *You look terrible. What's **wrong**?*
   *There's nothing **wrong** with me at all – I'm just tired.*
   *I think there's something **wrong** with the car.*
   ▶   Compare   **the matter**

c   *wrong* is often used as a COMPLEMENT:
   *I got my sums **wrong**. I'll have to do them again.*
   *We tried to bring the children up properly, and now look at them! Where did we go **wrong**?*
   *Something's gone **wrong** with the washing machine.*
   *Don't get me **wrong** (= misunderstand me). I'm not complaining . . .*

2   wrong: noun (C, U)

   *There are usually rights and **wrongs** on both sides.*
   *If I'm in the **wrong**, I'll apologise.* (= if I have done something **wrong**)
   *These people don't seem to know the difference between right and **wrong**.*

3 **wrongly**: adverb

wrong is the usual adverb in certain positions in a sentence, and when used with certain verbs (see **1c** above). *Wrongly* is used before a past participle, and as a sentence adverb:

*The letter was **wrongly** addressed, and my name was **wrongly** spelt.* (or . . . *was spelt **wrong/wrongly**.*)
*She was **wrongly** accused of being a terrorist.*
*They believed – quite **wrongly** – that the world was flat.*

---

year: noun

a The meaning is sometimes a calendar year (e.g. 1066, 1990) and sometimes a period of twelve months:

*That was the **year** we moved house.*
*I haven't seen Julia for nearly a **year**.*

b **last/next . . . year**   ▶ Compare **last**

We do not use *the* in the expressions *last year* and *next year*, when they are seen from now, the present moment:

*I haven't seen him since last **year**.*
*Count your cherry stones and see when you're going to get married – this **year**, next **year**, some time, never!*

We do need *the* when the meaning is 'final'.

*That was **the last year** tourists could get into Afghanistan.*

Notice also:

*See you in **the New Year**.* (= early in January)
*See you on **New Year's Day**.* (no *the* – a proper name)

---

yes

yes is the opposite of *no*

1 used to express willingness, to agree . . .
*'Is this book for language learners?' '**Yes**, it is.'*
*'It's a nice day, isn't it?' '**Yes**, lovely'.*
*'Aren't you ready?' '**Yes**, I'm just coming.'*
*'Please let me have this back by Friday.' '**Yes**, of course.'*

2 We use *yes* (not *no*) when we disagree with a negative statement and then add a positive affirmative one:
*'You don't like milk, do you?' '**Yes**, I do. I love it.'*

3 *yes* is also used to show that someone has heard what is being said:
*'Judith!' '**Yes**?'* (= What is it?)

---

or to encourage a speaker to continue:
'I was terribly unhappy. I simply didn't know what to do.'
'Yes, so what happened?'

---

yesterday ▶ See **tomorrow**

---

yet ▶ Compare **already; still**

1 yet: adverb

- up to this/that time:

a *yet* usually takes end position, though mid-position is possible, and is mainly used in questions and negative sentences. With action verbs, perfect tenses are used in British English when we are talking about now:
Have you written to your parents yet? (*Did you write . . . yet?* is possible in American English)
No, not yet.
'Is Paula all right?' 'We don't know yet. We haven't heard yet.'

b If we are talking about the past (with *yet* meaning 'up till then') again we use a perfect tense for an action or event, but a simple past for a state. Notice the preferred word order:
I was young then and hadn't yet decided on my career.
She wasn't yet 18 when she went to live in Paris.

c *yet* is possible in affirmative sentences – often with *be*, *have to* or a modal verb. Note the preferred word order. The meaning is rather like *still* but it is more formal:
We must save the rain forests while there is yet time.
I have yet to hear a good reason for taking drugs. (= I still have not heard . . .)
Granny died in 1967, but I can see her yet, sitting in her favourite chair by the window.

d We can also use *yet* with *again*, *another*, *more* and superlatives, as an emphasising word:
So Navratilova was Wimbledon champion yet again.
That's yet another reason why we need a strong defence policy.
You haven't heard half the story – there's a lot more yet.
Brookner's latest novel is her best yet.

e yet or **already**?
We often use *yet* to talk about things that we are expecting to happen, or that we think ought to happen. Somtimes this talk is neutral (we have no special opinion about it) but sometimes we are expressing surprise that the thing has not happened. We are surprised by the delay:
Aren't they married yet? They've been engaged for years.
Have you finished your homework yet? Do hurry up.

This contrasts with *already*, where we are often surprised that something has happened so soon:

*'I hear Madeleine's getting married.' 'Not again! She's been married three times **already**.'*
*Have you **already** finished it? That was quick.*

2 **yet**: conjunction

As a conjunction *yet* is a rather formal alternative to 'but'. Notice though that we can say *and yet*, and *but yet:*

*It's a beautiful picture, **yet** at the same time rather sad.*
*It was a horrible thing to do, **and yet** you can understand it.*
*I suppose he's honest, **but yet** you can never really rely on him, I feel.*

---

you: pronoun ▶ See **your; yours; yourself; yourselves**

Second person subject and object pronoun (singular and plural).

1 **you**: usage

a Unlike the other personal pronouns, which are either subject or object, *you* is both. It is also both singular and plural in meaning, though it must be followed by a plural verb:

__You__ are late again.
*If **you** want me to, I'll help **you**.*
*How very kind of **you**.*
*Somebody saw **you** take it.*
*'Who is this for?' '**You**.'*

b *you* (with plural meaning) can be followed by a NOUN, a NUMBER, *all* or *both*:

*It's time for **you** children to go to bed.*
*Hurry up **you** two, we're all waiting for you.*
*What do **you both** want to do?*
*I want **you all** to be here in fifteen minutes.*

c *you* is often used before *-ing* in structures where *your* is formally correct:

*I don't approve of **you**/**your** asking him.*

but only *you*, not *your*, is correct after verbs of the senses and some other verbs:

*We heard **you** asking him for money.*
*We don't want **you** worrying.*

d *you* + NOUN (singular or plural) is used in exclamations:

__You__ clever girl!
__You__ fools!
__You__ lucky people!

2 **you**: meaning ▶ Compare **one**

you, your, yours, yourself, yourselves can have several meanings.

a *you* being both singular and plural can refer to the person or the people spoken to – or the reader(s):

*Are **you** listening, Tom?*
*Both of **you** are right, of course.*

---

b *you* is often used in an impersonal way to mean people in general, but the speaker/writer and listener/reader are included. *You* is less formal than *one*, which could also be used here:

> *You can't believe everything you read in the papers.*
> *If you don't look after your health, you're in trouble.*

c *you* is also sometimes used when speakers/writers are actually talking about themselves, but perhaps they want to suggest that their experience is shared by other people:

> *No, when you leave your village as a young man, you leave it forever.*
> *'Did you enjoy living on a boat as a child?' 'Well, you got used to it.'*
> *The Prince added: 'You become very conscious that if you try to get to know anybody, the press will probably pursue them.'* (particularly if the newspapers think the Prince has found a new girl friend!)

---

young, younger, youngest: adjective ▶ Compare **new**; **old**

young is the opposite of *old*, mainly when talking about people, animals and plants (i.e. things that grow):

> *You're too young to get married.*
> *As I get older, the policemen look younger and younger.*
> *My sister's a year younger than me, and my brother Philip is the youngest in the family.*

---

your: possessive determiner
▶ See **you**; **yours**; **yourself**; **yourselves**

Second person possessive determiner (singular and plural)

a *How's your father?*
> *Your hands look cold – why don't you wear gloves?*

b *your* is formally and correctly used rather than *you* before some *-ing* patterns:
> *Fancy your/you expecting me to pay.*

c *your* is sometimes used to show that the speaker/writer is talking about some typical example or member of a group:
> *Your average teenager wants to look like everybody else of the same age.*

---

yours: pronoun ▶ See **you**; **your**; **yourself**; **yourselves**

Second person possessive pronoun (singular and plural)

a *I've found my luggage, but where's yours?*
> *I've still got that book of yours.*

b People write *Yours sincerely* or *Yours faithfully* (usually on more formal or business letters) or just *Yours* at the end of a letter before signing their name:

Best wishes,	Best wishes,
Yours,	**Yours sincerely,**
Sylvia	Sylvia Chalker

Second person reflexive pronouns (*yourself* = singular, *yourselves* = plural)

1 yourself/yourselves: reflexive

*Nobody's going to do it for you, Jane. You'll have to do it **yourself**.*
*Come on everybody. You can all help **yourselves** to food.*
*Audrey, you didn't come **by yourself**, did you?*
*I suppose it's lonely living **by yourself**, but some people choose to.* (Notice the general reference to people.)

2 yourself/yourselves: emphatic

*You **yourselves** might not use this dictionary but your children would.*
*But Donald, you said **yourself** (that) you needed a change.*
*You two surely didn't try and mend the car **yourselves**, did you?*

Glossary

active verb tenses are either active or passive. They are active in:
I posted the letter yesterday; *They have built another airport*; *We will send you more details later.*
They are passive in:
The letter was posted yesterday; *Another airport has been built*; *You will be sent more details later.*

adjective a word like *good, difficult, pretty* – used to describe people and things. See **attributive**, **predicative**.

adverb a word like *well, quickly, today, there* – which tells us how, when or where something happens. Other adverbs add to the meaning of adjectives (*very nice*), another adverb (*rather quickly*), or even the whole sentence (*Actually, I don't agree.*)

adverb clause a clause that has the same function in a sentence as an adverb, e.g. *I'll tell you when I see you.* (Compare: *I'll tell you tomorrow*). Other examples: *I'll do it if you ask me nicely* (adverb clause of condition); *I went out to get some fresh air* (adverb clause of purpose).

adverb phrase two or more words that are used in a sentence like an adverb: *at school, yesterday morning*.

affirmative also sometimes called positive – opposite of negative, as in *It is cold*; *I love you*.

agent in a passive sentence the agent is the person (or thing) that the action is done by: *We were shocked by the news*. We also have agents in phrases: *There's going to be a statement by the minister.* (i.e., a statement will be made by . . .).

article *a/an* are called indefinite articles: *the* is the definite article.

assertive some words are mainly used in affirmative statements – *some, plenty* . . . They are called assertive (to assert something means to say that it is definitely true). This is in contrast to words that are mainly used only in questions and negative sentences (*any, yet, at all*), which are non-assertive.

attributive adjectives are attributive when they come before their nouns – *a beautiful warm fur-lined raincoat, their elder son, the main idea*. See **predicative**.

auxiliary verb 1) *be, do, have* – used with other verbs to make questions, negatives and most of the tenses. 2) modal verbs are a special kind of auxiliary verb.

bare infinitive an infinitive without *to*, as in: *I can **hear** you*; *Make him **work***; *He does nothing but **watch** TV all day.*

clause 1) a group of words with a finite verb, and usually its own subject, that forms part of a sentence. See also **main clause**.
2) We can also have clauses with a non-finite verb, and often no subject. See **non-finite clause**. See also **adverb clause**, **noun clause**, **relative clause**.

cleft cleft means 'divided' and cleft sentences are divided into two parts by beginning the sentence with *It* or *What*: ***It's** a good sleep I need. **What** I need is a good sleep.*

collective noun a noun that refers to a group and that in its singular form can take a singular or plural verb: ***The committee** is/are* . . .

comparative the form of an adjective or adverb with *-er* added, or with *more* put in front of it: *better, quicker, more expensive.*

complement a word (or words) that helps to complete our information. A **subject complement** gives more information about the subject after verbs like *be, look, seem*: *That seems to be **all**, You look **beautiful***. An **object complement** gives information about the object: *He's painted his bicycle **blue**. They've made Muriel **president**.*

concession If we make a concession, we admit something, we 'allow' that something may be true. In grammar, *although, whereas* . . . introduce clauses of concession that admit that something is rather different from what the main part of the sentence says: *I love her, **although** she's a liar.*

concord sometimes called **agreement** – There are sometimes special verb forms according to what the subject is: *I **am**, you **are***; *they **know**, she **knows***. This is **verb concord**.

conditional conditional sentences refer to the conditions, the circumstances in which something could happen or be true. The condition itself is expressed in a conditional clause beginning with *if, unless* or a similar conjunction.

conjunction a word that joins clauses (and sometimes words) together: *and, but, because, if, when* . . .

connector a word (or words) that connects a sentence with the meaning of the previous sentence: *however, nevertheless, by the way.*

count noun (C) also called countable noun – a noun which can have a plural form and which can be used with *a/an* and numbers: *a book, six books, an idea, two good ideas, a man, men.*

defining clause See **relative clause**.

definite 1) definite article = *the*.
2) Although we think mainly of definite and indefinite articles,

other determiners and pronouns can show definite meaning (*this, those, my, yours . . .*) and indefinite meaning (*some, someone . . .*). Verb tenses and adverbs too can talk about definite time (*I saw him yesterday/in 1980*) and indefinite time (*Have you ever met him?*)

degree adverb the word degree is connected with measuring and how much. Degree adverbs include focusing adverbs, which often focus or concentrate on a particular word, or limit in some way (*I just wanted to know*; *He's only a child.*) and intensifying adverbs that emphasise words and make them stronger (*too difficult, very kind*) or weaker (*hardly possible, kind of difficult*).

determiner a word usually used before (ADJECTIVE+) NOUN. Determiners include articles (*a, an, the*), as well as words like *this, all, both, many, every, my . . .*

direct object the person or thing that is directly 'acted on' by the subject and verb: *Eat your lunch*; *I've bought a new car*; *Don't hurt your sister.*

direct speech When we repeat the exact words that somebody has said – and put them in quotation marks if we are writing – then this is direct speech – '*Have you ever loved anyone before?*' *he asked.* When we change the words, we are using indirect or reported speech: *He asked her if she had ever loved anyone before.*

emphatic pronoun a *-self* pronoun (*myself, themselves . . .*) when used to emphasise a noun or pronoun: *You yourself said . . .*

end position When an adverb is in end position it comes after the verb. End position does not mean the last word in a clause: *She spoke quietly about her amazing experiences.*

exclamation a phrase or sentence usually expressing surprise or some other emotion: *What a mistake! How awful! Sorry!*

finite a finite verb is a verb form (or verb phrase) showing a tense and referring to past or present or future time: *We saw Tim yesterday.* Compare **non-finite**.

first person *I, we, us, myself,* etc are first person words and refer to the speaker or writer, and in the plural, to other people the speaker or writer wants to involve in what he says.

focusing adverb See **degree**.

frequency adverb an adverb saying how often, how frequently something happens: *often, never, sometimes.*

front position when an adverb is in front position it comes before (in front of) the subject: *Tomorrow I'm going to do nothing all day. Actually, you never do anything, do you?*

gradable some words (particularly adjectives, adverbs and verbs) are gradable. We can grade them on a scale. We can say things/people are *more* (or *less*) *difficult*, or *fairly* or *very old*, or that something happened *rather* or *very unexpectedly*, or that we *quite like* something. Other words are ungradable. We do not say things are *more* or *less former* or *woollen*; or that something happened *very weekly*, or that we *rather walked*.

hypothesis, hypothetical a hypothesis is a theory, a suggestion about what could perhaps in some circumstances be true, and so hypothetical means 'perhaps theoretically possible, but unreal and imagined now.' Hypothetical conditions are conditions which are the opposite of the facts (*If I had lived in the nineteenth century . . . If I were a millionaire . . .*)

imperative the base form of a verb when used to give commands, orders etc.: *Listen! Come here. Be sensible.*

indefinite 1) *a* and *an* are indefinite articles. 2) For indefinite determiners and pronouns, and indefinite time – See **definite**.

indirect object (IO) the person or thing that receives the direct object of a verb: *Give your sister my love. I've brought you a present. Tell me (the truth).*

indirect speech (or **reported speech**) See **direct speech**. Indirect speech can also include sentences similar to reported speech, but with a 'thinking', not a reporting verb: *I am wondering if I should go/what to do.*

infinitive the base form of a verb (often with *to*), used after another verb (*We hope to see you*); after an adjective or noun (*Are you likely to come? I want a book to read*); and in quite separate clauses (See **non-finite**). See also **bare infinitive**.

-ing form the form of a verb when it ends with *-ing*.
1) Sometimes used like a noun: *Seeing is believing*, and always necessary after a preposition: *We look forward to seeing you.*
2) Also the present participle (See **participle**).

introductory sometimes we don't want to put the subject of a sentence at the beginning but later. So we introduce our sentence with an introductory *it* or *there*: *It's been marvellous seeing you again.* Introductory *it* as object is also possible.

inversion a pattern where the verb, or often just an auxiliary or modal comes before its subject: *Do you understand? Can I help? Here comes the bus.*

main clause a main clause contrasts with a subordinate clause as part of a longer sentence. Main clauses are often complete in themselves (*I was reading.*) Subordinate clauses – except *that*-clauses if we leave out the *that* – are not. Subordinate clauses are introduced by a conjunction – *that*, a *wh*-word, *if*, *because*, etc. (*. . . that the world's climate is changing./. . . what Professor Ozone thinks./. . . because I had nothing better to do.*) See also **subordinate clause**.

main verb a verb used as a finite verb (not as an auxiliary, and not an infinitive or participle). *Be*, *do* and *have* are sometimes used as auxiliaries, but in the following they are main verbs: *She is a doctor*; *What are you doing? We have had dinner.*

manner adverb an adverb that says how something is done. Many manner adverbs end in *-ly*: *beautifully, quickly*. But some do not: *well, fast*.

mass noun See **uncountable**.

mid-position mid-position adverbs come between the subject and the verb (*I absolutely love it, I never have enough. He eventually did the work.*) except when the main verb is a one-word part of *be*, and they then often come immediately after the verb (*You are generally right*). When the verb is a phrase, the adverb usually comes after the first auxiliary (*They don't always tell you. It has already been taken*). With passive verbs, manner adverbs sometimes come just before the last word in a verb phrase (*My shoes had been beautifully polished*).

modal verb modal verbs include 1) *can, could, may, might, must, shall, should, will, would*, and 2) *dare, need, ought to, used to*. The main modals (in 1) form negatives and questions in the same way as the auxiliaries *be, do, have*; they do not add *-s* for the 3rd person singular; they do not have infinitives or participles, and they do not have complex tenses. The 'semi-modals' (in 2) are partly like modals and partly like ordinary verbs.

negative opposite of positive. Negative words include *no, not, never, nobody, none, nothing . . .*

non-assertive See **assertive**.

non-defining See **relative clause**.

non-finite 1) A non-finite verb means an infinitive or participle, and cannot be the only verb in a sentence: *seeing, to see, having seen, to have seen*. 2) Non-finite clauses can form part of a bigger sentence: *Looking round, she saw a lion. To get away, she climbed a tree.*

non-gradable See **gradable**.

noun a word that can be used after *the* and other determiners as subject or object of a sentence. Nouns also include names of people and places (*James, London*).

noun clause a clause (usually with a finite verb) which can function like a noun, e.g. as subject or object of a sentence: *How she did it amazes me. She told me that she wasn't even trying.*

noun phrase a group of words containing a noun (or pronoun), and perhaps determiners, adjectives etc., and functioning in a sentence like a noun: *no other novelist*; *a beautiful green dress*; *the book you gave me*; *something like that* . . .

object (o) See **direct object** and **indirect object.** Words following prepositions are sometimes called objects of prepositions: *for you*, *at the station*.

participle verbs have so-called 'present' and 'past' participles, which are used in verb tenses, and by themselves in non-finite clauses. 1) The present participle ends in *-ing* and the meaning is usually active, but not in fact always present: *She was* **reading**. **Sitting** *by the fire, she fell asleep*. Compare present participles used as adjectives: *The film was* **boring/exciting/interesting.** 2) The past participle ends in *-ed* in regular verbs and often in an /n/ sound in irregular verbs (*gone, seen, spoken*. Also *drunk, rung, swum,* . . .). The meaning is usually passive, but not always past: *The roof is going to be* **repaired.** *These apples are good* **eaten** *with cheese*. (i.e., when eaten with cheese). *We are not* **amused.** Compare the passive meaning in: *We were very* **bored/excited/interested.**

passive See **active.**

past tenses we use past tenses:
1) to talk about past time: *It* **was raining** *all day yesterday, and I* **got** *very wet because I* **had left** *my umbrella at home.*
2) to talk about events and actions that are distant from the present because they are hypothetical: *If I* **knew***, I would tell you. I wish I* **had known** *then what I know now.*
3) for social reasons, such as politeness: *I* **was hoping** *(that) you would help me.*

perfect tenses these are tenses formed with *have*. We can also have perfect infinitives and participles. (See entry at **have.**)

personal pronouns *I, me, you, he, them*, etc.

phrase a phrase is a group of words that belong together, but is not usually as independent as a clause. We can have **adverb phrases**, **noun phrases** and **verb phrases.**

plural opposite of singular, and referring to more than one person or thing. Pronouns, determiners and nouns can be plural: *they, many, several*; *books, children*. Plural verb forms (*are, were*) are used with plural nouns and often with collective nouns.

positive 1) affirmative, opposite of negative. *I love you* is a positive sentence. In *You don't love me, do you?* the question tag is positive. 2) positive also contrasts with comparative and superlative in describing the 'base' form of adjectives and adverbs – *good, well, bad, badly* (Contrast *better, best, worse, worst.*)

possessive *my*, *our*, *their*, etc. are possessive determiners. *Mine*, *ours*, *theirs*, etc. are possessive pronouns. Nouns can also have a possessive form – *the country's, the children's, the girls', John's.*

predicative adjectives are in predicative position when they come after *be*, *look*, *seem* and a few other verbs: *It is cold. That looks expensive.*

preposition words like *at, below, by, for* when they are followed by a noun or pronoun are prepositions. Prepositions can also be followed by noun clauses beginning with a *wh-* word: *They complained about what I had said.* Some of these words can also be used without a noun/pronoun and are then adverbs.

prepositional phrase a preposition + its noun/pronoun is sometimes called a prepositional phrase. Prepositional phrases are sometimes like adverbs (*I went to school. I'll do it after dinner*), but they can also be used after nouns, rather like a relative clause with a describing (adjective-like) function; *a man in a white suit*; *the week after next.*

present tenses these can refer to actions and states happening:
at the present moment: *You are reading this book. Yes, I agree.*
at the present time in a more general sense: *Where are you living now?*
during much longer periods that include the present time: *I wear glasses. They go abroad every year. Water boils at 100°C.*
in the future, but the arrangements already exist now: *I'm going home next Tuesday. My plane leaves at 17.50.*
we also use present tenses in time and conditional clauses referring to the future: *Tell me when she arrives.*
in a period that extends to now: *I have finished my homework. I've known them all my life.*

progressive tenses also called continuous tenses – These are formed with *be* and *-ing*: *I am listening. They were working. It is being mended.* The meaning is often that there is some action in progress.

pronoun A pronoun is a word like *I, she, him, that, each, one, somebody* that can be used instead of a noun as subject, object or complement of a sentence.

proper noun or **proper name** nouns for definite people and places: *John, London, the Himalayas.*

question tag short question, consisting of an auxiliary (or modal) verb + a pronoun subject: *You like it really, don't you? It isn't wrong, is it? We must try again, mustn't we?*

reflexive pronouns all the *-self* words (*myself, themselves*) when used as objects: *Don't hurt yourself/yourselves.*

relative clause a clause often introduced by a relative pronoun. Relative clauses can be defining or non-defining. (See entries at **that**, **who**,

which, whose.) We can also have sentence relatives – See entry at **which**.

relative pronouns the words *that, who, whom, whose, which* when they introduce a relative clause.

reported speech also called indirect speech – See **direct speech**.

second person *you, your, yours, yourself, yourselves* – the person or people spoken to.

sentence adverb an adverb that makes a comment on the whole sentence. In *Clearly, this is a big problem, clearly* is a sentence adverb. In *I try to write clearly, clearly* belongs with *write* and is a manner adverb.

sentence relative See entry at **which**.

simple tense a simple tense is not progressive: *We go* (present simple). *We went* (past simple). *We have/had gone* (present/past perfect simple).

singular opposite of plural, and referring to only one. Pronouns and nouns can be singular: *I, he, she*, etc.; *book, idea*. Singular verb forms (*is, takes*) are used with singular and uncountable nouns.

stative verbs a label for verbs that refer to states, rather than actions, and are not usually used in the progressive: *belong, seem* . . .

subject the noun, pronoun, noun phrase (or noun clause) that comes before the verb in an ordinary statement: *The children enjoyed the party. The party was enjoyed by everyone there. What you are saying is very unkind.*

subjunctive a verb form or tense – not very common in English – used in certain cases where we want something to happen or have emotional feelings about something happening in contrast to tenses that talk about straight facts: *God Save the Queen. If I were you* . . . *They decided that the man be told.*

subordinate clause See **main clause**.

superlative the form of an adjective or adverb with *-est* added, or *most* + adjective/adverb: *best, quickest, most expensive.*

syllable a syllable is part of a word (sometimes a whole word) that has one vowel sound in it. *grammar* /'græmə/ has two syllables, and is stressed on the first syllable, *book* /bʊk/ is a one-syllable word.

tense a verb form or verb phrase showing the time of an action; or showing that the action is hypothetical; or in some other way showing the attitude of the speaker to it. Tense and time are not the same. For example, the so-called 'past tense' can refer to past, present or future time.

that-**clause** a clause introduced by the conjunction *that* (or which could have *that* in front of it) and often functioning as the object of a reporting or thinking verb: *He says/thinks (that) it's going to rain. That*-clauses can also be subjects: **That it will rain** *is quite possible.* The term *that*-clause does not include relative clauses beginning with relative pronoun *that*.

third person *he, she, they, him, herself* etc. – the person/people talked about (but not the speaker or listener).

to-**infinitive** See **infinitive**.

uncountable noun also called uncount noun or non-count noun or mass noun – a noun which has no plural, cannot be counted and does not usually take *a/an*: *bread, furniture, information.*

verb a word which follows a subject to made a simple clause. Most verbs are concerned with actions and events, or (stative verbs) with states.

verb phrase a group of words forming a tense: *could have happened, was not being done.*

wh-**clause** adverb or noun clause beginning with a *wh*-word. The term does not usually refer to relative clauses.

wh-**question** question beginning with a *wh*-word, in contrast to questions, sometimes called **yes/no questions**, that begin with an auxiliary or modal verb.

wh-**word** question word beginning with *wh*- (*what, when, where, which, who, whom, whose*) and *how.*

zero zero article means using a noun without any article: . . . *books,* . . . *men,* . . . *bread,* . . . *food.* Zero plural means a noun plural that is the same as the singular form (and does not add -*s*): *a sheep, two sheep.*

Phonetic symbols

Vowels and diphthongs

iː as in	meet	eɪ as in	make
ɪ	with	əʊ	no
e	went	aɪ	time
æ	sat	aʊ	out
ɑː	car	ɔɪ	boy
ɒ	got	ɪə	here
ɔː	saw	eə	air
ʊ	put	ʊə	during /ˈdjʊərɪŋ/
uː	too		American English /ˈdʊərɪŋ/
ʌ	sun		
ɜː	girl		
ə	*a*go		

Consonants

p as in	past	s as in	same
b	but	z	zoo
t	take	ʃ	shut
d	day	ʒ	decision /dɪˈsɪʒn/
k	car	h	happen
g	go	m	me
tʃ	*ch*oose	n	never
dʒ	just	ŋ	wro*ng*
f	fact	l	little
v	very	r	read
θ	think	j	yes
ð	that	w	want